The Judicial Protection of Human Rights in Botswana

The Judicial Protection of Human Rights in Botswana

Edited by
Emmanuel Quansah
and
William Binchy

CLARUS PRESS

Trinity College Dublin
with the support of the Irish Research Council for the Humanities and Social Sciences

Published by
Clarus Press Ltd,
Griffith Campus,
South Circular Road,
Dublin 8.

Typeset by
Amnet International
Pembroke House
28-32 Pembroke Street
Dublin 2
Ireland

Printed by
MPG Books Ltd
Victoria Square, Bodmin, Cornwall.

ISBN
978-1-905536-27-6

Table of Content

Appendices

Preface

In recent years the crucial role that the judiciary can play in the protection of human rights has become apparent. Most countries have written constitutions containing some acknowledgement of the rights of their citizens; most countries have judiciaries charged with the task of interpreting these provisions; fewer countries are fortunate enough to have a dispensation under which judges can act with complete independence as guardians of the Constitution, certain in the knowledge that the executive and legislature will comply with their decrees.

At a global level, the scope of application of human rights protection has been expanding. The argument that economic and social rights should be justiciable has gained wider support; the idea that, as well as States, non-State actors, notably transnational corporations, should be required to respect human rights has gained currency.

Botswana has been affected by these developments. Its Constitution is not in the first flush of youth yet the courts have on occasion shown that it is capable of dynamic interpretation in accordance with contemporary values. It is geographically and culturally close to South Africa, where the scope of judicial protection of human rights has been radically transformed at a fundamental constitutional level. The considerable textual differences between the Constitutions of Botswana and South Africa present challenges for judges who may be sympathetic to developing a jurisprudence based on values of dignity and equality.

This book seeks to identify the emerging issues relating to the judicial protection of human rights in Botswana. Most of the contributors are members of the Department of Law of the University of Botswana but they have been joined by others from South Africa and Ireland. The book emerged from a conference on the subject in Gaborone organised by the Department of Law of the University of Botswana and the Law School of Trinity College Dublin on 5th June 2008.

We are grateful to many people for their support for the project. In particular we must thank Vice Chancellor Bojosi Otlhogile for having opened the conference and shared his views on the theme of the conference which is included in the book. We appreciate the strong commitment of members of the Department of Law at the University of Botswana and we were delighted to receive contributions from Professor George Devenish and Mr. Magnus Killander from South Africa. Our publisher, Clarus Press, and David McCartney, its Managing Director, could not have offered more helpful and professional guidance.

The book is part of a research project on human rights and the judiciary in Africa, supported by the Irish Research Council for the Humanities and Social Sciences. We are very grateful to the Council for facilitating this publication.

Emmanuel Quansah
William Binchy

Table of Cases

Protection of Human Rights in Botswana: Emerging Issues

Prof. Bojosi Otlhogile*

The theme for this book, based on a conference organised by the Law Department of the University of Botswana and Trinity College, Dublin on 5 June 2008, involves a search for a workable, decent, affordable and efficient approach to emerging issues not covered by our Constitution. It is important for us in Botswana to continually remind ourselves of new and emerging trends in the human rights sphere for we came to independence on the basis of a constitution that did not cater for some areas of human rights that nowadays are commonly incorporated in newer constitutions. Some of us when we went to Law School found that Human Rights was not a core course of study but relegated to electives or options. Things have changed over the past few decades. On the other hand our judiciaries in the region are dominated by gentlemen (yes men) who like me studied law at a time when law schools teaching Human Rights were few.

There is another reason why books such as this are important. Southern Africa and indeed Africa's recent past history has been marked by unprecedented inhumanity. Time and again, human dignity was being crushed by wars, oppressive regimes and persistent denial of those elements which are essential to any civilised nations. That is, respect for freedom, justice and peace. Books like this one give us hope. Hope that there are still people and institutions that care for human dignity; that there are still many people out there who hunger for justice and freedom. The book affords us an opportunity to reflect not only on the emerging trends and issues of human rights but also to measure ourselves against these advances in international minimum standards.

I am particularly happy that a number of colleagues presented papers at the conference which have been incorporated in the book. They freely interrogate the state of human rights and their protection in Botswana. If our

* LLB (UBS), LLM, Phd (Cantab), Attorney (Botswana), Vice Chancellor, University of Botswana

Law Department cannot comment on these issues, nobody will. We have a duty to lead the discussion in a well researched, sober and scholarly manner.

Permit me to make one or two observation on some areas where I hope we could (in future) address our minds. First is the debate around HIV/AIDS. I am happy that it will be addressed in detail in one of the later sessions. Three issues have attracted debate, namely, how to deal (in policy or law) with HIV/AIDS in the workplace, ie should there be compulsory pre-employment testing; whether to move from routine testing to compulsory testing in the health facilities; and lastly the right to procreation.[1] The latter was raised once again by the Chairperson of National Aids Council (NAC):

> "Let me share with you some of my concerns as a citizen of Botswana, and as Chairperson of this Council. You will no doubt be aware of emerging undesirable trends associated with our treatment programme, among them repeated pregnancies among women on HAART. While we have no intention of interfering with individuals' rights to procreate, I believe that it should worry us when we see signs of unprotected sexual practices, including people on treatment. Many questions come to mind as a result of this observation: was this pregnancy sanctioned by a medical practitioner? Was the partner fully informed of this HIV status? Does the partner know that the other is on anti-retroviral treatment? In other words, was this a mutual decision between two consenting adults, having assessed the risk involved?"[2]

Second is the rights – human rights – of cross border migrants. I had occasion to address this issue some three years ago.[3] The bulk of what I have to say reflects what I raised at the time. However, some recent occurrences taking place in our region compel me to express my views again on the matter.

---

[1] At one stage some politicians likened HIV positive women on Highly Active Anti-Retroviral Therapy (HAART) who fall pregnant to a time bomb. However, it seems there is no medical reason why they can not choose to have children. See also a study by Botswana Network on Ethics, Law and HIV/AIDS (BONELA), on reasons why these women choose to have children –"Experiences of HIV Positive Women Accessing Sexual and Reproductive Health Services in Botswana" (2007).

[2] Former Botswana President Mogae at the meeting of National Aids Coordinating Agency (NACA) on 30th May 2008.

[3] Opening Remarks at Immigration Conference on Problems of Cross Border Migration, 6th December 2004.

Cross border migration is not a new phenomenon. It is as old as human existence itself. Human beings have always moved about – internally and externally. The Bible records two such early migrations. We are told that Jesus Christ was born in Bethlehem where his parents had gone for a census. In another incident Moses led his people across the Red Sea to the Promised Land.

Since the end of the Cold War, we have come to expect that there will be less movement of people across borders. When the balance of power was maintained between the two power blocs, those leaving their countries would often be under the control of one of the major power blocs. The migrants were more readily grouped as "them" or "us" depending on which power bloc they were fleeing. In our region the collapse of apartheid also, we believed, heralded the beginning of the end of cross border migration – be it refugees or others. Unfortunately this has not come to pass.

The past decade, and particularly the past few years, has seen more people crossing borders than ever before. The difference lies in that instead of being welcomed, all of them are now to be closely scrutinised. We also see more states unable to offer human rights protection to their citizens.

Since September 11, there is also greater difficulty and concern in easily permitting cross border migration. The issue is one of security risk. The security risk factor has blinded us to the realities of modern life. We live in a global world. One of the aspects of globalisation is that money and people are mobile. Unauthorised movement of people from one country to another, from insecurity to security, from persecution to protection, from famine to abundance, unemployment to employment, entrepreneurs, criminal syndicates etc, is to be expected.

In the past the cross border migrants were likely to be political refugees fleeing political persecution. In those years the migrants were welcomed and provided with safe haven until it was safe for them to be repatriated. Sometimes these migrants were integrated into the nation to which they fled seeking asylum or they were resettled in a third country.

The politics of Southern Africa have changed and cross border migration does not fit the old mould. Those who cross borders are generally seen as responding to the pull factors rather than the push factors of their own countries. Cross border migrants are more likely to be returned than being offered safe haven within our midst. The politics of fear has become a hallmark of many nations' politics this last decade. The fear of the foreigner, the fear of the "other" religions and cultures.

For countries with small population like Botswana, this fear is starting to be felt. The focus is on the migrants rather than the causes. Being a landlocked country, we do share land boundaries with other nations. The politics of our neighbours and the state of their economies do influence cross border movement of people – authorised and unauthorised. Those coming from deprived economies are likely to overstay their immigration permits. Some of those who overstay their immigration permits do so because they genuinely believe that there is no hope in returning to their home countries.

Of course, Botswana with its political stability and relatively strong economy has become attractive to cross border immigrants. The presence of these immigrants has put a strain on the government. We therefore cannot expect the government not to do anything. However, whatever we do let us not forget that this country itself has been founded on cross border migration – regulated or otherwise. Until the discovery of diamonds in the 1970s Botswana relied on remittances of our people who crossed the borders to work in the South African mines. At independence most of the educated Batswana obtained their education not in Botswana but across the border(s). The impact of cross border migration was celebrated in both song and dance. It was the late Sheleng[4] who immortalised the impact of migration in the society when he lamented the breakdown of the social fabric in Mahalapye. He lamented that migrant workers took their women:

> *"Ba okwa ke sepache go buduloga*
> *Ba re hitlhele re ntse re tshela ka nkutusa."*[5]

Today cross border migration has become a drain on our resources – human and financial. At enormous cost we are maintaining a reception (repatriation) centre in Francistown, and make shift ones throughout the country. Our police, prison and immigration officers are constantly being deployed to deal with unauthorised cross border migrants. The detainees are moved from around the country and kept at enormous cost before repatriation. It is not a cost we can afford in the long run.

Those who are not in the centre are kept in our prisons, thereby compounding the already deplorable conditions of our prisons – overcrowding. The police are diverted from their main function of combating crime to rounding up

---

4 Sheleng was one of Botswana's foremost guitarist and folk singer.

5 Literally meaning "attracted by bulging wallets and on their return to us to find us living as we have always done."

illegal immigrants. Immigration officers' time and efforts are diverting from processing other civil application by processing those to be repatriated.

Can our policies be reconciled with the international notions of human rights? There has already been controversy about the application of some of our actions and application of some of our laws to cross border immigrants. For instance, where a crime has been committed by an immigrant the application of corporal punishment by customary courts to these people has been a source of concern for those who are anti-corporal punishment. The mandatory detention of those awaiting repatriation, especially in prisons with seasoned and convicted prisoners without court order, has also come under the spotlight. These actions are regarded as offensive to the human rights of those detained. More so when children are involved. From a human rights point of view, the detention of children in the context of immigration procedures is contrary to international standards. Even from a practical point of view, this is undesirable. While in most cases, the parents of these children carry the main responsibility for ensuring the well-being of the children, and as such are to some extent responsible for the plight of the children; it would appear, nonetheless, obvious that detention of children for immigration purposes is not in their best interest. Despite the influx a more humane approach would certainly be desirable.

The influx of cross border migrants, especially from our northern neighbour, is a reality. It has to be addressed if not managed. Let me, however, point out from the onset that Botswana acting alone would not resolve it. No matter how much money we spend, no matter how many joint raids are conducted the problem will remain. We have the disadvantage of geography. We are landlocked; therefore we have to police long (and porous) borders. We do not have the luxury of going it alone because methods that deter access to a national territory merely shift the burden from one country to another. It is a very unneighbourly behaviour.

The solution lies in collective political action. Most of the cross border migrants in this region respond to the push factor than to the pull factors. The situations in our neighbours has steadily deteriorated, especially the economic one. The fact of the matter though is that the economic deterioration is a result of tumultuous political situations pertaining in these countries.[6]

[6] The economic meltdown in Zimbabwe coupled with political intimidation, for instance, is said to have displaced over three million Zimbabweans. The majority are living in neighbouring countries, especially South Africa.

Unless the political situation is settled or stabilised we will not cease to have cross border migration.

It is no use trying to justify our inaction on the basis of respect of our neighbours' sovereignty. The fact is that the sovereignty of the nation state is morally justifiable only if the nation state discharges its primary obligation to protect the human rights and uphold the dignity of its citizens. Non-interference in the affairs of other states is morally justifiable only if the international community makes provision for the protection of the human rights of those persons who are persecuted by their own State or their State selectively fails to protect them from the vagrancies of life.[7]

If our governments are not willing to embark on political solution to the problem, then there is no point in punishing those who have the temerity to turn up without proper travel documents or overstay their welcome. To do so is the equivalent of being charged for not having a parking permit when you have entered the car park while fleeing a bush fire. To arrest those who overstay is to equate bona fide bush fire victim with the car park cheat.

So, can their rights be protected within the limits of our Constitution?

I have taken the liberty to raise these questions knowing full well that I have no certain answers. But this book is a proper forum for similar issues to be addressed and debated.

---

[7] The argument was originally made by Secretary General Kofi A Annan in his *Millennium Report to the General Assembly* (2000) where he stated "... if humanitarian intervention is, indeed, an unacceptable assault on sovereignty, how should we respond to a Rwanda, to a Srebrenica – to gross and systematic violations of human rights that offend every precept of our common humanity?" See too, *The Responsibility to Protect: Report of the International Commission on Intervention and State Responsibility*, a Canadian Government Report of 2001.

The Role of International Law in Human Rights Litigation in Africa

Magnus Killander*

1 Introduction

Determining the content of human rights norms in national constitutions, international law – in the form of treaties, declarations and case law from international monitoring bodies, and comparative case law from other countries – is a subject often discussed in the judgments of domestic courts.[1]

This paper explores the extent to which international law has influenced domestic human rights case law in Africa.[2] The paper first explores how the human rights provisions of African constitutions came into being before turning to consider the role played by international law in the constitutional order of various African states and how treaties, declarations and findings of international monitoring bodies have been used in African countries to interpret and expand on constitutional human rights provisions.

---

*Researcher and LLD candidate, University of Pretoria, South Africa, magnus.killander@up.ac.za. Co-editor *African Human Rights Law Reports*, Associate Editor *International Law in Domestic Courts* (ILDC), http://www.oxfordlawreports.com.

[1] See generally cases in International Law in Domestic Courts (ILDC), http://www.oxfordlawreports.com. On the use of the case law of the Inter-American system in Latin American courts see Diálogo jurisprudencial available at http://www.juridicas.unam.mx/publica/rev/cont.htm?r=dialjur (accessed 24 April 2008). Case law cited in this paper is available in the African Human Rights Law Reports (AHRLR), http://www.chr.up.ac.za/centre_publications/ahrlr/ahrlr.html, ILDC, and from web site of the Southern African Legal Information Institute, http://www.saflii.org.

[2] For an overview focusing on the application of the African Charter on Human and Peoples' Rights by domestic courts in Africa, see F. Viljoen *International Human Rights Law in Africa* (2007) pp. 529–567. See also ME Adjami "African Courts, International Law, and Comparative Case Law: Chimera or emerging Human Rights Jurisprudence" (2002) 24 Michigan J. of Int'l L. 103, RF Frimpong-Oppong "Re-imagining international law: An Examination of Recent Trends in the Reception of International Law into National Legal Systems in Africa" (2007) 30 Fordham Int'l L.J. 296, K. Knop "Here and There: International law in Domestic Courts" (2000) 32 N.Y.U.J. of Int'l L. & Politics 501.

2 Constitutional Human Rights Provisions in Africa – a Historical Overview

Human rights norms have been included in the constitutions of all African countries.[3] The first Bill of Rights on the African continent was included in the Constitution of Liberia of 1847, with clear influence from the United States Bill of Rights.[4] More than a hundred years later, in 1953, the British government made a declaration extending the scope of the application of the European Convention on Human Rights to Basutoland (now Lesotho), Bechuanaland (now Botswana), Gambia, Gold Coast (now Ghana), Kenya, Mauritius, Nigeria, Northern Rhodesia (now Zambia), Nyasaland (now Malawi), Seychelles, Sierra Leone, Somaliland, Swaziland, Tanganyika, Uganda and Zanzibar.[5] When these countries gained their independence the European Convention ceased to apply to them, but nonetheless it came to have a lasting effect in that most of these countries in their independence constitutions included Bills of Rights which, as has been pointed out, "corresponded almost word for word with the Convention".[6] These Bills of Rights importantly provided for judicial review. Today only two countries retain the original Bill of Rights: Botswana and Kenya. The other countries that inherited the European Convention-inspired Bill of Rights have all adopted new constitutions with rewritten Bills of Rights. The Commonwealth countries which did not include a Bill of Rights in their independence constitutions, such as Ghana and Tanzania, have all included Bills of Rights in their current constitutions.

Many of the former French, Belgian and Portuguese colonies included human rights provisions in their independence constitutions. A few included a reference to the Universal Declaration of Human Rights in the preamble to their constitutions. However, most included a more detailed Bill of Rights, often with both civil and political rights and socio-economic rights in the Constitution. The inspiration of many of these provisions can be found in the often brief provisions of the Universal Declaration of Human Rights rather

---

[3] C. Heyns & W. Kaguongo "Constitutional Human Rights Law in Africa" (2006) 22 S. African J. on Human Rts 673.

[4] "The Liberian Constitutions", http://onliberia.org/con_1847.htm (accessed 25 April 2008).

[5] C. Heyns "African Human Rights Law and the European Convention" (1995) 11 S. African J. on Human Rts 252, 255.

[6] See C. Heyns, *op. cit.*, fn. 5 *supra*, 257. However, while the texts of these early Bills of Rights were very similar to each other, there were a number of major differences between them and the text of the Convention, for example with regard to the right to equality and non-discrimination. Compare Article 14 of the European Convention with Articles 3 and 15 of the Botswana Constitution of 1966 and Articles 70 and 82 of the Kenya Constitution of 1963.

than the more detailed European Convention. In general, judicial review of compliance with these bills of rights was not provided for.[7] All civil law countries in Africa have adopted new constitutions over the last decades, which have added provisions on human rights to those constitutions which lacked this at independence. However, provisions for judicial review at the request of individuals are still not included in all these constitutions.[8]

3 The Role of International Human Rights Law in the Legal Systems of Africa

3.1 Incorporation and Interpretation

African states have taken different approaches to the role of international law in their legal orders. Traditionally civil law countries are seen as monist and common law countries as dualist when it comes to incorporating international law into the domestic legal system. The monist approach involves automatic incorporation of international law into domestic law whilst the dualist approach does not incorporate international law into domestic law without specific national legislation to that effect.[9] Consequently, the constitutions of many civil law countries include a provision that ratified treaties form part of the law of the land,[10] mostly with a specific provision that they have a status superior to ordinary legislation.[11] This provision is provided for in the same wording in most Francophone constitutions and has its origin in the 1958 French Constitution.[12] Many of the Francophone African constitutions, in line with the 1958 French Constitution, provide that the domestic application of a treaty is subject to its application by the other party.[13] Arguably such a provision does not have any bearing on multilateral treaties, in particular

---

[7] For the text of most African independence constitutions see A.J Peaslee *Constitutions of Nations, Volume 1 – Africa* (3rd ed, 1965).

[8] For the current human rights provisions of African constitutions see C. Heyns (ed) *Human Rights Law in Africa Volume 2* (2004) and the web site of the Centre for Human Rights, University of Pretoria, http://www.chr.up.ac.za.

[9] See J.G. Starke, "Monism and Dualism in the Theory of International Law" (1936) 16 *Br.* Yrbk on Int'l L. 66 and C.J.R. Dugard, "Is International Law Part of Our Law?" (1971) S. African L. J. 135.

[10] Ethiopia (Article 9), Mozambique (Article 18), Somalia (Article 69, see also Article 14).

[11] Algeria (Article 132), Burkina Faso (Article 151), Cape Verde (Article 12), Central African Republic (Article 69), Chad (Article 222), Comoros (Article 10), Congo (Article 185), Côte d'Ivoire, Djibouti (Article 37), Egypt (Article 151), Tunisia (Article 32).

[12] Frimpong Oppong, *op. cit.*, fn. 2 *supra*, 308.

[13] E.g. DRC (Article 215), Guinea (Article 79), Mali (Article 116), Niger (Article 132), Rwanda (Article 190), Senegal (Article 98), Togo (Article 140).

human rights treaties. The Burundi Constitution makes this interpretation explicit by providing that the application of bilateral treaties is dependent on their application by the other party, while ratified multilateral treaties are applicable once they have entered into force.[14]

Despite the inclusion of international law as a source of law in these countries, references to such law in the adjudicating process have been quite limited. A case from Senegal provides an example of the reluctance of the courts to apply international law despite the monist framework. In 2002 the Court of Cassation decided that the former Chadian President Hissène Habré could not be charged in Senegal for atrocities allegedly committed in Chad based solely on the Convention against Torture, which had been ratified by Senegal. According to the Court, implementation legislation was needed before a Senegalese court could hear the case.[15] This position, where the courts consider a treaty not self-executing, has also been applied by other formally monist countries in Africa.[16] International treaties have been applied in a few cases in Ethiopia.[17] However, the lack of publication of treaties in the *Gazette* has been taken by some judges to mean that they are not applicable.[18]

Some African courts have been more willing to make use of international treaties. In *Military Prosecutor v Massaba*,[19] for example, the Military Tribunal of Ituri in the Democratic Republic of the Congo held that provisions in the Statute of the International Criminal Court, ratified by the DRC, could fill a lacuna in the Military Penal Code with regard to war crimes. In Benin the Constitutional Court often refers to provisions in the African Charter on Human

---

[14] Article 292.

[15] *Guengueng and Others v Habre* (2002) AHRLR 183 (SeCC 2001), ILDC 164 (SN 2001). The UN Committee against Torture subsequently held that Senegal had violated the Convention by not implementing Article 5(2) of the Convention which provides that states must "take such measures as may be necessary to establish its jurisdiction over such cases where the alleged offender is present in any territory under its jurisdiction and it does not extradite him".

[16] Viljoen, *op. cit.*, fn. 2 *supra*, 533.

[17] See *Dr Negaso Gidada v House of Peoples' Representatives and Another,* Federal Supreme Court, appeal, File Nos. 22980 and 22948, Judgment of 25 October 2006, cited in SA Yeshanew "Justiciability of Human Rights in the Federal Republic of Ethiopia" (2007, unpublished paper on file with author) and *Special Prosecutor v Col Mengistu Hailemariam, 173 others* ILDC 555 (ET 1995). See also judgment of the Federal Cassation Court in cassation file no. 23632, 6 November 2007.

[18] See Yeshanew, *op. cit.*, fn. 16 *supra*. Similarly the Constitutional Court of Benin has held that UN Convention on the Rights of the Child is not part of the law of Benin since it has not been published, decision DCC 03-009, 19 February 2003, cited in F. Viljoen *International Human Rights Law in Africa* (2007) 532.

[19] ILDC 387 (CD 2006).

and Peoples' Rights, a treaty which has been explicitly incorporated through the Constitution. However, the decisions are brief and, as in most civil law jurisdictions in Africa, there are no references to case law, whether national or international, in the judgments.[20] The Benin Constitutional Court has in some cases extended the scope of the African Charter. For example, in *Okpeitcha v Okpeitcha*[21] the Court held that Mr Okpeitcha had violated article 29(1) of the African Charter, dealing with the duty to "preserve the harmonious development of the family", since he did not pay child support. Provisions of international human rights instruments have been applied by some other courts in Francophone Africa but not as frequently as in Benin.[22] It should also be noted that international human rights provisions are often not applied on their own as in *Okpeitcha* but are cited to reinforce provisions included in the Constitution.

Constitutions which provide that international treaties form part of the law of the land often make no provision for their interpretation. Should they be interpreted in accordance with domestic rules on statutory or constitutional interpretation or should they be given the meaning as set out by international bodies which have been set up to interpret them? The few provisions on Bill of Rights interpretation in civil law constitutions give little guidance. For example, the Constitution of Mozambique provides that:[23]

> "The constitutional principles in respect of fundamental rights shall be interpreted and integrated in harmony with the Universal Declaration of Human Rights and with the African Charter of Human and Peoples Rights."

A more concrete provision is Article 48 of the Constitution of Seychelles which provides that the Bill of Rights

> "...shall be interpreted in such a way so as not to be inconsistent with any international obligations of Seychelles relating to human rights and freedoms and a court shall, when interpreting the provisions of this Chapter, take judicial note of –
>
> (a) the international instruments containing these obligations;
>
> (b) the reports and expression of views of bodies administering or enforcing these instruments;

---

[20] For collections of judgments from the higher courts of Francophone Africa see http://droit.francophonie.org and http://www.accpuf.org.

[21] (2002) AHRLR 33 (BnCC 2001); ILDC 191 (BJ 2001).

[22] See e.g. the application of CEDAW in the judgment of the Supreme Court of Chad in *Societé des Femmes Tchadiennes Transitaires v Ministère des Finances* (2005) AHRLR 104 (ChSC 2005).

[23] Article 43.

(c) the reports, decisions or opinions of international and regional institutions administering or enforcing Conventions on human rights and freedoms;

(d) the Constitutions of other democratic states or nations and decisions of the courts of the states or nations in respect of their Constitutions."

Although the dualist approach is favoured by most common law countries towards incorporation of international law into domestic law, a small number of them include constitutional provisions that automatically incorporate international law. A prime example is the Constitution of Namibia which provides in Article 144 that:

> "Unless otherwise provided by this Constitution or Act of Parliament, the general rules of public international law and international agreements binding upon Namibia under this Constitution shall form part of the law of Namibia."

In *Government of the Republic of Namibia and Others v Mwilima and Others,*[24] the Supreme Court held that "Article 14(3) (d) of the Covenant [on Civil and Political Rights] … creates an obligation in regard to all those cases where the interests of justice require that an indigent accused person be legally represented."

Courts in other Commonwealth African countries have been more hesitant to directly apply international law to extend the protection provided by a Bill of Rights. In Swaziland, for example, the High Court in November 2007, referring to a 2002 judgment of the Court of Appeal, that "unincorporated international agreements and treaties may be used as aids to interpretation but may not be treated as part of municipal law for purposes of adjudication in a municipal court."[25] The Court did not consider the provision in Section 238(4) of the 2005 Constitution of Swaziland, which provides that "[u]nless it is self-executing, an international agreement becomes law in Swaziland only when enacted into law by Parliament." Arguably many provisions in human rights treaties should be considered self-executing and therefore directly applicable as national law.

---

[24] [2002] NASC 8 (7 June 2002).

[25] *Jan Sithole N.O. (in his capacity as a Trustee of the National Constitutional Assembly (NCA) Trust and Others v Prime Minister of the Kingdom of Swaziland and Others)* (Civil Case No. 2792/2006) [2007] SZHC 1 (6 November 2007) citing *Gwebu Ray & Ano v Rex* (19/2002; 20/2002) [2002] SZCA 22 (1 November 2002).

The Constitution of South Africa in Section 231(4) provides that a self-executing provision of a treaty ratified by Parliament is law in the Republic unless it is inconsistent with the Constitution or an Act of Parliament. This is an exception to the general rule that an "...international agreement only becomes law in the Republic when it is enacted into law by national legislation". South African courts have not been keen to discuss what they consider to be a self-executing norm. However, in *Government of RSA and others v Grootboom and others*[26] the Constitutional Court held that, "where the relevant principle of international law binds South Africa, it may be directly applicable." In practice, the interpretation clause in Section 39, which provides that a court when interpreting the Bill of Rights "must consider international law" and "may consider foreign law", has proved to be more important than the incorporation provision in Section 231(4). International law has been discussed in the context of interpretation of the Bill of Rights in many South African cases. In *S v Makwanyane and another*[27] for example, Chaskalson P held that:

> "Public international law would include non-binding as well as binding law. They may both be used under the section as tools of interpretation. International agreements and customary international law accordingly provide a framework within which [the Bill of Rights] can be evaluated and understood, and for that purpose, decisions of tribunals dealing with comparable instruments, such as the United Nations Committee on Human Rights, the Inter-American Commission on Human Rights, the Inter-American Court of Human Rights, the European Commission on Human Rights, and the European Court of Human Rights, and, in appropriate cases, reports of specialised agencies such as the International Labour Organisation, may provide guidance as to the correct interpretation of particular provisions of [the Bill of Rights]."

The failure to mention of the decisions of the African Commission on Human and People's Rights in the above *dictum* may be explained on the basis that, at the time of deciding the case, the first decisions (communications) of the Commission had just been released and they mostly consisted of no more than a paragraph or two of text without any reasoning. However, although this situation has now changed, South African courts have not made frequent

---

[26] *Government of RSA and others v Grootboom and others* (CCT11/00) [2000] ZACC 19; 2001 (1) SA 46 (4 October 2000); ILDC 285, para. 26.

[27] (CCT3/94) [1995] ZACC 3; 1995 (6) BCLR 665; 1995 (3) SA 391 (6 June 1995); ILDC 647, para 35.

references to the decisions or resolutions of the African Commission on Human and Peoples' Rights.[28] They have in many cases, however, made references to case law and recommendations of other international courts and treaty monitoring bodies.[29]

It must be pointed out that the consideration of international law in the adjudicating process in South African courts has been inadequate in many cases. The courts have omitted from consideration relevant international instruments and case law which should have been considered.[30] For example in *Grootboom* the Court did not mention the African Charter on the Rights and Welfare of the Child to which South Africa is a party and did not sufficiently analyse the provisions of the UN Convention on the Rights of the Child, with regard for example to the "duty of the state to provide material assistance and support programmes in cases of need to parents of children".[31]

Malawi follows the traditional dualist model with regard to treaties ratified after the commencement of the Constitution in 1994. However, treaties ratified before that year automatically form part of the law of the land unless provided for otherwise by Parliament.[32] Many international human rights instruments were ratified before 1994. The international law-friendly nature of the Constitution is further evinced by its provision that in interpreting the Constitution courts should, "where applicable, have regard to current norms of public international law and comparable foreign case law".[33] It also provides that "no restrictions or limitations may be placed on the exercise of

---

[28] Viljoen, *op. cit.,* fn. 2 *supra*, 560. See, however, see *Mazibuko and Others v City of Johannesburg and Others (Centre on Housing Rights and Evictions as Amicus Curiae)* (06/13865) [2008] ZAGPHC 128 (30 April 2008) para 39 in which Tsoka J noted: "Article 16 of the African Charter on Human and Peoples' Rights guarantees the right to enjoy the best attainable standard of both physical and mental health. Failure by the State to supply basic services, such as safe drinking water and electricity, has been found by the African Commission to be violation of the Article." The judge provides no reference to the case in which the Commission made this finding, *Free Legal Assistance Group and Others v Zaire* (2000) AHRLR 74 (ACHPR 1995).

[29] See J Dugard *International law – A South African Perspective* (2005) pp. 336–340, with further references.

[30] With regard to the inadequate consideration of international law in cases dealing with socio-economic rights see S. Rosa & M Dutschke "Child Rights at the Core: The Use of International Law in South African Cases on Children's Socio-economic Rights" (2006) 22 S. African J. on Human Rts 224. See J Dugard, *op. cit.,* fn. 29, *supra*, pp. 336–340, with further references.

[31] Rosa & Dutschke, *op. cit.,* fn. 30 *supra*, 250.

[32] Section 211.

[33] Section 11(2)(c).

any rights and freedoms provided for in this Constitution other than those prescribed by law, which are reasonable, *recognised by international human rights standards* and necessary in an open and democratic society".[34] Furthermore, rights recognised in the Constitution may be derogated from only where such derogation is consistent with international law.[35] In *Attorney General v Misiska*[36] the Supreme Court held that the International Covenant on Civil and Political Rights forms part of the law of Malawi. In an earlier decision under the old Constitution the same Court recognised the Universal Declaration of Human Rights as part of Malawian law.[37] The Universal Declaration and the African Charter, ratified by Malawi in 1989, have been applied by the High Court in a few cases as tools of interpretation.[38] The courts have also applied international labour standards.[39]

In Zimbabwe, it has been argued that human rights treaties ratified by Zimbabwe before 1 November 1993 form part of the law of Zimbabwe. In *Kachingwe and Others v The Minister of Home Affairs and Others*[40] the Supreme Court held that this was probably true but that "the point was not sufficiently argued … to make a firm determination of this point". The *Kachingwe* case is also interesting in that it included a thorough examination of international case law with regard to conditions of detention. The Court discussed cases from the Inter-American Court on Human Rights, the European Court of Human Rights and the African Commission on Human and Peoples' Rights. The Court held that the police cells complained of in the case did not "comply with elementary norms of human decency, let alone, comply with internationally accepted standards" and that this constituted a violation of the prohibition of inhuman and degrading treatment in Section 15(1) of the Constitution.

The Nigerian Constitution explicitly provides in Section 12 that "[n]o treaty between the Federation and any other country shall have the force of law except to the extent to which any such treaty has been enacted into law by the

---

34 Article 44(2). (Emphasis added.)

35 Article 45(3)(b).

36 (MSCA Civil Appeal 42 of 1998) [2000] MWSC 6 (1 December 2000).

37 *Chihana v The Republic* MSCA Crim. App. No 9 of 1992, [1993] MWSC 1, cited in Viljoen, *op. cit.*, fn. 2 *supra*, pp. 548–549.

38 *Chakuamba v Attorney General* (MSCA Civil Appeal No. 20 of 2000) [2000] MWSC 5 (23 October 2000); *Jumbe and Another v Attorney General* [2005] MWHC 15 (21 October 2005).

39 *Kalinda v Limbe Leaf Tobacco Ltd* (Civil Cause No. 542 of 1995) [2003] MWHC 79 (21 November 2003).

40 (2005) AHRLR 228 (ZwSC 2005); ILDC 722.

National Assembly." Nigeria is the only dualist country in Africa to have formally incorporated an international human rights treaty, that is, the African Charter on Human and Peoples' Rights, *verbatim* into its domestic law.[41] In *Abacha v Fawehinmi* the Supreme Court held that the African Charter had a status higher than ordinary laws but lower than the Constitution.[42] In *Inspector General of Police v All Nigeria Peoples Party and Others*[43] the Court of Appeal held that the African Charter on Human and Peoples' Rights is "part of the domestic laws of Nigeria and like all other laws courts must uphold it. These rights are already enshrined in our Constitution". The case dealt with the freedom of assembly, recognised in both the Bill of Rights and the African Charter. What about rights recognised in the African Charter which are not recognised as justiciable rights in the Nigerian Constitution such as socio-economic rights which are only recognised as non-justiciable Directive Principles of State Policy in the Constitution? A view is held that socio-economic rights are not justiciable despite the incorporation of the African Charter into national legislation. This view is based on a decision of the Court of Appeal delivered prior to the incorporation of the Charter.[44] However, there have been some recent cases where the provisions on the right to health in Article 16 and the right to satisfactory environment in Article 24 have been successfully invoked before the High Court.[45] It must be pointed out that very often litigants choose to invoke concepts such as "natural justice, equity and good conscience" in vindicating their rights rather than use the provisions of international law.[46]

3.2 Development of the Common Law on the Relationship between International and National Law

Many African constitutions, in particular of common law countries, have no constitutional provisions on the relationship between national and international law. These include the constitutions of Botswana, The Gambia, Ghana,

[41] See the African Charter on Human and Peoples' Rights (Ratification and Enforcement) Act (Cap 10) Laws of the Federation of Nigeria 1990.

[42] (2001) AHRLR 172 (NgSC 2000); ILDC 21 (NG 2000).

[43] Appeal No: CA/A/193/M/05, Court of Appeal in the Abuja Judicial Division, 11 December 2007 (unreported, on file with author), p. 27.

[44] *Archbishop Okogie v The Attorney-General of Lagos State* (1981) 2 NCLR 350 cited in S Ibe 'Beyond justiciability: Realising the Promise of Socio-economic Rights in Nigeria (2007) 7 African Human Rts L. J. 225, 241–243.

[45] *Odafe and Others v Attorney-General and Others* (2004) AHRLR 205 (NgHC 2004), *Gbemre v Shell Petroleum Development Company Nigeria Limited and Others* (2005) AHRLR 151 (NgHC 2005).

[46] See Ibe *op. cit.*, fn. 44, *supra*, 243–244.

Kenya, Lesotho, Tanzania, Uganda and Zambia. The countries might, as Botswana, have Interpretation Acts which include international treaties as an aid of construction of an enactment. This notwithstanding, the courts, as will be seen from the discussion below, are particularly important in determining the relationship between national and international law within these jurisdictions.

In *Kanane v The State* the Court of Appeal of Botswana held that criminalisation of homosexual practices did not violate the Constitution.[47] It made reference to a number of foreign cases but did not discuss international human rights law. In particular the Court could have taken note of the jurisprudence of the Human Rights Committee with regard to the International Covenant on Civil and Political Rights to which Botswana is a state party. In *Toonen v Australia*[48] the UN Human Rights Committee had dealt with the issue of criminalisation of sodomy and held that the reference to sex in Articles 2 and 26 of the ICCPR should be interpreted to include a prohibition on discrimination on the grounds of sexual orientation.

The lack of discussion of international law in *Kanane* is surprising in light of the judgment of the Botswana Court of Appeal in *Attorney-General v Dow*,[49] where the Court held, in a case dealing with discrimination on the grounds of sex, that the Constitution should be interpreted in the light of international law. Amissah JP held that:

> "Botswana is a member of the community of civilised states which has undertaken to abide by certain standards of conduct, and unless it is impossible to do otherwise, it would be wrong for its Courts to interpret its legislation in a manner which conflicts with the international obligations Botswana has undertaken."[50]

Aguda JA went further and held that international instruments which had not been ratified could also be of relevance in constitutional and statutory

[47] [2003] 2 BLR 67 (CA). For commentary on this case see EK Quansah "Same-sex Relationships in Botswana: Current Perspectives and Future Prospects" (2004) 4 African Human Rts L.J. 201; KN Bojosi "An Opportunity Missed for Gay Rights in Botswana: *Utjiwa Kanane v The State*" (2004) 4 African Human Rts L.J. 466.

[48] Communication 488/1992, CCPR/C/50/D/488/1992 (1994).

[49] [1992] BLR 119.

[50] *ibid.,* at 154.

interpretation.[51] The majority of the Court read in the word "sex" in the prohibition on discrimination in Section 15(3) of the Botswana Constitution.[52] However, the main basis for this was the inclusion of "sex" in Section 3 of the Constitution and the notion that "all the relevant provisions bearing on the subject for interpretation be considered together as a whole in order to effect the objective of the constitution". International law was thus used to reinforce an interpretation already reached.

Kenya has taken a different approach to its identical constitutional deficiency and in a constitutional amendment in 1997 incorporated the word "sex" in Section 82(3) which corresponds to Section 15(3) of the Botswana Constitution. In 2006 the High Court of Kenya in *RM v Attorney-General* rejected the approach in *Dow* to read in "sex" in the prohibition of discrimination as "usurpation of the work of the Constitution framers".[53] The Court held that "the words of the Constitution or a statute should be accorded their natural and ordinary sense". On the role of international law the Court held that:

> "...where the national law is clear and inconsistent with the international obligation, in common law countries, the national court is obliged to give effect to national law and in such cases the court should draw such inconsistencies to the attention of the appropriate authorities since the supremacy of the national law in no way mitigates a breach of an international legal obligation which is undertaken by a country."

This was the approach taken by the Kenya Court of Appeal in *Echaria v Echaria*:[54]

> "It is now about seven years since this Court expressed itself in *Kamore v Kamore* [[2000] eKLR (31 March 2000)], but there is no sign, so far, that Parliament has any intention of enacting the necessary legislation on

---

[51] *ibid.,* at 170 where he opined that: "There is no evidence that Botswana is one of the 100 states that have ratified or acceded to the [Convention on the Elimination of All Forms of Discrimination against Women] but I take it that a Court in this country is obliged to look at the convention of this nature which has created an international regime when called upon to interpret a provision of the Constitution which is so much in doubt to see whether that Constitution permits discrimination against women as has been canvassed in this case."

[52] See now Section 4 of the Constitution (Amendment) Act, 2005 which has amended Section 15(3) to include the word 'Sex'.

[53] (2006) AHRLR 256 (KeHC 2006).

[54] [2007] e KLR. Civil Appeal 75 of 2001, 2 February 2007.

> matrimonial property. It is indeed a sad commentary on our Law Reform agenda to keep the country shackled to a 125-year old foreign legislation which the mother country found wanting more than 30 years ago! In enacting the 1968, 1970 and 1973 Acts, Britain brought justice to the shattered matrimonial home. Surely our Kenyan spouses are not the product of a lesser god and so should have their fate decided on precedents set by the House of Lords which are at best of persuasive value! Those precedents, as shown above are of little value in Britain itself and we think the British Parliament was simply moving in tandem with the times."

The Court of Appeal added that:

> "Human rights issues in particular women's rights issues, took centre stage on the global theatre from the 1960s. There were, for example, International Covenants on 'Civil & Political Rights' and 'Economic, Social and Cultural Rights' which were adopted in 1966 and came into force in 1976; the Convention on the Elimination of All Forms of Discrimination against Women (CEDAW), which came into force in 1981; and the African Charter on Human and Peoples Rights, which was adopted in 1981. Kenya has ratified all those international instruments and they therefore provide a source of law which, in appropriate cases, the courts in this country may tap from."

In an earlier case *Rono v Rono*, decided in April 2005, the Kenya Court of Appeal with reference to the Bangalore Principles held that "the current thinking on the common law theory is that both international customary law and treaty law can be applied by state courts where there is no conflicting existing state law, even in the absence of implementing legislation."[55] Waki JA went on to hold that "the central issue relating to discrimination which this appeal raises cannot be fully addressed by reference to domestic legislation alone. The relevant international laws which Kenya has ratified will also inform my decision."[56] Frans Viljoen has argued that the Court in this judgment directly applied the "equality provision" in CEDAW "apparently at odds with domestic law" to distribute the estate.[57] However, the Court simply distributed the estate, for which customary law did not apply,[58] more equitably than in the High Court under the discretion allowed under the

[55] Civil Appeal 66 of 2002, (2005) AHRLR 107 (KeCA 2005) para 21.

[56] *ibid.*, para. 24.

[57] Viljoen, *op. cit.*, n. 2 *supra* 535.

[58] (2005) AHRLR107, para 26.

Succession Act.[59] It is submitted that the Court was simply using the principle of application of international law when there is no conflicting domestic law.

In *Lemeiguran* the Kenya High Court gave a wide interpretation of the Constitution in dealing with the right to political participation of an indigenous people. In its discussion the Court took note of provisions in ILO Convention 169, which has not been ratified by Kenya, and the Draft Declaration on Indigenous Peoples.[60] Arguably the strongest endorsement yet in Kenyan courts of international law was in *Waweru v Republic*. The High Court examined the right to life in section 71(1) of the Constitution and held that "the denial of wholesome environment is a deprivation of life" in a case dealing with the effects on the lives of people living downstream from a source of pollution. In reaching this conclusion the Court referred to the declarations of the 1972 Stockholm Conference on the Human Environment and the 1992 Rio Conference on Environment and Development and article 24 of the African Charter on Human and Peoples' Rights which provides that: "All peoples shall have the right to a general satisfactory environment favourable to their development."[61]

The Court of Appeal of Lesotho could have taken a similarly broad approach to the right to life in its 2004 judgment in *Baitsokoli and Another v Maseru City Council and Others*,[62] dealing with the right to livelihood. The Court did not discuss international law, choosing only to refer to comparative foreign case law. However, a year later in *Ts'epe v The Independent Electoral Commission and Others* the Court of Appeal held that "where there is uncertainty as regards the terms of domestic legislation, a treaty becomes relevant, because there is a *prima facie* presumption that the legislature does not intend to act in breach of international law".[63] After a discussion of UN, regional and sub-regional treaties and soft law the Court held that "[i]t is accordingly evident that if regard is had to Lesotho's international law obligations, these, if anything, reinforce the interpretation of section 18(4) (e) of the Constitution…"[64]

---

[59] *ibid.,* para. 28.

[60] *Lemeiguran and Others v Attorney-General and Others* (2006) AHRLR 281 (KeHC 2006); ILDC 698.

[61] [2006] eKLR (Kenya High ct., 2 March 2006).

[62] (2004) AHRLR 195 (LeCA 2004).

[63] (2005) AHRLR 136 (LeCA 2005) para. 16.

[64] *ibid.,* para. 22.

The Tanzanian Constitution provides in Section 9(1)(f) that:

> "The State Authority and all its agencies are obliged to direct their policies and programmes towards ensuring that human dignity is preserved and upheld in accordance with the spirit of the Universal Declaration of Human Rights."

In *Director of Public Prosecutions v Pete*[65] the Court of Appeal held that:

> "...[s]ince our Bill of Rights and Duties was introduced into the Constitution under the Fifth Amendment in February, 1985, that is, slightly over three years after Tanzania signed the [African] Charter [on Human and Peoples' Rights], and about a year after ratification, account must be taken of that Charter in interpreting our Bill of Rights and Duties."

In some cases the courts have mentioned international human rights provisions seemingly to reinforce the findings of a violation of constitutional provisions.[66]

Similarly, The Supreme Court of Ghana in *New Patriotic Party v Inspector General of Police*[67] held that:

> "Ghana is a signatory to this African Charter and member states of the OAU and parties to the Charter are expected to recognise the rights, duties and freedoms enshrined in the Charter and to undertake to adopt legislative and other measures to give effect to the rights and duties. I do not think that the fact that Ghana has not passed specific legislation to give effect to the Charter means that the Charter cannot be relied upon."

However, the fact that treaties can be relied on also means that sometimes human rights must be balanced against provisions in other treaties. In *The Republic v Gorman and Others*,[68] the Supreme Court of Ghana partly relied

---

[65] (Criminal Appeal No. 28 of 1990) [1991] TZCA 1 (16 May 1991).

[66] See e.g. *Legal and Human Rights Centre (LHRC) and Others v Attorney General (1)* (Miscellaneous Civil Case No. 77 of 2005) [2006] TZHC 1 (24 April 2006).

[67] [1993] 1 N.L.P.R. 73, at 82. See Viljoen, "Application of the African Charter on Human and Peoples' Rights", (1999) 43 J. of African L. 1, at 5.

[68] (2004) AHRLR 141 (GhSC 2004) para 38, 50.

on the United Nations Convention on Narcotic Drugs and Psychotropic Substances in denying the right to bail. The Court noted that:

> "The Constitution adopts the view of human rights that seek to balance the rights of the individual as against the legitimate interests of the community. While the balance is decidedly tilted in favour of the individual, the public interest and the protection of the general public are very much part of the discourse on human rights in our Constitution."[69]

In Uganda, the Supreme Court has held, when dealing with freedom of expression in *Onyango-Obbo and Another v Attorney-General,*[70] that it was "instructive to look at definitions of the same freedom in international instruments, to which Uganda is party." After citing the African Charter, the Declaration of Principles on Freedom of Expression in Africa of the African Commission and the ICCPR, the Court held that:

> "From the foregoing different definitions, it is evident that the right to freedom of expression extends to holding, receiving and imparting all forms of opinions, ideas and information. It is not confined to categories, such as correct opinions, sound ideas or truthful information."[71]

Likewise, the Supreme Court of The Gambia in *Sabally v Inspector General of Police and Others* struck down the retroactive effect of an Act of Parliament as violating the Constitution. The Court held with regard to a decision by the African Commission on Human and Peoples' Rights that the 'principles laid down are pertinent and relevant to the instant case'.[72] This is one of the few domestic cases in Africa which has made reference to the Commission's case law.[73]

In Zambia the courts have generally been reluctant to engage arguments based on international human rights law raised by the parties to a case.[74] An exception is the case of *Longwe v Intercontinental Hotels*[75] where the High

---

[69] *ibid.,* para. 37.
[70] [2004] UGSC 1, ILDC 166 (UG 2004) para 18.
[71] *ibid.*, para. 21.
[72] (2002) AHRLR 87, para. 13.
[73] See also the Gambian High Court case of *Denton v The Director-General, National Intelligence Agency and Others* (2006) AHRLR 241 (GaHC 2006).
[74] See e.g. *Attorney General v Roy Clarke* (Appeal No. 96A/2004) [2008] ZMSC 4 (24 January 2008).
[75] [1993] 4 LRC 221.

Court made reference to provisions in international treaties in addition to the provision prohibiting discrimination in the Zambian Constitution.

4 Conclusion

The overall impression given by the cases discussed above is that international law is included in the judgments by way of *obiter dicta* and that it does not have any clear influence on the outcome of the case. This is quite obvious in cases which simply note that the State is also party to this or that convention which provides for an identical right to the one provided for in the Bill of Rights of the State in question.

The lack of a principled approach to the role of international law in domestic courts as set out in this paper is, however, not unique to Africa. For example, Stephen Toope has noted with regard to the use of international law in Canadian courts that:[76]

> "Although the Court often invokes international treaties as an aid to interpretation, particularly of the Charter [of Rights and Freedoms], it does so in a fluid, not to say unprincipled, manner. Treaty norms are alluded to but simply to provide context for the specific interpretations promoted by various Justices."

When the executive and legislature do not fulfil the role of incorporating an international agreement into national legislation as required under most international human rights treaties, the courts must ensure that the ratification of a treaty does not become just an empty promise. From the examples set out above it is clear that the questions whether a treaty has been formally incorporated is not very important when it comes to how most domestic courts apply international law. As Mirna Adjami has noted:

> "…classical dualism of common law systems should serve as a barrier to the invocation of international human rights norms in national courts… [However], courts draw parallels to international human rights norms, as expressed in treaties or statements of principles, and the pronouncements of foreign courts regarding these rights in order to determine the scope of their national constitutional guarantees. Most striking is that the courts do

[76] S Toope 'Canada and international law' (1998) 27 *Proc. Can. Council Int'l L.* 33 quoted in Knop, *op.cit.*, n. 2 *supra*, 512.

> so seamlessly, without noting or explaining the binding nature or level of persuasive authority of these international and comparative sources."[77]

It can be added that courts sometimes refer to "soft" law, such as declarations and recommendations of treaty bodies, without making any distinction between international law which is binding on the State and what is mere recommendations. However, interpretation of a treaty norm in the form of a General Comment, for example, is needed particularly in situations where the constitutional or treaty norm is in itself "soft" in the sense of being defined vaguely or not at all. It should also be noted that the determination of whether a provision in a constitution or statute is vague is often the first step a court takes before deciding whether to use international law as an aid of interpretation.

The need for courts to consider not only the often vague provisions of treaties but also how they have been interpreted by international monitoring bodies has been recognised in a few cases, but is not generally applied.[78] The question is whether judges should interpret a constitutional human rights provision in line with the interpretation of international monitoring bodies of similar provisions in treaties to which the State is a party.

Thomas Buergenthal has noted with regard to the impact of the European Court of Human Rights in Europe that:[79]

> "[i]ts judgments are routinely followed by the national courts of the states parties to the Convention, their legislatures, and their national governments. The Convention itself has acquired the status of domestic law in most of the states parties and can be invoked as such in their courts."

Similarly with regard to the Inter-American human rights system Buergenthal notes that "states find it increasingly necessary to bring their national legislation and judicial practice into conformity with the Convention to avoid being held in violation of it."[80]

---

[77] Adjami, *op. cit.,* n. 2 *supra*, 165–166.
[78] Viljoen, *op. cit.,* n. 2 *supra*, 565.
[79] T. Buergenthal "The Evolving International Human Rights System" (2006) 100 Amr. J. of Int'l L. 783, 793–94.
[80] *ibid.,* 797.

The case law of the European Court on Human Rights and the Inter-American Commission and Court can never have more than persuasive authority in African courts, similar to comparative case law from other national courts. The situation with regard to the case law, Comments and Recommendations of UN treaty monitoring bodies and the African Commission on Human and Peoples' Rights is less clear. It is submitted that though not strictly binding on the domestic courts these would be more important in that they are applicable to the State and non-compliance with a clearly established rule developed under such a treaty would lead to a finding of a violation by the treaty body if the case were brought before it. Domestic courts should always prefer an interpretation that would avoid making the State violate an obligation at the international level. Decisions from certain international bodies should be considered binding and applied in the same way as a precedent of the highest national court. This would apply to judgments of the African Court on Human and Peoples' Rights, regardless of whether a State has ratified the Protocol establishing this Court, and decisions of courts of Regional Economic Communities (RECs) of which the State is a party. At the time of writing the African Court had not handed down any judgments and the courts of the RECs have not been very active. Apart from the ECOWAS Court of Justice, they have decided few cases dealing with human rights, partly because of the limited jurisdiction with regard to human rights complaints these courts have.[81]

The use of international law is of course no guarantee that it will always be correctly applied by the courts. For example, in dealing with *locus standi* the Malawi Supreme Court of Appeal examined the position in various countries and before international bodies and held, overlooking the practice of the African Commission to allow *actio popularis,* that:[82]

> "The African Commission on Human and People's Rights takes its queue behind the European Convention on Human Rights and uses the same standard for standing. It allows only a victim of a violation of a human right or freedom, protected by the African Charter on Human and Peoples'

[81] See, however, the judgment of the East African Court of Justice in *Katabazi and Others v Secretary General of the East African Community and Another,* Ref No. 1 of 2007, judgment of 1 November 2007. See also *Mike Campbell (PVT) Limited and Another v Republic of Zimbabwe* [2008] SADCT 2 (28 November 2008).

[82] *Civil Liberties Committee v Ministry of Justice and Another* (MSC Civil Appeal No. 12 of 1999) [2004] MWSC 1 (8 April 2004). Cf the decision of the African Commission in *Social and Economic Rights Action Centre (SERAC) and Another v Nigeria* (2001) AHRLR 60 (ACHPR 2001), para. 49.

Rights, to submit a claim to the African Commission. *Actios popularis* are not entertained by the Commission."

Counsel have an important role to play in providing the court with requisite information. However, one should also recognise that the application of international law by domestic courts is not a one-way street from international to national but that both sides have something to learn from each other. Domestic courts are applying international human rights law much more than have been shown in this paper. Indeed, every time a domestic court interprets a provision in its Bill of Rights the court contributes to the understanding of the content of the right, something that is recognised in domestic courts across the world in their use of comparative national jurisprudence.

The Challenges of Human Rights Protection in Botswana in the 21st Century

Charles Manga Fombad*

1 Introduction

Each day that passes we hear over the radio, watch on television or read in the news papers accounts of discrimination, torture, murders, rape and other forms of violence in many countries. Whilst such horror stories are certainly not new in human history they raise one of the most fundamental and emotional issues of our times: the problem of human rights protection. An important measure of the political health of any country today is undoubtedly the extent to which its legal system effectively recognises, guarantees and protects the human rights of its citizens. Although this is fundamentally a domestic matter, today, as in the past, its international dimension is of critical importance. Countries with a poor human rights record are usually treated as pariahs of international society.

Most of the basic indicators show that Botswana's human rights record is fairly good. However, there is always a danger in falling into the trap of complacency. There are two fundamental reasons why examining the challenges to human rights protection is of fundamental importance to Botswana today.

First, the human rights protection *problematique* is not posed in terms of their recognition, violation or enforcement, for these have been taken care of, but rather in terms of the quality and quantum of protection that is provided. For example, although the 1966 Constitution does not provide for a right to education, measures have been taken to recognise this right but questions remain as to how deep and effective these measures are and as to whether they ensure quality education.

Second, the Constitution, to be meaningful, effective and relevant, cannot be immutable. Constitutional stagnancy is a recipe for revolution or chaos. It is now well established in constitutional theory that constitutions, although

*Licence-en-Droit (LLB) (Yaounde), LLM, PhD (Lond.), Professor of Law, Department of Law, University of Botswana.

enduring documents that should not be easily and whimsically altered, must be able to reflect the ever-changing realities of the day. They are thus living instruments rather than documents cast in stone. The necessary corollary to this is that constitutional rules protecting human rights must also be flexible and must change to reflect the new aspirations, desires and hopes of the people. In this regard, the history of human rights teaches us two important lessons. The first one is that the development of human rights principles is not an end game but rather part of a continuum which changes and adjusts itself with the needs and aspirations of the day. The second is that the very survival of humanity depends very much on how well human rights are protected.

The wind of change that hit the African continent in the1990s, following the collapse of the Berlin wall signalling the end of the Cold War, brought with it an explosion of human rights protection in the new or substantially revised constitutions that most African countries adopted. This also coincided with one of the most severe global economic recessions since the Great Depression of the 1930s, marked by increasing poverty, unemployment, violence, displaced persons and erosion of the environment, all of which have affected the protection of human rights in diverse ways. Human rights law has been further complicated by the relentless spread of the HIV/AIDS virus, the 11 September 2001 terrorist attacks in the US, globalisation and, more recently, the soaring prices of oil and foodstuffs, with the latter provoking bloody riots in many countries around the world.

2 Critical Issues

All these problems raise critical issues about the adequacy of the present regime for human rights protection in the world in general and Botswana in particular. Of particular importance is the need to:

1. Rethink the state's human rights obligations in a context where it may no longer be directly responsible for providing services traditionally provided by the state;
2. Develop human rights obligations on the part of states beyond their own national territories, that is the potential extraterritorial reach of human rights law;
3. Develop credible enforcement systems;
4. Rethink the role of customary law;

5. Reassess the present responses to the explosive migration crisis; and
6. Adjust to the emerging problem of global terrorism in the post 11 September 2001 era.[1]

This is by no means an exhaustive list of some of the burning issues which call for rethinking the national human rights legal framework. Why some of these issues need to be carefully examined sooner rather than later will now be briefly explained.

2.1 Rethinking the State's Human Rights Obligations

The existing human rights regime was developed at a time when the state monopolised power and was the main duty holder. The assumption was that the state, as primary actor, was responsible for creating the environment in which people can enjoy their human rights. The entire system was therefore based on obligations imposed on the state vis-à-vis individuals in society – a vertical system of responsibility. This is understandable as one of the most critical and distinctive functions of a constitution is that it attempts to define the powers and duties of the three organs of government: the legislature, the executive and the judiciary.

Today, serious debate amongst comparative constitutional law jurists focuses on the dissatisfaction with the present system of vertical application of constitutional law. There are at least two reasons for this dissatisfaction.

First, mainly as a result of globalisation, many private actors now exercise functions that were traditionally exclusively reserved to the state. Many services previously falling within the remit of the state have been or are in the process of being privatised, such as the provision of water, electricity and healthcare. The withdrawal of the state from the provision of some of these essential services does not free it from its duty to ensure that the citizens enjoy their right to health or right to education. Of necessity, it means that there is a duty on the state to oversee how these other actors now provide these services and ensure that they do not violate the citizen's human rights. The challenge that this poses is how to adjust the state's obligations to provide these critical services, especially to the poorest in society, whilst recognising the role and responsibilities of the new private actors.

[1] For an elaborate discussion of most of these issues, see generally, Koen De Feyter, *Human Rights. Social Justice in the Age of the Market*, Dhaka, University Press (2005).

There are other new important actors such as transnational corporations, international financial institutions and multilateral organisations both on the international and domestic scene whose powers sometimes dwarf that of the state and which have the potential to violate human rights.[2]

This raises the question as to the extent to which the normal vertical application of human rights law between the state and the individual could, as a result of globalisation, lead to a horizontal application of human rights, duties and responsibilities between individuals and non-state actors, even including the possibility that one individual enforces his or her rights against another.

Secondly, because most constitutions impose duties only on the state, the quality of human rights is considerably diminished because there are many abuses that are committed by non-state actors, especially private individuals. For example, section 15 of the Constitution of Botswana prohibits discrimination on grounds of "race, tribe, place of origins, political opinions, colour or creed," but this does not prevent a landlord from refusing to let a flat to a person on grounds of race, sex, gender or any other similar discriminatory grounds, however perverse or manifestly racist these grounds may be.

There is therefore a need for reforms that will address these problems and expand the quantum of human rights protection available by imposing duties on all these other potential or actual violators. The elaborate comparative constitutional law literature on this issue suggests two possible approaches to ensure a horizontal application of human rights to cover other actors.[3] One is the direct horizontal approach and the second is the indirect horizontal approach.

The direct horizontal approach is provided for in the South African Constitution[4] as well as the constitutions of a few other African countries

[2] See, e.g. Diane Orentlicher and Timothy Gelatt, "Public Law, Private Actors: The Impact of Human Rights on Business Investors in China," 14 Northwest J. of Int'l L. and Business 1 (1993).

[3] See Diane Orentlicher and Timonthy Gelatt, *op. cit.,* Alfred Cockrell, "Private Law and Bill of Rights: A Threshold Issue of 'Horizontality'," in *Bill of Rights Compendium*, Durban, Butterworths (2001), p. 3A–18 and Halton Headle and Dennis Davis, "The Application of the 1996 Constitution in the Private Sphere," 13 S. Afr. J. of Human Rts at 59–60 (1997).

[4] See for example, Alfred Cockrell, "Private Law and Bill of Rights: A Threshold Issue of 'Horizontality'," in *Bill of Rights Compendium*, Durban, Butterworths, p. 3A–18 (2001) and Halton Headle and Dennis Davis, *op. cit.*, at 59–60.

such as, Malawi, The Gambia, Cape Verde and Ghana.[5] Ireland is probably one of the best examples of a country where the Supreme Court has interpreted certain provisions of its Constitution as having a horizontal effect. The Court has held that provisions such as article 40.3.1 of the Irish Constitution which declares that "the state guarantees in its laws to respect, and, as far as practicable, by its laws to defend and vindicate the personal rights of the citizen," impose a positive obligation on all state actors, including the courts, to protect and enforce the rights of individuals. This has been taken to require the courts to permit an individual to invoke the Constitution directly as a source of a claim against another individual.[6]

---

[5] The most elaborate example of this is found in section 8 of the South African Constitution of 8 May 1996 which states:
"(2) A provision of the Bill of Rights binds a natural or a juristic person if, and to the extent that, it is applicable, taking into account the nature of the right and the nature of any duty imposed by the right.
"(3) When applying a provision of the Bill of Rights to a natural or juristic person in terms of subsection (2), a court –

(a) in order to give effect to a right in the Bill, must apply, or if necessary develop, the common law to the extent that legislation does not give effect to that right; and
(b) may develop rules of the common law to limit the right, provided that the limitation is in accordance with section 36(1).

"(4) A juristic person is entitled to the rights in the Bill of Rights to the extent required by the nature of the rights and the nature of that juristic person."
Besides this, section 9(4) imposes a duty on private individuals not to discriminate against others on the same comprehensive set of grounds that applies to the state. Another example is article 12(1) of the Ghanaian Constitution of 28 April 1992, which states as follows: "The fundamental human rights and freedoms enshrined in this chapter shall be respected and upheld by the Executive, Legislature and Judiciary and all other organs of government and its agencies and, *where applicable to them, by all natural and legal persons in Ghana,* and shall be enforceable by the Courts as provided for in this Constitution." (Emphasis added). Section 15(1) of the Malawian Constitution of 18 May 1994 puts it thus: "The human rights and freedoms enshrined in this Chapter shall be respected and upheld by the executive, legislature and judiciary and all organs of the Government and its agencies and, *where applicable to them, by all natural and legal persons in Malawi and shall be enforceable in the manner prescribed in this Chapter.*" (Emphasis added).

[6] See Andrew Butler, "Constitutional Rights in Private Litigation: A Critique and Comparative Analysis," 22 Anglo-American L. Rev. 20 (1996). Examples of particular constitutional rights that have been given full horizontal effect include the freedom of association (e.g. *Meskell v Coras Iompair Eireann* [1973] I.R. 121, where it was held that a trade union violated an individual's freedom of association by enforcing a closed shop agreement on existing employees), the freedom from sex discrimination (e.g. *Murtagh Propertiess Ltd v Cleary* [1972] I.R. 330, where an injunction against a trade union was issued for violating an individual's right to equality by objecting to the employment of women by the plaintiff publican), the right to earn a livelihood (e.g. *Lovett v Grogan* [1995] 1 I.L.R.M 12 and *Parsons v Kavanagh* [1990] 10 I.L.R.M. 560), and the right to due process (e.g. *Glover v B.L.N.Ltd* [1973] 1 I.R. 388 where damages where awarded to the plaintiff for violation by the defendant employer of his constitutional right to the fair procedures implied into his employment contract permitting dismissal for just cause.

The second approach is what is referred to as the "indirect horizontal effect" approach, or an intermediate or hybrid position which is situated between the vertical and the direct horizontal approach. Whilst recognising as a starting point that constitutional rights apply only directly to the state, this approach nevertheless allows for some indirect application to private actors. Following this approach, the Canadian Supreme Court has interpreted sections 32(1) and 52(1) of the 1982 Charter of Fundamental Rights and Freedoms, which make a distinction between constitutional "rights" and constitutional "values", as permitting some horizontal application of the Bill of Rights to private individuals because it gives the courts an inherent power to develop the common law in line with the constitutional values contained in the Charter. The Supreme Court, however, made it clear in *Retail, Whole & Department Store Union v Dolphin Delivery Ltd*,[7] that the Charter did not thereby create any new cause of action because private parties still did not owe each other any constitutional duties as such but only required that courts interpret and apply the common law in a manner consistent with the fundamental values enshrined in the Charter. Thus, whilst the Charter rights imposed duties only on the state, its values influenced the entire legal system.[8]

A similar approach was adopted in the South African case of *Du Plessis v De Klerk*,[9] a defamation action between a company and a newspaper, where a majority of the Constitutional Court held that, although the Bill of Rights in the interim Constitution neither had "general direct horizontal application," nor applied to private litigation based on common law, it nevertheless might and should influence the development of the common law governing relations between individuals.[10]

The jurisprudence of the German Constitutional Court is also worth noting.[11] In a series of decisions in the 1950s, the Court developed the doctrine that has come to be known as *Drikkwirkung* (or third-party effect

[7] [1986] 2 SCR 573.

[8] For a comprehensive analysis of two forms of horizontal application of constitutional rights, see Stephen Gardbaum, "The 'Horizontal Effect' of Constitutional Rights," 102 Michigan L. Rev. 387, esp. at 398–400 (2003).

[9] 1996 (3) SA 850 (CC).

[10] It is, however, important to note that South Africa has moved from indirect to direct horizontal effect between its interim and final constitution. Under the latter, only some of the bill of rights will have direct horizontal effect under section 8(2) of the Constitution. See generally, Stephan Gardbaum, *op. cit.*, at 411.

[11] See Kenneth M. Levan, "The Significance of Constitutional Rights for Private Law: Theory and Practice in West Germany," 17 Int'l & Comp. L. Q. 571 (1968).

of constitutional rights), which holds that, although constitutional rights bind only governmental organs, they apply directly to all private law and so have indirect effect on private actors whose legal relationships are regulated by law. Thus in Germany, unlike in Canada, all private law is directly subject to constitutional rights and is invalid if in conflict with them.

In the final analysis, unlike the direct effect of constitutional rights on private actors resulting from imposing constitutional duties on them in the fully horizontal position, indirect horizontal effect is achieved via the impact of constitutional rights on the private law that individuals invoke in civil disputes. This impact on private law can be either direct, where constitutional rights fully apply to it, or indirect, where courts are required to take constitutional values into account in interpreting and applying its provisions. The critical point is that the effect is indirect on the private actors rather than on the law.[12]

Nothing prevents the state from imposing human rights obligations on private actors within the domestic legal system. However, the climate of competition for investment may be no incentive to enact corporate human rights obligations. A leaf could, however, be borrowed from India's Supreme Court, which has been willing to provide constitutional rights protection against acts by private actors or industry.[13] Several international and regional courts and monitoring bodies have also emphasised the fact that states do have obligations to offer protection to persons falling under their jurisdiction whose human rights are threatened by others.[14] These decisions have, however, not gone as far as distributing responsibility between the state and the private actor or holding the private actor independently responsible. It has been suggested by some authors that there should be shared responsibility for human rights violations between the public and private actors.[15] Other writers have developed the theory of corporate complicity which tries to make distinctions between direct, beneficial and silent complicity.[16] All this clearly shows that the role

---

12 See Stephen Gardbaum, *op. cit.*, at 404.

13 See, for example, its decision in *Consumer Education and Research Centre v Union of India*, (1995) 3 SCC 42.

14 See, for example, *Velasquez-Rodriguez v Honduras,* Inter-American Court of Human Rights Judgment No. 7920 of 29 July 1988, paras 172–177.

15 See, for example, C. Scott, "Towards the Institutional Integration of the Core Human Rights Treaties," in I. Merali, & V. Oosterveld (eds.), *Giving Meaning to Economic, Social and Cultural Rights*, Philadelphia, University of Pennsylvania Press at p. 230 (2001).

16 See, for example, A. Clapham & S. Jerbi "Categories of Corporate Complicity in Human Rights Abuses," 24 Hastings Intl'l & Comp. L. Rev. *339 (2001).*

of other actors and their possible liability for human rights violations in this era of globalisation and privatisation is something that can no longer be ignored.[17]

2.2 Extraterritorial Impact of Human Rights

Traditionally, states have human rights obligations only towards those people within their borders and who are subject to their jurisdiction. The question may arise whether Botswana can be made responsible for human rights violations occurring in a third country either directly or through the policies that it promotes and sponsors within an international organisation.[18] This is not an abstract issue for Botswana is a member of the Southern African Economic Community (SADC) and in 1998 joined South Africa and, acting under the auspices of SADC, sent troops to Lesotho in an attempt to put down opposition to the government headed by Prime Minister Pakalitha Mosisili following seven weeks of violent protests over rigged elections.

In a limited number of international and regional cases, states were held responsible for human rights violations occurring outside their own territory.[19] This has usually been in clearly defined situations. For example, the European Court of Human Rights accepts that a state is responsible for what happens in another territory, if that state, "through the effective control of the relevant territory and its inhabitants abroad as a consequence of military occupation or through the consent, invitation or acquiescence of the Government of that territory, exercises all or some of the public powers normally to be exercised by that Government."[20] The Court refused to accept that "anyone adversely affected by an act imputable to a Contracting State, wherever in the world that act may have been committed or its consequences felt, is thereby brought within the jurisdiction of the State." In the case itself, the consequence was that Belgium and nine other NATO states involved in military operations

---

[17] Particular attention should be given to the question of individual criminal responsibility for the human rights behaviour of a corporate entity. There is already a move at international level in this direction. Although the Statute of the International Criminal Court does provide for corporate responsibility as such, it makes managers of a corporate entity individually accountable for certain crimes. This is not exactly new because the Nuremberg tribunals, established after the Second World War, convicted directors of certain German companies of their involvement in war crimes.

[18] See S. Skogly and M. Gibeney, "Transnational Human Rights Obligations," 24 Human Rights Q. 781 (2002).

[19] See Koen De Feyter, *op. cit.* pp. 54–57.

[20] See *Bankovic et al. v Belgium and nine other states* 11 BHRC 435 (ECHR, 12 December 2001), analysed by Matthew Happold, "*Bankovic v Belgium* and the Territorial Scope of the European Convenion on Human Rights", 3 Human Rts L. Rev. 77 (2003).

against Serbia could not be held responsible for killings of civilians that occurred as a consequence of the bombing of the Serb Radio and Television building in Belgrade.

Generally, the cases so far suggest that extraterritorial human rights responsibility is envisaged only when individuals are under the effective control of the agents of another state. It is debatable whether this principle can be applied to other decisions taken by an international organisation such as SADC or the IMF which adversely affect the human rights of individuals in Botswana or elsewhere. It would seem that there is no effective control by the member states of these organisations. Nevertheless, these are issues that need to be considered and possibly a specific duty imposed on the receiving state to prevent or take responsibility for human rights violations committed in the execution of projects carried out in the country by an international organisation, such as the IMF, of which it is a member.

2.3 Developing Human Rights Enforcement Systems

Current human rights law, at both domestic and global levels, shares the general weakness of international law, that the enforcement systems are not very effective. Compliance continues to depend very much on the good will of governments. In spite of all the sweet talk about democratisation, good governance and accountability, in almost all the new or substantially revised post-1990 African constitutions, the powers of the executive have been expanded. With this increase has come an expanded scope for interfering with human rights enforcement mechanisms. There is therefore a need for more imaginative ways to be thought of remedying this problem.[21]

2.4 Rethinking the Role of Customary Law

One very convenient route for escaping many of the obligations imposed by international human rights treaty obligations has for long been to take cover under customary law. This avenue for escape was widely opened by section 15 of the Constitution, which, whilst prohibiting discrimination on grounds of "race, tribe, place of origin, political opinions, colour or creed," specifically

[21] I address this theme further in "Enhancing the Judicial Role in Human Rights Protection in Botswana", *infra*, Chapter Seven.. See also Rekha A. Kunar, Constitutional Rights and Judicial Activism: Bridging the Gaps in Botswana", *infra*, Chapter Six and Badala Tachilisa Balule, "The Role of the Judiciary in Protecting Freedom of Expression: How Far Should the Courts Go?", *infra*, Chapter 13.

states in subsection 4 that this prohibition "shall not apply to any law so far as the law makes provision:

> "....
>
> (b) with respect to adoption, marriage, divorce, burial, devolution of property on death or other *matters of personal law*;
>
> (c) for the application in the case of members of a particular race, community or tribe *of customary law* with respect to any matter whether to the exclusion of any law in respect to that matter which is applicable in the case of other persons or not;..."[22]

The compatibility of African customary law with human rights has been widely debated but the effect of the above provisions is constitutionally to sanction discriminatory laws in areas of personal or family law, including the devolution of property or in the application of customary law in any matter to the members of a particular race or tribe exclusively. Besides this, section 15(2) of the Constitution, in only prohibiting people from being treated in a "discriminatory manner by any person acting by virtue of *any written law*,"[23] implicitly excludes the application of customary law, which is based on "*unwritten law*". The preservation of gender inequality[24] which is inherent in the continuous application of customary laws in many of the areas covered by section 15(4)(c) and (d) is a glaring anomaly and an anachronism which is difficult to reconcile with any modern and effective system of human rights protection.

The conflict between customary law and human rights also arises in matters concerning children's rights. Although Botswana has ratified two important human rights instruments dealing with children, the Convention on the Rights of the Child[25] and the African Charter on the Rights and Welfare of the Child 1990,[26] both of which are critical to the whole issue of children's rights, neither of these has been domesticated. It is clear that several aspects of customary law, such as matrimonial property, succession and the status of women and children, are out of touch with modern human rights

---

[22] Emphasis added.

[23] Emphasis added.

[24] It continues to defy all logic why Botswana and other African countries bothered to ratify the Convention on the Elimination of All Forms of Discrimination Against Women, adopted in 1979, only to retain many customary law practices that make nonsense of its provisions. Botswana acceded to this Convention on 13 August 1996.

[25] Adopted by the General Assembly of the UN on 20 November 1989. See G.A. Res. 44.25, Annex 44 UN GA, which Botswana ratified on 14 March 1995.

[26] See OAU BAB/LEG/24.9/49, which Botswana ratified on 10 July 2001.

jurisprudence. It is worthwhile pointing out that, whilst many of these apparent practices that can no longer be reconciled with basic human rights, principles have been practised in African societies since time immemorial, many of them countervailing and compensatory measures which traditionally made these practices less harsh. However, these have been eroded by factors such as Christianity, capitalism, industrialisation and urbanisation and exacerbated by growing poverty. Thus the traditional checks and balances which protected children and women have all disappeared and left them totally vulnerable.

Although it has been suggested that an imaginative and innovative process of deconstruction of customary law could eliminate some of its aspects which are antithetical to human rights, the ability for non-customary courts, which handle customary law matters only by way of appeals from customary courts, to do so is limited by the fact that so few appeals reach these courts.

The very composition and the nature of proceedings before customary courts raise huge human rights concerns. Some of these are:

I. The fact that these courts, although manned by people, generally without formal education or training in court procedures,[27] have the power to send people to prison for up to five years. Perhaps the most worrying fact is that most people in Botswana prisons today have been sent there by customary courts.[28]

II. Many of the fundamental rules of due process provided for in section 10(1) of the Constitution are not followed in these courts. For example, legal representation is not allowed,[29] there are no standardised rules of evidence, and the presumption of innocence has been reversed when

[27] It is difficult to reconcile this with section 10(8) of the Constitution which states that "no person shall be convicted of a criminal offence unless that offence is defined and the penalty therefore is prescribed in a written law." How can one realistically expect a person who is not educated, let alone trained in the technicalities of criminal law and procedure, to competently interpret and apply the Penal Code?

[28] Information obtained from the Prisons Service on 2 August 2007 shows that as at 2 August 2007, the total number of prisoners held was 5,954 (5,761 males and 193 females) and of these, 3,156 (that is 53 percent) had been committed to prison by customary courts.

[29] See section 10(12)(b) of the Constitution. See further Louise W. McKinney, "Access to Justice – Through Legal Aid – Is a Human Right: Why and How Botswana Must Protect This Right", *infra*, Chapter Nine.

dealing with certain offences such as stock theft which carry prison terms of up to five years.[30]

III. Sentences include corporal punishment such as lashings on the buttocks in public.

Customary law appears to have lost touch with its roots.[31] Few serious attempts have been made to radically adjust and adapt it to the dramatic changes that have taken place in the last fifty years and it is not surprising that it is increasingly difficult to reconcile many of its principles with fundamental human rights principles.

A complete reassessment of the role and place of customary law as a form and a system of law is necessary. Ultimately, the radical changes that are needed to bring customary law in line with modern human rights principles can be brought about only by way of legislation. The goal should not be to adjust human rights principles to accommodate customary law principles, as the cultural relativists think, but rather to adjust customary law to fit with the human rights principles that are now of universal application. In formulating any legislation towards this end, parliament must know that it has a special, if not sacred duty: to preserve customary law, not for the sake of it, but because it is able to provide a system of justice that is consonant with and resonates with the present human rights concerns of the people. It is not an easy task but it must be done. The survival of customary law as a form and a system of law depends on a conscious effort being made to eliminate many of its inherent anomalies that cannot be reconciled with the human rights

---

[30] In the Stock Theft Act 1996, section 3(1) provides for a sentence of "...not less than five years or more than 10 years without the option of a fine..." and section 4 provides that once it is proved to the satisfaction of the court that a person was for example found in possession of any stock or produce reasonably suspected of being stolen, "it shall be presumed that such person is guilty of an offence under section 3..."

[31] For example, there are several studies which have shown that customary law in the pre-colonial days contained better guarantees of procedural fairness than Western law. S.K.B. Asante, "Nation Building and Human Rights in Emergent African Nations," 12 Cornell Int'l L. J. 72, at 73–74 (1969) asserts: "The notion of due process of law permeated indigenous law; deprivation of personal liberty or property was rare; security of the person was assured, and customary legal process was characterized not by unpredictable and harsh encroachments upon the individual by the sovereign, but by meticulous, if cumbersome, procedures for decision-making. The African conception of human rights was an essential aspect of African humanism sustained by religious doctrine and the principle of accountability to the ancestral shades." But, as T.W. Bennett, "Human Rights and the African Cultural Tradition," 22 Transformation 30, at 31 (1993) observes, attributing this "utopian quality" to customary law may often be done "safely distant from any possibility of empirical verification."

values of today. Any reforms in this direction, far from our cultural heritage, would actually reinforce it.

2.5 Reassessing the Response to the Immigration Crisis

Section 15(4)(b) of the Constitution allows for making laws that discriminate against aliens. In 2003, a new Immigration Act was introduced which imposes stiff penalties for illegal immigrants. This does not seem to have discouraged the steady flood of illegal immigrants, mainly from Zimbabwe but also from other countries such as Malawi, Mozambique and Zambia.

The rapid increase in the number of illegal immigrants has coincided with a rising level of xenophobia.[32] Many politicians have exploited the issue of illegal immigrants, thus increasing the level of xenophobia.[33] Botswana, like most other countries, does not allow aliens to vote or be candidates in elections. It has also imposed restrictions on their right to own real property or to engage in employment in either the public or private sector and requires reciprocity from their countries of origin before they can be allowed to practice certain professions.[34] A matter of particular concern is the discrimination against lawful aliens in the provision of certain social services, to which they have contributed through the payment of taxes.[35] This is at present the situation with respect to the imposition of the payment of school fees in government schools as well as payment of hospital charges in government-owned clinics and other health facilities. It is a policy that does little to stem the rising culture of xenophobia in the country, particularly the hatred of blacks from other African countries that are referred to disparagingly as *makwerekwere*.[36]

---

[32] See generally Eugene K. Campbell, "Attitudes of Botswana Citizens toward Immigrants: Signs of Xenophobia?", 41 International Migrations 71 (2003), Eugene K. Campbell, Reflections on Illegal Immigration in Botswana and South Africa, 21 African Population Studies No. 2, 23 (2006).

[33] See Charles Manga Fombad, "The Constitutional Protection Against Discrimination in Botswana," 53 Int'l & Comp. L. Q. 139, at 160–162 (2004).

[34] See, for example, Sections 5 and 6 of the Legal Practitioners Act. This requires an alien who applies to practise law in Botswana to prove, *inter alia*, that there is a reciprocal law in his or her country of origin which will allow a Botswana citizen suitably qualified to practice law in that country.

[35] See generally, D.D.N. Nsereko, *Constitutional Law in Botswana*. Pula Press, Gaborone, p. 538 (2002).

[36] This is a derogatory term that denotes exclusion on the basis of perceived cultural differences. The word itself is meant to reflect the perceived "unintelligible noises" closely related to the languages black Africans from other countries north of Botswana speak, and is used to promote hatred on the basis of language, and incompetence and even calls into question the humanity of these other Africans. See further Sichone, "The Making of *Makwerekwere*," 14 SAPEM (2002).

From a human rights perspective, there have been numerous reports over the last eight years when the situation in Zimbabwe started to deteriorate, that the human rights of these migrants, especially those who have entered the country illegally, have been regularly and systematically violated by both private individuals and government officials, especially members of the security forces. These violations have ranged from assaults, deprivation of food in detention centres, rapes, and beatings, sometimes resulting in deaths. Most of the countries in the region, such as Malawi, Mozambique and Zambia, are in crisis but this is worse in Zimbabwe where rising violence, poverty and progressive economic meltdown[37] has steadily forced its citizens to flee. Botswana and South Africa, the richest countries in the region, will have to contend with the frustrations of having to deport someone today only for the person to return a day or two later.

The government must face up to the task of recognising and protecting the rights of migrants, particularly illegal immigrants. Growing hatred of migrants and the disregard of their human rights damages Botswana's image as a country that respects the human rights of those who live within its borders. The global economic slowdown has been having a serious effect on Botswana's otherwise robust economy and this may only raise the level of xenophobia. With the ravages on the country's limited manpower caused by the HIV/AIDS pandemic and the continuous dependence on foreign expertise, it is counterproductive in the long term to adopt the harsh measures it has taken against illegal immigrants and the barely tolerant attitude towards the legal migrants whose services it needs. There is need to urgently revise the laws dealing with aliens to ensure that these are consistent with internationally accepted norms.[38] A migrant in Botswana is made to feel and remain a migrant whose stay in the country remains very tenuous[39] whilst citizenship is reserved

[37] See Chris Boutet, "It's not just inflation — it's hyperinflation!" Posted on 16 April 2008 http://network.nationalpost.com/np/blogs/posted/archive/2008/04/16/primer-it-s-not-just-inflation-it-s-hyperinflation.aspx.

[38] The Universal Declaration of Human Rights, 1948, whose principles are today considered to have become part of customary international law, and the International Covenant on Civil and Political Rights confer the great majority of the rights they enumerate to "everyone". CEDAW and the Convention on the Rights of the Child make no distinction between citizens and non-citizens in the rights they establish. The 1985 UN General Assembly Declaration on the Human Rights of Individuals Who are not Nationals of the Country in which they Live also sets some standards of practice by states with respect to dealing with aliens.

[39] Under section 7(f) of the Immigration Act (Cap 25:02), the President has the right to declare any alien a "prohibited immigrant," and the exercise of this power is non-justiciable. See the famous case of *Good v Attorney-General* [2005] 2 BLR 337, and "Good's last moments," *Botswana Guardian*, Friday 3 June 2005.

as a special favour which does no more than make some a "special *makwerekwere*". Botswana needs to adjust to the age of the American lottery and similar special modern immigration programmes introduced in countries such as Canada, the UK, and Australia designed to attract and retain the best from other countries by ensuring that the skilled legal migrants that it attracts are encouraged to stay and have a stake in their new home. So far, Botswana has only pursued a misguided policy which enables it to attract skilled migrants and because of unreasonable migration policies only get out the chaff from them whilst other countries are left to reap the real benefits when these migrants mature and leave for other destinations offering better prospects.

2.6 Adjusting to the Post-September 11 2001 Era

The 11 September 2001 terrorist attacks on the US have suddenly woken the world to a new threat – globalised terrorism planned by a non-state actor in one state and perpetrated in another state. The US response to these attacks has posed serious problems not only for international human rights and humanitarian law but also for domestic human rights law.

Leaving aside the international reaction and subsequent events, most notably the joint US and UK invasion of Iraq, in flagrant violation of international law, it is the new US foreign policy of linking aid to the adoption of anti-terrorist measures in line with its anti-terrorist agenda,[40] that has raised human rights concerns which Botswana cannot ignore. This agenda has entailed measures such as:

i) Extraordinary rendition;[41]
ii) Repackaging of existing repressive human rights practices under the cloak of anti-terrorism;

[40] For example, recipients of funds for projects sponsored by certain governmental bodies such as USAID and Canada's International Development Research Centre usually sign an agreement which includes provisions that the project complies with the donor government's anti-terrorism principles.
[41] This refers to the US practice of shipping terrorism suspects to foreign prisons where they may be forced, often under torture, to make confessions in circumstances which would be illegal if obtained in the US. This process has involved other illegal acts such as CIA agents kidnapping foreign nationals in foreign countries and then flying them to secret prisons in other foreign countries. See, for example, the account of an Ethiopian student that the CIA kidnapped and tortured in Morocco. Paul Craig Roberts, "Bush's Rendition Policy," http://archive.newsmax.com/archives/articles/2005/12/13/134146.shtml.

iii) Encouraging states to adopt vague definitions of terrorism in domestic legislation, combined with sweeping powers for law enforcement officials with numerous other restrictions that go far beyond the normal permissible limitations to the exercise of civil and political rights;
iv) Tightening of immigration and asylum laws with restrictions designed to keep out applicants who come from countries considered to be supporting terrorism; and
v) Increasing military aid and building bases in countries that are deemed to be strategically important in the war against terror.

Whether Botswana will yield to the temptation to adopt any of these measures, it must nevertheless be remembered that the world has usually responded to atrocities such as Hitler's Holocaust by extending rather than restricting the scope of human rights protection to prevent such abuses. As Dworkin has argued, the proper response to international terrorism is to intensify rather than restrict the regime of human rights protection.[42]

3 Conclusion

For human rights law to remain relevant and effective in protecting citizens it must be seen as flexible and responsive both to the new and the old threats to human dignity and human existence. New principles, approaches and techniques have to be developed or existing ones adjusted and adapted to meet the changing needs of society. It is now well settled that the recognition and protection of human rights is one of the core elements of constitutionalism.[43] Without a credible framework for human rights protection the sustainability of a democracy will be very much in doubt.

The need to regularly reconfigure the system of human rights to address the diverse challenges that face Botswana today is not self-evident. This might be so because the present system, in spite of its numerous limitations, has

[42] Cited in Charles Manga Fombad, "The Protection of Human Rights in Botswana: An Overview of the Regulatory Framework," in Charles Manga Fombad (ed.), *Essays on the Law of Botswana,* Juta & Co., Cape Town p. 30 (2007).

[43] See Charles Manga Fombad, "Post-1990 Constitutional Reforms in Africa: A Preliminary Assessment of the Prospects for Constitutional Governance and Constitutionalism," in Alfred Nhema and Paul T. Zeleza, *The Resolution of African* Conflicts, OSSREA & James Currey, Oxford (2008), pp. 181–188.

worked rather well.[44] The fact is that Botswana has not faced any really serious political crisis that has tested the solidity of its constitutional framework. Bearing this in mind, it is fair to say that regular discussions and debates like this on what needs to be done provide sufficient material to close any loopholes and go a long way to provide a human rights system that addresses the current pre-occupations of the day.

[44] See generally, Charles Manga Fombad, "The Protection of Human Rights in Botswana: An Overview of the Regulatory Framework," in Charles Manga Fombad (ed.), *Essays on the Law of Botswana,* Juta & Co., Cape Town. pp. 1–31 (2007).

Expanding the Frontiers of Fundamental Human Rights: Judicial Protection of Human Rights in Botswana

Hon Justice Key Dingake*

1 Introduction

> "In the arguments in favour of a declaration of rights, you omit one which has great weight with me, the legal check which it puts into the hands of the judiciary. This is a body, which if rendered independent and kept strictly to their own department, merits great confidence for their learning and integrity…"[1]

The above quotation from one of the founding fathers of the United States of America is apposite in the context of the following discussion. In recent times there has been scathing criticism emanating from important constituencies, doubting the capacity and willingness of the judiciary in Botswana to uphold the Constitution and enforce fundamental human rights. It has even been suggested that the judiciary is not independent in that it is controlled and directed by the executive in its decisions. Unfortunately, this criticism is often couched in general and somewhat polemical terms, making it difficult to join issue with any specific concerns that may exercise the critics.

In this paper, it is proposed to make the point that the nature, character, applicability and enforcement of human rights have always been contested. At a global level, a close study of the human rights literature and jurisprudence shows that the applicability of human rights has always excluded certain individuals. For a long time, women and children were not considered as

*CERT IDS (Oslo); LL.B (UB); LL.M (Lond.); PhD (Cape Town); Justice of the High Court of Botswana.

[1] Thomas Jefferson, 1787, quoted by AT Mason & WM Beaney, *American Constitutional Law,* Englewood Cliffs, N.J.: Prentice-Hall, (6th ed. 1978), p. 555 and referred to by Aguda JA in *Petrus and Another v State* [1984] BLR 14 at 34.

bearers of rights. History is replete with many examples where declarations of equality and freedoms were often accompanied by explicit denials of equality and freedoms for large sections of society. The courts, especially, in constitutional democracies have tried to close the gap between the lofty declarations of rights and the actual practice thereof.

The point will be made that our Constitution, at its core, aims to protect the weak, the marginalised, the social outcasts and the victims of prejudice and stereotyping. These noble and lofty ideals will ring hollow if the judiciary is not committed to the actualisation of these values. A review of the case law hereunder will show that our judiciary has, in the main, lived up to the spirit and promise of the Constitution and has upheld human rights without fear or favour in accordance with the judges' oath of office.

The judiciary in Botswana has expanded the frontiers of fundamental human rights in a very creative way and has in the process developed the Constitution through a variety of techniques. It is this record that has entrenched the confidence of the people in the courts and enhanced its credibility. In order to appreciate how the judiciary in Botswana has upheld human rights it is important to sketch, in broad strokes, the significance of human rights in so far as the judicial function is concerned. The primary and overriding duty of a judge or judicial officer is to uphold the Constitution of Botswana. The judges are bound to breathe life into the Constitution, to interpret it in a manner that is consistent with the challenges of the time, to ensure above all that its promise is kept in practice. In this age it will be difficult to sustain the argument that judges play no role in shaping the law. It is the judges who infuse "life and blood into the dry skeleton painted by the legislature and creat[e] a living organism appropriate and adequate to meet the needs of society…"[2] The interpretation of the Constitution is and will always be a matter of law, but since the heart of the Constitution is often about human rights, the enterprise of constitutional interpretation is also about people, their hopes, fears, aspirations and dreams. A constitution is not simply a statute that mechanically defines the structure of government. It is much more fundamental than that. It has been correctly defined as "the mirror reflecting

[2] The Hon. Justice P.N. Bhagwati, "Domestic Application of Human Rights Norms", Judicial Colloquium in Abuja, Nigeria 9–11 December 1991: Developing Human Rights Jurisprudence, Volume 4 (Fourth Judicial Colloquium on the Domestic Application of International Human Rights Norms: Commonwealth Secretariat/Interights, June 1992), 23, at 27.

the national soul".[3] It is up to the judiciary to clarify the content, the location and the context of human rights and their application.[4]

2 The Approach of the Courts to Constitutional Interpretation

A constitution is the soul of the nation. It is by its very nature crafted in such away that it should serve generations yet unborn, and the courts have a sacred duty to breath life into it so as not to render it a "lifeless museum piece".[5] The principles of constitutional interpretation enjoin our courts not to approach constitutional interpretation as if it is the same thing as statutory interpretation. In the case of *Petrus and Another v The State,*[6] the court articulated the proper approach to constitutional interpretation in the following terms:

> "It was once thought that there should be no difference in approach to constitutional construction from other statutory interpretation. Given the British system of government and the British judicial set up, that was understandable, it being remembered that whatever statutes that might have the look of constitutional enactment in Britain, such statutes are nevertheless mere statutes like any others and can be amended or repealed at the will of parliament. But the position where there is a written Constitution is different."

In other words a constitution is superior to a mere statute and the principles of interpretation that apply to it are different. The Constitution, it has been said by numerous authorities, must be given a generous and purposive interpretation.[7] Such an interpretation must eschew an unjustified restrictive interpretation of constitutional provisions.

The principles of constitutional interpretation enjoin the courts to interpret the constitutional provisions in such a way as not to erode the rights and freedoms of individuals unless by very clear words such an interpretation is unavoidable.

---

[3] *S v Acheson* 1991(2) SA 805, at 813 (NM) at 813 (*per* Mohamed A.J.A.).

[4] *Diau v Botswana Building Society* [2003] 2 BLR 409.

[5] *Attorney General v Dow* [1992] BLR 119 at 166 (*per* Aguda JA).

[6] [1984] BLR 14 at 34 (*per* Aguda JA).

[7] See, for example, *Attorney-General v Moagi* [1982] 1 BLR 124 at 184 (*per* Kentridge JA), *Petrus & Another v The State op. cit.* at 34–35 (*per* Aguda JA), *Dow v Attorney-General* [1992] BLR 119 at 131 (*per* Amissah JP) and *Sejammitlwa &Others v Attorney-General & Others* [2002] 2 BLR 75 at 82 (*per* Tebbutt AJP).

In the case of *Petrus,*[8] the court referred with approval, to a quotation, from the Nigerian case of *Rafiu Rabiu v The State,*[9] which said that a constitution is:

> "...the supreme Law of the Land; that it is written, organic instrument meant to serve not only the present generation, but also several generations yet unborn...that the function of the constitution is to establish a framework and principles of government, broad and general in terms, intended to apply to the varying conditions which the development of our several communities must involve, ours being a plural, dynamic society, and therefore more technical rules of interpretation of statutes are to some extent inadmissible in a way as to defeat the principles of government enshrined in the Constitution".[10]

In order to bolster the above principles, our courts, in interpreting the Constitution have taken on board international human rights norms, embodied in the International Bill of Human Rights. This is so because human rights can not be said to be the exclusive concern of individual states.

It proposed at this juncture to give a few examples of the manner in which the judiciary in Botswana has sought to protect human rights.

3 A Review of Selected Case Law on Human Rights

The High Court has the primary role in protecting human rights. It performs its functions by considering cases brought before it, where the parties allege that their rights have been or are about to be infringed.[11] The courts decide these matters within the framework of the Constitution, for it must always be remembered that, whilst the judges are the guardians of the constitution, they are not its overlords. It is equally important always to bear in mind that the judicial function is distinct from the legislative function, and that there are matters that are properly the function of the courts and others that are properly the function of the legislature. At times these functions overlap, but in the main their areas of competence are not the same, and this distinction must be kept as such.

---

8 *ibid.,* at 34.

9 1981 2 NCLR 293.

10 [1984] BLR 14 at 34–35.

11 Section 18 of the Constitution of Botswana.

The attitude of the courts to protection of human rights can therefore be gleaned from the case law, a brief discussion of which follows hereunder.

3.1 The Right not to be Subjected to Inhuman and Degrading Treatment or Punishment

Petrus and Another v The State[12]

Petrus is one of the early cases where the judiciary signaled its intention to uphold the Constitution and protect human rights. Two accused persons were convicted by a magistrate court of house breaking and theft contrary to section 305(1)(a) of the Penal Code as amended by the Penal Code (Amendment) Act, 1982.[13] Each of the accused persons was sentenced to three years imprisonment and to corporal punishment as provided by the Criminal Procedure and Evidence Act.[14] The matter came before the High Court for review and was eventually referred to the Court of Appeal, where one of the central questions was whether corporal punishment as prescribed by section 301(3) of the Criminal Procedure and Evidence Act was unconstitutional as being in conflict with section 7 of the Constitution. The Court held that repeated and delayed infliction of corporal punishment is unconstitutional.

During the course of argument before the Court of Appeal the State sought to dissuade the Court from striking out the offensive sections of the Criminal Procedure and Evidence Act, on the basis that the National Assembly was supreme and the Court should not interfere with a law it passed. The Court's response was crisp and to the point:

> "Under a written Constitution such as we have in the Republic of Botswana, the National Assembly is supreme only in the exercise of legislative powers. It is not supreme in the sense that it can pass any legislation even if it is *ultra vires* any provision of the Constitution. I believe it is clear, and this point must be strongly made, that every piece of legislation is subject to the scrutiny of the courts at the instance of any citizen…who has the necessary locus to challenge the constitutionality of the legislation."[15]

---

[12] [1984] BLR 14.

[13] Act No. 20 of 1982.

[14] As amended by the Criminal Procedure (Amendment) Act 1982, Act No. 21 of 1982.

[15] [1984] BLR 14 at 33.

The court also drew inspiration for its view that corporal punishment amounted to inhuman and degrading punishment from the African Charter on Human and Peoples Rights and the Universal Declaration of Human Rights and emphasised that "...the concept of human rights has started to take on the garb of international customary law among civilized democratic states of the world."[16]

3.2 The Right to Non-Discrimination

Dow v Attorney General of Botswana[17]

As is now well known by many in the legal community, this case concerned a challenge by a female citizen of Botswana to certain provisions of the Citizenship Act, which she considered discriminatory against women. The Citizenship Act of 1984 provided that children born to a male citizen married to a female non-citizen were citizens, whilst those born to female citizen married to a male non-citizen were not granted citizenship.[18]

This challenge must be understood in the context of section 15 of the Constitution which prohibits discrimination on the grounds of race, tribe, place of origin, political opinions, colour or creed. The ground of sex is not mentioned. The absence of the specific ground of sex led the Attorney General, who argued on behalf of the State, to submit that the framers of the Constitution had intended to discriminate on the basis of sex; otherwise they would have included sex as a prohibited ground.[19]

The Court, however, took the progressive view that it could not accept that the word sex had been omitted in order to permit sex discrimination.[20] The Court placed reliance on international legal instruments such as the Organisation of African Unity's Convention on non-discrimination and pointed out that Botswana as a signatory to that Convention was bound by its terms, notwithstanding that the Convention had not been incorporated into national law. It is significant that the Court held that the courts in Botswana are obliged to interpret the Constitution in a manner that is consistent with Botswana's obligations under international law, unless such an approach is

[16] *ibid.*, at 37.
[17] [1992] BLR 119.
[18] See s. 4(1) of the Act.
[19] The Constitution (Amendment) Act 2005, s. 4, has now included 'sex' as one of the grounds on which discriminatory laws are prohibited under s. 15 of the Constitution.
[20] [1992] BLR, at 181.

expressly prohibited or impossible. It was, the Court found, difficult to accept that Botswana would deliberately discriminate against women in its legislation whilst at the same time internationally supporting non-discrimination against females. Earlier, the High Court had made the same point, with more devastating clarity, when it said, per Martin Horwitz Ag J:

> "I do not think I would be losing sight of my functions or exceeding them sitting as a Judge in the High Court, if I say that the time when women were treated as chattels or were there to obey the whims and wishes of males is long past and it would be offensive to modern thinking and the spirit of the constitution to find that the constitution was framed deliberately to permit discrimination on the grounds of sex."[21]

It must also be appreciated that earlier, the State had sought to bar the applicant access to the courts by arguing that she did not have *locus standi,* to sue. The Court refused to allow the case to be disposed on that ground. It was the contention of the State that the applicant lacked the standing to sue because she was not personally injured. The Court, in rejecting that contention, took a broader view that all that the applicant had to show was that the application of the law will affect her in some way. In the words of Amissah JP:

> "We here see an example of a case where constitutional rights should not be whittled down by principles derived from the common law, whether Roman-Dutch, English or Botswana."[22]

The logic espoused in the case of *Dow*, was recently embraced in the case of *Sarah Diau v Botswana Building Society.*[23] This case concerned an employee who was asked to undergo an HIV test by the employer and she refused. She was then advised that she would not be confirmed as a permanent and pensionable employee of the respondent. No reasons were advanced for such a decision. The employee brought the case before the Industrial Court alleging a number of constitutional violations.

The respondent sought to argue that the Constitution of Botswana does not apply to the Industrial Court, since it is a private entity. The Court held that the constitution of Botswana does not confine the applicability of the Bill of Rights to organs of the State only. It was the Court's firm view that the

[21] [1991] 2 BLR 231 at 244–245.

[22] [1992] BLR, at 156.

[23] [2003] 2 BLR 409.

absence of any limitation as to the applicability of the Bill of Rights means that the obligation lies in respect of all who would undermine the enjoyment of constitutional rights, be they public or private actors. In further amplification of its reasoning the Court observed that:

> "In today's world there are private organizations that wield so much power, relative to the individuals under them, that to exclude those entities from the scope of the Bill of Rights would in effect amount to a blanket licence for them to abuse human rights."[24]

According to the Court, a reasoning that seeks to confine the application of the Constitution to organs of the State only is not only unauthorised by the constitution, but is also a static approach in that it fails to take into account the realities of the modern distribution of power and influence. The clear message that the Court in the *Diau*, case was communicating is that it was not the intention of the framers of the Constitution that in guaranteeing fundamental rights, such rights must only be respected by organs of the State alone, but that obedience to the law is required of every entity, be it corporate or otherwise. It was further the clear message of the court that it is under a duty to act so as not to permit anybody, entity or individual residing in Botswana, to deprive another individual of his or her constitutionally guaranteed rights.

3.3 The Right to Administrative Justice

Peloewetse v The Permanent Secretary to the President and Others[25]

This case involved a challenge to the decision of the Permanent Secretary to the President, in terms of which the appellant had unsuccessfully applied to be the Director of Sports. He sought to review and set aside the appointment of Shaw Kgathi, who was the successful candidate on the basis that his appointment did not meet all the requirements set out in the advertisement for the job that was issued to the public. The court intervened and quashed the decision of the Permanent Secretary to the President to appoint Kgathi. In the course of its judgment the court made the following pertinent remark:

> "It would, in my opinion, be wrong and dangerous to uphold a principle to the effect that implemented decisions of government should never be disturbed because the consequences of disturbance are invariably

[24] *ibid.*, at 427.

[25] [2000] 1 BLR 79.

prejudicial to good administration. We have, in this case, heard submissions which seem to be predicated on the belief that whatever government does must be right. Such submissions are contrary to modern thinking on governance, and should be rejected."[26]

The court emphasised the point that judicial review of executive action contributes to promotion of good government, noting that it is the duty of the courts to scrutinise government actions to ensure that when government acts, it acts correctly. Although the right to just administrative action is not entrenched in the Constitution or any statutes, our courts as demonstrated in *Pelowetse* have always used their review power to ensure administrative justice.

3.4 Freedom of Movement

Sesana and Others v The Attorney General[27]

In this seminal case the Court afforded relief to members the Basarwa tribe who had been forcibly removed from the Central Kalahari Game Reserve. The applicants brought an application before the High Court, challenging, *inter alia*, the legality of their relocation by government from the Central Kalahari Game Reserve to a settlement outside the reserve, the government's refusal to issue special game licences and its refusal to allow them entry into the reserve unless they were issued with permits. The applicants succeeded in a number of respects. The Court held that the applicants had been forcibly removed from the reserve.[28] The court further held that the government's refusal to issue special game licences to the applicants, together with its refusal to allow them entry into the reserve unless they were issued with permits, was unlawful and unconstitutional.[29]

3.5 Freedom of Expression

Media Publishing (Pty) Limited v The Attorney General and Others[30]

In this case, the applicant contested the validity of a presidential directive, the effect of which was to prevent State or parastatal bodies from placing

[26] *ibid.*, at 92 (*per* Amissah JP).

[27] [2006] 2 BLR 633.

[28] *Per* Phumaphi and Dow JJ, Dibotelo, J. dissenting.

[29] *Per* Phumaphi and Dow JJ, Dibotelo, J. dissenting.

[30] [2001] 2 BLR 485.

advertisements with the Botswana Guardian and the Midweek Sun Newspapers. The applicant conceded, correctly so, that it did not have a right to receive advertisements from government, but argued that, once the government has decided to withdraw the benefit, it can not do so for purposes of showing disapproval to the applicant for the applicant's conduct that may not be acceptable to government or its officials.

In that case it is recorded that the purpose of the directive was to punish the applicants. The Permanent Secretary to the President is quoted as having said that:

> "The real reason for the decision was therefore to demonstrate Government's displeasure at irresponsible reporting and the exceeding of editorial freedom. The fact that the applicant's papers especially the Botswana Guardian sometimes exceeed parameters of editorial freedom and fair comment has been recognized by Mr Jones who is described in the papers as the sole Director and shareholder of the applicant."[31]

Lesetedi J held that it was not competent for the government to withdraw the benefit of advertising in the applicant's papers in order to punish the applicant for having published material not acceptable to government. In the course of his judgment,[32] the learned judge associated himself with the following statement from the United States of America case of *Hyland v Wonder*:[33]

> "That Hyland had no right, in the first instance, to serve as a volunteer and that he could have been terminated at will does not diminish his first amendment claim. Indeed, both the Supreme Court and this Court have repeatedly and emphatically rejected this argument.
>
>> 'This Court has made it clear that even though a person has no "right" to valuable governmental benefit and even though the government may deny him the benefit for any number of reasons, there are some reasons upon which the Government may not rely. It may not deny a benefit to a person on a basis that infringes his constitutionally protected interest – especially, his interest in freedom of speech. For if the Government could deny a benefit to a person because of his constitutionally protected speech or associations, his exercise of those freedoms would in

[31] *ibid.,* at 493.
[32] *ibid.,* at 496.
[33] 972 F 2d 1129 (1992).

> effect be penalized… Such interference with constitutional rights is impermissible.' "[34]

It is quite clear from a reading of the judgment in *Media Publishing* that the Court when called upon to adjudicate on the dispute took a clear stand and rejected an attempt by the executive to encroach on fundamental human rights.[35]

3.6 The Right to Protection of the Law

Kenneth Good v The Attorney General[36]

The decision of the court in the *Good* case has attracted some media criticism accusing the court of failing to protect the human rights of *Good*. The facts of the case bear stating briefly. The applicant was a professor of political science at the University of Botswana. He was an Australian national. He lived with his 17-year-old daughter, who attended school in Gaborone. The daughter was also an Australian national. On 18 February 2005, the President of Botswana, without affording the applicant an opportunity to be heard, declared him an undesirable inhabitant and liable to be deported from the country. The declaration was said to be in the interests of peace, stability and national security of Botswana. The applicant challenged the validity of the President's declaration in court, contending, *inter alia*, that the declaration was a nullity because the President had not acted lawfully in making the declaration, and further that he had failed to apply his mind properly to the facts and the law and had acted irrationally in making the declaration.

In the alternative it was argued that certain provisions of the Immigration Act were *ultra-vires* the Constitution and invalid. The Court held that the applicant's deportation had not been in breach of his constitutional rights,[37] and further that it had not been shown that the President had failed to apply his mind properly to the facts and the law and or had acted irrationally in making the declaration.

---

[34] *ibid.*, at 1136 (internal citation to *Perry v Sindermann*, 408 US 593, at 597 (1972)).

[35] For similar reasoning in other jurisdictions see the cases of : *The Free Press of Namibia (Pty) Ltd v Cabinet for the Interim Government of South West Africa* 1987 (1) SA 614 (SWA); *Chavunduku and Another v Minister of Home Affairs, Zimbabwe and Another* 2000 (4) 1 (ZSC).

[36] [2005] 1 BLR 462 (HC), [2005] 2 BLR 337 (CA). For an analysis and critique of the case, see B.T. Balule, "The role of the judiciary in protecting freedom of expression: How far should the court go?", *infra*, pp. 281-287.

[37] [2005] 1 BLR, at 474.

The case of *Good* must be understood within the context of the relevant legislative provisions that were implicated. In particular it must be borne in mind that section 36 of the Immigration Act expressly excluded the right to be heard either before or after a presidential decision under the Act. Authorities are legion that, where the legislation is silent on whether a party who stands to be adversely affected by a decision of an administrative body, that party must be afforded a hearing and the Court will not insist on the right to be heard where a statute expressly prohibits a hearing.[38]

In a future case in which the question of deportation having implications for children arises it may be that courts will have close regard to the Convention on the Rights of the Child, which Botswana has ratified, and the corresponding jurisprudence.

3.7 The Right to Non-Discrimination, Privacy and Freedom of Association

Kanane v The State[39]

The appellant was charged before the Magistrate Court in Maun with two offences. On the first count he was charged with "unnatural offence contrary to Section 164(c) of the Penal Code".[40] On the second and alternative count he was charged with "indecent practices between males contrary to Section 167 as read with Section 33 of the Penal Code". It was alleged in the particulars of the offence that the appellant had permitted one Norrie, being a male, to have carnal knowledge of him.[41]

The appellant contested the charge on the basis that the aforesaid section violated rights and or freedoms that the Constitution conferred on him, namely, the right to non-discrimination,[42] the right to privacy[43] and the right

[38] See for example, *R v Brixton Prison (Governor), Ex parte Soblen* [1962] 3 All ER 641 at 658 *per* Lord Diplock) and *Arbi v Commissioner of Prisons & Another* [1992] BLR 246 (CA) at 251 (*per* Puckrin JA).

[39] [2003] 2 BLR 67.

[40] Cap. 08:01.

[41] The charges against the appellant were framed in terms of the Penal Code before it was amended in 1998. In terms of the pre-1998 Penal Code, it was an offence to have carnal knowledge of another male person. This appeared to be applicable to males only. However, the 1998 amendment made the aforesaid offence gender neutral, with the result that females could be similarly charged.

[42] Section 15 of the Constitution of Botswana.

[43] Section 9.

to freedom of association.[44] It was argued on behalf of the appellant that the violation of the rights outlined above was not reasonably justifiable in a democratic society. It was argued by the appellant that it was within his right to liberty to choose how to engage in a consensual union without being punished as a criminal. With respect to the alleged violation of the right to privacy it was contended that the State has no business in seeking to regulate sexual activity between two consenting adults, which takes place in private and does not harm any of the parties involved. It was further contended that criminalising sexual activity unjustifiably discriminates against gay persons. The court found no merit in the constitutional attacks mounted by the appellant, holding in essence that Botswana is a conservative society which disapproves of homosexual activity.[45]

The judgment has been attacked by Chilisa, who writes that:

> "The *Kanane* case thus represents a major setback in terms of the development of Botswana's human rights jurisprudence. The Court's reasoning or lack thereof seems to suggest that the Court is prepared to engage in *ad hoc* decision-making rather than develop concrete principles of judicial precedence that will guide them in dealing with like cases in future."[46]

Chilisa continues:

> "Discrimination is often the result of ignorance, stereotyping and certain irrational prejudices held by the majority about the minority. It is not judicious for a Court to turn away a minority population that has sought its protection on the basis that the majority does not believe in their cause. In so doing, the Court is tolerating and perpetuating discrimination along with irrational stereotypes about the minority held by the majority. This is alarming because the courts are not majoritarian institutions; rather, they

---

[44] Section 13.

[45] This line of reasoning is consistent with the decision of the Supreme Court of Zimbabwe in the case of *Banana v The State* [2000] 4 LRC, 62, where the Court held that the criminalisation of consensual sodomy between males in private did not violate constitutional protection against discrimination. The Court indicated that in interpreting the constitution it has taken into account that Zimbabwe is a conservative society on matters of sexual behaviour. See EK Quansah, "Same-sex relationship in Botswana: Current perspectives and future prospects" (2004) 4 African Human Rts L. J. 201.

[46] Mboki Mbakiso Chilisa, "Two Steps Back for Human Rights: A Critique of the Kanane Case", in (2007) 1 *The Botswana Review of Ethics, Law and HIV/AIDS* 52.

> are entrusted with protecting constitutional liberties because they are intended to be impartial and beyond majoritarian politics."[47]

It is common for lawyers who contend that criminalisation of homosexual activity violates the right to privacy or equal protection of the law and or that such criminalisation is discriminatory to invoke the seminal decision of the South African Constitutional Court in the case of *National Coalition for Gay and Lesbian Equality v Minister of Justice.*[48] In that case the Court held that discrimination on the basis of "sexual orientation" is impermissible. It emphasized that the right to privacy essentially means the right to be left alone and further that it must be understood as encompassing the right of a person to express his or her intimate relationships without penalisation.

The point must never be missed, however, that the outcomes of the challenges similar to the one the appellant mounted depend to a large extent on the constitutional provisions. The one distinct difference between the Constitution of Botswana and that of South Africa is that the South African Constitution expressly prohibits discrimination on the basis of one's sexual orientation. The Botswana Constitution does not have a similar expression. It must also be said that it is entirely possible that a different court interpreting section 15 of the Constitution, may well come to the conclusion that the mere fact that among the grounds upon which it is not competent to discriminate, there is no ground called "sexual orientation" does not mean it is competent to discriminate on the said ground. This particular perspective was espoused in *Dow* Amissah JP, in holding that the list provided in section 15 of the Constitution is not exhaustive, remarked that he was:

> "Fortified in this view by the fact that other classes or groups with respect to which discrimination would be unjust and inhuman and which, therefore, should have been included in the definition were not. A typical example is the disabled. Discrimination wholly or mainly attributable to them as a group as such would, in my view, offend as much against section 15 as a discrimination against any group or class. Discrimination based wholly or mainly on language or geographical divisions within Botswana would similarly be offensive, although not mentioned….The main thrust of that definition in section 15(3) is that discrimination means affording different treatment to different persons wholly or mainly attributable to their respective characteristic groups."[49]

---

[47] *ibid.*, at 51.

[48] 1999 (3) SA 1.

[49] [1992] BLR 119 at 147.

3.8 The right to be Afforded Adequate Facilities for the Preparation of one's Defence

***The Attorney General v Ahmed*[50]**

In this case the Attorney General had appealed against the order of the High Court ordering the State to provide the respondent with copies of all state witnesses' statements and other relevant documentary evidence. The Court held that section 10(2) of the Constitution which entitled the accused to a fair hearing and adequate facilities for the preparation of his defence required that those statements and other relevant documentary evidence be furnished to the accused. It is clear that the Court gave the word 'facilities" in section 10(2) of the constitution a generous interpretation, holding that, in the absence of specific limitations to the section, there is no basis to interpret the word "facilities" narrowly or restrictively. The Court considered that the word "facilities" must relate to anything that will be required by the accused in order to prepare adequately for his defence.[51]

Ahmed concerns the procedural rights of an accused in a criminal trial. This case established for the first time in Botswana that an accused person has a right to police statements.

3.9 The Right to Fair Hearing Before Dismissal

***Phirinyane v Spie Batignolles*[52]**

Prior to the establishment of the Industrial Court in 1992, job security was perilous. The common law reigned supreme and employers could dismiss employees by simply giving notice in accordance with the contract of employment, without having to show the existence of a valid reason for the dismissal. Similarly, an employer was not bound to hear an employee before dismissing him or her. The employee had no remedy against an unreasonable decision of the employer to dismiss him or her, unless the dismissal was in breach of the contract, in which event the employee might sue for damages for breach of contract. With the advent of the Industrial Court, the open season of firing at will was brought to an end.

---

[50] [2003] 1 BLR 158.

[51] This conclusion is similar to a number of decisions in other countries such as the case of *S v Nassar* 1995 (2) SA 82 (NM) *S v Sithole* 1996 (2) ZLR 575 (Zimbabwe) and *Molpole v DPP* 1997 (8) BCLR 1154 (Lesotho).

[52] [1995] BLR 1(IC).

Although the Employment Act or the Trade Disputes Act does not require the existence of a valid reason and fair procedure for an employee to be dismissed, the Industrial Court has consistently ruled that dismissals have to be procedurally and substantively fair. In a number of decisions the Industrial Court declared dismissals that were not founded on any valid reason substantively unfair and those in which the employees were not afforded an opportunity to say their side of the story procedurally unfair.

The Court justified the applicability of the requirement of substantive and procedural fairness by reference to the principles of natural justice and International Labour Termination of Employment Convention No. 158 of 1982. Article 4 of the Convention provides that:

> "The employment of a worker shall not be terminated unless there is a valid reason for such termination connected with the capacity or conduct of the worker or based on the operational requirements of the undertaking, establishment or service."

The Industrial Court did not have to wait for Parliament expressly to legislate against unfair labour practices. The gap that existed in the legislative framework was filled by reference to ILO conventions. This progressive interpretation of the law has enhanced job security at the workplace. In this modern era, the right to work is not only a matter of the right to earn a living; it is a matter of human dignity too.

4 Conclusion

The above cases are only some of the examples chosen to demonstrate the crucial role which the judiciary in Botswana has played and continues to play in protecting human rights. The cases discussed show that the judges in this country are not timorous souls and that they possess the requisite judicial craftsmanship to mould and shape the provisions of the Constitution in accordance with contemporary circumstances and challenges. However, such craftsmanship has its limits and the judiciary is wary of crossing the boundary between the judicial and the legislative functions lest it be accused of encroaching on the legislature's domain. It is a reality of life that a great number of people either do not know their rights or if they do, have no means to enforce such rights. It is therefore the sacred duty of the judiciary to protect their rights against unwarranted encroachment by government or any entity. On the above evidence, one can categorically assert that the judiciary has not fallen short of this sacred duty.

Judicial Protection of Human Rights in Botswana and the Role of International Human Rights Law

Hon. Justice Onkemetse Tshosa*

1 Introduction

There is worldwide recognition of the need for the protection of human rights and fundamental freedoms. In order to meet this need, both national and international instruments have been adopted for the protection of human rights. Almost every national constitution protects rights of individuals in one form or another. Similarly, there is a plethora of international human rights instruments for the protection of human rights. The important thing though is that these instruments should complement each other in order to accord maximum protection to their beneficiaries: individuals.

The main challenge lies in the way in which human rights norms contained in international instruments are applied at national level. In this regard, the judiciary, as the principal enforcer of human rights at national level, has a critical role to play. The courts should not only enforce national human rights standards, they should invoke international human rights norms in doing so.

The general aim of this paper is to explore ways in which the judiciary in Botswana has protected the rights of individuals in national law. It further examines whether in the protection of national human rights the judiciary has been informed by international normative standards. The discussion will isolate some human rights that have been the subject of judicial activity and investigate whether or not their enforcement has been influenced by international human rights law.

---

*LLB (UB), LLM (Lond.), PhD (Edinburgh), Attorney (Botswana), Judge SADC Tribunal, Senior Lecturer, Department of Law, University of Botswana.

2 Legal Framework for Protection of Human Rights: An Overview

2.1 International Legal Framework: Brief Observatory Remarks

The protection of human rights is universally recognised.[1] It is articulated in a number of universal, regional and specialised instruments. The main universal instrument which protect fundamental human rights of individuals is the United Nations Charter.[2] One of the purposes and principles of the Charter is promote and encourage respect for human rights and fundamental freedoms for all without distinction as to race, sex, language or religion.[3] Similarly, the UN Charter enjoins the General Assembly to initiate studies and make recommendations for the purpose of realisation of human rights and fundamental freedoms for all without distinction as to race, sex, language or religion."[4] Thus the UN Charter aims at protecting human rights of all without discrimination whatsoever. The charter is a legal instrument which accords the human rights norms legal protection.

The other universal instruments that recognise and protect human rights are the Universal Declaration of Human Rights (hereinafter UDHR), 1948, the International Covenant on Civil and Political rights (hereinafter ICCPR), 1966, and the International Covenant on Economic, Social and Cultural Rights (hereinafter ICESCR), 1966 together commonly called the International Bill of Human Rights. All these instruments except the UDHR are hard law, which contain the legal rights of individuals. They are legally binding. The UDHR is a resolution of the United Nations General Assembly. It is in the form of *soft* law and is therefore not legally binding. However, there is universal consensus that the UDHR is an important instrument that has influenced the drafting of other international instruments, such as the ICCPR and ICESCR, and national constitutions. It is therefore obligatory to protect the human rights norms therein.

---

[1] See generally W. McKean, *Equality and Discrimination in International Law* (1983), pp. 166–193; Chihana, *op. cit.*; B. Wolfgang, B., *op. cit.*; Tornudd, K. *Finland and International Norms on Human Rights* (1986) Martinus Nijhoff Publishers, Dordrecht pp. 246–261; Kees van Raad, *Non-discrimination in International Tax Law* (1986) Kluwer Law and Taxation Publishers, No. 6, The Hague, pp. 7–16; DJ Harris., et al. *Law of the European Convention on Human Rights* (1995) London, Butterworths, at pp. 463–488.

[2] The UN charter was adopted in 1945 at the San Francisco Conference. For the text of the Charter, see Ian Brownlie, *Basic Instruments in International Law*, Oxford, Oxford University Press, p. 2.

[3] UN Charter, Article 1(3).

[4] *ibid.*, Article 13(1)(b). See also UN Charter, Article 55(c).

At a regional level, there is a host of human rights norms embodied in the European Convention on Human Rights and Fundamental Freedoms, 1950 (hereinafter ECHR)[5] the African Charter on Human and Peoples' Rights (hereinafter Banjul Charter), 1981 and American Convention on Human Rights and Fundamental Freedoms (hereafter AMR), 1969.[6] At a specialised level, there are a number of instruments that recognise and protect human rights. These include the Convention on the Elimination of Discrimination against Women (hereafter CEDAW), 1984 and the Convention of the Rights of the Child (CRC), 1989. These instruments protect human rights norms that are contained in the universal human rights instruments, and therefore complement the universal instruments in the protection of human rights of individuals. Thus there is a whole corpus of international law contained in international instruments aimed at protecting human rights of individuals. Significantly, Botswana is a party to most of these instruments and is thereby under a legal obligation to protect the rights contained in them.

It is worth noting that there are other human rights norms which have attained the status of customary international law and as such binding on states and certainly on Botswana irrespective of whether the country is a party to the specific instruments that recognise and protect them. Thus there has been both state practice (*usus*) and psychological element or mental disposition (*opinio iuris cive necessatatis*) that these rights are binding on states and should be protected at national level irrespective of whether the state is a party to the particular treaty protecting them. The human rights norms include prohibition against torture, slavery, genocide and non-discrimination.[7]

The most pertinent question, however, is whether this body of law has direct application in national law such that it can be invoked and utilised by national authorities especially the judiciary in the protection of human rights. This question raises the issue of the status of international law generally and in particular human rights treaties in the national legal order of Botswana. Thus, what is the place of international law in the national law of Botswana?

The place of international law in national law has been dominated by the rival theories of monism and dualism. Monism, or alternatively, the doctrine of automatic incorporation, posits that international law and national law belong

---

[5] See Article 14. For discussion of this article see DJ Harris, M O'Boyle and C Warbrick, *op. cit.*, pp. 462–487.

[6] See Article 1.

[7] J Harris, *Cases and Materials on International Law*, London, Sweet & Maxwell, 6th edition, 2004, p. 34. As for genocide see the *Genocide Case*, 1950 ICJ Reports, p. 1.

to a single normative system as interrelated parts of one legal structure.[8] Proponents of this theory view all law as a single normative system comprising of binding legal rules, whether these rules are obligatory on States or individuals, or on entities other than states.[9] Thus municipal courts are obliged to apply rules of international law directly without these rules being transformed into domestic law by legislation or adopted by courts.

Classical dualism, also known as the adoption or transformation theory, tends generally to treat international law and municipal law as two entirely distinct and separate normative orders. According to this theory, the two legal systems originate from different sources and regulate different legal subjects.[10] As such, rules of international law, particularly treaties become part of national law only when the State causes them to be so.[11] At a practical level, however, courts do not strictly adhere to this doctrinal division. In monistic countries, sometimes courts do not directly apply an international law rule where such rule conflicts with a clear legislative provision or judicial precedent. Similarly, the effect of international law generally and treaties in particular will always depend on a rule of domestic law, especially constitutional law. The basic principle in most legal systems is that, in line with the doctrine of sovereignty, the internal application of treaties is regulated by domestic constitutional law.

It should be noted that an attempt, albeit inconclusive, to assign international agreements a place and role in municipal law of Botswana has been made by the General Provisions and Interpretation Act of 1984 (hereafter the Interpretation Act).[12] The Act provides:

> "For the purposes of ensuring that which an enactment was made to correct and as an aid to the construction of an enactment a court may have regard

---

[8] T Maluwa, "International Human Rights Norms and the South African Interim Constitution," *S. African Yrbk of Int'l L. 14*, (1993/94), pp. 14–42; OB Tshosa, "Giving Effect to Treaties in the Domestic Law of Botswana," (1995) 10 Lesotho L.J. 205, Ian Brownlie, *Principles of Public International Law*, Oxford, Clarendon Press, p. 33; M. Shaw, *International Law*, Cambridge, Cambridge University Press, p. 102.

[9] This is the claim advanced by natural law theorists and lawyers who argue that individual human beings, not States, are the real subjects of international law. See Shaw, *op. cit.,* p. 102; Brownlie, *op. cit.,* p. 33; Maluwa, *op. cit.,* pp. 17–18.

[10] This view is associated with positivism according to which States, rather than individuals, are the primary subjects of international law. See Brownlie, *op. cit.,* pp. 32–33; Shaw, *op. cit.,* p. 102. See also G Erasmus, "The Namibian Constitution and the Application of International law," 15 *South Africa Yearbook of International Law*, (1989/90) pp. 81–100 at pp. 84–85; Tshosa, *op. cit.*, at p. 208.

[11] Maluwa, *op. cit.*, at pp. 16–17.

[12] Laws of Botswana, vol. 1, Cap. 01:01, 1984.

to any *relevant international treaty, agreement or convention* and to any papers laid before the National Assembly in reference to the enactment or to its subject matter, but not to the debates in the Assembly."[13]

The Interpretation Act authorises courts in Botswana to construe domestic legislation relating to a particular convention by reference to relevant international treaties, agreements or conventions. The Act serves as a basis for invoking international conventions in any sphere of international law to interpret and ascertain the meaning of ordinary domestic legislation. Moreover, the Interpretation Act can also be used to interpret constitutional provisions.[14] Thus, the Act empowers the judiciary in Botswana to have recourse to rules of international law embodied in treaties in discharging their role of interpreting ordinary domestic law and the Constitution.

It is worth stressing that, although Section 24(1) of the Interpretation Act authorises Botswana courts to construe national law by reference to international agreements, it clearly does not of itself make international agreements part and parcel of municipal law. It only means that, under certain circumstances, international conventions may be used to construe and ascertain the meaning of municipal law where that law is uncertain, unreasonable and vague or unclear in order to fill in the gaps in the law. Thus, according to the monist-dualist debate, the Act does not make international agreements part of municipal law of Botswana. They can only be used as an aid to the construction of national law and ensure that the country observes its international legal obligations. This was underscored by the *Attorney General v Unity Dow*[15] case.

2.2 Domestic Enforcement of Human Rights

The constitutionally entrenched Bill of Rights cyclostyled "Protection of Fundamental Rights and Freedoms of The Individual" recognises and protects a variety of human rights norms.[16] These rights include the right to life,

[13] *ibid.,* section 24(1) [emphasis supplied].

[14] The Constitution of Botswana, Laws of Botswana, Cap. 01, section 127(13). This clause provides that the General Provisions and Interpretation Act shall apply, with the necessary adaptations, for the purpose of interpreting the Constitution. For a discussion of the General Provisions and Interpretation Act, see *Attorney General of Botswana v. Dow* [1992] BLR 199 (*per* Justice Amissah).

[15] [1992] BLR 229.

[16] The Constitution of Botswana, Laws of Botswana, Cap. 01:01, sections 3–16. Generally, see AJGM Sanders, "Constitutionalism in Botswana: A Valiant Attempt at Judicial Activism" (1983) 16 CILJSA 351, C.M. Fombad,"The Protection of Human Rights in Botswana: An Overview of the Regulatory Framework," in C.M. Fombad, *Essays on the Law of Botswana*, 2007, Juta, Capetown, p. 1 at pp. 6–7.

personal liberty, the right to a fair trial, protection against cruel, inhuman or degrading punishment or treatment, non-discrimination and the right to property.[17] Most importantly, the Constitution entrusts the High Court of Botswana with the responsibility of enforcing the Bill of Rights. Section 18(1) stipulates that "subject to the provisions of subsection (5) of this section, if any person alleges that any of the provisions of sections 3 to 16 (inclusive) of this Constitution has been, is being or is likely to be contravened in relation to him, then, without prejudice to any other action with respect to the same matter which is lawfully available, that person may apply to the High Court for redress." The Court "may make such orders, issue such writs and give such direction as it may consider appropriate for the purpose of enforcing or securing the enforcement of any of the provisions of sections 3 to 16 (inclusive) of this Constitution following a determination in pursuance of subsection (1)." Sections 3 to 16 catalogue the various human rights norms embodied in the Bill of Rights. Therefore, the High Court has a constitutional mandate to protect human rights in the country.[18] Below is a discussion of some human rights in which the utilisation of international human rights norms has arisen.

A. Right to Life

The right to life is recognised and protected in municipal law of Botswana. According to Section 4(1) of the Constitution:

> "No person shall be deprived of his life intentionally save in the execution of the sentence of the court in respect of an offence under the law in force in Botswana of which he has been convicted."[19]

This clause does not protect the right to life in positive terms. It protects this right in negative terms by merely preventing the intentional deprivation of life.

The right to life in Botswana is recognised and protected subject to limitations. Section 4(a) to (d) of the Constitution recognises that this right may be violated in the execution of a sentence of the court, in self-defence, to suppress

[17] Sections 3–16.

[18] See *Kamanakao v. Attorney General* [2001] 2 BLR 654 (HC).

[19] See L. Lindholt, *Questioning the Universality of Human Rights: The African Charter on Human and Peoples' Rights in Botswana, Malawi and Mozambique*, Dartmouth, Ashgate, pp. 94–7; The Right to life is also recognised along with other rights by the preambular Section 3 of the Constitution of Botswana entitled "Fundamental Rights and Freedoms of the Individual."

a riot or prevent the commission of an offence. These exceptional instances ensure legality when deprivation of life is contemplated. This means that these exceptions should be narrowly interpreted in order to protect life.

The practical importance of the right to life clause is, however, minimised by the institution of the death penalty. The death penalty is specifically authorised by the Penal Code, which explicitly and unambiguously declares that ".. any person convicted of murder shall be sentenced to death."[20] Capital punishment is reserved only for most serious offences such as murder, treason[21] and murder committed in the process of committing piracy.[22] In terms of Section 26(1) of the Penal Code, execution is by hanging. In order to limit circumstances under which it may be meted out, the death sentence may not be imposed on persons below 18 years[23] and pregnant mothers.[24] It also may not be imposed where there are extenuating circumstances such as provocation, intoxication, youthfulness and absence of actual intention to kill.[25]

The institution of the death penalty has been a subject of judicial activity. In discussing it, the courts have made reference to international human rights standards. The challenge has mainly been with regard to its constitutionality. One of the cases in which it was challenged is *Mosarwana v State.*[26] The appellant, on substantial evidence, was convicted of murdering the deceased for calling him a thief. The High Court sentenced him to death in accordance with Section 203(1) of the Penal Code. It also found that there were no extenuating circumstances and in accordance with Section 26(1) of the Penal Code, ordered that the appellant be hanged. On appeal to the Court of Appeal, the appellant argued, *inter alia*, that Section 203(1) permitting the death penalty was *ultra vires* the Constitution since Section 4 thereof prohibits the intentional taking of life. The Court failed to analyse the general import and content, and the precise limits of Section 203(1). It merely held that, on

[20] Penal Code, Laws of Botswana, Cap. 08:01, Section 203(1). See generally DDN Nsereko, "Extenuating Circumstances in Capital offenses in Botswana," 1991 2 *Criminal Law Forum* at pp. 239–259; Lindholt, *op. cit.,* pp. 97–99.

[21] Penal Code, Laws of Botswana, Cap. 08:01, Section 34(1).

[22] *ibid.*, Section 63(2).

[23] *ibid.*, Section 26(2).

[24] *ibid.*, Section 26(3). See also Criminal Procedure and Evidence Act, Laws of Botswana, Cap. 08:02, Section 298(1).

[25] Other factors which the court can take into consideration are those, not too remote or indirectly related to the commission of the crime, which bear upon the accused's moral blameworthiness in committing it. These factors include ill-treatment of an employee, ailment such as epilepsy and economic plight. See Nsereko, *op. cit.*, pp. 244–60.

[26] [1985] BLR 258.

proper construction, Section 203(1) prescribing the death penalty was not inconsistent with, and thus not *ultra vires*, the Constitution. The Court noted that, while there was international sentiment, as reflected at the United Nations, to abolish the death penalty, it could not rewrite the Constitution in order to give effect to such sentiment. Its function in the interpretation of the Constitution was adjudicatory and not legislative. Relying strictly and narrowly on national law and jurisprudence, the Court confirmed the death sentence. It is submitted that this case presented an opportunity for the Court to utilise international human rights norms to determine the constitutionality of the death sentence, taking into account developments at the United Nations.

The death penalty was also a contentious issue in *State v Ntesang*.[27] The appellant was convicted of murder and sentenced to death by hanging. He appealed against sentence on the grounds, *inter alia*, that the death penalty breached the constitutional right to life clause. The Court of Appeal dismissed the appeal and confirmed the death sentence imposed by the High Court. It thus refused to declare capital punishment unconstitutional. The Court did take judicial notice of developments to abolish the death sentence at the international level and invited parliament to consider effecting appropriate changes at national level. It nevertheless refused to use these developments to determine the constitutionality of capital punishment and, if need be, outlaw it.

The death penalty was also an issue in *Marietta Bosch v The State*[28] in which the appellant was charged with the murder of a close friend in order to get married to her husband. In challenging the constitutionality of the death penalty the appellant's counsel relied, *inter alia,* on comparative jurisprudence and international human rights norms to convince the court not to impose the death penalty. However, the Court Appeal confirmed the death penalty imposed by the court of first instance.

Similarly, in *Lehlogonolo Kobedi v State*[29] the use of international law argument to convince the Court not to impose the death penalty was unsuccessful. The appellant shot and killed the deceased with a pistol for which he had no licence. He was found guilty of murder and, no extenuating circumstances being found, was sentenced to death.

---

[27] [1995] BLR 151 (CA).

[28] [2001] 1 BLR 71 (CA). See also *Maauwe v. State and Another* [1997] BLR 693 (CA).

[29] [2005] 2 BLR 76 (CA).

These pronouncements clearly demonstrate judicial restraint in Botswana in invoking and relying on international human rights standards to outlaw the death penalty. This form of restraint is an indirect judicial confirmation of the classical dualist theory that international and national laws are distinct legal orders, each governing a different legal sphere.

It is important to note that Botswana has not signed the Second Optional Protocol to the ICCPR Aiming at the Abolition of the Death Penalty and the ICCPR. It is, therefore, not legally obliged to outlaw the death sentence or submit reports under both protocol to the Human Rights Committee.

B. Personal Liberty

Personal liberty in Botswana is recognised and protected by Section 5(1) of the Constitution. This provision does not protect this freedom positively. It adopts a negativist approach. Nevertheless, it incorporates, both in form and content, the basic international standards for the safeguard of personal liberty.

The most controversial issue concerns arrest or detention by police officers on reasonable suspicion of the person's having committed an offence. Generally, police officers have powers to arrest any person on reasonable suspicion or grounds of having committed a crime.[30] The question that emerges is, what amounts to reasonable grounds or suspicion that a person has committed a crime? Or, what is the test of reasonableness in these cases? This issue was a point of contention in *Oakametse v Attorney-General and Another*.[31] The applicant was arrested by the Police in Serowe in the Central Administrative District on allegations that she had called the complainant a witch. She was detained. She challenged her detention in the High Court on the basis of Section 5(2) of the Constitution. The Court held that to arrest and detain someone without evidence of any offence which she has or was suspected to have committed is unlawful and intrusion of her physical liberty. It further held that, where an individual is arrested or detained on suspicion that she has committed an offence, the suspicion must be reasonable and based on real evidence but not mere allegations. It ordered her release. The Court did not, however, indicate whether the test of reasonableness should be judged by national or international human rights standards. It, nonetheless, based its decision only on the constitutional provision protecting individuals' right to liberty.

---

[30] For instance, see Criminal Procedure and Evidence Act, Laws of Botswana, Cap. 08:02, Section 28 (b)(1) to (111).

[31] Civil Trial No (F) 52 of 1987 (unreported).

C. Non-discrimination

The Constitution of Botswana outlaws discrimination. Section 3 thereof stipulates:

> "...whereas every person in Botswana is entitled to the fundamental rights and freedoms of the individual, that is to say, the right whatever his race, place of origin, political opinions, colour, creed or sex, but subject to respect for the rights and freedoms of others and the public interest..."

This provision should be examined conjunctively with Section 15, which regulates discrimination in greater detail. Section 15(1) declares that "subject to the provisions of subsections (4), (5) and (7) of this section, no law shall make any provision that is discriminatory either of itself or in effect." Subsection 2 states, in part, that "no person shall be treated in a discriminatory manner by any person acting by virtue of any written law or in the performance of the functions of any public office or any public authority." Significantly, Section 15(1) prohibits the enactment of any law that is discriminatory. In terms of Section 15(3), discrimination is described as:

> "...affording different treatment to different persons, attributable wholly or mainly to their respective descriptions by race, tribe, place of origin, political opinions, colour or creed whereby persons of one such descriptions are subjected to disabilities or restrictions to which persons of another such description are not made subject or are accorded privileges or advantages which are not accorded to persons of another such description."

These provisions completely prohibit, or rather outlaw discrimination in the municipal legal order of Botswana. There is a positive duty imposed on the National Assembly not to enact a law that discriminates against any individual both of itself and in its effect. Moreover, no individual acting on the basis of any written law or in an official capacity is supposed to discriminate against any person.

The issue of sex or rather gender-based discrimination arose in the landmark case of *Attorney General (Botswana) v Unity Dow*.[32] The applicant, Unity Dow, a female citizen of Botswana, was, on 7 March 1984, married to Peter Nathan Dow, a citizen of the United States of America who had lived in Botswana for a period of 14 years. By that time, Unity Dow had already

---

[32] [1992] BLR 119.

had a child born out of wedlock in 1979. Subsequently, two children were born of the marriage in 1985 and 1987. By virtue of Section 21 of the Constitution of Botswana, every person born in Botswana on or after 30 September 1966 shall become a citizen of Botswana at the date of his or her birth. The first child became a citizen of Botswana. Meanwhile, earlier in 1984, a new Citizenship Act had been enacted which repealed Section 21 of the Constitution. Section 4(1) thereof provided, *inter alia*, that "A person born in Botswana shall be a citizen of Botswana by birth and descent if, at the time of his birth (a) his father was a citizen of Botswana"; or (b) in the case of a person born out of wedlock, his mother was a citizen of Botswana. The last two children were, therefore, not citizens of Botswana because their father was not a citizen of Botswana. Unity Dow applied for an order declaring that Section 4 of the Citizenship Act was *ultra vires* the Constitution of Botswana since it violated her fundamental rights to pass her citizenship to her children. In particular, the provision discriminated against her in that, unlike male citizens of Botswana married to foreigners, she could not pass her citizenship to her children. Thus, she was discriminated against on the basis of sex. She based her argument on Sections 3 and 15 of the Constitution of Botswana.

The respondent, on the other hand, contended that the applicant not only lacked *locus standi* to litigate on behalf of her children, but had herself suffered no loss of guaranteed rights. Moreover, since discrimination on the basis of sex was not mentioned under Section 15 of the Constitution, it was not a breach of the Constitution. This argument was predicated on the fact that, whilst Section 3 of the Constitution of Botswana mentions the word 'sex' as one of the grounds of discrimination, Section 15 does not.

Both the High Court and the Court of Appeal invoked and relied upon provisions of international human rights instruments and treaties to reinforce their decisions. These included the European Convention on Human Rights and Fundamental Freedoms, 1950, the Convention on the Elimination of All Forms of Dissemination Against Women, 1979, the African Charter on Human and Peoples' Rights, 1981 and the International Covenant on Civil and Political Rights, 1966.

Justifying the court's reliance upon the international human rights agreements to construe constitutional human rights clauses, Aguda, J.A., it is submitted, quite correctly, noted:

> "In my view it is the clear duty of this court when faced with the difficult task of the construction of provisions of the Constitution to keep in mind

> the international obligation. If the constitutional provisions are such as can be construed to ensure the compliance of the state with its international obligations then they must be so construed".[33]

The Court of Appeal concluded that Sections 4 and 5 of the Citizenship Act infringed the fundamental rights and freedoms of the respondent conferred by Sections 3 and 15 of the Constitution and was indeed *ultra vires* the Constitution.

It is abundantly clear that the liberal and purposive approach adopted by the Court to constitutional interpretation of human rights clauses and reliance on international human rights treaties and instruments in construing constitutional human rights provisions influenced the court to outlaw the relevant discriminatory clauses of the Citizenship Act.[34]

Another case in which the Court discussed the issue of the right of women against discrimination is *Student Representative Council of Molepolole College of Education v Attorney General of Botswana*.[35] The point of contention in this case was whether the Teacher Training College Regulations requiring pregnant students to withdraw from colleges and to have their return to college conditioned by the approval of the Permanent Secretary of the Ministry of Education was discriminatory against the female students and, therefore, unconstitutional. In deciding this issue, the Court of Appeal had to construe the relevant Regulations in the light of the anti-discrimination clauses of the Constitution of Botswana with a view to finding out whether the regulations discriminated against the female students. In so doing, the Court adopted the reasoning *Attorney General of Botswana v Unity Dow*. Aguda, J.A., observed:

> "Any constitutional challenge in our courts on the basis of sex discrimination must begin with the examination of this Court's decision in the *Attorney General v Unity Dow*. (It was in that case that this Court held that discrimination based on sex is repugnant to sections 3 and 15 of the Constitution of Botswana)."[36]

---

[33] *ibid.*, at 234.

[34] Quansah, "*Unity Dow v Attorney-General of Botswana* – One More Relic of a Woman's Servitude Removed?", (1992) 4 RADIC 195, at 202.

[35] [1995] BLR 178 (CA).

[36] *ibid.*, at 182.

Justice Aguda proceeded to recall what he had said in *Dow* case. He noted that treatment of different sexes based on biological factors cannot be taken or is not *per se* discrimination for it may be one way of regulating the lives and affairs of one gender in a manner that is inapplicable to the other. But Justice Aguda issued this caveat:

> "When such a situation occurs, the law or regulation under consideration must be reasonable and fair, and made for the benefit of the welfare of the gender without prejudice to the other; it must not be punitive to the gender in question."[37]

Ultimately, the Court concluded that the regulations were not, as claimed by the College and accepted by the High Court, protective measures in relation to the mother and child, and an encouragement of a well planned maternity leave. Rather, they were designed to punish unmarried young mothers. This was particularly so since the recurrence of pregnancy resulted in permanent exclusion from colleges. Moreover, married students were not subjected to similar measures. Their cases were considered as "particular cases." The Court emphasised the fact that the whole intention of making regulations specifically for women was unreasonable and unfair, and struck down the Teacher Training College regulations as being discriminatory against unmarried female students.

The decision in *Attorney General of Botswana v Unity Dow* has also been embraced by the High Court in *Ishmael Dintwa v State*.[38] This case does not deal with the principle of non-discrimination or with women's rights. However, it illustrates the influential value of the decision in *Attorney General of Botswana v Unity Dow* in construing human rights clauses of the Constitution. The applicant was charged with rape. He was brought before the Francistown Magistrates Court and remanded in custody. He later decided to file an application for bail before the High Court in Francistown. When the matter went before the High Court, the applicant had already been freed and released from custody following the withdrawal of the charges against him. Nevertheless, it was upon the apprehension that his bail application would not succeed on account of the Penal Code (Amendment) Act No. 5 of 1998 that denies bail to persons charged with rape, that he sought to have the Act declared *ultra vires* the Constitution of Botswana.

---

[37] *ibid.*, at 182–183.

[38] [2000] 2 BLR 72. For an analysis of this case, see O. B. Tshosa, "The Influence of the European Convention on Human Rights and the Jurisprudence of the European Court of Human Rights in Botswana: An Emergent Trend," a paper presented at the Department of Law Seminar, University of Botswana, October 2000.

In arguing that the Penal Code (Amendment) Act was unconstitutional, the applicant invoked the provisions of international human rights instruments on the right to bail, including Article 6 of the Universal Declaration of Human Rights, 1948 and Article 9(3) of the International Covenant on Civil and Political Rights, 1966. In addition, the Court did not hesitate to rely on *Dow* as a guide to the interpretation of human rights provisions of the Constitution. Justice Mwaikasu poignantly observed:

> "As I search for the appropriate stand that this court should adopt in its application upon the constructing of the above cited provisions of the Constitution, I am minded of and find valuable guidance in the decision of their Lordships of the Court of Appeal of Botswana in that monumental Case of *Attorney General v. Unity Dow*, cited above. It is in that case that their Lordships went at great length in reviewing various cases from within and outside jurisdictions as to how courts are expected to interpret the provisions of a written Constitution in the course of the enforcement of fundamental rights and freedoms of the individual as enshrined and entrenched in a Constitution, which I have the privilege to adopt."[39]

The judge proceeded to observe: "I should therefore be forgiven for making frequent references to such cases in the course of my ruling."[40]

Relying on *Dow*, the High Court adopted a broad, generous and liberal approach, and declared that Section 142(1)(a) of the Penal Code, as amended by Penal Code (Amendment) Act No. 5 of 1998 was *ultra vires* Section 5(3(b)) of the Constitution of Botswana guaranteeing individuals the right to bail. In fact, the judge noted that *Dow* had greatly eased the work of the courts in interpreting the provisions of the country's Constitution in the process of enforcing fundamental rights and freedoms of the individual.

D. Freedom of Expression

The right to freedom of expression is also protected by the Constitution. Section 12(1) declares that:

> "Except with his own consent, no person shall be hindered in the enjoyment of his freedom of expression, that is to say, freedom to hold opinions without interference, freedom to receive ideas and information without

[39] [2000] 2 BLR, at 76.

[40] *ibid.*

interference, freedom to communicate ideas and information without interference and freedom from interference with his correspondence. The enjoyment of the freedom is subject public safety, public order, public morality or health and the rights of others."

Freedom of expression was discussed in *Kenneth Good v Attorney General*[41] The applicant, an Australian citizen, was employed as a lecturer in political science by the University of Botswana on periodical contracts renewed from time to time for 15 years. On 18 February 2005 the President, acting under the provisions of section 7(f) of the Immigration Act, declared the appellant to be an undesirable inhabitant of, or visitor to, Botswana. On the same day he was declared a prohibited immigrant and received a notice requiring him to leave Botswana within three days. The applicant made an urgent application to the court arguing that his deportation would be a violation of his constitutional rights guaranteed in Chapter 2 of the Constitution and obtained an interim order staying his expulsion pending the institution of the proceedings in terms of section 18 of the Constitution. One such right was freedom of expression. The President's sworn affidavit stated in part that:

"...in consequence of information received by me from sources I deemed to be reliable, I, in the exercise of the powers conferred upon and vested in me by the provisions of section 7(f) of the Immigration Act,... did, on 18 February 2005, declare Kenneth Good to be an undesirable inhabitant of or visitor to Botswana, in the interests of peace, stability and national security of Botswana..."

The court held that the President had the power to declare the appellant a prohibited immigrant based, *inter alia*, on the ground of national security and was not obliged to disclose the reasons for doing so.

Importantly, in this case the court made reference to international conventions protecting the rights of individuals, including non-citizens, such as the International Covenant on Civil and Political Rights, 1966 and the African Charter on Human and Peoples' Rights, 1981. Judge President Tebbutt observed:

"Botswana... is a signatory to a number of international treaties. It is trite and well recognised that signing such a treaty does not give it the power of law in Botswana and its provisions do not form part of the domestic law

[41] [2005] 2 BLR 337.

of this country until they are passed into law by parliament. Those treaties do not confer enforceable rights on individuals within a State."[42]

Justice Tebbutt further observed that:

"It must be remembered that treaties and conventions do not confer enforceable rights on persons within a state until parliament has legislated their provisions into the law of the land."[43]

Thus, international agreements do not, at least in principle, have automatic operation in Botswana's domestic law. They require legislative transformation to acquire a force of domestic law if they are to benefit individuals and be invoked and relied upon by national institutions particularly the courts.

E. Reasonable Time

Trial within a reasonable time is protected by section 10(1) of the Constitution. The clause declares: "If any person is charged with a criminal offence, then unless the charge is withdrawn, the case shall be afforded a fair hearing within a reasonable time..."

The issue of trial within a reasonable time was considered by the judiciary in *State v Merriweather Seboni.*[44] On 31 December, 1967 the accused was charged with theft of Government funds totalling 1,257 South African Rands. The trial took place on 3 February, 1969. It effectively meant that there was a delay of more than a year. The delay was wholly attributable to the State in that a great deal of time was taken in transmitting the record from the Magistrate, who presided over preparatory proceedings, to the Attorney-General for his decision whether to prosecute the accused in the High Court or remit the case to the Subordinate Court for trial. It was finally decided that trial should take place at the High Court. At the commencement of the proceedings, the accused raised a preliminary issue concerning his right to be tried within a reasonable time as provided for under Section 10(1) of the Constitution. He argued, *inter alia*, that this provision had been infringed in relation to him because he had to wait for approximately one year before his trial could commence. The State argued that the delay was not attributable to it.

---

[42] *ibid* at 334.

[43] *ibid* at 355.

[44] [1968–70] BLR 153. For an analysis of this case, See Neff. *Human Rights in Botswana, Lesotho and Swaziland: Implications of Adherence to International Human Rights Treaties,* Institute of Southern African Studies, 1986, Maseru, at pp. 29–30.

Rather, it had been caused by the shortage of staff and administrative inefficiency and as such the accused could not seek the benefit of Section 10(1).

The Court construed Section 10(1) and noted that although the question of whether there had been unreasonable delay depended on the circumstances of each case, nonetheless a delay of this magnitude was extremely unreasonable. It had flagrantly violated Section 10(1) of the Constitution and thus prejudiced the accused. The Court observed that administrative deficiency cannot be invoked as justification for failure to comply with this clause. Clearly, the Court's decision cannot be faulted in the light of the inordinate delay involved. It gave substance to Section 10(1). Significantly, the Court decided the matter not only on the basis of Section 10(1) of the Constitution. It also sought guidance from decisions of courts in other jurisdictions, notably *Baker v Wingo*[45], as well as Article 5(3) of the European Convention on Human Rights.

The Court dismissed the State's application and ordered a retrial. Article 5(3) of the ECHR formed, in part, the inspiration for the Court's decision.

However, subsequent court decisions do not reveal the same readiness to seek guidance from international human rights law and sources when construing Section 10(1) of the Constitution. In *Rapula Sello v State*[46] the accused was convicted of malicious injury to property and sentenced to three years imprisonment. One year lapsed before his appeal against sentence was heard by the High Court of Botswana. The Court, per Hayfron-Benjamin, C.J., pointed out that trial within a reasonable time did not end on conviction in the court of first instance. It also applied on appeal. The Court held that the delay in question was unreasonable. However, the Court relied purely on Section 10(1), and not international human rights norms, to declare that the delay was unreasonable. Similarly, in *S v Makwekwe*[47] a delay of two years and eight months was held to be unreasonable. The Court retorted that it is no small matter for a man to live for years with a serious charge hanging over his head. The delay of this nature inflicts mental suffering and must of necessity interfere with the freedom of movement, employment opportunities

---

45 407 U.S. 514 (1972)

46 Criminal Appeal No. 121 of 1977 (unreported). For a detailed discussion of this case, see Sanders. AJGM, "Constitutionalism in Botswana: a Valiant Attempt at Judicial Activism" (1983) 16 Comp. & Int'l L. J. of Southern Africa," at p. 356.

47 [1981] BLR 196.

and social life of the accused. However, as in *Rapula Sello v State*, the Court decided the matter purely and only on the basis of national law. It did not inform its decision by international human rights standards in order to reinforce its reasoning and broaden its approach to the concept of trial within a reasonable time.

Be that as it may, international human rights standards and sources were invoked and utilised to interpret Section 10(1) in *Johannes Kgolagano v Attorney-General.*[48] On 2 December 1992 the accused was charged with murder. He was admitted on bail. His trial in the High Court only commenced on the 8 June, 1995. This meant that there was a two-and-a-half year delay in bringing him to trial. At the commencement of the trial, his attorney invoked Section 10(1) of the Constitution and argued that the applicant had been denied the right to trial within a reasonable time. In determining whether the delay in question was unreasonable, the Court sought assistance and guidance from comparative case law in Zimbabwe and the United States interpreting similar clauses[49] as well as international human rights instruments.

With respect to international human rights instruments, the Court noted:

> "The right to be tried within a 'reasonable time' is also guaranteed by Article 6(1) of the European Convention for the Protection of Human Rights and Fundamental Freedoms. This right is also embodied in the African Charter on Human and People's Rights.. (see Article 7(1))."[50]

The Court then concluded that the embodiment of this principle in different constitutions and international instruments reflects a universal acceptance of the right to a speedy trial as an important factor in the concept of fair trial. It held that a two-and-a-half year delay was extremely unreasonable. Thus, unlike in previous cases, the determination that there had been unreasonable delay in this case was partly inspired by human rights treaties, particularly Article 6(1) of the ECHR and Article 7(1) of the ACHPR.

These decisions demonstrate the fact that instances in which international human rights law and sources in general and particularly human rights treaties have been invoked and relied upon to construe the right of accused persons

---

[48] [1997] BLR 914 (HC).

[49] *ibid.*, at 918. Additionally, the Court made reference to the Canadian Charter of Human Rights and Fundamental Freedoms.

[50] [1997] BLR, at 918.

to be tried within a reasonable time in Botswana have been irregular and inconsistent. They have also not been uniform. The courts have yet to develop a clear and consistent pattern of invoking international human rights norms to interpret this right. This approach lessens the effectiveness of international law in protecting the right of individuals to be tried within a reasonable time in national law. These cases presented an opportunity for the courts actively to invoke international human rights law when interpreting the concept of trial within a reasonable time so as to reinforce national human rights law and jurisprudence, and broaden the national protection system.

F. Legal Counsel

Another right that has been the subject of judicial activity is the right to legal counsel. This safeguard is protected by Section 10(2)(d) of the Constitution. The clause proclaims that "every person who is charged with a criminal offence shall be permitted to defend himself before the court in person or, at his own expense, by a legal representative of his own choice." Paragraph (e) thereof further requires that a person be "afforded facilities to examine in person or by his legal representative the witnesses called by the prosecution.."

This clause firmly guarantees the right to legal representation in criminal proceedings. In line with international normative standards, these clauses mandatorily entitle all persons adequate time and facilities to present their defence. The entitlement encompasses numerous individual rights.[51] First, the right to defend oneself in person. It is the primary, unrestricted right of everyone charged with a criminal offence to be present at the trial and to defend himself or herself. A person should not be tried *in absentia*. If unable to do so, the person can forgo this right and then, as a second right, can make use of defence counsel. The court is required to inform the accused of this right. In principle, the accused may engage an attorney of his or her own choosing. This implies that accused persons should not be compelled to be represented by legal counsel not of their choice.[52] The third issue relates to expenses. If able to afford it, the accused should meet his or her own legal expenses. This right should be available to the individual as soon

[51] M. Nowak. *U.N. Covenant on Civil and Political Rights: CCPR Commentary* (1993) Strasbourg, Kehl and Rhein, p. 258.

[52] However, in the interest of administration of justice, the Strasbourg organs have taken a relatively restrictive view of this right and have affirmed the right of States to assign defence counsel against the will of the accused. See Nowak, *op.cit.,* at p. 259.

as he or she gets in contact with the criminal justice system, that is, soon after the arrest.

The right to legal counsel is an important safeguard in the concept of a fair trial - especially in criminal proceedings in the national set up of these countries. The vast majority of the population is unable to read and, most significantly, does not understand the official language of the courts, which is English. This makes it all the more necessary for accused persons to be afforded legal counsel to ensure that they receive effective legal defence. This right guarantees effective protection of the rights of the defence. Any hindrance therewith may amount to breach of this right.[53]

In practice, however, the Government provides free legal assistance, particularly for serious cases such as murder and manslaughter. In other cases, this right is limited where the accused cannot afford high legal fees. However, the non-Governmental Organisations such as the University of Botswana Legal Clinic and Botswana Centre for Human Rights, Women and the Law in southern Africa whose responsibility involves, *inter alia,* human rights education provide free legal assistance to needy persons. However, they too operate under severe financial constraints.

Legal counsel has been a subject of judicial activity in Botswana. The opportunity arose in *Agnes Bojang v State*.[54] The Court not only invoked and relied on comparative national judicial decisions, but also sought assistance and guidance from provisions of international human rights instruments in determining whether the Magistrate's Court was under a legal obligation to inform the applicant of her right to legal counsel on a charge of stealing by a person employed in the public service. The Court noted that:

> "...due to paucity of case law in our courts, which should guide this court in solving the question which faces it, it should not be surprising that assistance is sought from... some of the international conventions designed to provide guarantees similar or near to those found in our Constitution or laws."[55]

After referring to these international conventions, the Court emphasised that the right to legal counsel is meant to ensure a fair hearing. Failure to protect this right renders other constitutional safeguards meaningless. It quashed the

---

[53] *S v Mwambazi* 1990 N.R. 353, at 355; *Golder v United Kingdom* 1 E.H.R.R. 524 (1975).

[54] [1994] BLR 146.

[55] *ibid.*, at 152. International conventions that the Court referred to are the American Convention on Human Rights (hereafter ACHR), the ECHR and the ACHPR.

conviction. Thus the court's decision was partly influenced by human rights normative standards in these treaties.

A peculiar aspect of the right to legal counsel in the country but which is not found anywhere in the international human rights instruments concerns the right to legal representation in customary or traditional courts.[56] Section 10(12)(b) of the Constitution excludes the right to legal representation in customary courts or proceedings in a subordinate court for an offence under customary law. This inroad into the right to counsel is further embodied in Section 27 of the Customary Courts Act.[57] Persons appearing before these courts who wish to exercise this right must apply to court to have their cases transferred to the Magistrates' Courts.[58] Failure by the court to accede to the application renders the trial a nullity. This clause is similar to section 18(3) of the Constitution of Zimbabwe, paragraphs (d) and (e) which exclude legal representation in proceedings before "local" or traditional courts.[59]

Exclusion of legal representation in customary courts is based on the assumption that the concept does not form part of the traditional justice system, or rather the indigenous system of jurisprudence. Moreover, the officers who preside over traditional courts have no formal training in the law and procedure of ordinary courts.[60]

Significantly, a great number of people in the country, and indeed in most countries in Southern Africa, are subject to, and governed by, customary law. Criminal and civil cases of a minor nature, which constitute the majority of cases before courts in the country, are dealt with in customary or traditional

---

[56] The domestic law of Botswana distinguishes between two types of courts: the ordinary and customary courts. The ordinary courts include the Court of Appeal, High Court and the various grades of Magistrates Courts. These courts administer the general law: mainly Roman-Dutch common law and statute law. Customary Courts administer customary or traditional law of the various tribes in the country. See generally Nsereko, DDN "The Right to Legal Representation in Botswana," (1998) *Israel Yrbk of Human Rts*, at pp. 211–15.

[57] The Laws of Botswana Cap 04:05. Section 27 provides as follows: "Notwithstanding anything contained in any other law, no advocate or attorney shall have a right of audience - (a) in any customary court; or (b) in any subordinate court in any criminal proceedings or in any civil proceedings which fall to be determined by customary law." Generally, see Sanders, *ibid.*, at pp. 366–7.

[58] Customary Courts Act, Cap 04:05, Section 30(1).

[59] The Zimbabwean Constitution defines a local Court as "any court constituted by or under any written law for the purpose of applying African customary law." See Constitution of Zimbabwe, Section, 113(1).

[60] Nsereko, *op. cit.*, p. 220; U.S. Department of State, "Botswana," In *1996 Human Rights Country Reports*, p. 3.

courts. This essentially means that exclusion of legal representation in these courts curtails and further compromises the accused's guarantee of a fair trial. The practice adversely affects the right of individuals to legal representation, especially those living under the system of customary law. This practice illustrates a conflict between international human rights norms and customary practices.[61] Most importantly, it shows that the country does not fulfil its obligations under international human rights law and specifically the African Charter on Human and People's Rights to ensure the enjoyment of this freedom by its citizens. Its municipal law diverges from international normative standards.

It is worth noting that legal representation under customary law has been questioned in Botswana courts. However, the courts have addressed it only on the basis of national law particularly the Constitution and not international law. It was questioned in *Moisakamo v Moisakamo.*[62] The case did not concern human rights law. Rather, it dealt with the division of matrimonial property following divorce. The parties had been married by Christian rites and their property was therefore governed by the Married Persons' Property Act (Cap 29:03 of the Laws of Botswana), Section 7 which applies to marriages between "Africans". The effect of Section 7 is that in the absence of another prior arrangement between the parties, their property rights are governed by customary law. Counsel for the defendant argued that this fact effectively excluded the jurisdiction of the High Court to entertain the action. The proper forum was the customary court. However, the High Court was of the view that it had jurisdiction based, *inter alia*, on the fact that legal practitioners have no right of audience in customary courts. The unhappiness of the High Court with exclusion of legal representation in customary courts, particularly in the criminal law field, was expressed thus:

> "Of course the provisions of the Customary Courts Act in so far as they purport to bar legal representation of persons charged with offences under the Penal Code before customary courts are of doubtful constitutional firmness and validity."[63]

---

[61] For a detailed discussion of difficulties concerning the interaction between international human rights norms and customary practices, see S.N. Preis, "Human Rights as Cultural Practice: An Anthropological Critique," (1996) 18 *Human Rts Q.*, at p. 287; Neff, *op. cit.*, pp. 331–347; C. Beyani, "Toward a More Effective Guarantee of Women's Rights in the African Human Rights System," in R. Cook,(ed)., *Human Rights of Woman: National and International Perspective,* Philadelphia, University of Philadelphia Press, 1994, pp. 285–306.

[62] [1978] BLR 22 (HC); See Sanders, *op. cit.,* p. 367.

[63] [1978] BLR, at 26.

It is submitted that the right to legal representation must also be accorded the accused in customary courts. The issues before these courts may be complicated for the accused to handle without the assistance of a legal practitioner. The presence of a lawyer may also be beneficial to the court itself in unknotting these issues. The fact that the accused fails to opt out of the customary court's jurisdiction when the case first came to these courts should not be held against him. He has the constitutional right to legal representation at any stage of the judicial process. Legal representation is vital in these courts as in ordinary courts. It is a universal and inherent right of every person whether indigent or rich and irrespective of whatever law he or she is subject.

At the implementation stage, the right to legal counsel is compromised by the fact that most people in these countries cannot afford the high fees charged by attorneys. However, the Government in the three countries has a policy of providing free legal assistance to individuals who cannot afford the high fees charged by lawyers.

Notwithstanding these issues, it is clear that except for the Botswana case of *Agnes Bojang v State*, courts have construed the right to legal representation predominantly on the basis of national law and jurisprudence. They have not actively and consistently sought assistance and guidance from international human rights standards and sources when interpreting this right in order not only to enrich national law with international standards but also to utilise these standards to broaden and extend the right to legal counsel to customary law.

G. Torture and Inhuman or Degrading Punishment or Treatment

The prohibition of torture and related practices is articulated in Section 7(1) of the Constitution, which declares that "no person shall be subjected to torture or to inhuman or degrading punishment or other treatment." The clause outlaws torture, inhuman punishment or punishment and degrading punishment or treatment. Judicial activity on these issues has taken place in relation to two practices: corporal punishment and hanging. The question has been whether these practices amount to inhuman or degrading treatment.

Whipping, both judicial and non-judicial, has been a major concern in an attempt to implement prohibitions against inhuman or degrading punishment or treatment in Botswana. Whipping as a punishment is reserved for offences such as rape, assault occasioning actual bodily harm, housebreaking and robbery. It can be imposed on adult males but not female offenders, males sentenced to death or those over forty years.

The constitutionality of whipping has been challenged in Botswana courts. Significantly, in trying to resolve the issue, the courts have invoked and relied on international human rights law. It was an issue in *Clover Petrus v State*.[64] The two accused were charged with and convicted by a Magistrate for house breaking and theft contrary to Section 305(10)(a) of the Botswana Penal Code (Amendment) Act of 1982. Each of the accused was sentenced to three years imprisonment and to corporal punishment as provided for by Section 301(3) of the Criminal Procedure and Evidence Act. This clause authorised the administration of corporal punishment at delayed and repeated intervals. The accused lodged an appeal with the High Court against both the conviction and sentence. On the issue of corporal punishment, they argued that such a penalty was contrary to Section 7(1) of the Constitution.

In arguing that the institution of corporal punishment or caning was unconstitutional, the appellants relied on the decision of the European Court of Human Rights in *Tyrer v United Kingdom*[65] and on a decision of the German Constitutional Court as well as other relevant international human rights instruments. In essence, the appellants wanted the Court to determine the constitutionality of corporal punishment against international human rights law embodied in these sources.

In resolving this point, the Court, per Aguda, J. A., also invoked and relied, in part, on these human rights treaties, that is, Article 5 of the ACHPR, Article 5 of the UDHR, the ACHR and the ECHR.[66] Justice Aguda noted that he relied on these instruments to demonstrate that human rights have matured into customary international law binding on all States including Botswana.

The Court also referred to the ECtHR decision in *Tyrer v United Kingdom*. Maisels, J.P., said:

> "I now deal with the reasons for the court's finding that corporal punishment as prescribed in section 301(3) of the CPEA is *ultra vires*...

---

[64] [1985] BLR 14. This case is fully discussion in Lindholt, *op. cit.*, 106.

[65] 2 EHRR 1 (1978).

[66] [1984] BLR, at 24.

> We were also referred to a decision of the European Court of Human rights, *Tyrer v. United Kingdom*, 2 EHHR 1..and to the decision of the German Court on 10th June 1963... A reading of the *dicta* in the various judgments ...leaves me in no doubt that the repeated and delayed infliction of strokes as enjoined by section 301(3), would be regarded as inhuman or degrading."[67]

The Court proceeded to observe that there was a universally recognised normative prohibition against corporal punishment. Moreover, as a "member of a comity of civilised nations," Botswana was legally bound to proscribe this form of punishment.[68] The Court finally held that the infliction of whipping in a delayed and repeated manner was inhuman and degrading punishment. It held, however, that whipping *per se* is not an inhuman or degrading punishment.[69] The important point for the present analysis is that the Court relied on international human rights treaties to outlaw instalmental whipping or corporal punishment by instalments.

International human rights law was also used to challenge whipping in *Desai and Modi v The State.*[70] The case involved an appeal to the High Court of Botswana against both conviction and sentences from a decision of the Senior Magistrate for Gaborone Administrative District in which the appellants had been charged with unlawful possession of a habit-forming drug, Mandrax, contrary to the Habit Forming Drugs Act of Botswana. Both appellants were each sentenced to 10 years' imprisonment, but the second appellant, Modi, received an additional three strokes with a cane and the first appellant, because of his age, 62 years, was spared the strokes. As in *Clover Petrus v State*, the second appellant argued as against the sentence of corporal punishment that the imposition of a long term of imprisonment in addition to corporal punishment amounted to an inhuman and degrading treatment and, as such, contravened Section 7(1) of the Constitution prohibiting that form of punishment. Both appellants also argued that the provisions of domestic legislation empowering the courts to impose a sentence of whipping were unconstitutional, hence null and void.

---

67 *ibid.*, at 24–25.

68 *ibid.*, at 25 (emphasis supplied).

69 However, Justice Akinola Aguda observed that he was convinced "beyond any shadow of doubt that the mere imposition of corporal punishment is under any circumstances at this time and age certainly degrading if not inhuman." *ibid.*, at 24–5.

70 [1985] BLR 582, aff'd [1987] BLR 55.

The Court rejected the argument that a sentence of strokes was inhuman and degrading. However, after referring[71] to *Clover Petrus v State* and the ECtHR's decision in *Tyrer v United Kingdom*, it noted that to combine strokes with a term of imprisonment amounted to an inhuman and degrading treatment. It ordered the deletion of the strokes. These cases may be contrasted with *Moatshe and Another v S,*[72] where the Court, after reviewing the two cases discussed above and other jurisprudence in the region, held that mandatory minimum sentences were not unconstitutional.

On the other problematic issue of hanging, the question that arises is: Does hanging, as a mode of executing the death penalty, in itself constitute a degrading and inhuman punishment or treatment? This institution was challenged in *Mosarwana v State,*[73] a decision that has already been considered in relation to the right to life provisions of the Constitution. The appellant contended, *inter alia*, that hanging to be visited on him on a murder conviction and subsequent death sentence contravened Section 7(1) of the Constitution prohibiting torture or inhuman or degrading punishment and was, as such, unconstitutional. He drew the Court's attention to the fact that the United Nations had urged its members, of which Botswana was one, to restrict the number of offences for which the death penalty might be imposed with a view to its final and complete abolition throughout the world. However, the Court simply ignored the submission premised on what was happening at the international level. It merely said that its function was adjudicatory but not legislative and cursorily held that execution by hanging was a lawful punishment.

Similarly, in *State v Ntesang*[74] which has also been discussed earlier in the context of the right to life provisions, it was argued on behalf of the appellant that the hanging that he was ordered to undergo by the High Court amounted to an inhuman and degrading punishment and was therefore contrary to Section 7(1) of the Constitution. The Court of Appeal construed this provision narrowly and restrictively, and held that hanging was saved by Section 7(2) of the Constitution. According to the Court, Section 7(2) created an exception to the prohibition on inhuman or degrading punishment or treatment which was lawful immediately before the Constitution came into operation. Thus,

---

[71] *ibid.*, at 587 (*per* O'Brien Quinn, C.J. See further *Raditlhose v State* (1990) BLR 166 (HC) where the Court of Appeal confirmed the inappropriateness of combining strokes with imprisonment by deleting six strokes from four years' imprisonment on a conviction for shop breaking and theft.

[72] [2003] (1) BLR 65.

[73] [1985] BLR 258. See also *Molale v The State* [1995] BLR 146 (CA).

[74] *Supra.*

since hanging had been a lawful mode of execution immediately before the Constitution came into force, it was not an inhuman or degrading punishment. It was *intra vires* the Constitution. Again, the Court took the view that, since its function was merely adjudicatory and not legislative, it could not outlaw hanging. A similar judicial position has been taken regarding death row phenomenon.

3 Conclusion

International law has a role to play in the domestic enforcement of human rights. It has an enriching effect on national human rights normative standards and assists in affording the individual maximum protection.

However, the Constitution of Botswana is silent on the domestic place and role of international law. The only legislative instrument that accords it a limited domestic role is the Interpretation Act, which enjoins the court to use international instruments to construe domestic legislation.

It is therefore important that international law should be accorded a specific place and role in national law especially in the Constitution so as to accord it a constitutional status. This notwithstanding, courts have a unique position of incorporating, albeit indirectly, international law in national law especially where the legislature fails to play its constitutional role, by invoking and utilising it in arriving at their decisions. There is an observable trend in Botswana that courts are discharging this role. However, this role has not been discharged adequately. Cases in which international law has been used to interpret national human rights law are few and isolated. The *Unity Dow* case is the one of those few cases and has thus earned itself a place in national legal order as a *locus classicus* in the protection and enforcement of human rights.

The courts have adopted a cautious approach to international law. Thus there is no deliberate and consistent pattern of vigorously invoking international human rights standards to interpret and enforce human rights at national law.

The Evolution and Development of a Value-Based and Teleological Interpretation of Statute and Common Law in South Africa as a Result of the 1996 Constitution

G. Devenish*

1 Introduction

In this paper I consider the interpretation of statute law, including the Constitution and the Bill of Rights,[1] as well as the common law. Jurisprudential principles that impact on interpretation, flowing from the Constitution apply to all three of these. Section 39(1) of the 1996 South African Constitution, which specifically addresses the seminal issue of interpretation, states that when interpreting the Bill of Rights, a court, tribunal or forum must promote the values that underlie an open and democratic society based on human dignity, equality and freedom; must consider international law; and may consider foreign law.[2] It is instructive to note that the ambit of section 39 as

*B.Sc, LL.B, LL.D (Unisa); LL.D. (Natal), TH.D (JCE), Senior Research Associate, University of KwaZulu-Natal (Durban), South Africa.

[1] See *Nyamakazi v President of Bophuthatswana* 1994 (1) BCLR 92 (B) for suggested rules of interpretation as formulated by Friedman J. See also *Ntenteni v Chairman, Ciskei Council of State* 1994 (1) BCLR 168 (Ck); *Matinkinca v Council of State, Ciskei* 1994 (1) BCLR 17 (Ck); *Rattigan v Chief Immigration Officer* 1995 (1) BCLR 1 (ZS); and *The Attorney-General v Dow* 1994 (6) BCLR 1 (Bot). See also Botha "Interpretation of the Constitution" 1994 *SAPL* 257; Devenish "The Interpretation of Justiciable Rights in South Africa's Interim Constitution" 1995 *De Jure* 249; Binnie "Constitutional Interpretation" 1995 *Consultus* 8(2), 8; Carpenter "Constitutional interpretation by the existing judiciary: Can New Wine Be Successfully Decanted into Old Bottles?" 1995 *CILSA* 322; and de Bruyn "Judicial Interpretation of the Interim Constitution: A Review of the First Year" 1995 *SAPL* 504.

[2] The corresponding provision in the interim Constitution was Section 35(1) which read: "In interpreting the provisions of this Chapter a court of law shall promote the values which underlie an open and democratic society based on freedom and equality and shall, where applicable, have regard to public international law applicable to the protection of the rights entrenched in this Chapter, and may have regard to comparable foreign in case law." See *Shabalala v The Attorney-General of Transvaal* 1994 (6) BCLR 85 (T) where it was held that the power contained in Section 35(1) of the

a whole is, however, not restricted merely to the interpretation of Chapter 2 of the Constitution, dealing with the Bill of Rights. This is manifestly clear from section 39(2) which states:

> "when interpreting any legislation, and developing the common law[3] or customary law, every court, tribunal or forum must promote the spirit, purport and objects of the Bill of Rights".[4]

It should be noted that section 39(2) requires that the Bill of Rights must be applied indirectly where it cannot be applied directly.[5] This is of singular importance in relation to the process of interpreting legislation in general. Section 39 has brought about a fundamental change in the way legislation should be interpreted and applied in South Africa. It mandates that we move away from the traditional literal method of interpretation inherited from English law and jurisprudence, based to a great extent on positivism, to a

---

interim Constitution to have regard to comparable foreign law should be exercised with circumspection, since the resort to case law of foreign jurisdictions by persons not fully acquainted with the practice in those jurisdictions or with the concepts and techniques of foreign systems entails a real risk that a foreign legal position would be misinterpreted. It is necessary to take into account the accumulated experience of what does and does not work satisfactorily in the administration of justice in South Africa. See *Nortje v Attorney-General of the Cape* 1995 (2) BCLR 236 (C). See also *Park-Ross v Director, Office for Serious Economic Offences* 1995 (2) BCLR 198 (C), where it was held that the different historical background against which other constitutions were drafted presents a danger of unnecessarily importing doctrines associated with foreign constitutions which are inappropriate in a South African setting.

3 See *Rivett-Carnac v Wiggins* 1997 (4) BCLR 562 (C). This case dealt with the corresponding provision in the interim Constitution, that is, s 35(3). In this regard the court in a defamation matter held that s 35(3) was mandatory and therefore obliged every court to reconsider the rules of the common law so as to render them congruent with the underlying principles of the interim Constitution. These principles were to be gleaned from the constitutional text itself and stemmed from the desire to attain an open and democratic society based on freedom and equality. Cf *S v Friedman* 1996 (3) BCLR 347 (W), where the court held that the common law definition of fraud, embracing misrepresentations that could cause only potential prejudice rather than actual prejudice, was not repugnant to the interim Constitution. See *Motala v University of Natal* 1995 (3) BCLR 374 (D), which also dealt with the corresponding provision in the interim Constitution. In this case the court held that it is the task of the courts to define the limits of fundamental rights where they appear to encroach upon one another and simultaneously blend them into the common law, modifying the common law whenever necessary to achieve a harmonious amalgam. This was the task of the courts and not the legislature. See also *Holomisa v Argus Newspapers Ltd* 1996 (2) SA 588 (W).

4 See *Bux v The Officer Commanding the Pietermaritzburg Prison* 1994 (4) BCLR 10 (N), in which Didcott J held that a construction which is in keeping with the spirit of the Constitution and which furthers its altruistic and benevolent aims applies essentially to civil rights and liberties and its bearing on procedural provisions is much less pronounced.

5 See *Mkhize v Commission for Conciliation, Mediation and Arbitration* 2001 (1) SA 338 (LC).

purposive/value-based method of interpretation, involving an unqualified contextual methodology and natural law jurisprudence, or at least jurisprudence akin to natural law.

It must be borne in mind that the scarcity of local precedents securing fundamental rights makes it necessary that international and foreign case law be used to resolve jurisprudential issues precipitated by the justiciability of the provisions of the Bill of Rights. This does not mean that indigenous values should be neglected. Indeed, there is a need for indigenous concepts like that of *ubuntu* to find appropriate expression in constitutional law judgments so that our jurisprudence can have an autochthonous character.[6] Furthermore, in the development of our common law, the principle of tolerance and the recognition of the plural nature of our society must be taken into account.[7] Public policy and the *boni mores* which our courts apply in developing the common law should not merely reflect the view or presumed views of only one group in a plural society, as was indeed the position under our previous discredited constitutional and political constitutional system, since it is inimical to all the values encapsulated in the Constitution for one group to impose its values on another. Therefore what is contrary to public policy is accordingly to be ascertained by reference to those universal values in a multi-cultural society that are shared by all right-thinking members of the community as distinct from only one section of it.[8]

2 The Theory and Methodology of Interpretation that Applies in South Africa Today

The South African jurisprudence has used legal precedents from other countries, particularly in relation to human rights jurisprudence, which according to section 39(1) requires the consideration of foreign law in the interpretation process. Our experience may be of value to the legal community in Botswana. We can also learn from Botswana's jurisprudence. This is manifestly clear from the Court of Appeal judgment in *Attorney-General v*

[6] See in this regard the judgments of Mokgoro J and Langa J in *S v Makwanyane* 1995 (3) SA 391 (CC) paras 300, 307–308, 223–227 respectively.

[7] See *Ryland v Edros* 1997 (1) BCLR 77 (C).

[8] *ibid.*, at 90.

Dow,[9] and also from that involving Prof Kenneth Good.[10] The process is therefore reciprocal and we are mutually enriched by our respective jurisprudential experiences.[11] The *Good* case is of great significance as far as human rights jurisprudence is concerned and needs to be penetratingly discussed. It certainly impacts on emerging issues pertaining to human rights, which the very essence of this book. The *Dow* judgment is very interesting and relevant because the court stretched its 'powers of statutory interpretation

[9] [1992] BLR 119. In this case the Botswana Court of Appeal held that a provision in the Citizenship Act of that country, entitling the legislature to discriminate in regard to children born of a citizen mother and an alien father by withholding citizenship from them, while conferring citizenship on children of a citizen father and an alien mother, constituted a violation of the right not to be unfairly discriminated against, in a constitutional provision omitting gender from the list of unacceptable bases on which different treatment might be afforded to different categories of persons. In his judgment Amissah JP adopted a cogent value-based approach to constitutional interpretation, using in effect analogous interpretation and therefore implicitly ignoring the *casus omissus* rule. The appellant, however, contended that any reference to gender had been deliberately omitted from the definition of discriminatory treatment because the intention was that gender discrimination would be condoned by the Constitution. The appellant further contended that the whole fabric of customary law in Botswana was based upon its society being patrilineal and it thereby being gender discriminatory. The respondent argued persuasively that the existence of important international agreements, before and after the date of passing on the Botswana Constitution, to which Botswana was a party, showed that the majority of the world was opposed to discrimination against women on the grounds of sex and therefore it could not lightly be assumed that the framers of the Constitution would not intend to outlaw gender discrimination.

Puckrin JA, who in a polished dissenting judgment adopted a qualified contextual approach to the interpretation of provisions of the Constitution, observed that when courts are called on to interpret such provisions they do not have a wide and unfettered discretion to deviate from the literal meaning of words used where there is no inherent ambiguity. He claimed that his approach reflects a purposive method of interpretation, which in his view is the "correct means of interpretation". It is,however, submitted that purposive interpretation in this case does have patent limitations, since as Eskridge points out it "cannot be accepted as a general theory because it neglects other critically important values". Furthermore, as Mureinik observed, "if the policy of a statute is iniquitous, a purposive interpretation may well foster iniquity". Gender discrimination, *par excellence,* is the prejudicial consequence of the purposive approach adopted by Puckrin JA, since it is universally regarded as unacceptable. See Coldham S "Human Rights in Botswana: *Unity Dow v Attorney-General (Botswana)*" [1992] *J. of African L.* 91; Quansah "*Unity Dow v Attorney - General of Botswana* - One more relic of Woman's Servitude removed?" (1992) 4 Afr. J. of Int'l & Comparative L/RADIC also 5 Afr. J of Int'l & Comparative L/RADIC 169; Tshosa. "The Application of Non-discrimination in Botswana in the Light of *Attorney-General of Botswana v Unity Dow*: Judicial Approach and Practice" (2001) 5 *Int'l J of Discrimination and the Law* 189.

[10] See *Communication Submitted for the Consideration under article 56 of the African Charter of Human and People's Rights.* The Commission declared the communication admissible.

[11] See Aguda "Discriminatory Statutory Provisions and Fundamental Rights Provisions of the Constitutions of Botswana, Lesotho and Swaziland" (1972) 89 SALJ 299.

to the limits'.[12] This was also the position in the South African judgment in *S v Mhlungu*.[13] Lastly in this regard, the legal position relating to Basarwa is of interest.[14]

Professor Christo Botha[15] explains that the following three basic and kindred principles apply to the contemporary process of statutory interpretation as a result of the new constitutional dispensation in South Africa:

(1) Interpretation must take into account that South Africa has a supreme constitution with a justiciable bill of rights that constitutes the cornerstone of the new legal order, of which interpretation is an integral part;

(2) As a result of this the most important principle of interpretation is to determine and apply the purpose of the legislation in the light of the Bill of Rights and its values; and

(3) This requires that the interpreter must study the legislative text to ascertain its initial meaning and, while bearing in mind the presumptions of interpretation, construe the text by striking a balance between the text and context of the legislation.

The question arises in this regard as to what theory applies and how do we designate it? It is submitted that "purposivism" or a mere purposive approach should not be accepted as a general theory of interpretation in South Africa[16] because it neglects certain critically important values.[17]

---

[12] See Fombad "The Constitutional Protection Against Discrimination in Botswana" (2004) *53 Int'l & Comp L Q* 139 at 143.

[13] 1995 (7) BCLR 793 (CC).

[14] "No water for Bushmen" in the *Daily News* 13 May 2008. In this report it is stated that the Botswana Government has banned the Central Kalahari Game Reserve from accessing their own water but has given permission for a tourist lodge to do so. Survival International Director Stephen Corry said "Despite the Botswana High Court ruling that the Busmen have a constitutional right to live in the Central Kalahari Game Reserve, the government is doing everything to keep them out, denying them access to water and the right to hunt for food." See Ng'ong'ola "Land rights for Marginalised Groups in Botswana, with Special Reference to the Basarwa" (1997) *J. of African L* 1.

[15] *Statutory Interpretation* (2005) 66.

[16] Cf Rautenbach and Malherbe *Constitutional Law (1999)* 290; Hogg *Constitutional Law of Canada* 814–815; and *S v Gqozo* (2) 1994 (1) BCLR 10 (Ck).

[17] See Eskridge and Frickey "Statutory Interpretation as *Practical Reasoning*" *(1990) 42 Stanford L. Rev.* 321, at 337 and also the views of Mureinik in (1986) 103 *SALJ* 615, 620–623 in which he commented that the purposive theory has certain limitations in that it fails to "aspire to higher coherence: the coherence of the legal system as a whole". Cf *De Klerk v Du Plessis* 1994 (6) BCLR (T) 124, at 128 where it was held that if the proper approach to interpretation is described as a "generous and purposive" one then the terms generous ought to be read as qualifying "purposive" and not relating to a separate concept.

What is required is a value-based theory of interpretation which must, in terms of section 39(2), "promote the spirit, purport and objects of" the fundamental rights encapsulated in Chapter 2 of the Constitution. The word "spirit", which is used in conjunction with the words "purport and objects", clearly indicates that we are dealing with a method of interpretation that is wider and more comprehensive than that of the purposive approach.[18] Obviously the courts do not have licence to deal with interpretation as they please. What is required is a process of teleological evaluation[19] involving a judicious weighing-up of linguistic and jurisprudential considerations. Therefore, it is clear that the curial interpretation in many circumstances of human rights, which are broadly conceived and formulated with a high degree of abstraction, must involve "an overt value judgment, amounting to an act of creation and imagination".[20]

In this regard Davis, Cheadle and Hayson comment that:

> "There is recognition that constitutions are not simply about a mechanical execution of plain words, howsoever defined, and that the engagement with values, and the debate thereon, is the key to constitutional inquiry."[21]

Therefore, in an interpretative conflict the core values of, *inter alia*, equality, freedom and dignity should triumph over a particular contrary purpose inferred from a specific provision of the Constitution, thereby rendering the interpretation compatible with the overall purpose of the Constitution as a whole, as a constitution of liberty. This is indeed the essence of Mahomed J's bold and imaginative judgment in *S v Mhlungu*.[22] This does not mean that a particular purpose of a section of the Constitution is irrelevant, but that it should not be regarded as determinant, and therefore that it should be considered as one factor, albeit an important one, in the process of teleological evaluation, used in the methodology of interpretation, which should be ambulatory[23] and involve an unqualified contextual approach,[24] by which is

[18] See *Qozeleni v Minister of Law and Order* 1994 (3) SA 625 (E); *Baloro v University of Bophuthatswana* 1995 (4) SA 197 (B). In the last-mentioned case, the court *per* Friedman JP held that the courts should play a proactive role in changing society in accordance with the aims and spirit of the Constitution.

[19] See Devenish *Interpretation of Statutes* (1992) 52.

[20] Bennett, *Human Rights and African Customary Law* 41. See also *Matiso v Commanding Officer, Port Elizabeth Prison* 1994 (3) BCLR 80 (SE).

[21] Davis, Cheadle and Haysom *Fundamental Rights in the Constitution* 20.

[22] 1995 (7) BCLR 793, (CC).

[23] See Devenish *op.cit.,* fn. 19 *supra*, 32.

[24] *ibid.*, 75.

meant that even words that are prima facie clear and unambiguous, should be read in context.

It can be argued that a value-based approach opens the door to subjective judicial decision making and that a principled and effective restraint on judicial powers is essential.[25] This will indeed occur if the value-based approach is coupled with teleological evaluation and an unqualified contextual methodology. The quintessence of such a theory and methodology of interpretation is astutely captured by Dworkin's concept of a "Constitution of Principle", which he describes as one enforced by independent judges [that] is not undemocratic. On the contrary it is a precondition of legitimate democracy that government is required to treat individual citizens as equals and to respect their fundamental liberties and dignity. Unless those conditions are met, there can be no genuine democracy because, unless they are met, the majority has no legitimate moral title to govern.[26]

Finally, there is another important reason why a value-based interpretation is preferable to a pure purposive one. The 1996 Constitution itself mandates such interpretation. This is clear from, *inter alia*, first, the preamble, which calls for the establishment of "a society based on democratic values, social justice, and fundamental rights". Furthermore, section 1 proclaims that the seminal values of human dignity, the achievement of equality and the advancement of human rights and freedom, non-racialism and non-sexism as well as accountable, responsive and open government must be promoted by the Constitution. Lastly, in this regard, section 39(2) enjoins a court to interpret Chapter 2 so as to promote these values.

A generous interpretation may prove to be too wide and a purposive one too narrow in certain circumstances. Both these methods of interpretation are defective in that they tend to be one-dimensional. Furthermore, the Bill of Rights encapsulates universal moral and ethical values and therefore in its application and its interpretation it has an important moral dimension to it. It is for this reason that a value-based theory of interpretation is the most satisfactory one. This approach is also compatible with the discipline of hermeneutics, in relation to philosophy and theology, which is not merely technical, but is concerned with "[v]alues, particularly as to right and wrong [that] are always to be referred back to the context of the value, [and] that of

---

[25] See Du Plessis "The Legitimacy of Judicial Review in South Africa's New Constitutional Dispensation: Insights from the Canadian Experience" unpublished research project (1997) 25.

[26] Dworkin, *Life's Dominion* (1993) 123.

the pre-existent whole, whether that whole or totality be that of community or in more specific circumstances, that of a religious, political or legal tradition".[27] Lastly, in this regard it is clear from the wording of the judicial oath that in the process of interpreting the law judges "should believe that they are engaged in a moral activity".[28] This means in effect that, in expounding and interpreting the law, a judge is involved with a moral function. The judicial function is different from the legislative one, in which legislators make the law in a primary sense. However, in a secondary sense judges do make the law in a very creative way, by refining and developing the law to apply in a particular set of circumstances. In putting into effect universal values they indeed fulfill a profound moral role. The theory and methodology of the contemporary interpretation are explored and evaluated below in greater detail.

3 Value-Based Interpretation

Froneman J[29] observes in relation to contemporary statutory interpretation in South Africa that the "intention of the legislature" does not apply in a system of judicial review based on the supremacy of the Constitution, for the reason that the Constitution is sovereign and no longer parliament. This effects a metamorphosis in relation to the purpose and method of statutory interpretation. The purpose is to test legislation and administrative action against the values and principles encapsulated in the Constitution. The interpretation of the Constitution must be directed at ascertaining the foundational values inherent in the Constitution, whilst the interpretation of particular legislation must be directed at ascertaining whether legislation is capable of sustaining an interpretation which is compatible with the fundamental values or principles of the Constitution. According to Froneman J,[30] "[c]onstitutional interpretation in this sense is therefore primarily concerned with the recognition and application of constitutional values and not with a search to find the literal meaning of the statute". For South African constitutional law and interpretation of statutes, which tended to be very literal in character, this constituted not merely a significant change but a "Copernican revolution,"[31] as it entailed "a pivotal role for the South African judiciary as the guardian of the

[27] Goodrich *Reading the Law* (1986) 135.

[28] Devenish *op.cit.*, fn. 19, *supra*, 10.

[29] *Matiso and Others v Commanding Officer, Port Elizabeth Prison and Others* 1994 (3) BCLR 80, at 87 (SE).

[30] *ibid.*

[31] Du Plessis "The Politicisation of the Judiciary. Or the Judicialisation of Politics", (1993) 20 Politikon 46, at 47. See also Tarnas *The Passion of the Western Mind* (1996) 249 *et seq.*

Constitution and the democratic values enshrined in it".[32] It introduced an exciting era of creative jurisprudence for our courts.

The meaning of a provision of the Constitution is therefore not to be located in the intention of its drafters, which in effect "is a decoding of the written text".[33] The interpretation of a Constitution is not concerned with the determination of a psychological intention. Indeed even in relation to ordinary statutes what is relevant is an "institutional intention", since the legislature is a composite body and not an individual.[34] Constitutional interpretation is involved with giving expression to the universal ethical and moral values that are encapsulated in the Bill of Rights, which reflects a new political morality in South Africa, based on equality, human dignity and liberty.

The high water mark of a values-based interpretation is, it is submitted, to be found in the incisive judgment of Mahomed DP in *S v Mhlungu and Others*,[35] in which the Constitutional Court had to interpret the scope and ambit of section 241(8) of the Interim Constitution in relation to cases pending at the 27 April 1994. According to Mahomed DP the only purpose of this section was to preserve the authority and legitimacy of the pre-Constitutional courts to continue to function and operate for the purpose of adjudicating in pending cases. Therefore, the words "shall be dealt with as if this Constitution had not been passed", were held to be intended only to mean that pending cases should proceed to finality as if the Constitution had not impacted on the authority of a pre-Constitution court to continue to function as a court, and that such words do not preclude a party in a case which was pending as at 27 April 1994 from relying on any of the fundamental rights provisions of Chapter 3 of the Interim Constitution. This is clearly a values-based interpretation, in contrast to the more semantic or literal interpretation adopted by Kentridge AJ in the minority judgment, in which Chaskalson P, Ackerman and Didcott JJ concurred. Mahomed DP explains the jurisprudential defects of a more literal approach and why it should be rejected:

> "The literal interpretation would invade all these objectives in its arbitrary selection of one category of persons who would become entitled to enjoy the human rights guarantees of the Constitution and the arbitrary exclusion

---

32 *ibid.*

33 See Kentridge and Spitz "Interpretation" in Chaskalson *et al. eds., The Constitutional Law of South Africa* 11–16.

34 See "Legislative Intention" in G E Devenish *op.cit.*, fn. 19, *supra*, 11 et seq.

35 1995 (7) BCLR 793 (CC).

> of another group of persons from such entitlement. The Courts must strive to avoid such a result if the language and context of the relevant provision, interpreted with due regard to the objectives of the Constitution, permits such a course."[36]

It is true that Mahomed DP's interpretation is, according to his admission, "not entirely free from difficulties",[37] but as a manifestation of "a purposive and mischief-orientated reading as against a purely literal one, [it is one that] always involves a degree of strain on the language," as explained by Sachs J in his judgment.[38] In contrast, Kentridge AJ adopts the view in his polished and in many respects most certainly not entirely unconvincing judgment that "when language is clear it must be given effect to".[39] He observes that the "reluctance of some judges to give effect in particular cases to the language of section 241(8) is no doubt understandable ... [n]onetheless, there are some provisions, even in a constitution, where the language used, read in its context, is too clear to be capable of sensible qualification."[40] He concludes by commenting that although it is the duty of all courts, in terms of section 35 of the Interim Constitution, to promote the values which underlie a democratic society based on freedom and equality, in the long run those values are not promoted "by doing violence to the language of the Constitution in order to remedy what may seem to be hard cases".[41] What to Sachs J is "a strain on language" is to Kentridge AJ "violence to the language". It must, however, be asked which is the lesser of two evils: violence to language or violence to fundamental rights? If an election is indeed called for, it is submitted that the preservation of fundamental rights is more important than avoiding 'violence to language', if this indeed be the position.

4 Contextual Interpretation

A constitution must be interpreted in its contemporary political and social context, and not according to the situation that prevailed when it was adopted, "otherwise it will cease to take into account the growth of the society which it seeks to regulate".[42] This is an ambulatory approach, which requires that a

---

36 *ibid.*, at 799.
37 *ibid.*, at 811.
38 *ibid.*, at 843.
39 *ibid.*, at 828.
40 *ibid.*, at 831.
41 *ibid.*
42 *Nyamakazi v President of Bophuthatswana* 1992 (4) SA 540 at 567 (*per* Friedman J).

statutory instrument must be considered as always speaking.[43] Another important reason for an ambulatory approach to the interpretation of a constitution is that, because constitutions are usually difficult to amend in a formal way, amendments are infrequent and consequently the courts have an important role to play in ensuring that the application of the constitution keeps up with changing socio-economic and political realities. This means, as De Ville and Du Plessis[44] explain, that "[i]nterpretations may therefore change, without thereby implying that earlier interpretations were necessarily 'wrong' at the time when they were given". This ambulatory approach to constitutional interpretation was given exemplary recognition by the Zimbabwean Supreme Court in *S v Ncube, S v Tshuma, S v Ndhlovu,*[45] when it had to decide whether the whipping of adult offenders violated the proscription on inhuman and degrading punishment contained in the Zimbabwean Constitution. In this regard the court reasoned as follows:

> "Punishments which are compatible with the evolving standards of decency that mark the progress of a maturing society or which involve unnecessary and wanton infliction of pain are repugnant. Thus a penalty that was permissible at one time in our nation's history is not necessarily permissible today. What might not have been inhuman or degrading decades ago may be revolting to new sensitivities which emerge as civilization advances."[46]

It is submitted that it is clear from the above that both the theory of original intent and even the purposive theory should be rejected as a basis for the interpretation of a constitution and that instead a values-based theory should be used. The actual method of construction should be an open-ended and imaginative one of elucidation and careful evaluation which explores, "reads into, derives and attaches significance to every word, section or clause in relation to the whole context".[47] What is required is a holistic method, involving an unqualified contextual weighing up of linguistic, legal and juristic considerations.[48] The process of interpretation always starts with the ordinary grammatical meaning of words, but should never end with it. This

---

43 See Devenish *op.cit.*, fn. 19, *supra*, 32. See du Toit "The Dimension of Futurity: Towards a Renewal of the Theory of Interpretation" 1977 *TRW* 11–21.

44 "Bill of Rights Interpretation in the South African Context (2): Prognostic Observations", (1993) 4 Stellenbosch L Rev 199, at 212.

45 1988 (2) SA 702 at 715 (ZS).

46 Quoted by De Ville and Du Plessis *op. cit.*, fn. 44, *supra*.

47 *Nyamakazi v President of Bophuthatswana* 1992 (4) SA 540 (BGD), at 566 (*per* Friedman J).

48 Devenish *op.cit.*, fn. 19, *supra*, 55.

idea of holistic interpretation is elucidated by the famous German scholar Hans-Georg Gadamer who comments that "the anticipated meaning of the whole is understood through the parts, but it is in the light of the whole that the parts take on their illuminating function".[49]

5 Methodology of Interpretation of the Bill of Rights

1. The sources that must be consulted in the process of interpretation are the following:
   (a) The text of the provision in question interpreted against the Constitution as a whole;
   (b) The values that underpin an open and democratic society based on human dignity, equality and freedom;
   (c) International and foreign law;
   (d) The principles with which the Constitution had to comply;
   (e) Contextual evidence in relation to the process of constitutional negotiations that gave rise to the 1996 Constitution; and
   (f) The history of human rights violations.

In the process of interpretation, whether it is of the Constitution or any other statute, the words of the text of the Bill of Rights or any other part of the Constitution must be engaged as the starting point. In this regard, Kentridge AJ commented as follows in *S v Zuma*:[50]

> "While we must always be conscious of the values underlying the Constitution … it cannot be too strongly stressed that the Constitution does not mean whatever we may wish it prohibits."[51]

---

[49] Gadamer "The Problem of Historical Consciousness" in P. Rabinow and W. Sullivan eds., *Interpretive Social Science - A Reader* (1979) 146.

[50] 1995 (2) SA 642 (CC).

[51] Emphasis added. See also *Park-Ross v Director, Office for Serious Economic Offences* 1995 (2) BCLR 198 (C), where it was held that while the fundamental rights provisions of a constitution call for a special method of interpretation, the specific language in which the provisions are couched cannot be overlooked and that due regard must be paid to the specific words chosen and their meaning in accordance with existing usages. In *DTA of Namibia v Prime Minister of the Republic of Namibia* 1996 (3) BCLR 310 (Nm), the Namibian High Court *per* Hannah J, with O'Linn J dissenting, held that the court is not concerned with the justice or injustice of a provision in question and that if the law is within the scope of the power conferred on the legislature and does not violate a restriction on that power, the court must uphold the law whatever it may think of its merits or demits. This, it is submitted, is a very technical approach to interpretation and the dissenting view of O'Linn J is to be preferred.

As part of this process, the Constitution further provides that, in interpreting the Bill of Rights, international law must be considered.[52] For this purpose the courts must consider all relevant international instruments, be they declarations or conventions. The Constitution also stipulates that customary international law is to be regarded as law in South Africa, unless it is inconsistent with the Constitution or an Act of Parliament.[53]

Finally, in this regard, the Constitution also provides that in interpreting the Bill of Rights, foreign law *may* be considered.[54] Although it is correct, as the courts always emphasise,[55] that foreign law cannot be decisive in the process of interpreting and applying the South African Bill of Rights, such law has indeed been extensively researched and quoted in many judgments,[56] which have thereby been greatly enriched.

The Constitution and the Bill of Rights cannot be construed in a political and social vacuum. They must be interpreted in a particular political and historical context, against the background of the remarkable transformation that has occurred in South Africa from a dispensation involving human rights violations on an inordinate scale to a new democratic era with its vast potential for the realisation of political and social justice, as reflected in the provisions of the Bill of Rights. In this regard the Constitutional Court perceives it function, and indeed the wider curial one, to be a remedial and healing one.[57]

6 Some Other Important Principles of Interpretation that have Emerged as a Result of the New Constitutional Dispensation

It is important to note that the ordinary rules and maxims[58] of interpretation of statutes continue to be used.[59] However, what is important is the way they are applied, which is obviously influenced by section 39(2) of the Constitution,

---

[52] See Botha "International Law in the Constitutional Court" 1995 *SA Yrbk of Int'l L.*222.

[53] See in this regard the discussion of the corresponding provision in the interim Constitution, Section 35(1): Dugard "International Human Rights" in Van Wyk *et al Rights and Constitutionalism* (1995) 191–195; and "Public International Law" Chaskalson *et al Constitutional Law of South Africa* (1996) 13.

[54] Section 39(1)(*c*).

[55] See Rautenbach and Malherbe *op.cit.* fn.16, *supra*, 289.

[56] See e.g. *S v Williams* 1995 (3) SA 632 (CC) para 23.

[57] See *S v Mhlungu* 1995 (3) SA 867 (CC) paras 7 and 111.

[58] See *Kusa Kusa CC v Mbele* 2003 (2) BCLR 222 (LCC) at 229 para 15, where reference is made to the well known maxim *generalia specialibus non derogant*, which means general provisions do not derogate from special provisions.

[59] See in this regard the view of Flemming DJP in *Beta Eiendomme (Pty) Ltd v Ekple-Epoh* 2000 (4) SA 468 (W) in which he stated that

which makes it clear that "pre-constitutional legislation must be read in the light of the Constitution and the need to give effect to its fundamental values...".

6.1 Constitutions must be Interpreted in a Liberal Spirit

Of seminal importance is the catholic legal sentiment that constitutions must be interpreted in a liberal spirit. This requires that the interpretation of, particularly, a Bill of Rights calls for a "special judicial frame of mind".[60] Examples of this can be found in the interpretation of the constitutions of the United States, Australia, Pakistan and Sri Lanka.[61] In the past, courts in the Commonwealth held "that they would apply the rules of statutory interpretation in construing their constitutions",[62] as they did, in regard to ordinary legislation. This has, however, changed and there are judicial acknowledgments that constitutions are not to be restricted in their interpretation to "strict and illiberal rules of statutory interpretation".[63] Fombad expresses the position as follows:

> "[C]onstitutions are now regarded as *sui generis*, requiring generous and purposive interpretation. To avoid what has been called 'the austerity of tabulated legalism' the ordinary rules of statutory interpretation and presumptions are not rigidly applied".[64]

Provisions intended to protect fundamental rights are especially to be accorded a liberal construction.[65] Courts should give a broad and liberal interpretation to those constitutional provisions designed to safeguard fundamental rights, such as life, liberty and property. As Professor Hogg[66] observes, the courts, in interpreting the Canadian Charter, "should avoid narrow, legalistic

"...The Constitution of the Republic of South Africa Act 108 of 1996 and subsequent legislation must be approached on the basis that normal legal principles of interpretation of statutes will be applied to resolve ambiguities and to avoid diminution of rights which is not spelt out with adequate clarity. When passing the statute parliament accepted that existing law - which includes the legal principles of interpretation of statutes - is generally speaking not abolished or abrogated...".

60 De Ville and Du Plessis *op.cit.*, fn.12, *supra*, at 65.

61 Groves, *Comparative Constitutional Law: Cases and Materials* (1963).

62 Antieau *Constitutional Construction* (1982) 52.

63 *ibid.*

64 See Fombad *op.cit.*, fn.12, *supra*, at 145.

65 Antieau *op.cit.*, fn.62, *supra*, 35.

66 *op.*cit., fn.16, *supra*, 814–815.

interpretations that might be appropriate to a detailed statute". Hogg[67] further indicates his preference for a purposive approach by commenting that:

> "The Court has generally assumed that a 'purposive' approach and a 'generous' approach are one and the same thing – or at least are not inconsistent. Indeed statements of the purposive approach have nearly always been accompanied – often in the same sentence – by statements of a generous approach. In the case of some rights, that is correct: a purposive approach will yield a broad scope for the right. In case of most rights, however, the widest possible reading of the right, which is the most generous interpretation, will 'overshoot' the purpose of the right, by including behaviour that is outside and unworthy of constitutional protection. The effect of a purposive approach is normally going to be to narrow the scope of the right. Generosity is a helpful idea as long as it is subordinate to purpose."

As indicated above, "purposivism" as such should not be accepted as a general theory of interpretation because it may, in certain circumstances, neglect critically important values.[68] What is required is a values-based theory of interpretation which must, in terms of section 39(2), "promote the spirit, purport and objects of" the fundamental rights encapsulated in chapter 2 of the Constitution. What is required is a process of teleological evaluation,[69] as explained below.

6.2 The Presumption of Constitutionality

In regard to the seminal issue of the constitutionality of legislation, the jurisprudence of United States of America, which initiated and pioneered judicial review, has the most complete system of rules that can provide beneficial guidance for our courts. According to Groves,[70] the most important single rule is the presumption of the validity of the statute under review.[71] This deference to the legislature is premised on an important policy consideration that the democratically elected legislature acts and speaks on behalf of the electorate, which in general is entitled to have its desires made into law at any given time, with the exceptions that relate to an amendment to the constitution, requiring a special procedure.

---

67 *ibid.*

68 See Eskridge and Frickey *op. cit.*, fn. 17, *supra*, at 37.

69 See Devenish *op. cit.,* fn. 19, *supra*, 52.

70 *op. cit.*, fn. 61, *supra*, at 5.

71 See e.g. *Gitlow v New York* 268 US 652 (1925).

The presumption of constitutionality requires that, should a statute be capable of being interpreted in more than one way, one resulting in validity and the other in invalidity, the court should presume that the legislature intended to act in a way that is compatible with the Constitution.[72] This does not necessitate that the Constitution be interpreted restrictively in order to accommodate the impugned statute. The Constitution should, as indicated above, be interpreted liberally, after which the relevant statute should be analyzed to determine whether it can be construed in a manner that is in accordance with the provisions, values and principles of the Constitution.[73]

This linchpin presumption of the constitutionality of a statute features in most countries with constitutions incorporating a supremacy provision.[74] In Canada,[75] for instance, Hogg observes[76] that "[t]here should be, in other words, a presumption of constitutionality. In this way a proper respect is paid to the legislators, and the danger of covert (albeit unconscious) imposition of judicial policy preferences is minimised". Hogg[77] comments further that this presumption transfers from the law of evidence the idea that a burden of demonstration lies upon those who would challenge the validity of the statute which has emerged from the democratic process. Hogg explains that in Canadian constitutional law there are three consequences of the presumption of constitutionality:

(i) In choosing competing, plausible characterizations of the law, the court should normally choose that one which would support the validity of the law;

(ii) A finding of fact need not be strictly proved by the government; it is sufficient that there should be a rational basis for the finding; and

(iii) Where the language of a statute is equally capable of two constructions, one of which would be in conflict with the Constitution and the other compatible with it, the latter should be preferred. This interpretational technique is known as "reading down".

---

72 Section 232(3) of the Interim Constitution provided for the presumption of constitutionality. See Kentridge and Spitz "Interpretation" in Chaskalson *et al.* eds *The Constitutional Law of South Africa* (Original Service, 1996), 11-14.

73 De ville and Du Plessis *op. cit.*, fn. 44, *supra*, at 213. See *Minister of Home Affairs v Bickle* 1984 (2) SA 439 (ZS) at 448; and *Zimbabwe Township Developers v Lou's Shoes (Pvt) Ltd.* 1984 (2) SA 778 (ZS) at 783.

74 See Ireland: *The National Union of Railwaymen v Sullivan* [1947] IR 77. Australia: *Federal Commissioner of Taxation v Munro* 38 CLR 153 (1926).

75 See *Nova Scotia Board of Censors v McNeil* [1978] 2 SCR 622; Magnet "The Presumption of Constitutionality" (1980) 18 *Osgoode Hall LJ* 87.

76 Hogg, *op.cit.*, fn.16, *supra*, 123.

77 *ibid.*, 390.

The presumption of constitutionality means that courts of law, in a constitutional dispensation involving a testing right, will not lightly invalidate an act of parliament, but will rather endeavour to interpret a provision in such an act in a way that is compatible with the Constitution by using the technique of restrictive interpretation or modification of language or even the addition of words by implication. The last mentioned technique was used by the Canadian courts in *Haig v Canada*.[78] The application of the presumption of constitutionality was considered in two Zimbabwean decisions; *Minister of Home Affairs v Bickle & Others*[79] and *Zimbabwe Township Developers (Pvt) Ltd v Lou's Shoes (Pvt) Ltd*.[80] The presumption has always been applied in relation to the interpretation of subordinate legislation in South Africa.[81]

In the United States the presumption of constitutionality is eschewed when statutes affecting fundamental liberties are impugned, because the protection of these liberties occupies a preferred place in the constitutional jurisprudence of that country.[82] As far as the Canadian Charter is concerned,[83] the presumption of constitutionality takes the form as indicated above, of

---

78 (1992) 9 OR (3d) 495 (CA): see Cachalia et.al., *Fundamental Rights in the New Constitution* (1994), 122. In this case the Ontario Court of Appeal held that the *Canadian Human Rights Act* which proscribed discrimination in employment violated s15 of the *Canadian Charter* because the Act's definition did not include an express prohibition of discrimination on the grounds of sexual orientation. In interpreting the provision the court in effect corrected the defect by holding that the Act had to be construed as if it contained a reference to omitted prohibition.

79 1984 (2) SA 439 (Z).

80 1984 (2) SA 778 (ZS) Georges CJ (*ibid.*, at 783) explained how the presumption operates in the process of interpretation:

> "Clearly a litigant who asserts that an Act of Parliament or a regulation is unconstitutional must show that it is. In such a case the judicial body charged with deciding that issue must interpret the constitution and determine its meaning and thereafter interpret the challenged piece of legislation to arrive at a conclusion as to whether it falls within that meaning or it does not. The challenged piece of legislation may, however, be capable of more than one meaning. If that is the position then if one possible interpretation falls within the meaning of the constitution and others do not, then the judicial body will presume that the lawmakers intended to act constitutionally and uphold the piece of legislation so interpreted. One does not interpret the Constitution in a restricted manner in order to accommodate the challenged legislation. The Constitution must be properly interpreted,.... Thereafter the challenged legislation is examined to discover whether it can be interpreted to fit into the framework of the Constitution."

See *In re: Munhumeso and Others* 1995 (2) BCLR 125 (ZS); *Minister of Home Affairs v Bickle* 1983 (2) ZLR 431 (SC) at 441; *S v Juvenile* 1989 (2) ZLR 61 (SC) at 89.

81 Steyn *Uitleg van Wette* (1981) 123.

82 See *United States v Carolene Products Co* 304 US 144, 152 n 4 (1938).

83 cf. Magnet, *op. cit.*, fn. 75, *Supra,* at 91.

"reading down", as explained above. De Ville and Du Plessis[84] explain, that where the presumption of constitutionality prevails, its operation is restricted to the context within which a court exercises its function of justiciability. They emphasise that it cannot exonerate the court from its primary duty of ascertaining whether the provisions of the Bill of Rights are compatible with a provision of a statute, allegedly violating the former, and as a consequence to pronounce on the constitutionality of such a provision. The presumption is therefore an aid to assist the court in reaching a reasoned decision and not a "device facilitating the circumvention of its duty".[85] Reading down is therefore the interpretation of statutory provisions to avoid conflicts with the Bill of Rights.[86] In effect it constitutes an indirect application of the provisions of the Bill of Rights and the Constitution, as mandated by section 39(2).

Besides the interpretative technique of reading down referred to above, there is also the technique of reading in. This was used for the first time in *National Coalition for Gay and Lesbian Equality v Minister of Home Affairs*[87] where the Constitutional Court used the power to read words into legislation to correct constitutional deficiencies in it. At issue was section 25(5) of the Aliens Control Act,[88] which the court had declared unconstitutional because it discriminated unfairly on the grounds of sexual orientation and marital status. The problem with the provision "was that it was under-inclusive".[89] It conferred a benefit on married persons that it did not confer on same sex life partners. This meant that the remedy of national severance was inappropriate.[90] In the case of an omission, the court held, there was no reason why courts should not confine themselves to the remedy of striking down and suspension of the order of invalidity. The court therefore reconstructed the provision by reading in appropriate words and thereby conferred the missing benefit on same-sex partners. So the Constitutional Court explained that "[s]ection 25(5) of the Aliens Control Act 96, of 1991, is to be read as though the following

---

[84] "Bill of Rights Interpretation in the South African Context (1): Diagnostic Observations" (1993) 4 Stellenbosch L Rev. 63, at 72.

[85] *ibid.*., at 73.

[86] See in this regard *South African Association of Personal Injury Lawyers v Heath* 2001 (1) SA 883 (CC); *S v Mamabolo (ETV Intervening)* 2001 (3) SA 409 (CC); *Govender v Minister of Safety and Security* 2001 (4) SA 273 (SCA).

[87] 2000 (2) SA 1 (CC) 2000 (1) BCLR 39.

[88] 96 of 1991.

[89] See Currie "Bill of Rights Jurisprudence" *Annual Survey of South African Law 2000* at 45.

[90] At paras 63–4.

words appear therein after the word 'spouse': 'or partner, in a permanent same-sex life relationship'".[91]

In *S v Manamela*[92] a majority of the court held that the remedy of reading in is not necessarily confined to cases in which a provision has been found to be underinclusive. There was no reason why it could not be used as part of the process of narrowing the reach of a provision that was unduly invasive of a protected right. The court skilfully used this remedy to convert a reverse onus presumption into an evidential presumption. In *S v Niemand*[93] the court's power to read in was used to correct an omission in legislation providing for the indefinite imprisonment of habitual criminals.[94]

However, there are limits to the use of this remedy. So, for instance, in *Dawood v Minister of Home Affairs*[95] the court refrained from using its new-found power to cure an omission in legislation. It did so in deference to the doctrine of separation of powers. Where different policy options are available to the legislature to remedy a constitutional defect in legislation, it is *par excellence* inapposite for a court, by employing its "reading in" power, to elect one of the options concerned.[96] In such circumstances, the more satisfactory remedy is a declaration of invalidity and suspension pending legislative correction.

6.3 A Court should Decide no more than is Absolutely Necessary for the Adjudication of a Particular Case.

The courts of law must be acutely attentive to the politically sensitive role they are called upon to fulfil in a delicately balanced power structure where a constitution embraces a supremacy clause, as the 1996 Constitution does.[97] This is even more pertinent in a federal or quasi-federal system where the courts must adjudicate in regard to the distribution of powers between central and provincial administrations. In these circumstances a prudential modality of interpretation, referred to and discussed below, which involves a careful balancing of competing jurisprudential interests, becomes of seminal importance and precipitates rules of "statutory construction, not necessarily applicable in

[91] See also *Satchwell v President of the Republic of South Africa and Another* 2002 (9) BCLR 986 (CC) para 37.
[92] 2000 (3) SA 1 (CC).
[93] 2002 (1) SA 21 (CC).
[94] See Currie "Bill of Rights Jurisprudence" *Annual Survey of South African law* 2001 at 59.
[95] 2000 (3) SA 936 (CC).
[96] *ibid.*, para 64.
[97] Section 2.

other forms of government."[98] It is therefore a salutary rule that in general a court should decide no more than is necessary for the adjudication of a particular case. Such a rule is particularly important in constitutional matters, with the result that "[c]onstitutional law ...should be developed cautiously, judiciously and pragmatically if it is to withstand the test of time".[99]

6.4 Outflanking Strategies or the Doctrine of Avoidance

For good reasons, courts that have the power to exercise judicial review are reluctant to do this and have therefore developed skilful outflanking strategies for avoiding the problematic task of review. The United States Supreme Court has held that "the most fundamental principle of constitutional adjudication is not to face constitutional questions but to avoid them, if at all possible."[100] It directly avoids matters which it considers to be political.[101] This is also the position with the Indian courts, which are careful to demarcate legal from political questions, refusing to adjudicate upon the latter.[102] The Indian Supreme Court limits constitutional decisions as much as possible. It has therefore indicated that

> "it is hardly necessary to emphasise that in dealing with constitutional questions courts should be slow to embark upon an unnecessary wide or general enquiry and should confine their decisions as far as may be reasonably practicable within the narrow limits of the controversy arising between the parties in a particular case."[103]

For the same reason, courts should also avoid deciding on speculative issues in relation to hypothetical questions.[104] Therefore, in the South African decision of *Zantsi v Council of State, Ciskei and Others,*[105] the Constitutional Court held that it was undesirable that courts should anticipate questions or decide upon them in advance of the necessity of such a decision. Where it is

---

[98] Groves *op.cit.*, fn. 61, *supra*, 4.
[99] *Kauesa v Minister of Home Affairs and Others* 1995 (11) BCLR 1540 (*per* Dumbutshema AJA). (NmS). See also *M M Pathak v Union of India* (1978) 3 SCR 334 in which Bhagwati J (as he then was) commented as follows in relation to the practice of the Supreme Court of India: "It is the settled practice of this Court to decide no more than what is absolutely necessary for the decision of a case".
[100] *United States v Lovett* 328 US 303 at 320 (1946).
[101] See *Baker v Carr*, 369 US 186 (1962).
[102] *R. C. Poundyal v Union of India* AIR 1993 SC 1804.
[103] *Atiabari Tea Co v State of Assam* AIR 1961 SC 232 at 251.
[104] *Central Bank of India v Their Workmen* AIR 1960 SC 12 at 28.
[105] 1995 (10) BCLR 1424 (CC).

possible to dispose of a case without addressing any potential constitutional issue, that course should indeed be followed by the court. This is a salutary rule worthy of emulation by all courts since it allows for the orderly development of the law.[106] Courts should refuse to decide issues on the grounds of lack of ripeness or of mootness when the issue is too late.[107] A case which no longer presents an existing or live controversy is therefore moot.[108]

Watchenuka and Another v Minister of Home Affairs and Others,[109] a case dealing the rights of refugees, is a good example of the principle of outflanking strategy. The issue in this case was resolved without considering the alleged violation of rights and the "accompanying limitation limitations analysis". The issue in this case was resolved by considering non-constitutional law requirements for the legality of regulation relating to refugees.

The doctrine of avoidance has been recognised by the Constitutional Court in *National Coalition for Gay and Lesbian Equality v Minister of Home Affairs*[110] in which the Court stated that "where it is possible to decide any

[106] *ibid.*, at 1429 (*per* Chaskalson P.). See also the Canadian case of *Borowski v Canada* 57 DLR (4th) 231 (1989). In relation to the *Borowoski* case Chaskalson comments that the Canadian Supreme Court held that although the general policy or practice was that courts may decline to decide cases which merely raise hypothetical or abstract questions, they have a discretion to lay down precise criteria for the exercise of such discretion except to emphasise that the Court has to take into account the rationale behind the general policy against deciding moot issues. First, in an adversary system, issues are best decided in the context of a live controversy. The second consideration is based on concern for judicial economy and the last is that it is generally undesirable and possibly an intrusion into the role of the legislature for a Court to pronounce judgment on constitutional issues in the absence of a dispute affecting the rights of parties to litigation. The Court ultimately dismissed the appeal stating that: "[T]he mere fact, however, that a case raising the same point is likely to recur even frequently should not by itself be reason for hearing an appeal which is moot. It is preferable to wait and determine the point in genuine adversarial context unless the circumstances suggest that the dispute will have always disappeared before it is ultimately resolved."

[107] See in this regard *Freedom of Expression Institute v President, Ordinary Court Martial* 1999 (2) SA 471 (C); *President, Ordinary Court Martial v Freedom of Expression Institute* 1999 (4) SA 682 (CC) and Currie "Bill of Rights Jurisprudence"*Annual Survey of South African Law* 1999 at 43–44.

[108] A good example of this is found in *Janse van Rensburg NO & another v Minister of Trade and Industry* 2001 (1) SA 29 (CC) para. 9. However, in this regard the courts have discretion that must be exercised according to the interests of justice. See *Independent Electoral Commission v Langeberg Municipality* 2001 (3) SA 925 (CC) and *President, Ordinary Court Martial v Freedom of Expression Institute* 1999 (4) SA 682 (CC) 1999 (11) BCLR 1219.

[109] 2003 (1) BCLR 62 (C).

[110] 2000 (2) SA 1 (CC), para 21.

case, civil or criminal, without reaching a constitutional issue, that is the course which should be followed". Currie argues persuasively that this approach to interpretation "translates into a principled preference for decisions in constitutional cases that are shallow and narrow (minimally reasoned and confined in their impact on subsequent cases) as opposed to deep and broad (widely reasoned and with wide implications for subsequent cases)".[111]

6.5 Rules of Severability

Rules of severability have been devised where a court is obliged to invalidate a part of an impugned statute.[112] Severance is also used in Canada in "cases where there has been a holding of unconstitutionality, [and] the vice infected only one or a few provisions of the challenged statute; those 'were severed' from the rest of the statute, enabling the rest to survive".[113] In Canada severance is not favoured in regard to cases relating to federalism, which involve the distribution of power between the central and provincial governments, but is favoured in regard to Charter cases.[114] The concept of severability is sound and has been employed in relation to subordinate legislation. The Constitutional Court has held that severance is not merely confined to the deletion of words from a legislative provision.[115] This can also be achieved by so-called "notional severance" which involves leaving the language of the provision intact, but subjecting the provision to a condition for its application. An exemplary illustration of this is found in *Ferreira v Levin NO.*[116] In this judgment of the Constitutional Court a legislative provision was effectively rewritten.

In *S v Lawrence*[117] the Constitutional Court explained the extent of its interpretative remedial powers as follows:

> "In effect what the appellant has asked this Court to do is to amend the Liquor Act so as to make provision for 'grocer's wine, beer and cider licence' as an exception to the prohibition imposed by section 40 of the Act.

[111] Currie "Bill of Rights Jurisprudence" *Annual Survey of South African Law* 2001 at 45. See also Currie "Judicious Avoidance" *SAJHR* 138 at 147 and *Minister of Education v Harris* 2001 (4) SA 1297 (CC); 2001 (11) BCLR 1157.

[112] See *R M D Chamarbaugwalla v Union of India* AIR 1957 SC 628.

[113] Hogg *Constitutional Law of Canada* 808.

[114] *ibid.,* 393.

[115] See Currie "Bill of Rights Jurisprudence" *Annual Survey of South African Law* 2000 at 45.

[116] 1996 (1) SA 984 (CC); 1996 (1) BCLR 1.

[117] 1997 (4) SA 1176 (CC) para 80.

A court can strike down legislation that is unconstitutional and can sever or read down provisions of legislation that are inconsistent with the Constitution because they are overbroad. It may have to fashion orders to give effect to the rights protected by the Constitution, but what it cannot do is legislate."

Notional severance, as explained above, appears to erode the principles of separation of powers. Nevertheless, there are limits to the court's remedial powers in this regard, as will be explained below, when the notion of reading in is discussed. As indicated above, notional severance entails leaving the language of the provision intact, but subjecting it to a proper or remedial application. The order of the court *a quo* in *South African Defence Union v Minister of Defence*[118] employed notional severance in relation to a provision of the Defence Act by stating that "[s]ection 126B(2) of the Defence Act 44 of 1957 is declared unconstitutional and invalid to the extent that it refers to acts of public violence".[119] In its confirmatory decision the Constitutional Court held that, while notional severance is permissible, where actual severance can achieve the same result it is generally to be preferred.[120]

6.6 The Role of Legislative History

Let us turn to consider an aspect of our law relating to the interpretation of statutes that has undergone an important change. Our courts have held that it is in general permissible when interpreting a statute to have regard to the purpose and background of the legislation in question.[121] In South Africa, the English law rule excluding parliamentary history, which had its origin in *Millar v Taylor,*[122] was initially adopted.[123] Despite this, it was, however, permissible to take notice of a report of a judicial commission of inquiry for the limited purpose of ascertaining "the mischief aimed at [by] the statutory enactment in question".[124]

---

118 1999 (2) SA 735 (T).

119 *ibid.*, at 756.

120 *South African Defence Union v Minister of Defence* 1999 (4) SA 469 (CC), para 16.

121 See *S v Makwanyane* 1995 (6) BCLR 665 (CC) at 677 and *Jaga v Dönges NO* 1950 (4) SA 653, 662–663 (A).

See also Corder and Du Plessis "What Value the Background in Constitutional Interpretation? A Response To Matthew Chaskalson" (1995) SAJHR 587.

122 (1769) 4 Burr 2303, at 2332, 98 ER 201, at 217.

123 See *Mathiba v Moschke* 1920 AD 354, at 362.

124 *Attorney-General, Eastern Cape v Blom* 1988 (4) SA 645, at 668–669 (A) and *Westinghouse Brake and Equipment (Pty) v Bilger Engineering (Pty) Ltd* 1986 (2) SA 555, at 562C–563 (A).

It is, however, important to note that, in English law, the House of Lords has relaxed the exclusionary rule and held, in the judgment in *Pepper (Inspector of Taxes) v Hart* that:[125]

> "Reference to Parliamentary material should be permitted as an aid to the construction of legislation which is ambiguous or obscure or the literal meaning leads to an absurdity. Even in such cases references in court to Parliamentary material should be permitted where such material clearly discloses the mischief aimed at or the legislative intention lying behind the ambiguous or obscure words."[126]

In Australia and New Zealand the exclusionary rule has also been relaxed.[127] Legislative history is used extensively in the United States,[128] and in Continental countries such as France and Germany.[129] The *travaux preparatoires* are extensively used for the purpose of interpreting treaties.[130] Chaskalson P[131] came to the conclusion, after an examination of the position in Germany, Canada, India, the European Court of Human Rights, the United Nations Committee on Human Rights and the United States that legislative history may be consulted as an aid to interpretation in certain circumstances

---

[125] [1993] AC 593 (HL).

[126] *Per* Lord Browne-Wilkenson, who in addition observed that "as at present advised I cannot foresee that any statement of the minister or other promoter of the Bill is likely to meet these criteria". See also in this regard Steyn *op. cit.*, fn. 81, *supra*, 134–136. See also the judgment of Leon AJA in *Ex parte Attorney-General, Namibia: In re The Constitutional Relationship between the Attorney General and the Prosecutor-General* 1995 (8) BCLR 1070 at 1080 (NmS). In this regard Leon AJA observes:

> "In the United Kingdom it has been authoritatively held that parliamentary debates may be looked at as a guide to the construction of statutes *only* where: (a) legislation is ambiguous or obscure; or leads to an absurdity; (b) the material relied upon consists of one or more statements by a Minister or other promoter of the Bill together, if necessary, with such other parliamentary material as is necessary to understand such statements and their effect; and (c) the statements relied upon are clear."

[127] See Devenish *op. cit.*, fn. 19, *supra* 126.

[128] See Singer *Sutherland Statutory Construction* (4th ed., 1984) vol 2A para 13, n72.

[129] See Sacks "Towards Discovering Parliamentary Intent" 1982 *Statute L Rev* 143 at 144.

[130] See Art. 32 of the Vienna Convention of Treaties 1969, 8 *ILM* 679 (1969). In this regard see *Cox v Canada*, The United Nations Committee on Human Rights, Communication No 539/1993 3 November 1993, 19, states: '. . . when giving a broad interpretation to any human rights treaty, care must be taken not to frustrate or circumvent the ascertainable will of the drafters. Here the rules of interpretation set forth in Article 32 of the Vienna Convention on the law of treaties help us by allowing the use of *trauvaux preparatoires*' (quoted by Chaskalson P in *S v Makwanyane* 1995 (6) BCLR 665 (CC) para 16).

[131] *S v Makwanyane, supra*, at 680.

in relation to the interim Constitution.[132] He did, however, observe that caution is called for in respect of "the comments of individual actors in the process, no matter how prominent a role they might have played".[133]

7 The Interpretation and Development of the Common Law

That South African common law does indeed require development in certain areas is manifestly clear from the remarkable judgment of the Constitutional Court in *Carmichele v Minister of Safety and Security and another.*[134] In this case the plaintiff had been viciously assaulted by a man named Coetzee, who had a history of assault. At the time of the attack Coetzee had been facing a charge of rape. Interested parties had endeavoured to persuade the police and the senior prosecutrix that he should not be released on bail or warning pending his trial for rape. This was all to no avail. While at liberty after being released on bail, he assaulted the plaintiff. As a result she instituted action against the two relevant ministers for alleged dereliction of duty by the police and the prosecutrix. The High Court granted absolution from the instance on the basis that a duty of care had not been *prima facie* established. The plaintiff's appeal to the Supreme Court of Appeal was also unsuccessful. The Constitutional Court in giving judgment on further appeal held that both the High Court and the SCA had relied only on the extant common law understanding of wrongfulness which had been developed by our courts over many years.[135]

The specific issue was whether the High Court and the Supreme Court of Appeal ought to have broadened the concept of "wrongfulness" as understood on the law of delict in the light of the State's constitutional duty to safeguard the rights of women. In a unanimous decision (*per* Ackermann and Goldstone JJ) the Constitutional Court granted the applicant leave to appeal and upheld

---

[132] He declined (678 par 15) to express any opinion on whether this *modus operandi* should be used to interpret 'ordinary legislation'. As he indicated, a constitution is no ordinary statute. In relation to the interpretation of the interim Constitution he observed: "Such background material can provide a context for the interpretation of the Constitution and, where it serves that purpose, I can see no reason why such evidence should be excluded. The precise nature of the evidence, and the purpose for which it may be tendered, will determine the weight to be given to it."

[133] Cf *Hewlett v Minister of Finance* 1982 1 SA 490, at 492 (ZS); and *In re Motor Vehicle Act* [1982] 2 SCR 486. where the Canadian Supreme Court cautioned against adherence to legislative history and concluded that it had little interpretive weight. See also Davis, Cheadle and Haysom *Fundamental Rights in the Constitution* 338.

[134] 2001 (10) BCLR 995 (CC).

[135] *ibid.*, at para 38.

the appeal. The Court held that, although the major engine for law reform should be legislation, the courts were under a general duty to develop the common law where it deviated from the spirit, purport and objects of fundamental rights provisions. The constitutional issues had not been addressed before either the High Court or the Supreme Court of Appeal. That fact did not, however, detract from the obligation resting on those courts to develop the common law if it was appropriate to do so in a particular case.[136] The Constitutional Court therefore set aside the order of absolution from the instance and referred the matter back to the trial court to continue the trial.[137]

Mthembi-Mahanyele v Mail and Guardian Limited and Another[138] is another judgment in which the common law in relation to the law of defamation was brought into line with the Constitution as far as freedom of expression is concerned and removed the "chilling effect" in this regard.[139] Another very important recent case in this regard is that of *Masiya v Director of Public Prosecutions, Pretoria and another.*[140] In this case the constitutional court extended the scope of the common law crime of rape to include, in addition to penile non-consensual penetration of the complainant's vagina, such penetration of her anus. The court held that this was necessary in order to duly recognise a woman's right to dignity, equality and freedom of security of person, which are respectively protected by sections 10, 9(1) and 12 of the South African Constitution. This creative interpretation and development by the Constitutional Court is viewed by a noted commentator as "a dangerous precedent".[141]

---

136 *cf Phoebus Apollo Aviation CC v Minister of Safety and Security* 2003 (1) BCLR 14 (CC). In this case, which involved alleged vicarious liability of the Minister for wrongful acts of policemen, the Constitutional Court, *per* Kriegler J, held that there was no convincing argument to show why the common law should be developed so as to impose an absolute liability on the State for the conduct of its employees committed dishonestly and in pursuit of their own interests.

137 See Currie "Bill of Rights Jurisprudence" *Annual Survey of South African Law* 2001 at 43.

138 2002 (12) BCLR 1323 (W).

139 *SA Associated Newspapers Ltd v Estate Pelser* 1975 (4) SA 797 (A) had diluted the principle established in *Die Spoorbond and Another v South African Railways; Van Heerden and Others v South African Railways* 1946 AD 999 to the effect that for reasons of public policy the government cannot sue for defamation.

140 2007 (5) SA 323 (CC). See in this regard C R Snyman "Extending the scope of Rape - A Dangerous Precedent" (2007) *SALJ* 677.

141 C R Snyman, *op.cit.*, at 685.

8 Conclusion

Teleological interpretation is of importance for both South Africa and Botswana. Both these countries are committed to human rights and have democratic credentials. As far as Botswana is concerned, Amissah JP declared in the *Dow* judgment:

> "Botswana is a member of the community of civilized states which has undertaken to abide by certain standards of conduct and, unless it is impossible to do so otherwise, it would be wrong for its courts to interpret its legislation in a manner which conflicts with international obligations Botswana has undertaken."[142]

Although the new constitutional dispensation has heralded a purposive/ value-based approach to interpretation, unfortunately, several judgments have been delivered since the new dispensation has come into effect where the traditional approach to interpretation has been employed. So, for example, although the theory of literalism is generally said to have been on the wane for many years, it is, according to Du Plessis,[143] still "alive and kicking" and is most certainly not dead like the proverbial dodo. Although jurisprudentially discredited, the literal theory still has exponents in the higher courts of the land. So, for example, Smalberger JA observed in *Public Carriers Association & others v Toll Road Concessionaires (Pty) Ltd & others*[144] "it must be accepted that the literal interpretation principle is firmly entrenched in our law and I do not seek to challenge it".

In more recent times, the Appellate Division (now the Supreme Court of Appeal) in *Swanepoel v Johannesburg City Council*[145] relied once again on the orthodox literal or plain meaning process of statutory construction and declared as follows:

> "The rules of statutory [exegesis] are intended as aids in resolving any doubts as to the legislature's true intention. Where this intention is proclaimed in clear terms either expressly or by necessary implication the assistance of these rules need not be sought."

142 [1992] BLR 119 at 154 as quoted by Fombad *op. cit.*, fn.12, *supra*, at 143.

143 See L M du Plessis *Re-Interpretation of Statutes* (2002) 94.

144 1990 (1) SA 925, at 943 (A).

145 1994 (3) SA 789, at 794.

The above quotation is *par excellence* a manifestation of primitive literalism. As recently as 2001, expression has been given to this theory and methodology of interpretation. In *Commissioner, SARS v Executor, Frith's Estate*[146] the Supreme Court of Appeal gave expression to the traditional rules of interpretation, encapsulating the intention of the legislature and the so-called well-known golden rule, initially expounded in English law, by stating:

> "The primary rule of construction of a statutory provision ...is to ascertain the intention of the legislator, and ...one seeks to achieve this, in the first instance, by giving words under consideration their ordinary meaning, unless to do so would lead to an absurdity so glaring that the legislature could not have contemplated it".

Once again this is a clear example of literalism in its most basic form.[147]

The literal theory and methodology are associated with the sovereignty of parliament and primitive legal positivism of the by-gone era, of imperialism, colonialism and white minority rule, epitomised by the simplistic jurisprudential idea, propounded by John Austen, that law is the command of the sovereign,[148] which has now been superseded. Our jurisprudence has progressed to something far more intellectually and morally sophisticated that is compatible with the universal values reflected in the Bill of Rights, which forms an integral part of a supreme constitution.

As indicated above, the provisions of the Bill of Rights are stated in general and broad terms in a way which allows "for the evolutionary interpretation and the growth of the instrument which entrenches fundamental rights and freedoms."[149] Most of them are not absolute[150] and they may, to a greater or lesser extent, be limited by legislation which accords with section 36 of the Constitution. The Constitutional Court is given, as a result of the general and vague terms used in the provisions of chapter 2, considerable latitude and opportunity for innovative, imaginative and creative jurisprudence. Certain seminal moral and jurisprudential issues are not explicitly answered.[151]

---

[146] 2001 (2) SA 261, at 273 (SCA).

[147] See also the judgment of Schutz JA in *Standard Bank Investment Corporation Ltd v Competition Commission* 2000 (2) SA 797 at 811 and LM du Plessis *Re-Interpretation of Statutes* 103.

[148] See D Johnson, S Pete and M du Plessis *Jurisprudence A South African Perspective* (2001) 72.

[149] Fundamental Rights, 5th Report, 1993-06-11 3 (49).

[150] Freedom from torture in international law is absolute, non-derogable and unqualified. See Cachalia et al *Fundamental Rights in the New Constitution* 37.

[151] See Mureinik "NP Conspicuous by its Failures" *The Star*, 23 November 1993.

Therefore, the Bill of Rights did not provide an express answer to the legal status of abortion and capital punishment.[152] In relation to the latter the Constitutional Court came to the conclusion that capital punishment was incompatible with the Interim Constitution.[153] The Constitutional Court will have to give finality on all these and many other vexed moral and jurisprudential questions.

The process of interpretation of statutes and of the 1996 Constitution must inevitably become profoundly and manifestly jurisprudential and not merely or apparently technical, as was the position in regard to the methodology of interpretation and the philosophy of law that previously prevailed in South Africa, which in effect constituted a primitive positivism based on and white domination.

The nature of the methodological approach required for the interpretation and application of a Constitution is perceptively explained by Van Diykhorstj in *De Klerk and Another v Du Plessis and Others*[154] as follows:

> 'In my view one must apply the purposive approach to interpretation of our Constitution, determining from it as a whole what the aim of Chapter 3 and its constituent sections individually, what problems and aspirations did it seek to address, and what does it have in mind for our society. In short, what are the values and norms our society cherishes and intends to uphold?'

The purposive approach described above is not merely a technical exercise. It involves values and hence value judgments. Interpretation, is however, an eclectic process greatly dependent on the jurisprudential disposition of the judge or judges involved. Constitutional interpretation does however require a jurisprudential and hermeneutic coherence. In this regard Michelman suggests that "on the constitutional level, legal interpretation succeeds by construing legal words, intentions, and purposes, yes, but by construing them decidedly in the light of consequences, and by appraising consequences decidedly in the light of an emergent national sense of justice to which the

---

152 See "Death penalty moratorium" *Daily News,* 6 June 1994. In an Appellate Division murder case involving Mr Pieter John van der Merwe, Kumbleben JA found that it was inappropriate to conclude an appeal matter that involved the death penalty and the case was adjourned pending a decision of the Constitutional Court.

153 *S v Makwanyane* 1995 (6) BCLR 665 (CC).

154 1994 (6) BCLR 124, at 128 (T).

interpretations are themselves, contributing".[155] In effect such interpretation involves a jurisprudential and teleological evaluation of all the issues involved and not merely a linguistic exercise.[156] This makes the process of interpretation highly creative and jurisprudentially fascinating and exciting.

Although South Africa has made a remarkable transformation from apartheid to multi-party democracy, there remain many serious human rights defects in our body politic such as the scourge of poverty, vast unemployment, the AIDS/HIV pandemic and racism. We need critical self-examination. I have no doubt that such as approach is also necessary for Botswana.[157] Intellectual honesty is essential in this regard and is reflected in the words of Tshosa in 1994 that the "on-going praise of Botswana as the bastion of multi-party democracy may not be entirely accurate".[158] In the light of the *Good* case,[159] referred to and cited above, these words are particularly poignant at the present time.

[155] "A Constitutional Conversation with Frank Michelman" 11 *SAJHR* 477, at 482 (1995).

[156] See Devenish *Interpretation of Statutes* (1992) 55.

[157] See O B Tshosa "Freedom of Political Activity in Botswana" (1994) *CILSA* 371.

[158] *ibid.*, at 382.

[159] See *Communcation Submitted for the Consideration under Article 56 of the African Charter of Human and Peoples' Rights.* The Commission declared the communication admissible. There has not had a decision on the merits. That is likely to come in about year's time - the Commission being a fairly slow moving body.

Constitutional Rights and Judicial Activism: Bridging the Gaps in Botswana

Dr. Rekha A. Kumar*

1 Introduction

Botswana is one of the few countries in Africa with a relatively stable, multi-party democracy and an enviable human rights record. Botswana's liberal democracy and universal respect for, and observance of, human rights and fundamental freedoms are anchored in the foundations of Tswana traditional polity which emphasised the devolution of governing authority of local political units and popular participation in decision-making processes.[1] Protection of the constitutional rights of the people has been one of the prime objectives of the framers of the Constitution, who ensured that certain rights, inalienable to all citizens, were protected against state infringement by their incorporation into the Bill of Rights, albeit subject to certain restrictions. They also provided that, in the protection of the guaranteed rights, germane to that in a democracy, all the three organs of the state, the legislature, the judiciary and the executive, would have their distinct roles to play.

2 The Basic Framework of Constitutional Rights in the Constitution of Botswana

Basic principles of democratic government were embodied in Botswana's Constitution, adopted at independence in 1966. The underlying purpose was to create a limited government out of the ashes of the colonial order. The powers of government were separated into three co-ordinate branches, none of which was supposed to encroach on the other.[2] Executive powers of

---

*LLB (MD University), LLM, PhD (Delhi), Advocate (India), Lecturer, Department of Law, University of Botswana.

[1] M.L.M. Mao, "Constitutional Government and Human Rights in Botswana," in Nasal S. Ramble and Evince Kaluga (eds.), *Constitutional Government and Human Rights in Africa: Proceedings of a Workshop on Constitutional Government and Human Rights in Africa, Maseru, Lesotho, 4–8 October, 1989*, INTWORLSA, Roma Lesotho, 1991, p. 179.

[2] *ibid.*, p. 180

the Republic were entrusted to the President who was both head of the State and head of the Government. Executive actions were required to conform to the Constitution and to the laws enacted in accordance therewith. The courts were given the power of judicial review of executive actions. Chapter II of the Constitution enshrined a Bill of Rights fashioned on the Universal Declaration of Human Rights (UDHR) and the European Convention of Human Rights (ECHR).

The doctrine of separation of powers is an indivisible part of the progression of democracy itself. The doctrine, which provides for checks and balances amongst the organs of the State, is one of the most characteristic features of Botswana's constitutional scheme. The Constitution lays down the structure and defines the limits and prescribes the role and functions of every organ of the State including the judiciary and establishes norms of inter-relationship. The obvious consideration is to preserve and protect the basic rights of the people and recognise the supremacy of the popular will in the governance structure.

The responsibility for identifying and defining people's rights and for providing statutory sanction for them has thus been thoughtfully bestowed on the Parliament which represents the people of the nation as a whole. All institutions of governance in a democracy are required to remain accountable to the people directly or indirectly. It is this notion of abiding accountability to the people which holds the key to the success and sustenance of democracy. The constitutional set-up has enabled the judiciary to place in abeyance not only laws passed by the Parliament but also executive actions which are not in consonance with the rights of the people under its Constitution.[3]

The Constitution of Botswana provides for an independent judiciary. The safeguards instituted at independence are still maintained. The Chief Justice and the President of the Court of Appeal are appointed by the President in his discretion and Judges of the Court of Appeal and Judges of the High Court are appointed by the President acting in accordance with the advice of the Judicial Service Commission.[4] It is imperative to emphasise here that the essence of judicial independence is not segregation from the other branches

---

[3] Constitution of Botswana, Chapter II.

[4] *ibid.*, Ss. 96 and 100.

of government but the preservation of a separate institution that can adjudicate cases or controversies impartially without fear or favour.[5]

Botswana's human rights record has been widely praised as one of the best in the World.[6] Section 3 of the Constitution delineates the basic human rights and fundamental freedoms in a preambular form:

> "Whereas every person in Botswana is entitled to the fundamental rights and freedoms of the individual, that is to say, the right, whatever, his race, place of origin, political opinions, colour, creed or sex, but subject to respect for the rights and freedom of others and for the public interest to each and all the following, namely:
>
> (a) life, liberty, security of the person and the protection of the law.
>
> (b) Freedom of conscience, of expression and of assembly and association; and
>
> (c) Protection for the privacy of his home and other property and from deprivation of property without compensation…"

In addition to this preambular declaration, the Constitution goes on to protect the fundamental rights and basic freedoms of the people in Botswana by means of specific prohibitions provided in sections 4 to 16. According to these provisions, "any person" can seek protection for his or her rights. The claimant need not be a citizen of Botswana and may be a natural or juristic person. What is decisive is that any of his or her rights, contained in these sections of the Constitution, "has been, is being or is likely to be contravened *in relation to him or her*." He or she thus must be a victim of the contravention or anticipated contravention of the rights. At the same juncture the Constitution recognises that, intrinsically, one's human rights cannot be guaranteed in absolute terms. It provides that a person's entitlement to the enumerated rights is "subject to respect for the rights and freedom of others and for the public interest". Every recognised right is followed by a list of exceptions (known as claw-back clauses). Because these clauses restrict the realisation of protected rights, the courts interpret them strictly.[7] Therefore, while Parliament has powers to enact laws restricting the exercise of the protected

---

[5] *op. cit.*, n. 1, p. 197.

[6] See A. Molokomme, "Political Rights in Botswana: Regression or Development", paper presented to the Symposium on Democracy in Botswana, 3 August 1988.

[7] See *Petrus v The State*, [1984] BLR 14.

rights, it does not thereby have a *carte blanche* to enact laws that totally annul those rights.[8]

Section 18 of the Constitution entrusts to the High Court original jurisdiction to enforce the protective provisions enumerated under sections 3 to 16. Sub-section (3) of section 18 provides further that, when in any subordinate court any question arises as to the contravention of sections 3 to 16 of the Constitution, the presiding judge in the court may (and shall if the party to the proceedings so requests) refer the matter to the High Court.

Archibald Cox rightly observed that a perfect constitution is not an adequate protection of civil liberties. Constitutional guarantees are statements of principle to which adherence can be assured only when the political culture engenders respect for the Constitution and there are institutionalised means for forcing the government to respect it.[9]

The essential point here is that the sphere of human rights comprises an indivisible and interdependent whole. No right has its own independent existence. In this respect, although Botswana has an excellent record as regards political and civil rights, it must address the vital question of the interrelationship between widespread poverty and the full enjoyment of economic, social and cultural rights. Social progress and economic development are key factors in the promotion of such rights and fundamental freedoms. A starting point, as asserted by Mbao, could be the satisfaction of the basic needs of society, in particular those of the most vulnerable groups and individuals, for if a man is unable to feed or clothe himself how can he assert any of his fundamental rights?[10]

3 Judicial Activism

Protection and enhancement of people's rights in a democracy will advance their empowerment within the system. It is in creating conditions for people to enjoy their basic rights that the legislature is expected to play the most crucial role in a democracy and, conversely, it is in safeguarding those rights that the judiciary has to play its vital role.[11]

---

[8] D.D.N. Nsereko, *Constitutional Law in Botswana*, Pula Press, Gaborone, p. 271 (2001).

[9] A. Cox , *The Court and the Constitution* New Delhi, Asian Books (Pvt) Ltd., p. 15 (1987).

[10] *op. cit.*, fn. 1, p. 204.

[11] N. L. Belekar Memorial Lecture on The Role of Legislature and Judiciary in Protecting and Enhancing the People's Rights in our Democracy, Nagpur, India, 18 February 2008.

As Thomas Sowell has aptly noted, "judicial activism" like any other catchword, has acquired various meanings so as to obscure more than it reveals.[12] Since abandoning the term is not a viable option, a clarification becomes imperative. *Merriam-Webster's Dictionary of Law*[13] defines judicial activism as:

> "...the practice in the judiciary of protecting or expanding individual rights through decisions that depart from established precedent or is independent of or in opposition to supposed constitutional or legislative intent."

David Strauss and Harry Wyatt have argued that judicial activism can narrowly be defined as one or more of the following three:

- overturning laws as unconstitutional;
- overturning judicial precedent; or
- ruling against a preferred interpretation of the Constitution.[14]

4 Living Constitution

The U.S. Supreme Court is probably the most activist tribunal on earth, with Canada fast becoming a runner-up.[15] In the United States legal discourse, the "living" Constitution is a theory of constitutional interpretation premised on the view that the Constitution is, to some degree, dynamic. As the direct counter to originalism, which centres on textual meaning at the time of ratification, the theory of a "living" Constitution suggests a document that is in a relationship of interdependence with the society that implements it. Its proponents thus argue that societal progress should be taken into account when interpreting key constitutional phrases.[16] The term originally is derived

[12] T. Sowell, *Judicial Activism Reconsidered*, Essays in Public Policy No. 13, Hoover Institute Press, 1989, Stanford, p. 1.

[13] *Merriam-Webster's Dictionary of Law* (1996), Merriam-Webster.

[14] D. Strauss, Harry N. Wyatt, *Common Law and the Constitution*, University of Chicago Law School, Cambridge University Press, Cambridge (2006).

[15] C. Michael Macmillan and Raymond Tatalovich, "Judicial Activism vs. Restraint: The Role of the Highest Courts in Official Language Policy in Canada and the United States", 33 American Review of Canadian Studies 239 (2003).

[16] W. Adam. "A Revolution Too Soon: Woman Suffragists and the 'Living Constitution'", 76 N.Y.U.L. Rev. 1456, at 1463 (2001): "Based on the idea that society changes and evolves, living constitutionalism requires that constitutional controversies, in the words of Justice Oliver Wendell Holmes Jr., 'must be considered in the light of our whole experience and not merely in that of what was said a hundred years ago.'"

from the title of a 1937 book of that name by Howard McBain.[17] The earliest efforts at developing the concept in modern form have been credited to such influential figures as Oliver Wendell Holmes, Louis D. Brandeis and Woodrow Wilson.[18]

5 A Word of Caution

In *Michigan v. Long*[19], Justice John Paul Stevens expressed the belief that:

> "…a policy of judicial restraint, one that allows other decisional bodies to have the last word in legal interpretation until it is truly necessary for this Court to intervene, enables this Court to make its most effective contribution to our federal system of government."

Various cases and judicial shifts throughout the U.S. Supreme Court's history have prompted accusations of judicial activism or over-reaching.[20]According to Douglas H. Ginsburg, the courts are not democratically elected, and for good reason. They should use their authority to override or constrain the will of the elected political branches of government very sparingly, lest the genius and harmony of constitutional architecture be lost. However, as Ginsburg notes, the courts must preserve from majoritarian government the individual rights that the Constitution vests in the people. Insofar as the rights of individuals, as clearly established in the Constitution, are threatened by such government, criticism of judicial activism is misplaced. Ginsburg warns that the courts should be circumspect, sceptical and cautious of some newly discovered individual right implicit, rather than explicit, in the Constitution; for, once thrust in the Constitution, that right must be vigorously protected against encroachments from the government. In this way, as the rights of individuals expand, the rights of the majority contract, but it is not for each new judge, or even each new generation, to strike anew the balance between these conflicting rights, he explains. According to him, the framers of the

---

17 Howard L. McBain, *The Living Constitution*, Macmillan (1937).

18 Wilson often referred to the Constitution as a "vehicle of life". See Michael Kammen, *A Vehicle of Life: The Founders' Intentions and American Perceptions of Their Living Constitution*. Proceedings of the American Philosophical Society, Vol. 131, No. 3, A More Perfect Union: Essays on the Constitution (Sep., 1987).

19 463 U.S. 1032 (1983).

20 See for illustration *Marbury v. Madison* 5 U.S. (1 Cranch) 137 (1803); *Chisholm v. Georgia* 2 U.S. (2 Dall.) 419 (1793); *Dred Scott v. Sandford*, 60 U.S.393 (1857); *Hans v. Louisiana*, 134 U.S.1 (1890); *Goodridge v. Dept. of Public Health*, 798 N.E.2d 941 (Mass. 2003).

Constitution did that once, and left it for future generations to amend a process not judicial, but legislative, in character.[21]

These arguments by Ginsburg are formidable in forcing us to hesitate before embracing some simplistic notion of judicial activism. Activism towards *what?* Restraint in relation to *what?* The contexts in which this activism or restraint may call for exercise include the following areas of focus:

1. the current popular majority;
2. the legislature representing the current popular majority;
3. the statutes passed by present or past legislatures;
4. the acts of current of past executive or administrative agencies;
5. the meaning of the words in the Constitution;
6. the principles or purposes of those who wrote the Constitution; or
7. the precedents established by previous judicial interpretations of the Constitution.[22]

Other commentators have raised further questions. Thomas Sowell calls on us to reflect on the terms "judicial activism" and "judicial restraint". Sowell explains that activism or restraint toward one of these does not imply the same toward all the others and may in some instances imply the opposite.[23]

It is not mere activity or passivity that is at issue, but the basis of that activity or passivity. In a constitutional government, a jurist is said to be activist to the extent that he or she settles cases on grounds *extrinsic to the Constitution.* It is ultimately the Constitution towards which the jurist is "activist" or "restrained."[24] One of the most obvious obstacles to following what the Constitution says is the difficulty of knowing what it intends. The magnitude of this problem is crucial.[25] The question is not whether a term is comprehensively definitive but whether it is sufficient to dispose of the issue in the case at hand.[26]

---

[21] Ginsburg's Legal Philosophy, New York Times, 5 November, 1987.

[22] *op. cit.* fn. 12.

[23] *ibid.* See also Thomas Sowell, *Knowledge and Decisions*, Basic Books Publications, New York, pp. 298–99 (1996).

[24] *cf.* Blackstone, *Commentaries on the Laws of England*, vol. 1, Elibron and Elibron Classics, London. pp. 59–61 (2005).

[25] *ibid.*, p. 6.

[26] Holmes, *Collected Legal Papers,* The Lawbook Exchange Ltd. Clark, New Jersey, p. 177 (2006).

6 The Case of Botswana

Rights entrenched in the Constitution possess several obvious advantages over common law and statutory rights: they cannot readily be repealed or overridden and they derive their moral and legal force directly from the will of the people. In the past forty years, Botswana has witnessed a moderate development in certain areas of the Bill of Rights and Individual Freedoms. Lately, there has been growing debate about the function of courts and their role in the development of constitutional rights. Interestingly, the Constitution of Botswana does not confer an over-arching authority on any one organ. No organ has any power to superintend over the exercise of powers and functions of another, unless the Constitution strictly so mandates.

The courts in Botswana have power of judicial review so as to ensure executive compliance with the Constitution and laws enacted in accordance with the Constitution.[27] The courts are not a substitute for administrative authorities and their value judgments, but rather have the role of scrutinising methods of proper operation.[28]

As regards legislative initiatives, the Constitution bestows broad powers on the judiciary in appropriate cases to strike down legislation that runs counter to the human rights provisions of the Constitution. Nsereko observes that the High Court's powers derived under the Constitution to review executive, legislative and even private persons' actions run parallel and sometimes overlap with its powers to review administrative action derived from the common law.[29]

The role of the courts in the protection of human rights also depends on interpreting the human rights provisions of the Constitution. By its nature the Constitution often formulates human rights in general, imprecise or indefinite terms. It leaves to the courts, when an opportunity shows itself, the task of filling in the gaps. In so doing the courts help the Constitution to develop and

---

[27] See *Clover Petrus* v. *The State*, [1984] BLR 14 (CA); *Desai and Modi* v. *The State*, [1987] BLR 55 (CA); *Mooi, Mbali and Mbulani v. The State*, Criminal Appeal No. 25 of 1986; and *Kgamenyane* v. *The State*, [1986] BLR 62.

[28] See *Alfred Chilinde Mokgoeng v. The Attorney-General*, Civil Appeal No. 8/1987; *Mtetwa v. O. C. State Prison, Lobatse*, [1976] 1 BLR 1; *Student Representative Council v. University of Botswana and others*, [1989] BLR 396.

[29] Nsereko, *op. cit.*, fn. 8.

grow, for it is indeed a live and organic instrument. The observation made by Aguda JA, in *Attorney General v Unity Dow*[30]is well-fitted here:

> "The Constitution is the supreme law of the land and it is meant to serve not only this generation but also generations yet unborn. It cannot be allowed to be a lifeless museum piece; on the other hand the courts must continue to breathe life into it from time to time as the occasion may arise to ensure the healthy growth and development of the State through it."

On the role of courts he states further:

> "…the primary duty of the judges is to make the Constitution grow and develop in order to meet the just demands and aspirations of an ever-developing society which is part of the wider and larger human society governed by some acceptable concepts of human dignity."[31]

If the implications of these observations are carried out, the scope of judicial activism in Botswana would stand on par with that in the United States of America. These instances amply illustrate the operation of the principle which has emerged (albeit slowly) as a useful weapon in the hands of superior courts. It would be naive to ignore the possibility that rights previously unknown to the common law and unwritten in the Constitution might yet emerge from the cases of the High Court.

Section 7 of the Constitution prohibits "torture and inhuman and degrading punishment"; it does not define these terms. It is the task of the courts to engage in that process and to determine what forms of punishment or treatment fall afoul with the Constitution.[32] In *Clover Petrus v. State*[33] the Court of Appeal had to determine whether corporal punishment constituted "inhuman and degrading punishment". It defined "inhuman and degrading treatment" as treatment that was "devoid of human kindness or barbaric". It went on to hold that corporal punishment *per se* was not inhuman. Such punishment became inhuman, however, when administered in instalments. Section 10 of the Constitution provides that an independent and impartial court must try an accused person "within a reasonable time". It does not elaborate on what

[30] [1992] BLR 119, at 166.

[31] *ibid.* See also Nsereko, *op. cit.*, fn. 8, p. 276.

[32] *ibid.* p. 277.

[33] [1984] BLR 679.

constitutes "reasonable" or "unreasonable time" is. The courts have the task of defining these terms in the context of a given situation. In *State v. Merriweather Seboni*[34] the High Court held that the question whether there has been unreasonable delay in bringing the accused to trial is one which depends on the circumstances of each case. The Court also suggested the possible remedies available to a person whose right to trial within a reasonable time has been violated. In *State v Makwekwe*[35] it held that unreasonable delay must be a factor to be considered when sentencing. Going further, being a court of unlimited jurisdiction, the High Court, in *Ditshwanelo v Attorney General & Anr.,*[36] granted the applicants a stay of execution and leave to lead further evidence even though their appeal to the Court of Appeal had been unsuccessful.

There has been a striking paucity of constitutional litigation in Botswana but it may be expected that in coming years the position will change radically with the increasing interest in comparative constitutional jurisprudence, an enhanced consciousness of rights in the community, the growth of numbers of lawyers and the ease of access through the internet to international legal materials.

7 International Human Rights Standards: the Role of the Judiciary

The Nesereko study about the courts in Botswana is profound. He states that, in discharging their tasks, the courts draw on the wisdom of the day, taking into account public opinion, current social morality and data and contemporary experience. According to him, they also draw on the experience of foreign courts and other international judicial bodies that might have had to interpret provisions in their constitutions or instruments that are *in pari materia* to Botswana's. He mentions further that the courts do not have recourse to a foreign or an international precedent where the constitutional or statutory provisions in question are clear and unambiguous or where there exist local precedents on the points at issue. They only have such recourse in cases of ambiguity, lacuna or absence of local precedent. The author strongly suggests that such recourse is justifiable on two grounds. The first is that human rights are universal. The second is that international instruments embody international

[34] [1968–70] BLR 153 referred from Nsereko, *op. cit.,* fn. 8, p. 277.
[35] [1981] BLR 196 See also Nsereko, *op. cit.*, fn. 8, p. 277.
[36] [1999] 2 BLR 56.

standards, which all nations of the world must strive to attain and maintain.[37] The justifications given by the learned author open the gates for Parliament to enact legislation to fulfil that obligation. However, there is a discrepancy between theory and practice in the application of international human rights law in the domestic legal system of Botswana, according to Tshosa.[38] The author is cautious to avoid giving the impression that the domestic application of international law should take place without taking into account the need to preserve the legislative sovereignty of the countries in which it is applied. In his words, "an unqualified domestic application of customary international law is not a preferable option".[39]

The regulation of international law by the countries in which it is to be applied is also necessitated by the fact that international treaties, including human rights treaties, are often formulated in very general terms and their effective implementation in domestic legal systems requires specific legislative action by national legislatures.[40] Tshosa notes that, although substantive provisions of the Bill of Rights contained in the Constitution of Botswana are essentially in consonance with international human rights standards, internal human rights practice has not always been consistent with the requirements of international treaties.

So far as the application of international law in Botswana is concerned, according to Tshosa, it has been hindered by several factors, among which is the failure of domestic forums to apply international law in a consistent manner. He recommends that, in their legal proceedings, domestic courts should move away from excessive reliance on national law and jurisprudence and instead invoke international law more often and consistently. They should also go beyond this and use international human rights law to invalidate practices in domestic legal systems that violate fundamental human rights. In short, he strongly advocates judicial activism as opposed to restraint in the domestic application of international human rights law. The author's recommendations about how the role of international human rights law can be enhanced and more effectively enforced in domestic legal systems seem

---

[37] Nsereko, *op. cit.*, n. 8, p. 276.

[38] Onkemetse Tshosa, *National Law and International Human Rights Law: Cases of Botswana, Namibia and Zimbabwe*. Aldershot: Ashgate Publishing, 2001, p. 202.

[39] *ibid.*, p. 68.

[40] *cf.* Tapiwa Zimudzi. "Review of Onkemetse Tshosa, *National Law and International Human Rights Law: Cases of Botswana, Namibia and Zimbabwe*", H-SAfrica, H-Net Reviews, March, 2002. See also Geoffrey Robertson, *Crimes Against Humanity: The Struggle for Global Justice*, London: Penguin Books, (2000).

to give the judiciary and parliament, as opposed to the executive, a leading role in the protection of human rights. He argues that judicial activism is crucial to effective implementation of human rights norms and treaties in domestic legal systems.[41]

Human rights laws that cannot be enforced are of no substance, especially given that some human rights scholars have argued that the 21st century signals a new era in human rights, which they have termed the age of enforcement.[42] However, there seems to be a new aura in the commitment by the new president of the Republic of Botswana, H.E. Lieutenant General S.K.I. Khama, who recently, in his inauguration address, stated:

> "Democracy, has served our country and its people well. It is an important cornerstone of good governance and prudent economic management. Only democracy guarantees human rights, the rule of law, accountability and basic freedom that we have enjoyed over the years."[43]

8 Conclusion

Sustenance of a vibrant parliamentary democracy all these years, no doubt, has been one of Botswana's most significant achievements of the first four decades of independence. There are also several areas where Botswana has not yet been able to achieve what has widely been expected. A great deal more needs to be done to address such issues as women's empowerment, wider employment opportunities, the preservation and expansion of the rights of the workers, comprehensive social reforms and universal education. Certainly, there are constitutional provisions for women's empowerment and participation at the grassroots level of governance in the country; but it is time we went beyond that. None of the civil, political, economic and social rights can be exercised unless a certain minimum of education is proffered. It is the primary vehicle by which the economically and socially marginalised can lift themselves out of the mire of poverty and obtain the means to participate fully in community affairs. More vigorous efforts are required to remove the obstacles that deny children access to school and completion of schooling. These are some areas in which the Parliament has not functioned powerfully and productively. One certainly should acknowledge the significant

---

[41] *ibid.*

[42] *ibid.* See also *Geoffrey* Robertson, *op. cit.*, n. 40, pp. xiii–xxi.

[43] Inauguration address by the President on 1st April 2008, para 10.

role the judiciary can play in protecting and enhancing the rights of the individual in a democracy.

There is every need to address the question of whether the judiciary has been able to make a positive difference in the life of the ordinary man and woman, where constitutional rights are concerned. Unfortunately, the enthusiasm demonstrated in drafting these rights has not always been matched by a commitment to consummate implementation. Many of the progressive legislative initiatives with far-reaching goals are, perhaps, not made widely known to potential beneficiaries. The vast majority of citizens, especially in rural areas, are apparently not aware of their constitutionally guaranteed rights even today. The judicial branch, no doubt, has to take some of the responsibility for this gap between the objectives set and their delivery and in this sphere an alert civil society and the media can also play a vital role.

Enhancing the Judicial Role in Human Rights Protection in Botswana

Charles Manga Fombad*

1 Introduction

The explosion in human rights awareness in Africa in the last two decades has meant that the spotlight is less on the recognition and protection of these rights and more on how effective the mechanisms for their enforcement are. This has focused the limelight squarely on the judiciary. Standing firmly between the individual citizens and the wielders of power, the judiciary has become the ultimate arbiter in the arena of human rights. For a judiciary, which in most parts of Africa was sidelined before the 1990s, its sudden emergence at the heart of human rights adjudication has posed enormous challenges. Human rights litigation encourages an examination, not only of the quality, prestige and legitimacy of the judiciary but also the human rights and democratic credentials of the country. Judgments on human rights questions are often carefully scrutinised by an increasingly restive and assertive civil society as well as an international community that has come to consider human rights protection as one of the critical *sine qua non* conditions for political stability and economic development.

The judiciary has not been immune from the forces of globalisation which have affected all areas of political, social and economic life. The inward-looking culture which was characteristic of the old judiciary is gradually being abandoned as judges come to see themselves as members of a global legal community where knowledge and ideas are exchanged across jurisdictions. Because of its inherent dynamic and international character, it is inevitable that national human rights laws have been substantially influenced by global developments in human rights protection. Judges can no longer examine human rights issues without looking at developments in other jurisdictions. It is contended that this calls for a new judicial approach to human rights adjudication which requires judges to adopt a fresh, innovative and principled approach to reflect adequately the dynamic changes in human

---

*Licence-en-Droit (LLB) (Yaounde) LLM PhD (Lond), Professor of Law, Department of Law, University of Botswana.

rights recognition and protection that have taken place in the last two decades.

In Botswana, the main source of human rights recognition and protection is the 1966 Constitution. This paper will start by considering the role it reserves for the courts. On the premise that the dynamic nature of human rights requires a more proactive judicial approach, a number of ways will be examined in which, it is argued, the judicial role could be made more effective. It will be suggested that enhancing the judicial role in human rights protection entails a bold, more imaginative approach to adjudication and depends on issues such as judicial leadership, judicial independence, judicial attitude, judicial integrity, judicial activism, judicial training, advocacy and the positive intervention of human rights organisations. It will be shown that, much as the extent of human rights protection today in Botswana is substantially determined by law, judges play a very important part in defining the scope of this law and the way it is enforced through the manner in which they interpret and apply the law.

2 The Constitutional Basis of Judicial Intervention

Constitutions generally, and Bills of Rights in constitutions specifically, do not implement themselves. The ultimate responsibility for interpreting and applying the "fundamental rights and freedoms of the individual"[1] rests on the High Court and, by way of appeal, the Court of Appeal. The scope of these powers is defined in section 18 as follows:

> "(1) Subject to the provisions of subsection (5) of this section, if any person alleges that any of the provisions of sections 3 to 16 (inclusive) of this Constitution has been, is being or is likely to be contravened in relation to him, then, without prejudice to any other action with respect to the same matter which is lawfully available, that person may apply to the High Court for redress.
>
> (2) The High Court shall have original jurisdiction –
>
> (a) To hear and determine any application made by any person in pursuance of subsection (1) of this section; or
>
> (b) To determine any question arising in the case of any person which is referred to it in pursuance of subsection (1) of this section and *may make such orders, issue such writs and give direction as it may consider appropriate for the purpose of enforcing or securing*

[1] As defined in Chapter II, sections 3 to 19 of the 1966 Constitution.

the enforcement of any of the provisions of sections 3 to 16 (inclusive) of this Constitution.

(3) If in any proceedings in any subordinate court any question arises as to the contravention of any of the provisions of sections 3 to 16 (inclusive) of this Constitution, the person presiding in that court may, and shall if any party to the proceedings so requests, refer the question to the High Court unless, in his opinion, the raising of the question is merely frivolous or vexatious.

(4) Parliament may confer upon the High Court such powers in addition to those conferred by this section as may appear to be necessary or desirable for the purpose of enabling that court more effectively to exercise the jurisdiction conferred upon it by this section.

(5) Rules of court making provision with respect to the practice and procedure of the High Court for the purposes of this section may be made by the person or authority for the time being having the power to make rules of court with respect to the practice and procedure of that court generally."[2]

Four important comments need to be made about the scope and breadth of this provision.[3] First, any aggrieved party may bring an action not only in cases of actual violation of the rights conferred by the Bill of Rights but also in cases of potential or threatened violations. This right of action does not prevent the aggrieved party from bringing "any other action which is lawfully available on the same matter." It is, however, not very clear what possible concurrent actions can be brought on the same matter here.

Secondly, although the High Court is conferred primary original jurisdiction in such matters, this does not prevent any other subordinate court, which clearly means the magistrates' courts, before which an issue concerning the interpretation of the Bill of Rights may arise, from dealing with the matter, provided that the person presiding over that matter "may, and shall if" any party to the proceedings so request, refer the matter to the High Court. Whilst the matter must be referred to the High Court if the parties so request, the discretion of the person presiding to refuse a referral only arises where he or

---

[2] Emphasis added.

[3] See further, Charles Manga Fombad, "The Protection of Human Rights in Botswana: An Overview of the Regulatory Framework," in Charles Manga Fombad (ed.), *Essays on the Law of Botswana*, Cape Town, Juta & Co pp. 16–19 (2007).

she comes to the conclusion that the raising of the matter is merely frivolous or vexatious.

Thirdly, there is a clear advantage in raising these issues before the High Court rather than the Magistrates' Courts because section 18(2)(b) gives the former very wide powers in terms of the remedies that it can impose. The High Court may "make such orders, issue such writs and give such direction as it may consider appropriate for the purpose of enforcing or securing the enforcement" of these provisions. These are very significant powers which the High Court has probably been too timid to use. For example, after the Court of Appeal declared certain provisions of the Citizenship Act unconstitutional in the *Attorney-General v Dow*,[4] it took the government several years to repeal the section. The same delay has been evident with respect to the amendment of other Acts which had certain provisions declared unconstitutional by the courts.[5]

The implications of these delays are not difficult to imagine; a person or group of persons could be deprived of their fundamental rights for the length of time that it takes the government to repeal the provision in an Act declared unconstitutional for violating the Bill of Rights. Whilst it is clear that once a provision in a law is declared unconstitutional, it becomes in law *pro non scripto* and of no force and effect, even if the government does not repeal it formally, the reality is that civil servants who act on instructions they receive will continue to implement the old law until they receive new instructions even if they are aware that the law has been declared unconstitutional.[6]

Section 18(2)(b) gives the courts considerable powers that can be used to overcome governmental inertia by, for example, issuing "constructive" orders or directions, which order or direct that the unconstitutional provision should be amended either in a certain way or within a specified time or, even more generally, advise the government on better ways of implementing the Bill of Rights. In fact, as we shall see later, Botswana judges can develop imaginative measures, such as the structural interdict, which South African judges have

[4] [1992] BLR 119.

[5] See, for example, *Kamanakao I & 2 Others v Attorney-General & Another* [2001] 2 BLR 654.

[6] There were reports in the papers that after the *Dow* case, many parents rushed to the immigration department to have the status of their children rectified. For quite a while, immigration officials could do nothing until they received new instructions whilst the law itself was changed only many years later. For more on this, see EK Quansah, *"Unity Dow v Attorney-General of Botswana – The Sequel,"* 5 *African Journal of International and Comparative Law* 189, at p. 206 (1999) and the *Botswana Guardian* Friday 12 June 1992.

adopted in some situations to ensure that the government complies with their decisions. Such measures are dictated by the practical realities and, whatever reservations the judiciary may have to such apparently intrusive or interventionist orders, it must be accepted that government needs sometimes to be nudged out of its slumber.[7] Finally, perhaps to underscore the importance given to human rights protection, the Bill of Rights gives Parliament the discretion to confer upon the High Court such powers in addition to those conferred by section 18 that they consider necessary.

There have since 1966 been numerous cases in which the courts have had the opportunity to interpret and apply various provisions of the Bill of Rights. Most of the cases have dealt with the protection of the law,[8] freedom from discrimination[9] and freedom of association.[10] Others have involved the protection from inhuman treatment,[11] protection from deprivation of property,[12]

---

[7] Another glaring example of governmental inertia is the *Kamanakao* case decided in 2001. It was only on 8 June 2007 (six years later) that government introduced a *Bogosi* Bill, 2007, which states as follows in clause 4 of the Memorandum: "In a recent decision of the High Court in the case of *Kamanakao and Others v The Attorney-General and Others*, it was held that the definitions of the words 'chief' and 'tribe' contained in the Chieftainship Act (Cap. 41:01) were too restrictive and discriminatory, and as such offended against section 3(a) of the Constitution. The High Court went on further to recommend that the Chieftainship Act should be amended by redefining those words in order to accord equal treatment to all tribes in the country." It is noteworthy that a court decision handed down six years previously is referred to as "recent" and raises the fundamental question whether it requires such a long time to repeal an unconstitutional law.

[8] See *State v Merriweather Seboni* [1968–1970] BLR 158: *State v Monyoso* [1964–1967] BLR 249; *Maposa v State* [1989] BLR 556; *Samaribela v State* [1987] BLR 37; *Molathegi v State* [1990] BLR 477; *Marumo v State* [1990] BLR 659; *Lesetedi & Another v State* [2001] BLR 393; *Bojang v The State* [1994] BLR 146; *Rabana v Attorney-General & Another* [2003] 1BLR 330; *Masuku v State* [2004] 2 BLR 239; *Charles v State* [2005] 1 BLR 421; *Basupi v State* [2000] 2 BLR 1; *Basima v State* [1999] BLR 202; *Standard Chartered Bank of Botswana Ltd v Jotia* [1999] 2 BLR 1; *Motshwane & Others v State* [2002] 2 BLR 368; *Ahmed v Attorney-General* [2002] 2 BLR 431; *Attorney-General v Muzila* [2003] 1 BLR 471; *Kelaotswe v Attorney-General* [2005] 1 BLR 306; *Otlhomile v State* [2002] 2 BLR 295; *Sejammitlwa & Others v Attorney-General & Others* [2002] 2 BLR 75; and *Tlhogo v State* [1993] BLR 287.

[9] See *Attorney-General v Dow* [1992] BLR 119; *Makuto v State* [2000] 2 BLR 130; *Good v Attorney-General* [2005] 1 BLR 462; and *SRC of Molepolole College of Education v Attorney-General* [1995] BLR 178.

[10] *BPC Workers' Union v BPC* [1999] BLR 159; *Zachariah & Another v BPC* [1994] BLR 492; *Zachariah & Another v BPC* [1996] BLR 710.

[11] See *Petrus & Another v The State* [1984] BLR 14; *Desai v The State* [1987] BLR 55; and *Moatshe & Another v State* [2003] 1 BLR 65.

[12] See *Azad Hauliers (Pty) Ltd v Attorney-General* [1985] BLR 144.

freedom of expression,[13] the right to personal liberty,[14] freedom of conscience[15] and the right to life.[16] It is beyond the scope of this chapter to go into any critical review of these cases; nevertheless, they do show that Batswana have freely resorted to the courts whenever they felt that their constitutionally recognised and protected freedoms have been violated or threatened.

Until the enactment and coming into force of the 1966 Constitution with its Bill of Rights, the protection of human rights was largely left to the common law and statute. The limited human rights protection that the colonial administration could allow Batswana to enjoy was based on common law, which was essentially a mix of English common law principles developed by English judges to protect civil liberties and the Roman-Dutch principles applied to Botswana during the colonial period via the Cape Colony in South Africa.[17] Section 2(1) of the Botswana Independence Act 1966 and section 4(1) of the Independence Order saved existing laws, including the common law. It is clear from this that the Bill of Rights does not deny the existence of any other rights or freedoms that are recognised or conferred by common law, customary law or legislation, as long as these are not inconsistent with the Constitution.

A further basis for the continuous application of common law principles is provided by section 127(12) of the Constitution, which states that "the Interpretation Act, 1889 shall apply, with the necessary adaptations, for the purpose of interpreting this Constitution ..." With the power conferred by sections 18 and 105 to interpret the Constitution, the resulting judicial decisions constitute precedents which, as a result of the English doctrine of *stare decisis*, were received as part of the general reception of English law during the colonial period and constitutes a separate and independent source of law. Many judicial decisions interpreting the Constitution have laid down important principles that have developed not only human rights and

---

[13] See *State v Mbaiwa* [1988] BLR 314, *Zachariah & Another v BPC* [1994] BLR 492; *Media Publishing (Pty) Ltd v Attorney-General* [2001] 2 BLR 485; *Zachariah & Another v BPC* [1996] BLR 710. and also see, B Maripe, "Freezing the Press: Freedom of Expression and Statutory Limitations in Botswana," 3 African Human Rights Journal 52 (2003) and Charles M. Fombad, "The Protection of Freedom of Expression in the Public Service Media in Southern Africa: A Botswana Perspective," 65 *Modern Law Review* 649 (2002).

[14] See *Serurubele v Attorney-General* [1998] BLR 661; *Botswana Cooperative Bank Ltd v Noor & Others* [1990] 1 BLR 248, aff'd [1991] 1 BLR 443.

[15] See *Zachariah & Another v BPC* [1996] BLR 710.

[16] See *Ditshwanelo & Others v Attorney-General &Another* [1999] 2 BLR 56.

[17] For a full discussion of the origins of the Botswana legal system, see CM Fombad and EK Quansah, *The Botswana Legal System*, Durban, LexisNexis Butterworths (2006).

constitutional law but also other areas of the law, the most famous being *Attorney-General v Dow*.[18]

Common law principles on human rights also still have relevance in those areas not covered by the Bill of Rights. This is on the premise that common law human rights principles are residual in the sense of being what is left after the Bill of Rights principles are exhausted. In this respect, they can be used to fill any gaps that appear in the Bill of Rights. However, the ability of common law human rights principles to effectively fill any such gaps is inherently limited because of their residual character in that they can easily be overridden and extinguished by a simple Act of Parliament.

In considering the judicial role in human rights protection, two conclusions are inescapable. First, that section 18 of the Constitution generally, and 18(2)(b) in particular, give judges considerable leeway in dealing with human rights cases. Second, that the ability of the common law principles to fill in the gaps in the Constitution, for example, in many aspects of economic, social, cultural and solidarity rights, depends very much on the judicial willingness to recognise these rights. It is therefore contended that the quality and quantum of human rights protection enjoyed depends not only on the scope of protection provided for in the relevant laws but also the way these laws are interpreted and applied by the judges. Improving the quality of human rights protection will depend as much on expanding the scope of legal protection as well as enhancing the judicial role. It is this latter aspect that is of concern to us here.

3 Methods of Enhancing the Judicial Role in Human Rights Adjudication

Judges are just one of several groups of actors who play an important role in the protection of human rights. Others include government departments and their officials, human rights groups and other civil society organisations, and business organisations. The judicial role is crucial. Judges may simply legitimise egregious practices under the pretext of applying the letter of the law or use the law in an imaginative way to check governmental abuses. The critical issue here is not about how the judiciary in Botswana should help in protecting human rights, for they are already doing this, but rather how their role can be enhanced. An agenda for enhancing the judicial role in human

[18] [1992] BLR 119.

rights protection is premised on a bold and imaginative approach centred on the following features: judicial leadership, judicial independence, judicial attitude, judicial integrity, judicial activism, judicial training and the activities of legal practitioners and human rights organisations.

3.1 Judicial Leadership

The issue of judicial leadership has hardly attracted any serious research or writing because of the assumption that the judicial role is essentially passive and judges only react to situations. Leadership by judicial officers plays an important role in adjudication, especially in an area as sensitive as human rights. This leadership role can take place on at least three levels, each of which can be critical in human rights adjudication.[19] First, it can take the form of leadership in the judicial process, that is, the process of judging and making decisions. Second, it can take the form of leadership in chambers, in the organisation and functioning of the particular court of which the judge is a part. Finally, it can take the form of leadership among the other branches of government in defence of the rule of law and respect for law and legal institutions.

Leadership in the judicial process is inextricably linked with the inherited common law principle of *stare decisis*. The obligation to adhere to the precedents laid down by the superior courts means that the quality of the common law principles that emerges from the courts depends very much on the quality and credibility of the Judges of the superior courts, especially the highest court, the Court of Appeal. Carefully articulated judicial opinions do more than clarify the law and set precedents. They also enhance the respect for the law by making it difficult for governments to ignore such judgments. Perhaps the best example of this is the famous *Dow* case, where the power of the reasoning was such that the government, in spite of initial hesitation, nevertheless complied with the decision. The superior courts therefore can provide a clear sense of direction not only to inferior courts but also to the government and other actors through carefully reasoned and forceful arguments.

Leadership in chambers relates to the way judges manage cases. In the last few years, there have been numerous complaints about the hardships caused

[19] James Apple, "The Role of the Judicial Independence and Judicial Leadership in the Protection of Human Rights," in Eugene Cotran & Adel Omar Sherif (eds.), *The Role of the Judiciary in the Protection of Human Rights*, Kluwer Law International, London, pp. 201–207 (2007).

by delays and bottlenecks in the disposal of cases.[20] The human rights of litigants are bound to be affected by any delays for, as it is often said, justice delayed is justice denied. The introduction of a case management system is one giant step that will enable the judiciary to have control over pre-trial, trial and appeal processes and ensure the prompt and speedy disposal of cases. Effective case management by judges is therefore another means by which judges can ensure efficiency in the administration of justice and the protection of human rights of litigants.

Judicial leadership can also be manifested in a way that it will affect not only the other branches of government but also individuals and other institutions and organisations outside government. In many respects, the judiciary is the weakest branch of government since it neither has the power of the purse nor the power of the sword. The best way the judicial branch can create and maintain its strength and independence is through the power of the pen which is applied in specific cases and judicial opinions as well as the force of advocacy of its judicial leaders.[21]

But, over and above this, the fact that the Constitution in section 18 specifically reserves all matters dealing with fundamental human rights to the superior courts of record, namely the High Court and the Court of Appeal, underscores not only the importance it attaches to such disputes but also the fact that it expects these courts to assume a leadership role in dealing with such disputes. These are often delicate disputes that sometimes deal with sensitive issues of political and social importance, particularly concerning the validity of the actions of government officials, and must of necessity be handled by the experienced judges who sit in these superior courts. It is the quality of leadership provided by the superior courts, especially the Court of Appeal, that will lay down the standards to be followed by the judges in the lower courts.

---

[20] For example, *State v Keodirile Kelapile* Criminal Appeal F 47 of 2001(Unreported) a simple case of stealing of money by an employee in the public service which took almost ten years to dispose of. A major cause of the delays has been the difficulties of attracting and retaining the services of suitably qualified and experienced magistrates and judges. With the recent introduction of a scarce skill retention allowance by a Presidential Directive of April 2008, which has the effect of increasing the salaries of magistrates and judges by 35–40 percent, there is an expectation that more judicial personnel will be attracted and retained.

[21] See James Apple, *op. cit.*, at 207, who points out that judicial advocacy of matters relating to the strength of the judiciary and court administration is not a violation of the principle of separation of powers.

3.2 Judicial Independence

Human rights can not be adequately protected unless there is a fully functional independent judiciary. Both the Universal Declaration on Human Rights 1948 and the International Covenant on Civil and Political Rights 1966 indicate that an independent judiciary is one of the essential elements for safeguarding human rights.[22] An independent judiciary can be considered as one that is free to render justice on all issues of substantial legal and constitutional importance, fairly, impartially, in accordance with the law, without threat, fear of reprisal, intimidation or any other undue influence or consideration.[23] Nevertheless, it is necessary to note that there is no absolutely independent judiciary and the whole idea of judicial independence hinges on the ability of the judiciary to deal with cases impartially and in accordance with the law, especially those touching on certain sensitive legal and constitutional issues that matter in the country. Recent comparative studies have shown that the Botswana judiciary is reasonably independent.[24]

Nevertheless, a few aspects of this judicial independence, that depends largely on the character of the judges themselves, which are often taken for granted, need to be underscored. First, there is the need for it to be seen that the orders, decisions and judgments made by judges are entirely based on the law and the application of recognised and established legal principles and rules and have not been influenced by the status of one of the parties or the dictates or influence of some person within or without the government or by the direction or influence of some government or non-government official or agency.

Second, judges should decide matters based entirely on their understanding of the law and their conscience. They should disagree where the need arises and not feel compelled to agree with the majority. The use of *obiter dicta* as a means to persuade parliament to change the law or guide it on how to change the law or even just to establish a climate of opinion in which the law can be changed is very useful. For example, the recent amendments to sections 77, 78 and 79 of the Constitution were certainly influenced by the

---

22 See Articles 8 and 14, respectively, of each of these instruments.

23 See Charles Manga Fombad, "A Preliminary Assessment of the Prospects for Judicial Independence in Post-1990 African Constitutions," 2 *Public Law*, at 235 (2007).

24 See Linda Van de Vijver and Democratic Governance and Rights Unit, UCT, *The Judicial Institution in Southern Africa. A Comparative Study of Common Law Jurisdictions*, Siber Ink, Cape Town pp. 14–33 (2006).

reservations expressed about these provisions in the *Kamanakao I v The Attorney-General & Another*.[25]

Finally, judicial independence includes the right of the court to get its decision wrong as well as right. The appellate processes will hopefully correct any errors. In the final analysis, without an independent judiciary to protect it, the substance of human rights law becomes virtually meaningless. The vital role that judicial independence plays has been underlined in some recent empirical studies which show that the extent of judicial independence does have an actual impact on the state of human rights behaviour in any country.[26]

3.3 Judicial Attitude

The judicial role in human rights protection will be enhanced if judicial officers adopt an attitude that respects and upholds human rights in every aspect of their lives and professional work. The Hon. Justice Michael Kirby of the High Court of Australia, in an *ex curia* address, illustrates how judges can earn the acceptance of their role as defenders of human rights with this example about one of his colleagues on the bench:

> "One of my judicial colleagues…was given to making inappropriate jests at the expense of women and minorities [in court]. When next he attempted such a remark…I observed that he neither spoke for me nor the Court. Soon his jests were a thing of the past…"[27]

A positive human rights-conscious attitude is particularly important in *ex curia* writings. Judges are often invited to give addresses at academic and other public ceremonies and many write for legal and popular publications. These provide opportunities for judges not only to influence public opinion but also to plead with and persuade parliament on certain issues of law reform. It would be unethical to deal with issues which are before the courts but nothing excludes judges from expressing their opinions on the current state of the law and on how it should be reformed. Many judges can therefore,

---

[25] [2001] 2 BLR 654.

[26] See Linda Keith, "Judicial Independence and Human Rights Protection Around the World," 85(4) *Judicature* 195 (2002) and Cross, "The Relevance of Law in Human Rights Protection," 19 *Int'l Rev. of L. & Economics* 87 (1999).

[27] "Strengthening the Judicial Role in the Protection of Human Rights – An Action Plan," paper delivered at the "Inter-Regional Conference on Justice Systems and Human Rights," 20 September 2006, Brasilia. http://www.hcourt.gov.au/speeches/kirgyj/kirgyj_20sep06.pdf.

through scholarly treatises[28] or even public speeches, contribute to shaping the way the law is interpreted or influence legal reforms.

3.4 Judicial Integrity

Judges have no physical force or financial means to enforce their will and, if either branch ignores their decisions, they will end up becoming paper tigers. Their legitimacy depends on public support which itself is determined by the confidence the public has in the judiciary. This confidence cannot be imposed but must be earned. In a modern age, which places a high premium on accountability, one of the main ways of promoting judicial integrity, especially in dealing with human rights cases, is by displaying openness, efficiency, competence and transparency in adjudication. The common law tradition requires that judicial decisions be clear, discursive and detailed. It is unlikely that a judge who takes time to explain every aspect of his or her decision can easily get away with a biased or wrong decision. As pointed out earlier, a well reasoned decision not only enhances the reputation of the judiciary but makes it easier for their decisions to be accepted by the parties, especially by governments.

3.5 Judicial Activism

The classical role of the judge, according to the positivist jurists, such as Austin, is that of the mechanical interpretation of the law as enacted by parliament. Such an approach gives extreme deference to the value judgments of parliament and only in exceptional cases must judges go against the judgment of parliament.

In the rights-conscious environment of today, judges can no longer content themselves with a simple mechanical literal interpretation of the law. Nor can they invoke the doctrine of judicial self-restraint and passive interpretation of the law. Since the middle of the twentieth century, courts throughout the world have moved away from the positivist approach and are increasingly more activist. The ever fast changing nature of human rights issues has forced courts in some countries, especially in the United States, India and South Africa, to devise a number of novel strategies to expand the scope and

[28] For example, the late Justice Aguda, former president of the Botswana Court of Appeal, was a leading author in the law of evidence and procedure in Nigeria and published more than a dozen books. See http://www.gov.bw/cgi-bin/new.cgi?=20010920.

quality of human rights protection.[29] Before considering some of these strategies, it is worthwhile pointing out that there are at least two reasons why it can be argued that this activist approach is imperative on judges in Botswana.

First, the proviso to 18(2)(b) gives a court considerable flexibility with respect to the enforcement measures it may take to ensure that its decisions on human rights disputes are enforced when it states that courts "may make such orders, issue such writs and give such direction as it may consider appropriate for the purpose of enforcing or securing the enforcement of any of the provisions of section 3 to 16 (inclusive)." As argued above, the judiciary, relying on section 18(4), can put pressure on parliament to "confer upon the High Court such powers in addition to those conferred" by the Constitution as "may appear to be necessary or desirable for the purpose of enabling that court more effectively to exercise the jurisdiction conferred upon it," in dealing with issues of fundamental human rights and freedoms under the Constitution. In other words, an activist judiciary is sanctioned by the Constitution.

Second, far from being a document that contains "time-worn adages or hollow shibboleths,"[30] or a "lifeless museum piece,"[31] a constitution must be regarded as a living document designed to serve the present and future generations as well as reflect and embody their fears, hopes and aspirations. In making it clear that the method to be used in interpreting a constitution is definitely different from that to be used in interpreting an ordinary piece of legislation, Amissah J.P. in the *Dow* case quoted Lord Wright who in the Australian case of *James v Commonwealth of Australia* said:

> "It is true that a Constitution must not be construed in any narrow and pedantic sense. The words used are necessarily general, and their full import and true meaning can often only be appreciated when considered, as the years go on, in relation to the vicissitudes of fact which from time to time emerge. It is not that the meaning of the words changes, but the

---

[29] Recent developments in these countries are analysed in Brice Dickson ed., *Judicial Activism in Common Law Supreme Courts* (2008). See further the Hon. E.D. Bayda, "Judicial Activism", 70 *Saskatchewan L. Rev.* 225 (2007), Lord Justice Thorpe, "The Case for Judicial Activism", 9 *Euro. J. of L. Reform* 1 (2007), Luc Tremblay, "The Legitimacy of Judicial Review: The Limits of Dialogue between Courts and Legislatures", 3 *Int'l J. of Constitutional L.* 617 (2005).

[30] *Trop v Dulles* 356 U.S. 86, at 103 (*per* Warren C.J., 1958).

[31] *Attorney-General v Dow* [1992] BLR 119 at p. 166 (*per* Aguda J.A.).

changing circumstances illustrates and illuminates the full import of that meaning."[32]

Amissah JP also quoted with approval Kentridge JA who, in *Attorney-General v. Moagi*,[33] had pointed out that a constitution such as the Constitution of Botswana, embodying fundamental rights, should, as far as its language permits, be given a broad construction.

With such pronouncements from our highest court, composed as it was in the *Dow* case, with some of the best legal minds who have ever sat on the bench in Botswana, it can not be gainsaid that there is clear authority for adopting an open, liberal and progressive approach in dealing with human rights adjudication under the Botswana Constitution. In fact, the lesson that this and other authorities from the Commonwealth teach us is that the broad and generous approach to be adopted in the interpretation of a constitution inevitably involves some judicial activism.

Besides the two grounds above, there are a number of ways that have been tried in other jurisdictions which, it is contended, can be adopted in Botswana by the judiciary for strengthening the regime of human rights protection.

A major obstacle to the effective enforcement of human rights in Botswana, as in most African countries, is the daily fact that too many people whose constitutionally protected human rights have been violated have, due either to ignorance, poverty, marginalisation or some other social or economic disadvantage, been unable to approach the courts for relief. There are many imaginative methods that the courts can adopt to help them. For example, the Supreme Court of India has given a very broad interpretation to article 32 of the Indian Constitution, which appears in the chapter on fundamental rights and confers powers on the court to issue directions, orders or writs for the enforcement of such rights to depart from the traditional rule of *locus standi* and to broaden access to justice to the poor and disadvantaged in society. It has taken the view that, where a person or class of persons is by reason of poverty or other form of social, economic or political disability unable to approach the courts for relief, any member of the public or social action group, acting *bona fide*, can maintain an application in the court seeking judicial redress for the legal wrong or injury caused to such a person or class of persons. The Supreme Court effectively evolved what is known as

[32] [1936] AC 578, at 614.
[33] [1982] 2 BLR 124 at 184.

epistolary or open-letter jurisdiction, where the fundamental rights jurisdiction of the court can be activated just by addressing a simple letter on behalf of the disadvantaged group without insisting on the normal expensive court formalities.[34] The proviso to section 18(2)(b) of the Botswana Constitution is couched in similar language and can be so interpreted to facilitate access in human rights cases to the poor, the down-trodden and illiterate of our society. Besides this, there have been many instances, not only in India, but also in Britain and in the United States, where courts, after reading newspaper items and conducting initial investigations, have on their own motion opened up inquiries into the violation of human rights.[35]

The Indian Supreme Court has even gone further in its attempts to help the poor and needy vindicate the violation of their fundamental rights.[36] The court found that the adversarial process could operate fairly and produce just results only where the two parties were evenly matched in strength and resources but, given that the poor often lacked the social and material resources, they were bound to be at a disadvantage in producing all relevant evidence before the court. It also noted that quite often the social action groups that tried to assist the poor themselves may not have adequate resources to gather all relevant material to place before the court. The court decided to abandon the *laissez-faire* approach in the judicial process and devised a strategy and procedure for ascertaining, establishing and articulating the claims and demands of the poor by appointing socio-legal commissions of inquiry. In fact, the practice of appointing socio-legal commissions of inquiry for the purpose of gathering relevant material and information bearing on the case put forward on behalf of a disadvantaged individual or section of a community in social action litigation has now been institutionalised as a result of the Indian Supreme Court judgment in *Bandhua Mukti Morcha v Union of India*.[37]

---

[34] For a full discussion of this and similar developments in India, see P.N. Bhagwati, "Social Action Litigation: The India Experience," in Neelan Tiruchelvam and Radhika Coomaraswamy (eds.), *The Role of the Judiciary in Plural Societies*, London, Frances Publishers, pp. 20–31 (1987).

[35] *ibid.*, at p. 128.

[36] See Vijayashri Sripati, "Constitutionalism in India and South Africa: A Comparative Study from a Human Rights Perspective", 16 Tulane J. of Int'l & Comp. L. 49, at 98–104 (2007), H. Kwasi Prempeh, "*Marbury* in Africa: Judicial Review and the Challenge of Constitutionalism in Contemporary Africa", 80 *Tulane L. Rev.* 1239, at pp. 1300–1301 (2006).

[37] AIR, 1984 Supreme Court 802 and see generally, P.N. Bhagwati, *op. cit.*, Jamie Cassels, "Judicial Activism and Public Interest Litigation in India: Attempting the Impossible?" 37 *Am. J. of Comp. L.* 495 (1989), Burt Neuborne, "The Supreme Court of India", 1 *Int'l J. of Const. L.* 476, at 500–504 (2003).

The proviso to section 18(2)(b) also provides the flexibility for expanding the existing remedies available to the courts in dealing with human rights cases. The effectiveness of the Bill of Rights depends very much on the orders and decisions of the courts being enforced and respected. The decisions and other orders made by the courts are not self-executing. They have to be enforced through state agencies and if these refused to co-operate, as is often the case in many African countries, the ends of justice will be defeated. Although the record of government compliance in Botswana with court decisions is good, the delay, particularly in repealing provisions declared unconstitutional, has left violations unremedied for several years until the government found it politically convenient to act. Section 18(2)(b), it is contended, gives the courts considerable flexibility to compel the government to comply with its decisions but they have so far not been used in an imaginative way. There is no better statement explaining the scope of this power than the following *dicta* of the full bench of the High Court in the *Kamanakao I v The Attorney-General & Another* case:

> "It can readily be seen that the remedies available to the court are wide and varied. Such remedies are not spelt out in any precise language, but they are couched in broad terms indicating by what processes the court may require the provisions contravened to be enforced, i.e. the breach to be corrected. Thus the court is empowered to consider issuing orders or writs or making directions, all for the purpose of enforcing or securing the enforcement of the relevant provisions of the Constitution.

[T]he Constitution intended to give the High Court power to order the immediate enforcement of the provisions contravened, or where appropriate to give such directions as to recognise that other things will have to be done leading ultimately to the enforcement of the provision breached. The diversity of the methods of enforcement given to the court indicates the flexibility which the Constitution has granted to the court in order to deal with the circumstances of each case."[38] Ironically, earlier in the same judgment, the court had declared:

> "We have now come to the point where we can deal with the requirements of the applicants for orders designed to compel the Government of Botswana to take positive steps to appoint and recognise Wayeyi Chiefs…

[38] [2001] 2 BLR 654, at 678–679.

As a matter of judicial policy the courts are reluctant to issue orders for carrying out of works and other activities which require their supervision. It is obvious that for a court to issue orders requiring positive action on the part of the government on a continuing basis is a mammoth task. The performance by government of required activities to fulfil the orders sought by the applicants must involve inter alia, careful planning, budgeting and funding, manpower and other inputs on the part of the State.

The court, in our view, would be incapable of supervising the required activities and would thus be unable to judge whether the performance is adequate, or to know whether the person ordered has wilfully disobeyed the order, in the event of a complaint of lack of execution. Now it is a well known rule of our law that courts should not issue orders for doing things which they would not be capable of supervising."[39]

Is this so-called "judicial supervision," so complex and near impossible as the court suggests? The South African courts offer examples of how the Botswana courts could exercise the enormous powers given to them for very good reasons under section 18(2)(b) of the Constitution. It is submitted that the effectiveness of court decisions can be enhanced by the application of the concept of structural interdict, which has been used with great success by the South African Constitutional Court. In its judgment in *August & Another v Electoral Commission & Others*,[40] the court for the first time made use of a structural interdict, which directs a violator to take steps to rectify a violation of rights under the court's supervision. This followed a holding that the Electoral Commission had violated prisoners' rights to vote by failing to take steps to allow them to register as voters on the national voters' roll. The court ordered the Commission to make arrangements for them to register and once registered to vote in the election. A similar order was given by the Witwatersrand High Court in *Strydom v Minister of Correctional Services*,[41] in which the prison authorities were ordered to report on affidavit to the court

[39] *ibid.*, at 676–677 (Emphasis added.)

[40] 1999 (3) SA 1 (CC). The decision has influence Canadian jurisprudence: see *Sauvé v Canada (Chief Electoral Officer)*, [2002] 3 S.C.R. 519. See also the decision of the Grand Chamber of the European Court of Human Rights, *Hirst v United Kingdom (No. 2)*, 42 E.H.R.R. 41 (Application no. 74025/01) (2006). More generally, see Cormac Behan and Ian O'Donnell, "Prisoners, Politics and the Polls", 48 *Br. J. of Criminology* 319 (2008).

[41] 1999 (3) BCLR 342 (W).

within a month of the order, setting out a timetable for the upgrading of the electrical system in the Johannesburg prison.[42]

Without compliance within a reasonable time by the State with court orders and decisions not only will the system of human rights protection be undermined but also the administration of justice would fall into disrepute. The Indian Supreme Court provides another option through its policy of setting up a monitoring agency which would continuously check and report on the implementation of its decisions. In the *Bandhua Mukti Morcha* case referred to earlier, the court made an order giving various directions for identifying, releasing and rehabilitating bonded labourers, ensuring minimum wage payments, observance of labour laws, providing good drinking water and setting up dust-sucking machines in the stone quarries. It also set up a monitoring agency to check continuously and report on the implementation of these directions. In another case, it gave a State government instruction to prepare annual reports detailing implementation of the Court's decisions.[43]

It must be recognised that the effectiveness of the Bill of Rights depends very much on the ability of judges to breathe life and relevance to its provisions to ensure that they are not frozen in time. Courts in Botswana can not run away from the gradual but progressive "internationalisation" of constitutional law, especially in matters dealing with human rights. This means going beyond the normal common law judicial liberalism which enables judges to refer to, cite and rely on the decisions of courts in other common law jurisdictions as persuasive authorities. Because of the commonality not only in the provisions of many of the Bills of Rights but also the fact that they have been inspired by the same philosophy, it is now not just possible but actually imperative that judges, in dealing with human rights problems, investigate how these problems have been solved in other jurisdictions, both by national and international courts. Although the judicial outcome depends as much on how thoroughly the counsel on both sides have done their research, the fundamental character of the common law as a system in which judges draw their inspiration from the basic conceptions of justice and fairness should remain the driving force. In interpreting the law, judges must try to keep in step with the standards and values of the times. As the former Chief Justice of Zimbabwe, Gubbay,

[42] See further Danielle Elyce Hirsch, *A Defense of Structural Injunctive Remedies in South African Law*, Berkeley Electronic Press (bepress) Paper 1690 (2006); http://law.bepress.com/expresso/eps/1690.

[43] See P.N. Bhagwati, *op. cit.*, pp. 28–29.

has rightly observed, "a judicial decision has greater legitimacy and will command more respect if it accords with international norms that have been accepted by many jurisdictions, than if it is based upon the parochial experiences or foibles of a particular judge or court."[44] Such was the approach adopted in the *Dow* case and there is need for more of such purposive and progressive interpretation of the Bill of Rights. In the words of Aguda JA in the *Dow* case:

> "…it is the primary duty of the judges …. to make the Constitution grow and develop in order to meet the just demands and aspirations of an ever developing society which is part of the wider and larger human society governed by some acceptable concepts of human dignity."[45]

However, Botswana's contract system of judicial appointments is clearly unsatisfactory and there is evidence to suggest that the contracts of some of the judges who displayed strong traits of judicial and constitutional activism were not renewed.[46]

Nevertheless, the recognition and enforcement of human rights also depends on other factors such as the standards of judicial training and the willingness and ability of human rights lawyers and bar generally, to raise human rights issues before the courts, which cannot on their own invoke and enforce human rights laws.[47] This leads us to the issue of judicial training and the standards of legal advocacy before the courts in the country.

---

[44] In "Foreword," 1 *Commonwealth Human Rights Digest*, at p. 1 (1996).

[45] [1992] BLR 119, at p. 166. The *dicta* in this case sit rather uneasily with the recent view of Tebbutt JP in *Good v Attorney-General* [2005] 2 BLR 337 at p. 357 where the learned Judge President said: "The rule of law is also the cornerstone of the domestic law of the country and its application is not dependent upon some concept of a quality of law inherent in the articles of international treaties or conventions, which were not in existence when the Botswana Constitution was framed." This *dictum* is questionable not only because it throws into doubt the relevance and value of the international human rights system on which the national regime is substantially built but also appears to suggest that "international treaties and conventions" such as the Universal Declaration of Human Rights, which came into existence before Botswana became an independent state with its own Constitution in 1966, are of no relevance.

[46] See generally Bojosi Otlhogile, *A History of the Higher Courts of Botswana 1912–1990*, Gaborone, Mmegi Publishing House, pp. 92–92 (1994) and AJGM Sanders, "Constitutionalism in Botswana," 16 *CILSA* 350 (1983).

[47] See further Mac Darrow and Philip Alston, "Bills of Rights in Comparative Perspective," in Philip Alston (ed.), *Promoting Human Rights Through Bills of Rights: Comparative Perspectives* 473 (1999).

3.6 Judicial Training

Unlike in the civil law tradition that is prevalent in Francophone and Lusophone Africa where judges undergo a formal two-year training, in the English common law system which prevails in Botswana, this is not the case. There is no formal training as such and judges are appointed from the ranks of practicing attorneys or teachers of law of at least 10 years' standing.[48] Too many people in the common law world had taken too seriously Lord Devlin's view that judicial training might become a means of propaganda by the executive and thus intrusive into the independence of judges.[49] This attitude is now changing and in many common law jurisdictions, there are courses organised to train judges, especially on their first appointment to the bench.

Two pertinent points need to be made here. First, that frequent training of judges is necessary to enable them to be exposed to new thoughts, recent developments and new experiences and, above all, to enable them share their experiences. Second, in the globalised judicial world of today, there is need for the judiciary to be familiarised with the techniques and pitfalls of comparative legal research. Once it is accepted that a consideration of foreign law is not only unavoidable but absolutely necessary, the question then arises as to what approach to adopt in assessing the relevance and applicability of such foreign law. Too often, judges have simply accepted and adopted legal principles from other common law jurisdictions without heeding Watson's warning that that in law, as in medicine, transplants carry the risk of rejection.[50] For example, in a number of dicta,[51] the Botswana courts have cautioned against the excessive reliance on foreign authorities. In *Mohalenyane* v *The State*, Amissah J.A. warned:

> "There is also a danger in the use of foreign authorities of which we should all be aware, and that is, decisions on construction of statutory provisions of one country bearing a superficial resemblance to statutory provisions in this country may be given weight which is undue or might even lead to confusion when the actual foreign statute is not available to us and its extent, therefore cannot be gauged. It is even more difficult

[48] Section 96(3) Legal Practitioners Act 1996 and further, Charles M. Fombad and Emmanuel K. Quansah, *The Botswana Legal System*, Durban, LexisNexis Butterworths pp. 129–133 (2006).
[49] *The Judges*, Oxford, Oxford University Press, pp. 36–47 (1979).
[50] See A.J.G.M. Sanders, "Ten Years of the Botswana Matrimonial Causes Act – Further Proposals for Divorce Reform," 26 *J. of African L.* at 165 (1982).
[51] See e.g., *State* v *Mankurwane* [1985] BLR 168 at p. 172 (*per* O'Brien-Quinn C.J.).

> when the foreign authority is in a language not used in our courts. In the interpretation of a statute, our primary consideration should be the Botswana statute…"[52]

The universality of human rights principles is no longer in doubt. A court can hardly deal with a human rights dispute without being invited by counsel to consider one foreign authority or another. More often than not, the reliance on these foreign authorities has been rather eclectic with scant or at most superficial reference to the techniques of comparative law. Although, as a discipline, comparative constitutional law is still very much in its infancy and its techniques are still lacking in methodological coherence, it is increasingly necessary for judges to be conscious of its existence and to make efforts to study, understand and apply its methods and techniques when considering the relevance and applicability of foreign legal authorities. For as Julia Laffranque, in making it clear that judicial borrowing has a much wider significance, points out, "it means to broaden one's vision," and that "it does not necessarily need to result in copying foreign examples, but learning from them and using international… comparative law as tools in domestic adjudication."[53] In borrowing from foreign sources there are therefore skills and techniques which judges must acquire. Unless the judiciary is ready to learn about how to deal with current developments both nationally and internationally, judicial decisions will retain a rigid, positivist orientation which is bad for both human rights protection and social justice.[54]

Lord McCluskey in the opening paragraph of his book, *Law, Justice, and Democracy*, highlights some of the challenges when he says:

> "If I were to be asked what temptations any new judge is exposed to, I should have to admit that they include arrogance, self-esteem and impatience. That answer must alarm all who know that the principal qualities a judge must possess are humility, modesty and tolerance. But just think of the facts. He has been elevated to a position in which he wields a royal authority. The apparatus of state lies ready to enforce his orders. The visible symbols of his office, the way he dresses, the place in which he sits, the manner in which he is addressed, the respect which he

---

[52] [1985] BLR 542 at 548.

[53] In "Judicial Borrowing: International and Comparative Law as Nonbinding Tools of Domestic Legal Adjudication," http://www.coe.int/t/dg1/legalcooperation/judicialprofessions/ccje/meetings/discours/1…

[54] See *ibid.*, p. 4, where the author points out that "comparative law has been proving extremely useful in the countries of Central and Eastern Europe in reconstructing their legislation and legal order."

is accorded, all are designed to buttress that authority, to intimidate those who might wish to challenge or evade it."[55]

Judges must therefore resist the intoxicating notion that they know it all and be prepared to keep up with the latest developments in the law. The ability of judges to adopt this approach depends on the standards of advocacy at the Bar in the country.

3.7 A Proactive Bar

The creative intervention of the judiciary in human rights adjudication depends as much on the skilled, independent and activist quality of the Bar. The legal profession plays a vital role in the defence of human rights because it is they who choose the cases that come before the courts and prepare all the necessary arguments. If the cases are well researched and powerful and irresistible arguments made before the judge, the latter will be bound to consider these arguments seriously.

These are matters to which the Botswana Law Society is yet to fully address its mind. The legal profession in Botswana has played a rather limited role insofar as human rights protection and activism is concerned. There are at least two reasons for this. First, although the Bill of Rights guarantees a right to legal representation[56] there is no legal assistance available to poor persons in society who wish to present a defence except those who are charged with murder. In spite of Botswana's impressive economic growth rates in the last decades, a majority of its population are poor and unable to afford adequate legal services. Section 56(a) of the Legal Practitioners Act 1996 in dealing with the membership of the Law Society states:

> "The membership of the Society shall consist of –
>
> any person who holds a practising certificate issued under this Act and has paid any prescribed subscription and undertakes to do *pro deo* or *pro bono* work;"

There is no evidence that the Law Society actually insists on an undertaking to do *pro deo* or *pro bono* work or that, when such an undertaking has been made, it follows up to actually ensure that this is done. One of the direct consequences of this is that *pro deo* representation for now mostly occurs in

---

[55] In *Law, Justice, and Democracy*, London, Sweet & Maxwell, p. 1 (1987).

[56] See section 10(1)(d) of the Constitution.

murder cases. Even then it is problematic because the amount paid to the lawyers who do such work is minimal as compared to the average fee paid to private lawyers. As a result, the *pro deo* cases are usually handled by "lawyers who lack the skills, resources and commitment to handle such serious matters."[57] This means that because many of these people cannot afford adequate legal services they are unable to fully benefit from the right to legal protection provided in section 10 of the Constitution. Secondly, the right to legal representation is qualified by section 10(12)(b) of the Constitution, which excludes legal representation in customary courts. Yet it has been suggested that as many as 90 percent of civil cases and 85 percent of criminal matters are heard or tried by these customary courts and some have the powers to impose sentences of up to five years of imprisonment.[58] Because these courts involve adjudicators who have no legal training, there has been concern about the quality of justice that these customary courts provide and the possible effect that this has on the human rights of those who appear before them, particularly in the light of the full implications of the protection of the law guaranteed in section 10 of the Constitution.[59]

The legal profession in general and the Law Society in particular have a crucial part to play in influencing the judicial role in promoting and protecting human rights and social justice. They are the watchdog for the respect for the rule of law, advocates for legal reforms and those who articulate the diverse and intricate legal and social issues that the judges need to consider in deciding cases. Hence, one can rightly say that the judiciary in Botswana is only as good as the Bar that serves it; an activist Bar will inevitably lead to an activist judiciary and the converse is also true.

3.8 Civil Society Organisations

The judicial role can also be enhanced when there are vibrant civil society organisations that are ready to speak up for the weak, the poor and other voiceless members of society through *amicus curiae* representation in court.

The most active NGO in the country has been the *Ditshwanelo-The Botswana Centre for Human Rights*, an advocacy organisation that was

[57] See http://www.ditshwanelo.org.bw/index/Current_Issues/Legal_Aid.htm.

[58] *ibid.,* The Court of Appeal has shown sensitivity to the issue: see *S. v Ntwayame*, [2008] BWCA 37.

[59] See further Louise W. McKinney, "Access to Justice through Legal Aid – Is a Human Right: Why Botswana Must Protect This Right", Chapter 10, *infra*.

founded in 1993 and has as its mission to educate, research, counsel and mediate human rights issues, with particular reference to people who are marginalised and disempowered.[60] It has been at the forefront of the campaign to abolish the death penalty in Botswana.[61]

Another institution worth mentioning is the Legal Clinic operated by the staff and students of the Law Department of the University of Botswana, which provides some free legal advice service. The Clinic provides the only social service of its kind in Botswana. It tries to cater for those who cannot afford the services of a lawyer and uses a means test to decide whether a person qualifies for assistance. Although the Legal Clinic tries to advise indigent clients on all problems, it does not usually accept criminal matters and concentrates on issues such as divorce, maintenance and other family problems, housing problems, hire purchase, employment, including worker's compensation, motor vehicle insurance claims, debt collection and attachment and insurance. It therefore plays a limited role in dealing with human rights issues.

Botswana is one of the few countries in the region without a human rights commission. A human rights commission is absolutely critical to the promotion and protection of human rights and ensuring that people can obtain redress in the face of injustice. It can canvass in the courts some of the policy implications of different interpretations of the Bill of Rights without necessarily representing the interests of either litigant before the court. It could also exercise promotional and advisory functions aimed at both State and non-state actors. In fact, the South African Human Rights Commission, in terms of its structure, functions and powers, provides a good model from which Botswana can learn.

4 Conclusion

Courts stand as the last hope and the haven of refuge for those who might otherwise suffer because they are poor, helpless, weak, outnumbered, marginalised or victims of prejudice. There is no longer any doubt that the legitimacy of the judiciary in any country will depend to a large extent on how it is able to ensure that the courts can effectively operate as havens of refuge for the downtrodden against governmental lawlessness. The need for

60 See http://www.ditshwanelo.org.bw/.

61 See http://www.ditshwanelo.org.bw/index/Current_Issues/Death_Penalty.htm.

strengthening the judicial role in human rights protection in Botswana, it should be emphasised, is not motivated by any actual or apparent failures of the latter in this respect. All objective studies and reports have rightly acknowledged Botswana's good human rights record and the judiciary have certainly played a major part in this success. Nevertheless, changing circumstances such as globalisation and the terrorist attacks on the US on 11 September 2002 and a host of other issues have raised new and complex human rights problems.

It is contended that many of the post-Cold War and post-September 11 human rights problems of today call for a new kind of judge, a novel kind of judging involving more imaginative and innovative uses of judicial powers. When dealing with human rights issues, there is need for the courts to be seen as the courts for Batswana rather than the courts of Botswana. As Lord Devlin said in the *Heaton's* case,

> "if judges are to do more than decide what the law means, if they are also to speak for it, their voice must be the voice of the community; it must never be taken for the voice of the government or the voice of the majority."[62]

Although the judiciary stands out as the weakest and most vulnerable part of the democratic triad, if it is ready to and able to protect the fundamental human rights of the people, especially against enormous and often overbearing powers of government, then it will certainly enjoy a high level of public support that will protect it against interference from the executive and legislature.

In conclusion, an agenda for an enhanced judicial role that would likely improve the quality of human rights protection in Botswana will entail the following:

First, judicial leadership by the High Court and Court of Appeal which provides clear, well researched and articulated judgments that makes their enforcement by the parties irresistible.

Second, maintaining judicial independence by judges acting and being seen to decide cases impartially, without fear or favour for any of the parties, especially the government.

---

[62] Quoted in *The Judges*, *op. cit.*, p. 24.

Third, a strong commitment to the defence of human rights manifested by the judges especially in their public speeches or academic or other publications.

Fourth, adopting a liberal, progressive and creative approach to interpreting the fundamental rights provisions in the Constitution by regarding them as "living organisms" with universal principles that need to be interpreted in the light of changing national and international circumstances. In particular, judges should take advantage of the broadly worded provisions of section 28(2)(b) of the Constitution, which provide considerable scope for the introduction of novel procedures and remedies that can tremendously improve the lot of poor people.

Fifth, exploring the methods and techniques of comparative constitutional law to help judges understand the relevance and applicability of foreign law.

Sixth, displaying an attitude that will encourage a more activist Bar and civil society in vigorously pursuing the claims of the poor, knowing that the courts are receptive and sensitive to such disputes.

Finally, it must be said that it is time the government consider establishing a specialised constitutional bench within a permanent Court of Appeal and making a deliberate attempt to ensure that the members of this court are capable of providing strong judicial leadership. Some thought must be given to ensuring that it is constituted with a good mix of academics and practitioners on the one hand and judges with common law and Roman-Dutch law backgrounds on the other.

Dignity as a Core Constitutional Concept

William Binchy*

This paper attempts to discern the place of dignity in the Constitution of Botswana and to assess whether developments in the constitutional jurisprudence of other countries have any implications for Botswana.

The subject is timely.[1] Constitutions throughout the world have been rushing to embrace respect for dignity.[2] Human dignity[3] is, moreover, the core value of international human rights instruments.[4] The Preamble to the Charter of the United Nations in 1945 and the Preamble to the Universal Declaration on Human Rights in 1948 refer to 'the dignity and worth of the human person'. Both the International Covenant on Civil and Political Rights and the International Covenant on Economic, Social and Cultural Rights recognise 'the inherent dignity and …the equal and inalienable rights of all members

---

* BA, BCL, LLM (NUI), MA (Dublin), FTCD, Barrister, Regius Professor of Laws, Trinity College, Dublin.

1 Among the vast literature, reference should be made to McCrudden, "Human Dignity and Judicial Interpretation of Human Rights", 19 European J of Int'l L. 655 (2008), which presents a magisterial analysis of the subject. Also particularly helpful are: David Feldman, "Human Dignity as a Legal Value" [1999] *Public Law* 682; [2000] *Public Law* 61; Gay Moon & Robin Allen, "Dignity Discourse in Discrimination Law: A Better Route to Equality?" (2006) *EHRLR* 610, Denise Reaume, "Indignities: Making a Place for Dignity in Modern Legal Thought" (2002) 28 *Queen's LJ* 61.

2 In recent years dignity has been enshrined at a constitutional level in Europe in many countries: for example Belgium (Article 23), Estonia (Article 10), Finland (Articles 1, 7 and 19), Greece (Articles 7 and 106), Hungary (Article 54), Latvia (Article 95), Lithuania (Article 21), Poland (Preamble, Article 30), Portugal (Articles 1, 26(2) and 59), the Slovak Republic (Articles 12(1) and 19(10), Slovenia (Articles 12(10) and 19(1)), Slovenia (Articles 21 and 34) and Spain (Article 10): Catherine Dupré, "Human Dignity and the Withdrawal of Medical Treatment: A Missed Opportunity?" (2006) *EHRLR* 678, at 687, note 38, European Parliament, LIBE (Committee on Civil Liberties, Justice and Home Affairs), Freedom, Security and Justice: An Agenda for Europe, Charter of Fundamental Rights of the European Union, Article 1, Human Dignity (www.europarl.europa.eu/comparl/libe/elsj/charter/art01/default_en.htm). In the aftermath of the Nazi era, human dignity was enshrined as a foundational value in the German Constitution.

3 See David Kretzmer and Eckart Klein eds, *The Concept of Human Dignity in Human Rights Discourse* (Klewer Law International, 2002), David Feldman, "Human Dignity as a Legal Value" [1999] *Public Law* 682; [2000] *Public Law* 61.

4 See Klaus Dicke, "The Founding Function of Human Dignity in the Universal Declaration of Human Rights" in Kretzmer and Klein eds, note 4, at 111.

of the human family' as the foundation of freedom, justice and peace in the world.

Dignity has a central role in the African Charter on Human and Peoples' Rights. Article 5 proclaims that every individual "shall have the right to respect of the dignity inherent in a human being…"[5] The Protocol[6] of the Charter on the Rights of Women in Africa recognises in its Preamble the crucial role of women in the preservation of African values based on principles which include that of dignity. Article 3 provides that "[e]very woman shall have the right to dignity inherent in a human being…" It goes on to require States parties to adopt and implement appropriate measures to ensure that protection of every woman's rights to respect for her dignity. Articles 22 to 24 in which States' parties undertake to produce special protection for elderly women, women with disabilities and women in distress, require that they ensure that these women have the right to be treated with dignity.

The concept of human dignity is of an ancient pedigree.[7] Its philosophical origins may be found in Greek philosophy and in Judeo-Christian insight into the unique value and equal worth of every human being.[8] At the

[5] Cf. Lilian Chenwi, *Towards the Abolition of the Death Penalty in Africa: A Human Rights Perspective,* (2007): "The right to respect of one's dignity is the only right in the African Charter described as 'inherent in a human being'."

[6] The Protocol has generated considerable analysis. See eg. Banda "Blazing a Trail: The African Women's Protocol Comes into Force", 50 J of African L 72 (2006), Mengesha, "Reconciling the Need for Advancing Women's Rights in Africa and the Dictates of International Trade Norms: The Position of the Protocol on the Rights of Women in Africa", 6 African Human Rts LJ 166 (2006), Dyani, "Protocol on the Rights of Women Protection of Women from Sexual Violence During Armed Conflicts", 6 African Human Rts LJ 166 (2006), Durojaye, "Advancing Gender Equity in Access to HIV Treatment through the Protocol on the Rights of Women in Africa", 6 African Human Rights LJ 188 (2006).

[7] See Hubert Canick, "'Dignity of Man' and '*Persona*' in Stoic Anthropology: Some Remarks on Cicero, *De Officiis I*, 105–107" in Kretzmer and Klein eds, note 4, at 19.

[8] *Cf* Christian Starck, "The Religious and Philosophical Background of Human Dignity and Its Place in Modern Constitutions" in Kretzmer and Klein eds, note 4, at 179, 180–18; John Coughlin, "Pope John Paul II and the Dignity of the Human Being" (2003) 27 *Harv J of L & Public Pol'y* 65; Jean Bethke Elshtain, "The Dignity of the Human Person and the Idea of Human Rights: Four Inquiries" (1999) 14 *J of L & Religion* 53; William Joseph Wagner, "Universal Human Rights, The United Nations and the *Telos* of Human Dignity" (2005) 3 *Ave Maria L Rev* 197; Lorne Sossin, "The Supremacy of God, Human Dignity, and the *Charter of Rights and Freedoms*" (2003) 52 *UNBLJ* 227; Izhak Englard, "Human Dignity: From Antiquity to Modern Israel's Constitutional Framework" (2000) 21 *Cardozo L Rev* 1903; Kevin Hasson, "Religious Liberty and Human Dignity: A Tale of Two Declarations" (2003) 27 *Harv J of L & Public Pol'y* 81, Eibach, "Protection of Life and Human Dignity: The German Debate between Christian Norms and Secular Expectations", 14 Christian Bioethics 58 (2008).

outset it is useful to acknowledge the elusive and contested character of the concept.

Its meaning depends greatly on the philosophical premises of those who invoke it[9]; the range of such premises is so broad that "dignity" can have completely opposing connotations. Thus, for example, from one philosophical standpoint, dignity is exemplified by a person's enduring suffering; from another, it is exemplified by his or her choosing to end that suffering by an autonomous act. From one such standpoint, dignity derives from one's essential humanity; from another, dignity may be lost by circumstances external to that humanity. From one standpoint, dignity is rooted in social interrelationship; from another, it is a characteristic of the deracinated individual.

Apart from these differences in philosophical premises affecting the meaning of dignity, it is clear that the word "dignity" has more than one meaning in general discourse. Thus it is possible, for example, for one who understands dignity as involving the inherent worth of every human being nonetheless to speak of situations, or actions, as involving "a lack of dignity" or to differentiate between actions on the basis of the degree of dignity they manifest.

When it comes to the legal acknowledgment or protection of human dignity still greater complexities arise. Gay Moon and Robin Allen helpfully observe:

> "There are at least three different roles that dignity can play – as a value, as a principle and as a basis of defined rights … In our view [a discussion as to *when* any particular role is appropriate] is important for three reasons…
>
> First, the use to which it is put will alter the nature and effect of the concept.
>
> The appeal to respect for human dignity can be made to assert a value that ought to be shared by all; to invoke a principle to stand alongside other fundamental principles (including in particular the principle of equal treatment) to help determine how that other principle should be applied; and to claim a remedy for the violation of a self-standing right. This chameleon-like quality of dignity had meant that reference to it has often

[9] See Pullman, "Universalism, Particularism and the Ethics of Dignity", 7 Christian Bioethics 333 (2001).

> been made without any express consideration of which role is in play and which is the most apt, and importantly, how therefore the concept *works.*
>
> Secondly, it is obviously necessary, for an effective critical point of view to be established, that the utility of this concept should be judged in the context in which it is deployed.
>
> Thirdly, whenever it is asserted that there is a right to respect for dignity which has been violated in some context, it is likely that there will be pressure from the supposed violator to persuade the court to limit the concept. Without clear conceptualisation this is a pressure which is likely to have some effect, perhaps with a consequential rigidity. On the other hand if respect is asserted only as a value or a principle, the way in which a court moulds it to the seeming justice of the case will be less likely to give rise to a rigidity in the law. Applying a principle or value in a specific context will not create the kind of precedent which ossifies the concept. The value will enhance the process of reasoning and the principle will set a boundary to the discourse which must be obeyed or negotiated."[10]

1 Dignity as a feature of constitutions in Southern Africa

Dignity features in many of the other constitutions of Southern Africa.[11] The most striking example is, of course, South Africa. Section 1(a) of the Constitution of 1996 identifies dignity as one of the values on which the Republic of South Africa is founded. Section 7 "affirms the valu[e] of human dignity…" Section 10 provides that "[e]veryone has inherent dignity and the right to have their dignity respected and protected." Section 36(1) requires that limitations on rights be "reasonable and justifiable in an open and democratic society based on human dignity, equality and freedom". Section 39(1)(a) requires the courts, when interpreting the Bill of Rights, to promote the values that underlie such a society.

In the Namibian Constitution, the first recital of the Preamble acknowledges that recognition of the inherent dignity and of the equal and inalienable rights of all members of the human family is indispensable for freedom, justice and peace. It identifies the desire of the People of Namibia "to promote amongst all of us the dignity of the individual." Article 8(1) provides that "The dignity

[10] Moon and Allen, note 1, at 615.

[11] See Rory O'Connell, "The Role of Dignity in Equality Law: Lessons from Canada and South Africa", 6 Int'l J. of Constitutional L. 267 (2008).

of all persons shall be inviolable" and[12] Article 8(2)(b) guarantees that in any judicial proceedings or in other proceedings before any organ of the State, and during the enforcement of a penalty, respect for human dignity shall be guaranteed.

One of the fundamental underlying principles on which the Malawian Constitution is founded is that:

> "[t]he inherent dignity and worth of every human being requires that the State and all persons shall recognize and protect fundamental human rights and afford the fullest protection to the rights and views of all individuals, groups and minorities whether or not they are entitled to vote."[13]

Section 19(1) provides that "[t]he dignity of all persons shall be inviolable" and section 19(2) involves the guarantee of respect for human dignity in any judicial proceedings or in any other proceedings before any organ of the State, and during the enforcement of a penalty.[14]

---

[12] Cf. *Government of the Republic of Namibia v Getachew* [2008] NASC 4 (unlawful detention held to violate Article 8(1)), *McNaband v Minister of Home Affairs NO* [2007] NAHC 50 (prison conditions held to violate dignity, though claim for damages failed on procedural grounds), *Minister of Health and Social Services v Lisse* [2005] NASC 8 (refusal by Minister of authorisation for doctor to practice at a State hospital held to violate Article 8(1)).

[13] Section 12, para (iv).

[14] In *Kafantayeni v Attorney General* [2007] MWHC 1 (27 April 2007), the High Court of Malawi held that the mandatory death penalty for murder violated the constitutional guarantees of rights under section 19 (and other sections) of the Constitution. In *Palitu v Republic* [2001] MWHC 43 (19 September 2001) Mwaungulu J considered "it offensive to public policy and human dignity" for the judicial process to use evidence obtained by a confession made under duress. In *Jumbe v Attorney General* [2005] MWHC 15 (21 October 2005) a reverse onus provision in the Corrupt Practices Act was struck down as violating the right to a fair trial guaranteed by section 42(2)(f)(iii). *Per* Katsala J:

> "Admittedly corruption is bad... and it has to be rooted out of our society ... Those that engage in corruption in a way violate the citizens' right to development as enshrined in section 30 of the Constitution. They ... divert for their own use public resources thereby depriving the general public the benefit from such resources. Such people are selfish and greedy at the expense of everyone else. Surely, if caught, they must be dealt with firmly.
> However, inasmuch as we may harbour hatred for such people, we can only show and prove to the whole world and indeed to ourselves that we are an open and democratic society and that we cherish and promote the values that underlie such a society if we treat those we suspect of committing heinous crimes with dignity as fellow human beings and afford them all the protection that accused persons enjoy under the Constitution. I do not see any justification for limiting their right to be presumed innocent bearing in mind that they are mere suspects and have not been convicted of the alleged crimes."

Persons who are detained, including sentenced prisoners, have the right to be detained "under conditions consistent with human dignity, which shall include at least the provision of reading and writing materials, adequate nutrition and medical treatment at the expense of the State."[15] Children arrested for, or accused of, the alleged commission of an offence are entitled to be treated in a manner consistent with the promotion of their "sense of dignity and worth…"[16]

The Preamble to Zambia's Constitution involves a pledge by the people of Zambia to ensure that the State shall respect "the rights and dignity of the human family…."

Section 18(1) of Swaziland's Constitution provides that "[t]he dignity of every person is inviolable". Section (6) requires the State and society to recognize the right of persons with disabilities to respect and human dignity.

Section 28(a) of the Constitution of Lesotho requires the state to adopt policies aimed at securing that education is directed to "the full development of the human personality and sense of dignity…"[17]

2 Dignity and the Constitution of Botswana

The Constitution of Botswana does not in express terms incorporate dignity as a core right or value. But this does not mean that dignity has no place in

---

In *In re Adoption of Children Act (Cap. 26: 01); In re: David Banda (Adoption Cause No. 2 of 2006)*, [2008] MWHC 3, Nyirenda J, noted that the human rights provisions in the Constitution were "purposely there contained to enhance and uphold the rights of all manner of people in our nation in order to preserve their dignity." He considered that section 19(1) "in particular" stressed that the dignity of all persons should be inviolable and he added that "in order to preserve the dignity of all persons section 30 of the Constitution in turn obligates the State to ensure the right to development at every stage and level of humanity…"

[15] Section 42(1), para (6).

[16] Section 42(2), sub-para (g)(iv).

[17] The two Lusophore constitutions of Southern Africa are also enthusiastic about respect for dignity. Article 20 of the Constitution of Angola requires the State "to respect and protect the human person and human dignity." Article 19(1) of the Mozambican Constitution expresses Mozambique's solidarity with the struggle of the African peoples and states for "unity, freedom, dignity and the right to economic and social progress". See further Binchy, "The Constitution of Timor-Leste in Comparative Perspective", Chapter 10 of William Binchy ed., *Timor-Leste: Challenges for Justice and Human Rights in the Shadow of the Past* (2009), at 264–265.

the constitutional jurisprudence of Botswana. One must surely give significant weight to Aguda JA's observation in *Attorney General v Dow*[18] that, in his understanding:

> "[g]enerous construction means... that you must not interpret the Constitution to whittle down any of the rights and freedoms unless by very clear and unambiguous words such as interpretation is compelling... I would conceive it that the primary duty of the judges is to make the Constitution grow and develop in order to meet the just demands and aspirations of an ever developing society which is part of the wider and larger human society governed by some acceptable concepts of human dignity."

The constitutional centrality of dignity was also acknowledged by Dingake J in *Lemo v Northern Air Maintenance (Pty) Ltd.*[19]:

> "The view I hold is that once an employee is dismissed because he is HIV positive, as in this case, the constitution is immediately implicated, in particular s 7(1) which prohibits inhuman and degrading treatment. This is so because to dismiss an employee because he is HIV positive is a violation of his right to dignity.
>
> "The value of dignity as a core value of our constitution cannot be overemphasised. Recognising the right to dignity is an acknowledgement of the intrinsic worth of a human being. It is therefore plainly impermissible to dismiss an employee because he is HIV positive, when such a status has not been shown to incapacitate him. The era of routine dismissals because an employee is HIV positive, if ever there was, is now past. It is offensive to modern thinking and must not be tolerated. The courts, need to assert and enforce this right, so as to inform the future, and invest in our legal and constitutional order the intrinsic worth of all human beings.'
>
> "In the context of an individual, human dignity means having a sense of self respect and self-worth. It is concerned with physical and psychological integrity. Human dignity is harmed by unfair treatment or discrimination based on personal traits or circumstances which have no relationship to individual capacities....There can be no doubt in my mind that the values of human dignity and elimination of discrimination are the very essence of our constitution."

---

[18] [1992] BLR 119, at 165–166.

[19] [2004] (2) BLR 317 at 328–329 (Industrial Ct, Gaborone).

Is it possible to argue with any credibility that dignity is a value that requires respect under the Constitution of Botswana and that actually shapes the contours of rights and obligations? Perhaps the most attractive immediate response is that it is not. The stark fact is that Botswana's Constitution – in contrast to the constitutions of many of its neighbours – contains no express reference to dignity. If it is now thought desirable that dignity should develop as a core constitutional concept, the solution, it may be said, is to replace the existing Consitution by a new one rather than achieve that goal by judicial stealth.

As against this, some opposing arguments may be marshalled. First, comparative consitutitonal scholarship makes it plain that a rich constitutional jurisprudence on dignity may be built on inferential foundations. The experience of the United States of America is a prime example.[20] Secondly, dignity explains the reason for constitutional protection of rights and gives guidance as to how those rights should be interpreted. That is why Aguda JA's observations in *Dow* are so important. They do not represent some sterile technical rule of constitutional interpretation but rather inspire us to the realisation that constitutional provisions are based on a philosophy of the human person and that the rights of human beings to have their unique worth recognised and respected on an equal basis.

One should retain a sense of realism and acknowledge that the constitutional jurisprudence of Botswana has yet to demonstrate a judicial disposition to interpret the Constitution by reference to such broad values. The general tendency has been to adopt a more cautious approach, largely eschewing grand constitutional theory, as favoured in the Supreme Courts of Canada, the United States of America and South Africa, for example, and to give full force to the qualifications and provisos in the text of the Constitution.

It is therefore useful to consider a more contextualised question, as to whether respect for dignity is a value that *enlightens judicial understanding of rights specifically guaranteed under the Constitution of Botswana*.[21] The answer is that it clearly does; the more difficult question, yet to be fully addressed by the courts, relates to the extent which this respect should have on the contours of these rights.

[20] See Goodman, "Human Dignity in Supreme Court Constitutional Jurisprudence", 84 Nebraska L. Rev. 740 (2006).

[21] In *Dawood v Minister of Home Affairs* 2000 (3) SA 936, the Constitutional Court of South Africa strongly endorsed this approach. O'Regan J stated (para. 35):

3 Dignity and equality

The essence of the concept of dignity is the unique inherent value of every human being. This value does not depend on age, capacity or social position. Human beings are understood to have a relational and social dimension: human flourishing is not possible without regard to this interpersonal perspective which generates a large tapestry of rights and obligations as between individuals, groups and society.

This understanding of dignity clearly has significant implications for constitutional jurisprudence of equality and non-discrimination. Indeed this is demonstrated unambiguously by the constitutional experience in a range of countries. In Ireland, in an important decision of the Supreme Court, *Quinn's Supermarket v Attorney General*,[22] Walsh J said that the provision in the Constitution relating to equality involved was:

> "a guarantee related to their dignity as human beings and a guarantee against any inequalities grounded upon an assumption, or indeed a belief, that some individual or individuals or classes of individuals, by reason of their human attributes or their ethnic or racial, social or religious background, are to be treated as the inferior or superior of other individuals in our country."

This passage is of crucial importance in providing such a clear acknowledgment of the relationship between dignity and equality. It recognises the radical equality that underlies our inherent value as human beings and seeks to ensure that any inequalities grounded on an assumption or belief that contradicts this equality will not withstand constitutional scrutiny.

"Human dignity … informs constitutional adjudication and interpretation at a range of levels. It is a value that informs the interpretation of many, possibly all … rights … Section 10 … makes it plain that dignity is not only a value fundamental to our Constitution: it is a justiciable and enforceable *right* that must be respected and protected. In many cases, however, where the value of human dignity is offended, the primary constitutional breach occasioned may be of a more specific right such as the right to bodily integrity, the right to equality, or the right not be subjected to slavery, servitude or forced labour".

See also *Republic v Minister for Home Affairs* [2008] eKLR (Kenya High Ct., Nyamu J, 18 April 2008):

"Human dignity is of fundamental importance to any society including Kenya and indeed is a foundational value which informs the interpretation of many and perhaps all other fundamental rights."

22 [1972] IR 1, at 13.

It is not the proper function of the judiciary to engage in a political agenda of social justice. It is, however, the entitlement and obligation of our courts to vindicate constitutionally-protected rights and values. This may require courts to engage critically with their society and to scrutinise what the political consensus may regard as the natural order. Of course, courts must do this in fidelity of the requirements of the separation of powers, but when cases come along, in which human dignity has been compromised, the courts should engage more energetically in interrogating the assumptions of the powerful so as to vindicate the constitutional rights of those lacking strong political leverage.

The experience in South Africa is useful in demonstrating that it is possible for courts charged with the task of vindicating social and economic rights to develop a rich jurisprudence in which respect for dignity enlightens judicial understanding of equality.[23]

In *Government of the Republic of South Africa v Grootboom*,[24] the Constitutional Court held that, although the State had a good national housing plan, it was deficient in failing to have particular regard for the very urgent need of homeless people who were living in appalling conditions on land which they had no permission to occupy. The court invoked section 26 of the Constitution, under which everyone had a right to have access to adequate housing and held that the State was required to take reasonable legislative and other measures, within its available resources, to achieve the progressive realisation of this right. Yacoob J (for the Court) observed that:

> "section 26 is not the only provision relevant to a decision as to whether state action at any particular level of government is reasonable and consistent with the Constitution. The proposition that rights are interrelated and are equally important is not merely a theoretical postulate. The concept has immense human and practical significance in a society founded on human dignity, equality and freedom. It is fundamental to an evaluation of

---

[23] See Liebenberg, "The Value of Human Dignity in Interpreting Socio-Economic Rights," 21 S. Af. J on Human Rts 1(2005), Govender, "Economic, Social and Cultural Rights in South Africa: Entitlements, Not Mere Policy Options", in B. Goldewijk, A. Baspineiro & P. Carbonari eds., *Dignity and Human Rights: The Implementation of Economic, Social and Cultural Rights* (2002), 75.

[24] 2000 (11) BCLR 1169. For analysis see Pierre De Vos, "*Grootboom,* the Right of Access to Housing and Substantive Equality as Contextual Fairness" (2001) 17 *S Afr J on Human Rts 258*, Daniel Schneider, "The Constitutional Right to Housing in South Africa: *The Government of the Republic of South Africa v Irene Grootboom*" (2004) 2 *Int'l J of Civil Soc'y L* 45.

the reasonableness of state action that account be taken of the inherent dignity of human beings. The constitution will be worth infinitely less than its paper if the reasonableness of state action concerned with housing is determined without regard to the fundamental constitutional value of human dignity. Section 26, read in the context of the Bill of Rights as a whole, must mean that the respondents have a right to reasonable action by the state in all circumstances and with particular regard to human dignity. In short, I emphasise that human beings are required to be treated as human beings. This is the backdrop against which the conduct of the respondents towards the appellants must be seen." [25]

A similar approach towards dignity and equality is apparent in the Canadian constitutional jurisprudence.[26] In the leading decision of *Law v Canada*[27], the Supreme Court of Canada interpreted the purpose of section 15 of the Canadian *Charter of Rights and Freedoms* as being:

"to prevent the violation of essential human dignity and freedom through the imposition of disadvantage, stereotyping, or political or social prejudice, and to promote a society in which all persons enjoy equal recognition at law as human beings or as members of Canadian society, equally capable and equally deserving of concern, respect and consideration. Legislation

[25] Irish decisions on issues similar to those arising in *Grootboom* have generally not been encouraging though there are some instances in which the courts have shown sensitivity to the dignity of the homeless.

One decision showing a commendable awareness to the dignity of the indigent is *Redmond v Minister for the Environment*, [2001] 4 IR 61, where Herbert J held that provisions of the electoral code that candidates for election to the Parliament had to pay a €1,000 deposit violated Article 40.1 of the Constitution. Having quoted the crucial passage from Walsh J's judgment in *Quinn's Supermarket*, Herbert J stated:

"In my judgment a law which has the effect, even if totally unintended of discriminating between human persons on the basis of money is an attack upon the dignity of those persons as human beings who do not have money. This is far removed for instance from issues such as alleged rights to wage parity or increases or issues of the uneven impact of taxation upon citizens in various marital or non-marital relationships or on farmers or householders or occupiers. The history of poverty and of social deprivation in Ireland, but by no means exclusively in Ireland, demonstrates overwhelmingly the extent to which the essential dignity of persons as human beings is involved. In my Judgment this is exactly the type of discrimination for which the framers of the first sentence of Article 40 Section 1 of the Constitution were providing."

[26] See Essert, "Dignity and Membership, Equality and Egalitarianism: Economic Rights and Section 15", 19 *Can. J. of L.* & Jurisprudence 407 (2006), Greschner, "Does *Law* Advance the Cause of Equality?" 27 *Queen's L.J.* 299 (2001), Fyfe, "Dignity as Theory: Competing Conceptions of Human Dignity at the Supreme Court of Canada", 70 *Saskatchewan L. Rev.* 1 (2007).

[27] [1999] 1 S.C.R. 497, para. 51.

which effects differential treatment between individuals or groups will violate this fundamental purpose where those who are subject to differential treatment fall within one or more enumerated or analogous grounds, and where the differential treatment reflects the application of presumed group or personal characteristics, or otherwise the effect of perpetuating or promoting the view that the individual is less capable, or less worthy of recognition or value as a human being or as a member of Canadian society."

Although African courts outside South Africa tend to hesitate before recognising the justiciability of economic and social rights, it may be suggested that the spirit of *Dow* is entirely consistent with the jurisprudence on dignity that has emerged from the courts of South Africa and Canada.

4 Dignity and the Right to Life

Dignity has played a crucial role in enlightening the understanding of courts as to the philosophical basis and contours of the right to life. This is particularly noteworthy in relation to the death penalty[28] where respect for dignity, either as a free-standing right or as one implicating the right not to be subjected to cruel or inhuman punishment, has led courts in the United States of America, Canada and South Africa to hold capital punishment unconstitutional in at least some circumstances. In *State v Makwanyane*[29], where the South African Constitutional Court struck down legislation providing for the death penalty, dignity was at the centre of the judges' analysis. Mokgoro J observed:

"In the past legal order, basic human rights in South Africa, including the right to life and human dignity, were not protected in a Bill of Fundamental Rights and Freedoms, in a supreme constitution, as is the case today. Parliament then was sovereign, and could pass any law it deemed fit. Legislation was supreme, and due to the absence of judicial review, no court of law could set aside any statute or its provision on grounds of

[28] See Lilian Chenwi, *Towards the Abolition of the Death Penalty in Africa – A Human Rights Perspective* (2007), William Schabas, *The Abolition of the Death Penalty in International Law* (3rd ed., 2002), Chapter 9, Roger Hood & Carolyn Hoyle, *The Death Penalty: A Worldwide Perspective* (4th ed., 2008), 73–84, van Zyl Smit, "The Death Penalty in Africa", 4 African Human Rts L J 1 (2004).

[29] [1995] 1 LRC 269.

violating fundamental rights. Hence, Section 277 of the Criminal Procedure Act, 51 of 1977, could survive untested to this day.

Our new Constitution, unlike its dictatorial predecessor, is value-based. Among other things, it guarantees the protection of basic human rights, including the right to life and human dignity, two basic values supported by the spirit of *ubuntu* and protected in Sections 9 and 10 respectively. In terms of Section 35, this Constitution now commits the state to base the worth of human beings on the ideal values espoused by open democratic societies the world over and not on race colour, political, economic and social class. Although it has been argued that the currently high level of crime in the country is indicative of the breakdown of the moral fabric of society, it has not been conclusively shown that the death penalty, which is an affront to these basic values, is the best available practical form of punishment to reconstruct that moral fabric. In the second place, even if the end was desirable, that would not justify the means. The death penalty violates the essential content of the right to life embodied in Section 9, in that it extinguishes life itself. It instrumentalises the offender for the objectives of state policy. That is dehumanising. It is degrading and it violates the rights to respect for and protection of human dignity embodied in Section 10 of the Constitution.

Once the life of a human being is taken in the deliberate and calculated fashion that characterises the described methods of execution the world over, it constitutes the ultimate cruelty with which any living creature could ever be treated. This extreme level of cruel treatment of a human being, however despicably such person might have treated another human being, is still inherently cruel. It is inhuman and degrading to the humanity of the individual, as well as to the humanity of those who carry it out.

Taking the life of a human being will always be reprehensible. Those citizens who kill deserve the most severe punishment, if it deters and rehabilitates and therefore effectively addresses deviance of this nature. Punishment by death cannot achieve these objectives. The high rate of crime in this country is indeed disturbing and the state has a duty to protect the lives of all citizens – including those who kill. However, it should find more humane and effective integrated approaches to manage its penal system, and to rehabilitate offenders.

The state is representative of its people and in many ways sets the standard for moral values within society. If it sanctions by law punishment for killing by killing, it sanctions vengeance by law. If it does so with a view to deterring others, it dehumanises the person and objectifies him or her as a tool for crime control. This objectification through the calculated killing

> of a human being, to serve state objectives, strips the offender of his or her human dignity and dehumanises, such a person constituting a violation of Section 10 of the Constitution."[30]

We shall presently consider the specific question of the relevance of dignity to the death penalty in Botswana. Here we may note, in relation to the right to life, that some courts internationally have invoked dignity when interpreting the right to life broadly so as to encompass a range of social and economic entitlements which are the necessary substratum to a life lived with dignity. The most famous example is the Supreme Court of India.[31]

A similar approach has been adopted in Pakistan. In *Zia v WAPDA*[32] Akhtar J, noting that the Constitution of Pakistan guaranteed the dignity of man and also the right to life under Article 9, went on to observe that:

> "if both are read together, [the] question will arise whether a person can be said to have dignity of man if his right to life is below [the] bare necessity line without proper food, clothing, shelter, education, healthcare, clean atmosphere and [an] unpolluted environment."

---

[30] *ibid.*, at 380–381. See also O'Regan J (at 384):

"The importance of dignity as a founding value of our new Constitution cannot be over-emphasised. Recognising a right to dignity is an acknowledgment of the intrinsic worth of human beings: human beings are entitled to be treated as worthy of respect and concern."

[31] Among the rich jurisprudence, leading decisions include *Mullin v Administrator, Union Territory of Delhi*; AIR 1981 SC 746, *Tellis v Bombay Municipal Corporation* AIR 1986 SC 180, *Bandhua Mukti Morcha v Union of India* AIR 1984 SC 802, *Jain v State of Karnataka* (1992) 2 SCC 666. See Muralidhar, "Judicial Enforcement of Economic and Social Rights: The Indian Scenario", in Fons Coomans ed., *Justiciability of Economic and Social Rights: Experiences from Domestic Systems* (2006), 237, Nihal Jayawickrama, *The Judicial Application of Human Rights Law: National, Regional and International Jurisprudence* (2002), 258–260, Neuborne, "The Supreme Court of India" 1 Int'l J of Constitutional L 476, at 500–504 (2003), Rajamani, "Public Interest Environmental Litigation in India: Exploring Issues of Access, Participation, Equity, Effectiveness and Sustainability", 19 J of Environmental L 293 (2007), Young, "The Minimum Core of Economic and Social Rights: A Concept in Search of Content", 33 Yale L J of Int'l L 113 at 128–130 (2008), Deva, "Human Rights Realization in an Era of Globalization: The Indian Experience", 12 Buffalo Human Rts L Rev 93, at 119–132 (2006), Sripati, "Constitutionalism in India and South Africa: A Comparative Study from a Human Rights Perspective", 16 Tulane J of Int'l & Comp L 49, at 98–104 (2007), Ní Chuilleanáin, "Opening Up the Courts to the Marginalised: The Uses and Usefulness of Public Interest Litigation in India", 6 Trinity College L Rev 18 (2003).

[32] PLD 1994 SC 693. See further Martin Lau, "Islam and Judicial Activism: Public Interest Litigation and Environmental Protection in the Islamic Republic of Pakistan", Chapter 14 of Alan Boyle & Michael Andereson eds., *Human Rights Approaches to Environmental Protection* (1998).

In Africa, some courts have favoured an expansive interpretation of the right to life. In *Waweru v Republic*[33], a decision of the Kenyan High Court, Nyamu J gave a broad meaning to the concept of "life" in the environmental context. Inspired by a range of international initiatives, including the Stockholm Declaration of 1972, Principle 1 of which refers to man's fundamental right to freedom, equality and adequate conditions of life, in an environment "of a quality that permits a life of dignity and well-being", Nyamu J considered it:

> "...quite evident ...that the word life and the environment are inseparable and the word life means much more than keeping body and soul together".

Not every African court has taken the same approach. In *Baitsokoli v Maseru City Council*[34], the Lesotho Court of Appeal rejected the argument that the right to life, protected by Section 5(1) of the Constitution of Lesotho, should be interpreted as encompassing the right to a livelihood. Gauntlett JA thought it impossible that there should be "an absolute right to livelihood"[35] where "the core right – the entitlement to exist as a human being" – was itself derogable under Section 5(2). He was of the opinion that the Principles of State Policy contained in Chapter III of the Constitution, in particular section 29(1),[36] represented the limits of constitutional recognition of the right to a livelihood.

The decision of the High Court of Botswana in *Sesana v Attorney General*[37] is consistent with an expansive interpretation of the right to life. Dow and Phumaphi JJ held that the termination by the Government of essential services to the applicants in the CKGR was unconstitutional, breaching their right to life. In Phumaphi J's view, the simultaneous stoppage of the supply of food rations and the issuing of Special Game Licences was "tantamount to condemning the remaining residents of the CKGR to death by starvation."

---

[33] [2006] eKLR (High Ct of Kenya, Nyamu J, 2 March 2006).

[34] [2005] LSCA 13 (Lesotho Court of Appeal, 20 April 2005).

[35] Gauntlett JA did not enlarge on why the right to a livelihood should be described as "absolute". While not qualified by some express exception, as under Section 5(2), a right of this kind must be understood as less than absolute insofar as its contours are moulded by the exigencies of the limits to the state's resources.

[36] "Lesotho shall endeavour to ensure that every person has the opportunity to gain his living by work which he freely chooses or accepts".

[37] [2006] 2 BLR 633, analysed by Lebotse, "Perspectives on the Interface between Human Rights and the Environment in Botswana in the Light of the Barawa case", Chapter 15, *infra*.

Dow J observed that the case was "ultimately about a people demanding dignity and respect. It is a people saying in essence, 'our way of life may be different but it is worthy of respect …'"

5 Torture, Inhuman or Degrading Punishment or Treatment

Does dignity enlighten judicial understanding of the prohibition of torture or inhuman or degrading punishment or other treatment contained in section 7(1) of the Constitution? The answer is clearly in the affirmative. In *S v Ndou*[38], Moore JA quoted this "terse"[39] provision and went on to observe:

> "The proscribed elements of torture and inhuman or degrading punishment or other treatment are pregnant with meaning and are powerful concepts reaching down to the very depths of a person's humanity and to his right not to be treated in a manner which robs him of his human dignity and worth."[40]

6 The Death Penalty in Botswana

Let us now turn to consider the question of the death penalty. Can any argument be made that respect for dignity as a value renders capital punishment unconstitutional in Botswana? It has to be acknowledged that the express language of sections 4(1)[41] and 7[42] of the Constitution makes it hard to have any confidence in such an argument's meeting with judicial approval in the future, so far as it would seek to outlaw capital punishment in all cases. There remains, however, the possibility that respect for dignity may affect — and

[38] [2008] BWCA 60 (24 July 2008).

[39] *ibid.*, Para. 58.

[40] *ibid.*, Para. 59.

[41] Section 4(1) provides that:

> "[n]o person shall be deprived of his life intentionally save in execution of the sentence of a court in respect of an offence under the law in force in Botswana of which he has been convicted."

[42] Section 7 provides as follows:

> "(1) No person shall be subjected to torture or inhuman treatment or degrading punishment or other treatment.
>
> (2) Nothing contained in or done under the authority of any law shall be held to be inconsistent with or in contravention of this Section to the extent that the law in question authorizes the infliction of any description of punishment that was lawful in the country immediately before the coming into operation of this Constitution."

at least narrow — the constitutionality of the death penalty in a range of particular circumstances.

In *The State v Ntesang,*[43] the Court of Appeal had little difficulty in rejecting the argument that the death penalty prescribed by section 203 of the Penal Code violated section 4 of the Constitution. Aguda JA noted that the Court was being urged:

> "to perform a surgical operation on Section 4(1) of the Constitution by sustaining the first nine words of that Section and deleting all the other words…
>
> "In this case the appellant is not only asking us to segregate one provision and interpret it in isolation, but indeed to segregate it and cut it in two, and thereafter refuse to give effect one of the two parts into which we should have cut the provision. In my view we cannot do this; and all the words of Section 4(1) of the Constitution must be given to full effect."

That represented the essence of the Court's rejection of the attack on the constitutionality of the death penalty under section 4. The right to life guarantee in section 3 was not considered strong enough to eclipse the clear language of section 4 conferring constitutional validity on the deprivation of life in execution of the sentence of a court in respect of an offence under the law in force in Botswana of which he had been convicted.

Aguda JA went on to reject the attack on the constitutionality of the death penalty based on section 7(1). Such an attack overlooked section 7(2) which "apparently" saved any law that authorised the infliction of any description of punishment that had been lawful in Botswana immediately before the Constitution came into operation. The death penalty by hanging was such a punishment. As in respect of Section 4, in the absence of very compelling reasons the Court could not hold that one provision of the Constitution was contradictory and opposed to another and hence refuse to give effect to the one in favour of the other:

> "The result, of course, is that despite the [fact that] the death penalty may be considered, as it apparently has been elsewhere, to be torture, inhuman or degrading punishment or treatment, that form of punishment is preserved by sub-section (2) of Section 7 of the Constitution. I have no doubt in my

[43] [1995] BLR 151.

mind that the Court has no power to re-write the Constitution in order to give effect to what the appellant has described as progressive movements taking place all over the world, and to give effect to the Resolutions of the United Nations as to the abolition of the death penalty. I, however, express the hope that before long the matter will engage the attention of that arm of the Government which has responsibility of effecting changes in the Statutes for its consideration and changes which it may consider necessary to further establish the claim of this country as one of the great liberal democracies of the world."

The textual analysis of the provisions of Section 7 is perfectly logical: one may respectfully suggest that the conclusion is not quite so inevitable as the judgment indicates. Indeed, when one examines the subsequent decision of the Botswana Court of Appeal in *Kobedi v The State,*[44] which on its face appears to offer a ringing endorsement of *Ntesang*, one can discern important qualifications to the breadth of the constitutionality of the death penalty. In *Kobedi*, the Court of Appeal discussed in detail the Privy Council decision of *Reyes v The Queen,*[45] which held that a mandatory death penalty for 'Class A' murder offences in Belize, which included murder by shooting, violated Section 7[46] of the Belize Constitution by virtue of its mandatory character, which "precluded any judicial consideration of the humanity of condemning [the convicted person] to death".[47] The Judicial Committee quoted with approval Saunders JA (Ag)'s observation in *Spence v The Queen and Hughes v The Queen*[48] that:

> "[t]he dignity of human life is reduced by a law that compels a court to impose death by hanging indiscriminately upon all convicted of murder, granting none an opportunity to have the individual circumstances of his case considered by the court that is to pronounce the sentence ..."

In *Kobedi*, Tebbutt JP interpreted *Reyes* as "serv[ing] .... to reinforce" *Ntesang* in that both decisions had sanctioned the death penalty and had held that "the questions of whether the passing and implementation of the sentence

---

44 [2003] BWCA 22.

45 [2002] 2 AC 235.

46 Section 7 provides that "[n]o person shall be subjected to torture or to inhuman or degrading punishment or other treatment." It has no equivalent to the proviso contained in Section 7(2) of the Constitution of Botswana.

47 [2002] 2 AC, at 256.

48 East Carribbean Court of Appeal, 2 April 2001 (consolidated appeals from St. Vincent and the Grenadines and Saint Lucia), para. 215 of Saunders JA (Ag)'s judgment.

of death are themselves inhuman and degrading" did not, and could not, arise under the respective constitutions of Belize and Botswana. In holding that murder by shooting should be treated as falling within Class B, the Privy Council had impliedly considered that that category did not offend the Belize Constitution in section 203(2) of the Botswana Penal Code, which likewise provided that, where there were extenuating circumstances, a sentence other than death might be imposed, "should therefore also be considered as not being unconstitutional".

This last observation is hugely significant. It suggests that, if a mandatory death penalty were introduced in Botswana, it could well be unconstitutional. This is consistent with the international trend of decisions: a mandatory death penalty has been rejected as it has been by the Privy Council[49] and by courts in Malawi[50] Uganda,[51] India[52] and the United States of America,[53] as well as by international human rights bodies,[54] though not by the Court of Appeal of Singapore.[55]

---

[49] *Reyes v The Queen, supra*, *Roodal v The State of Trinidad and Tobago* [2005] 1 AC 328, *Bowe v The Queen*, [2006] 1 WLR 1623. See Lilian Chenwi, *supra*, 51–52, Broadbent, "Bahamas: Mandatory Death Penalty; Constitutionality", 71 J of Crim L 215 (2007).

[50] *Kafantayeni v Attorney General*, *supra*, analysed by Nkhata, "Bidding Farewell to Mandatory Capital Punishment: *Francis Kafantayeni and Others v Attorney General*", 1 Malawi L J 104 (2007).

[51] *Kigula and 417 others v Attorney General*, [2009] UGSC 6.

[52] *Mithu v State of Punjab*, AIR 1983 SC 473. See Chandrasekharan Pillai, "Supreme Court and Abolition of Death Sentence: An Evaluation of Techniques of Interpretation", Chapter 10 of Janak Raj Jai *ed.*, *Death Penalty* (2005), at 80–83. The Supreme Court's response to legislation that effectively ignored its holding in *Mithu* has been cautious: see Amnesty International and People's Union for Civil Liberties (Tamil Nadu & Puducherry), *Lethal Lottery: The Death Penalty in India; A Study of Supreme Court Judgments in Death Penalty Cases 1950-2006* (2008), 139–144.

[53] *Woodson v North Carolina,* 428 US 280 (1976), *Roberts v Louisiana*, 431 US 633 (1976), *Sumner v Shuman*, 483 US 66 (1987).

[54] *Lubuto v Zambia*, Human Rights Committee, Communication No. 390/1990 (1995), *Thompson v Saint Vincent and the Grenadines*, Human Rights Committee, Communication No. 806/1998 (2000), *Rolando v Philippines,* Human Rights Committee, Communication No. 1110/2002 (2004), *Bastide v Granada*, Inter-American Commission on Human Rights, Case 11.743, Report No. 38/00 (1999), *Hilaire, Constantine and Benjamin v Trinidad and Tobago,* Series C, No. 94 (21 June 2002). See further William A. Schabas, *The Abolition of the Death Penalty in International Law* (3rd ed., 2002), 323–324, Carozza, "'My Friend Is a Stranger': The Death Penalty and the Global *Ius Commune* of Human Rights", 81 Texas L Rev 1031 (2003). Tittemore, "The Mandatory Death Penalty in the Commonwealth Caribbean and the Inter-American Human Rights System: An Evolution in the Development and Implementation of International Human Rights Protections", 13 Wm & Mary Bill of Rts J 445 (2004).

[55] *Nguyen Tuong Van v Public Prosecutor* [2005] 1 Sing L R 103 (CA). Analysed by Lilm, "The Constitution and the Reception of Customary International Law: *Nguyen Tuong Van v Public Prosecutor*", [2005] Singapore J of Legal Studies 218. For an analysis published before the judgment of the Court of Appeal was handed down, see Hor, "The Death Penalty in Singapore and International Law", Singapore Yrbk of Int'l L (2004) 105.

As well as the question of the mandatory death penalty raising a constitutional issue in Botswana, it may be argued that the Constitution may also be engaged in cases where the legislature imposes the death penalty for a relatively trivial offence. In such circumstances, the death penalty would constitute an inhuman punishment, contrary to Section 7(1) and its constitutional validity would not be saved by Section 4(1) or Section 7(2).

It is worth noting in this context that the United States Supreme Court has accepted the argument that the death penalty must have regard to proportionality. In *Kennedy v Louisiana,*[56] the Court, by a five to four majority,[57] held that the capital punishment for the rape of a child violated the Eighth Amendment. Kennedy J, for the majority, observed that "[e]volving standards of decency must embrace and express respect for the dignity of the person, and the punishment of criminals must conform to that rule."[58] He noted that the Court had in an earlier decision explained that capital punishment must "be limited to those offenders who commit 'a narrow category of the most serious crimes and whose extreme culpability makes them 'the most deserving of execution"[59].

Finally, in regard to *Kobedi*, it is worth noting that the Court of Appeal endorsed the principle that the constitutional validity of the death penalty is subject to due expedition in its execution. Tebbutt JP accepted that "if an inordinate delay in carrying out a sentence of death occurs after a condemned prisoner has exercised his rights of appeal this may constitute a violation of his right to protection under Section 7(1) of the Constitution."

Courts in Uganda[60] and Zimbabwe[61] have taken the same approach. Dignity lies at the heart of their analysis. The holding in *Kobedi* has been criticised[62] for discounting from its computation of the period of the delay the time that

---

[56] 128 S. Ct. 2641 (2008), critically analysed in "The Supreme Court – Leading Cases", 122 Harvard L Rev 122, at 296–206 (2008).

[57] Kennedy J, joined by Stevens, Souter, Ginsburg and Breyer JJ; Alito J dissenting, joined by Roberts, C., Scalia and Thomas JJ.

[58] Kennedy J's judgment, p 9.

[59] *Roper v Simmons*, 543 U.S. 551, at 568 (2005), quoting from *Atkins v Virginia* 536 U.S. 304, at 319 (2002).

[60] *Kigula and 417 others v Attorney-General, supra.*

[61] *Catholic Commission for Justice and Peace in Zimbabwe v Attorney General, Zimbabwe*, 1993 (4) SA 239 (ZS).

[62] Bojosi, "The Death Row Phenomenon and the Prohibition against Torture and Cruel, Inhuman or Degrading Treatment", 4 African Human Rts LJ 303, at 313–314 (2004).

is attributable to the convicted person's pursuit of an appeal, but the larger point – that delay can in principle render an execution in Botswana unconstitutional – should not be ignored.

Let us now consider a question the answer to which must at first sight seem easy. Is a sentence of life imprisonment, without parole, contrary to the Constitution of Botswana? The easy answer might seem to be that it is not. A Constitution that permits capital punishment surely cannot be inconsistent with the lesser penalty of life imprisonment. Further reflection suggests that the answer is less easy though it may well be the same.

The German Federal Constitutional Court has held that such a sentence would violate the Basic Law:[63]

> "The State strikes at the very heart of human dignity if [it] treats the prisoner without regard to the development of his personality and strips him of all hope of ever earning his freedom. The legal provisions relating to the granting of pardons do not sufficiently guarantee this hope, which makes the sentence bearable in terms of human dignity…"[64]

The Supreme Court of Namibia took a similar view in *S. v Tcoeib.*[65] Referring with approval to the German decision, Mohammed J observed:

> "It seems to me that the sentence of life imprisonment in Namibia can … not be constitutionally sustainable if it effectively amounts to an order throwing the prisoner into a cell for the rest of the prisoner's natural life as if he was a 'thing' instead of a person without any continuing duty to respect his dignity (which would include his right not to live in despair and helplessness and without any hope of release, regardless of the circumstances)."[66]

---

[63] Bundesverfassungsgericht 21 June 1977, 45 BVerfGE 187 (F.R.G.), translated by Donald P. Kommers, *The Constitutional Jurisprudence of the Federal Republic of Germany* 306 (2nd ed., 1997). See Miller, "The Shared Transatlantic Jurisprudence of Dignity" 4 German L.J. 925, at 929–930 (2003).

[64] Kommers, *op. cit.*, 309.

[65] [1996] NASC 1 (6 February 1996).

[66] The Court did not lend that the sentence of life imprisonment in Namibia was *per se* unconstitutional as the relevant legislation permitted release on parole in appropriate circumstances.

The Constitutional Court of South Africa, in *S v Dodo*[67] upheld the constitutionality of legislation prescribing life imprisonment for certain very serious offences save where the sentencing court was satisfied that substantial and compelling circumstances existed which justified the imposition of a lesser sentence. It was clear that legislation which lacked a qualification of this kind would offend against the Constitution. Ackermann J observed:

> "To attempt to justify any period of penal incarceration let alone imprisonment for life ..., without inquiring into the proportionality between the offence and the period of imprisonment, is to ignore, if not to deny, that which lies at the very heart of human dignity. Human beings are not commodies to which a price can be attached; they are creatures of infinite worth; they ought to be treated as ends in themselves, never merely as means to an end. Where the length of a sentence, which has been imposed because of its general deterrent effect on others, bears no relation to the gravity of the offence.... the offender is being used essentially as a means to another end and the offender's dignity assaulted."[68]

It is interesting to note that in *Kobedi v The State,*[69] Tebbutt JP, when distinguishing the Privy Council decision of *Reyes v The Queen,*[70] observed that the legislation in Belize prescribed a mandatory sentence of life imprisonment for Class B murders in contrast to section 203(2) of the Botswana Penal Code, which enabled Botswana courts to "impose any appropriate punishment". One should not read too much into this *obiter*

---

[67] 2001 (3) SA 382 (CC).

[68] Para. 38 of Ackermann J's judgment. Ackerman J's analysis of the interrelationship between the norms of "cruel, inhuman or degrading" treatment and human dignity (*id.,* para. 35) are worth recording:

> "In the phrase 'cruel, inhuman or degrading' [in section 12(1)(e)] the three adjectival concepts are employed disjunctively and it follows that a limitation of the right occurs if a punishment has any one of these three characteristics. This imports notions of human dignity .... The human dignity of all persons is independently recognized as both an attribute and a right in section 10 of the Constitution, which proclaims that '[e]veryone has inherent dignity and the right to have their dignity respected and protected.' It is also one of the foundational values of the Constitution [citing sections 1(a) and 74(1) and Chaskalson, "Human Dignity as a Foundational Value of Our Constitutional Order", 16 S.A.J. of Human Rts 193 (2000)] and is woven, in a variety of other ways, into the fabric of our Constitution [citing sections 7(1), 36(1), 37(5)(c) and 39(1)(a) as examples]. While it is not easy to distinguish between the three concepts of 'cruel', 'inhuman' and 'degrading', the impairment of human dignity, in some form and to some degree, must be involved in all three. One should not lose sight of the fact that the right relates, at least in part, to freedom."

[69] *Supra.*

[70] *Supra.*

observation but it certainly is consistent with the notion that constitutional values are better protected by a non-mandatory sentence of life imprisonment.

7 Corporal Punishment

Dignity has played an important role internationally in the judicial determination of the constitutionality of laws permitting corporal punishment, whether in prisons, reformatories, schools or home environments. The international human rights norms are in a state of radical transition. The Committee on the Rights of the Child's General Comment No. 8[71] opposes corporal punishment of any type in any context, public or domestic.

In *S. v Williams*[72] the Constitutional Court of South African struck down as unconstitutional the corporal punishment of juveniles. Langa J (with whom the other ten judges of the Court concurred) stated:

> "Whether one speaks of 'cruel and unusual punishment' as in the Eighth Amendment of the United States Constitution and in article 12 of the Canadian Charter, or 'inhuman or degrading punishment' as in the European Covention and the Constitution of Zimbabwe, or 'cruel, inhuman or degrading punishment' as in the Universal Declaration of Human Rights, the ICCPR and the Constitution of Namibia, the common thread running through the assessment of each phrase is the identification and acknowledgement of society's concept of decency and human dignity....
>
> The enactment of the Constitution has created a framework within which significant changes can be brought about in the criminal justice system. The rights entrenched in Chapter 3 are available to 'every person'; that includes children and adults, women and men, prisoners and detainees. The Constitution clearly places a very high premium on human dignity and the protection against punishments that are cruel, inhuman or degrading; very stringent requirements would have to be met by the State before these rights can be limited.
>
> In addressing itself specifically to punishment, the Constitution ensures that the sentencing of offenders must conform to standards of decency

[71] Committee on the Rights of the Child, General Comment No. 8 (2006), *The right of the child to protection from corporal punishment and other cruel or degrading forms of punishment.*
[72] 1995 (3) S.A. 632.

> recognised throughout the civilised word. Thus it sets a norm; measures that assail the dignity and self esteem of an individual will need to be justified; there is no place for brutal and dehumanising treatment and punishment. The Constitution has allocated to the State and its organs a role as the protectors and guarantors of those rights to ensure that they are available to all. In the process, it sets the State up as a model for society as it endeavours to move away from a violent past. It is therefore reasonable to expect that the State must be foremost in upholding those values which are the guiding light of civilised societies. Respect for human dignity is one such value; acknowledging it includes an acceptance by society that … even the vilest criminal remains a human being possessed of common human dignity."[73]

It is worth noting that in *State v Petrus,*[74] the Botswana Court of Appeal was not invited to hold unconstitutional the provisions of the legislation prior to Botswana's attaining independence, in view of section 7(2) of the Constitution. The Court's disapproval of corporal punishment was plain. Moreover, there was a willingness to adopt a narrow interpretation of section 7(2) which opens the door to further judicial creativity.

Aguda, J.A. observed:

> "In my view the phrase 'any description of punishment' must bear its ordinary meaning. I hold that it will be referable to a species or kind of punishment, not to the details of such punishment. This approach appears to me the only reasonable approach possible if the Court was not to open a flood gate to variations of punishments which the makers of the Constitution had never had in mind nor could have contemplated. To drive home the point I am trying to make, I shall give only two examples. 'Capital punishment' was lawful in the country as at 29th September 1966. Even if one holds that capital punishmennt is saved by the sub-section, but by no stretch of the imagination can anyone hold that the killing by instalments of a person convicted of an offence for which that description of punishment was available is saved by the sub-section. 'Capital punishment' can be carried out by starvation, by slow poisoning, by guillotine, by progressive cutting off the parts of the body, by decapitation and so on. But no one, I am sure, can reasonably argue that these methods of effecting capital punishment are saved by the sub-section (2). Again,

[73] Paras 35, 76–77, citing *Furman v Georgia* 408 U.S. 238, at 273 (*per* Brennan J., 1972).

[74] [1985] L.R.C. (Const.) 699.

'corporal punishment' was lawful in the country as at 29th September 1966. It cannot be argued, I hope, that, flowing from this, any form of whipping whatsoever and whereever, is permitted by the sub-section. In my view all that is permitted is the generic term 'corporal punishment'. Any Act which is passed in purported exercise of the permissive provision of that sub-section must, in the final analysis, be subjected to the over-riding provision of sub-section (1)."[75]

8 Dignity and Sexual Orientation

Let us turn to the sensitive question of the relevance of dignity to the constitutional analysis of issues relating to sexual orientation. This is an area of intense international debate.[76] In *Kanane v The State*[77] considerable emphasis was laid by the Court of Appeal on cultural attitudes to the subject of homosexuality in Botswana.[78] The question arises as to whether the *Kanane*[79] decision could conceivably have been decided differently if greater emphasis had been placed on the relevance of the issue of dignity.

South African jurisprudence on the question is saturated with a concern for dignity, ranging well beyond the contexts of equality, the death penalty and corporal punishment. In *National Coalition for Gay and Lesbian Equality v Minister of Justice*[80] where the Constitutional Court struck down

---

[75] *ibid., at* 730–731.

[76] See Murray and Viljoen, 'Towards Non-Discrimination on the Basis of Sexual Orientation: The Normative Basis and Procedural Possibilities before the African Commission on Human and Peoples' Rights and the African Union', 29 Human Rts Q. 86 (2007), Sunit Baudh, *Human Rights and the Criminalisation of Consensual Same-Sex Sexual Acts in the Commonwealth, South and Southeast Asia (*South and Southeast Asia Resource Centre on Sexuality Working Paper 1 May 2008), International Commission of Jurists, *Sexual Orientation and Gender Identity in Human Rights Law: References to Jurisprudence and Doctrine of the United Nations Human Rights Systems* (3rd updated ed., 2007).

[77] *Kanane v The State* [2003] (2) BLR 67, analysed by Bojosi, 'An Opportunity Missed for Gay Rights in Botswana: *Utjiwak Kanane v The State*', 20 S. Afr. J. on H. Rts 466 (2004), Chilisa, 'Two Steps Back for Human Rights: A Critique the *Kanane* Case', 1 Botswana Rev. of Ethics, L. & HIV/AIDS 45 (2007), Odunsi, 'A Need to Re-Examine the Voice of the People? Reflections on the Interplay of Homophobia and the HIV/AIDS Pandemic in Botswana', *id.* 33, Quansah, 'Same-Sex Relationships in Botswana: Current Perspectives and Future Prospects', 4 Afr. H. Rts. L.J. 201 (2004).

[78] See BONELA, "The Violations of the Rights of Lesbian, Gay, Bisexual and Transgender Persons in Botswana: A Shadow Report".

[79] *Kanane v The State* [2003] (2) BLR 67.

[80] 1999 (1) S.A. 6 (C.C., 1998).

legislation criminalising consensual homosexual conduct, dignity was the central concept that guided the Court. Ackermann J noted that the right to dignity was 'a cornerstone' of the South African Constitution. The symbolic effect of the criminal prohibition was[81]:

> "to state that in the eyes of our legal system all gay men are criminals. The stigma thus attached to a significant proportion of our population is manifest. But the harm imposed by the criminal law is far more than symbolic. As a result of the criminal offence, gay men are at risk of arrest, prosecution and conviction of the offence of sodomy simply because they seek to engage in sexual conduct which is part of their experience of being human. Just as apartheid legislation rendered the lives of couples of different racial groups perpetually at risk, the sodomy offence builds insecurity and vulnerability into the daily lives of gay men. There can be no doubt that the existence of a law which punishes a form of sexual expression for gay men degrades and devalues gay men in our broader society. As such it is a palpable invasion of their dignity and a breach of section 10 of the Constitution."[82]

Sachs J commented:

> "In the case of gays, history and experience teach us that the scarring comes not from poverty or powerlessness, but from invisibility. It is the tainting of desire, it is the attribution of perversity and shame to spontaneous bodily affection, it is the prohibition of the expression of love, it is the denial of full moral citizenship in society because you are what you are, that impinges on the dignity and self-worth of a group.... At the heart of equality jurisprudence is the rescuing of people from a caste-like status and putting an end to their being treated as lesser human beings because they belong to a particular group. The indignity and subordinate status may flow from institutionally imposed exclusion from the mainstream of society or else from powerlessness within the mainstream; they may also be derived from the location of difference as a problematic form of deviance in the disadvantaged group itself, as happens in the case of the disabled. In the case of gays it comes from compulsion to deny a closely held personal characteristic. To penalise people for being what they are is profoundly disrespectful of the human personality and violatory of equality.

[81] Para. 28.
[82] *ibid.*

This aspect would not be well captured, if at all, by the Centre's approach, which falls to be rejected."[83]

Of course the South African Constitution is quite different from that of Botswana, not only in its express provisions relating to dignity but also, importantly, in its express prohibition on discrimination on the ground of sexual orientation. No simple transposition of the South African jurisprudence is therefore possible. A more subtle analysis must be made. This would involve a critique of the Court of Appeal's analysis in *Kanane* on the basis, first, that it lays no emphasis on concern for dignity and secondly that it fails to examine the possiblity of a constitutional prohibition on discrimination on the basis of sexual orientation as at least capable of being envisaged under the approach adopted in *Dow*.[84]

9 Concluding observations

My purpose of this paper is to provoke debate on the relevance of dignity to the constitutional jurisprudence of Botswana. The outcome of such a debate is hard to assess. Perhaps no discernible change in judicial outlook will follow from it. Yet the experience internationally is so consistently in the direction of an enhanced judicial receptivity to the concept that it seems reasonable to anticipate at least modest change in Botswana in forthcoming years.

---

[83] *ibid., paras* 127, 129.

[84] See Chilisa, *op. cit.,* at 49–51.

Access To Justice — Through Legal Aid — Is a Human Right: Why and How Botswana Must Protect This Right

Louise W. McKinney*

1 Introduction

This paper provides background for why Botswana must have a legal aid system. Its primary purpose is to provide the legal basis for establishing a system of legal aid that opens the doors to the justice system for people who have seen only closed doors or who have not even seen any doors because they are too poor or too distant or too disempowered to enter the halls of justice. Many have truthfully said that legal professionals, particularly lawyers, hold the keys to the courts. Lawyers hold a special place in the entire systems of the rule of law. But, as important as lawyers are, just providing lawyers is not enough. In order to provide access to justice, legal aid or legal assistance must include much more. This paper will also describe some of that "much more" that Batswana[1] need to participate in the benefits of their human rights and the rule of law.

2 The Results of Lack of Legal Assistance Are Dire

In Africa, there is much information to describe what happens when a criminally accused poor person does not receive legal assistance. "The prisons are filled with fine defaulters and people too poor to pay the surety for their next appearance in order to be allowed home on bail. The prisons are full – not of dangerous people (though there are some), but of poor people, the majority of whom have not committed the types of offenses that require their removal from society."[2]

* BA (Heidelberg), JD (Case Western Reserve), Professor of Law, Case Western Reserve School of Law, fulbright Scholar, Department of Law, University of Botswana.

[1] "*Motswana*" is "a person from Botswana"; the term "*Batswana*" means more than one *Motswana*.

[2] Penal Reform International & Bluhm Legal Clinic, Northwestern University School of Law, "Access to Justice in Africa and Beyond: Making the Rule of Law a Reality," NITA (2007) [hereafter, "NITA"], p. 8; for instance, the percentage of remand prisoners in comparison with convicted prisoners in some countries was: 70 percent Benin (2003); 64.7 percent Mali (2003); 60 percent Angola (2003) 60 percent Uganda (2004); 80 percent Cameroon (2004); 22 percent Malawi (2004); 40 percent Kenya (2003); 97 percent Liberia (2006); 50 percent Tanzania (2003).

In Botswana, the majority of people in prison are there by order of customary courts.[3] Botswana prisons are designed for a maximum of 3,994 but hold 6,074.[4] Magistrates in Botswana say that probably 50% of convicted persons would be acquitted if they had legal assistance; they are there because they are poor.[5] In Botswana, there is one police officer for every 266 members of the population; there is one private attorney for every 8,421 members of the population.[6]

No attorneys are permitted in Botswana's Customary Courts, where a high percentage of criminal cases are heard.[7] In common law courts, there is no right to appointed defence counsel, except in capital cases. Even in capital cases, the experience of the lawyer is not required to be commensurate with the alleged crime and potential penalty.[8]

In non-penal cases, poor people's lack of access to the justice/legal systems through legal assistance is even more staggering throughout the world. In the state of Wisconsin in the USA, 11 judges filed an amicus curiae brief, to support the need for appointed counsel for civil litigants, saying that "*pro se*[9] litigants represent a significant and growing burden on a judicial system which is not well-equipped to deal with them."[10] They wrote that: "*Pro se* litigants are a significant and growing part of … trial courts' caseloads." "Unsophisticated and inexperienced *pro se* litigants complicate the process and burden the entire system." "*Pro se* litigants complicate not only their own cases but can increase the burden and transaction costs of other parties, represented or not." They gave an example of a man who tried, *pro se*, for 12 years to remove a maintenance order because he was indisputably not the father. Which of these assertions are inaccurate for Botswana?

---

[3] Report of Chief Magistrate Lot Moroka, Access to Justice Workshop, 30 April 2008, Gaborone, Botswana. The workshop, 29–30 April 2008, was sponsored by the UNDP/Government of Botswana Governance Programme, Access to Justice/Legal Aid Project and was co-ordinated by the Attorney General's Chambers, Law Society of Botswana and University of Botswana Law Department.

[4] U.S. Department of State, Country Reports on Human Rights Practices – 2007 (released March 11, 2008) http://www/state/gpve/g/drl/rls/hrrpt/2007/100467.htm (2 of 14)> last visited 5/30/2008.

[5] Author's conversations with several magistrates in Gaborone, Botswana (2008).

[6] NITA, p. 12, Table 1.

[7] Customary Courts Act, CAP 04:05, Sec. 32.

[8] NITA, p. 12–13, Tables 2 and 3.

[9] "*Pro se*" litigants are parties in a court action who have no legal representation and are therefore representing themselves "for themselves".

[10] Amicus Brief, *Kelly v Warpinski*, Wisconsin Supreme Court, reproduced in "Judges' Views of *Pro Se* Litigants' Effect on Courts," 40 Clearinghouse Review (No. 3–4, July-August 2006), pp. 228–229.

Justice Dunstan Mlambo described the challenges of the unrepresented litigant: "...the complexity of the case; the lack of knowledge of the law and relevant procedures especially in civil matters; inexperience in presenting the relevant evidence especially relating to the leading and cross examination of witnesses; inequality of arms."[11]

In addition, in Botswana court fees bar poor people from even entering the courts. The courts will waive fees only if the potential litigants surmount hurdles that require legal acumen not available to the common poor litigant. Almost never is free legal representation available for court, despite the high incidence of poverty in the country.[12] Nobody is ever required to provide free legal assistance for poor people.

Alternative dispute resolution, which may be less costly, is available only in scattered areas of the law and practice, including some customary dispute resolution procedures, employment disputes in under the Employment Act and some commercial disputes. The University of Botswana Legal Clinic, which provides only legal advice and assistance and does not go to court with people except in the Industrial Court,[13] is overwhelmed with demand for legal assistance. The demands on the Legal Clinic are great even though it assists only people whose monthly income is no more than 500 pula[14] and the Legal Clinic is located only in the capital city, Gaborone, on the University of Botswana campus.

Let us remind ourselves as to the crucial importance of legal aid. The Dakar Declaration on the Right to a Fair Trial in Africa states the reality in stark and simple terms:

> "Access to justice is a paramount element of the right to a fair trial. Most accused and aggrieved persons are unable to afford legal services due to the high cost of court and professional fees. It is the duty of governments to provide legal assistance to indigent persons in order to make the right to a fair trial more effective."[15]

---

[11] Access to Justice Workshop, 29–30 April 2008, presentation by Justice Dunstan Mlambo, Justice of the Supreme Court of South Africa and Chairperson of the Legal Aid Board of South Africa.

[12] In 1993/94 47 percent of people in Botswana had incomes below the poverty line. Vision 2016 Section 3.c.(i)

[13] With few exceptions, non-lawyers are not permitted to appear to represent people in common law courts in Botswana; one exception is in the Industrial Court.

[14] A Botswana Pula is worth about US$.16 or Euro.09.

[15] Dakar Declaration and Recommendations on the Right to a Fair Trial in Africa, Section 9 (Legal Aid), adopted at the African Commission on Human and Peoples' Rights meeting at its 26th Ordinary Session, in Kigali, Rwanda, 1–15 November 1999.

In criminal cases, without fully engaged, competent legal representation, there is an overwhelming risk of loss of liberty (through a sentence or for inability to pay fines or bail) or life (through capital punishment) or bodily integrity (through corporal punishment). In non-penal cases, the risks to relationships (e.g., parental rights, marriage/divorce) and of loss of property (e.g., through contracts, succession/estates) and of loss of employment are equally great and potentially more devastating than some of the punishments meted out in criminal procedures. As the President of Botswana recognised, "I am sure you will agree that no one should be subjected to the indignity of losing, for example, their property or reputation simply because they are ignorant of the law, or they cannot afford to pay a lawyer to enforce their right."[16]

3 Access to Justice – Through Legal Aid – Is a Human Right Under International Law

3.1 "Access to Justice" Defined

"Justice" is a term that is so broad that it can mean many things to many people. Or it can mean almost nothing. Justice has been defined as "a moral ideal that the law seeks to uphold in the protection of rights and punishment of wrongs. Justice is not synonymous with law – it is possible for a law to be called unjust."[17]

For the purposes of this paper, which deals with access to justice through legal aid, "justice" really means "justice systems" and is a short-hand way of referring to "the systems that provide a range of legal and semi-legal solutions to disputes or to breaches of the public safety or peace." Although we know that "law" and "justice" are not automatically the same and may be opposites,

---

[16] Access to Justice Workshop, 29–30 April 2008, Opening by His Excellency Lieutenant General Seretse Khama Ian Khama, President of Botswana, printed in Mmegi newspaper, 30 April 2008, p. 22–23. See also the observations of Justice Dunstan Mlambo at the same Workshop:

> "Legal representation enables people to exercise their right to access to justice in a meaningful way. Legal representation is a basic human right to which all are entitled. Most accused persons are not able to exercise their right without legal assistance. Where accused are indigent and substantial injustice would otherwise result, provision of state funded legal aid is of critical importance in enabling accused to adequately enforce these rights."

[17] Alice Mogwe, Ditshwanelo (The Botswana Centre for Human Rights), Proceedings of Workshop on Alternatives to the Pro Deo System 'From Arrangement to System', 18 November 2004, Gaborone, Botswana.

the paper will go no further in defining "justice" than to define it as "justice or legal systems".

"Access to justice" means "access to justice/legal systems". It means opening up the entire justice systems equally to all those who want to use them and to all those who are brought to them involuntarily. The forums within which justice happens in Botswana include common or general law courts (e.g., High Courts, Magistrate Courts, Industrial Court), Special courts (e.g., military tribunals), customary courts, administrative tribunals (e.g., land boards) and alternative dispute resolution sites (e.g., Division of Labour mediation, which, if successful, avoids proceeding to Industrial Court).

These forums follow procedures and apply law in various ways. If individuals do not know the law, they will not try to use the justice systems and will not have access to them for that reason. If individuals are not skillful in the procedures, they will not be able to obtain the remedy that is available and will not have access to the justice systems for that reason. Access to justice is not the only way to ensure justice and implementation of the rule of law; but without access to justice, there can be no implementation of the rule of law.

"Legal aid" is another term that may have many meanings to many people. In this paper "legal aid" includes a wide range of activities that provide legal information, education, skills, advice, assistance, representation, generally at no cost to the individual who receives the benefit. It is not limited to legal representation in a particular court proceeding. "Legal aid" is a substantial part of the full range of activities that are necessary to ensure equal access to the legal systems, regardless of the poverty or disadvantage of the recipient of the legal aid services.

4 International Human Rights Law Requires Access to Justice through Legal Assistance

4.1 The Universal Declaration of Human Rights

The Universal Declaration of Human Rights, 1948,[18] has set out basic human rights that are recognised by all members of the United Nations. Although the UDHR does not specifically mention a right to counsel, let alone a right to appointed counsel, it describes human rights, many of which would not be

[18] Adopted and proclaimed by the United Nations General Assembly resolution 217 A (III) of 10 December 1948.

enforced without access to a country's justice systems, with the assistance of legal aid. Human rights most pertinent for this paper include:

Article 2. Everyone is entitled to all the rights and freedoms set forth in this Declaration, without distinction of any kind, such as race, colour, sex, language, religion, political or other opinion, national or social origin, *property*, birth or other status.....[19]

Article 3. Everyone has the right to life, liberty and security of person.

Article 7. All are equal before the law and are entitled without any discrimination to equal protection of the law.....

Article 8. Everyone has the right to an effective remedy by the competent national tribunals for acts violating the fundamental rights granted him by the constitution or by law.

Article 9. No one shall be subjected to arbitrary arrest, detention or exile.

Article 10. Everyone is entitled in full equality to a fair and public hearing by an independent and impartial tribunal, in the determination of his rights and obligations and of any criminal charge against him.

Article 11(1). Everyone charged with a penal offence has the right to be presumed innocent until proved guilty according to law in a pubic trial at which he has had all the guarantees necessary for his defence.

Article 12. No one shall be subjected to arbitrary interference with his privacy, family, home or correspondence, nor to attacks upon his honour and reputation. Everyone has the right to the protection of the law against such interference or attacks.

Article 16. The family is the natural and fundamental group unit of society and is entitled to protection by society and the State.

Article 17(1). Everyone has the right to own property alone as well as in association with others. **(2)** No one shall be arbitrarily deprived of his property.

[19] Emphasis added.

4.2 The International Covenant on Civil and Political Rights

The International Covenant on Civil and Political Rights (ICCPR), 1966,[20] is more specific than the UDHR. It amplifies some of the human rights in the UDHR and sets up mechanisms for monitoring compliance with its standards. The ICCPR specifically requires appointment of counsel for indigent criminal defendants "where the interests of justice so require". The ICCPR is clear that any criminally accused person has the right to counsel of his or her choice.

Article 14(1) All persons shall be equal before the courts and tribunals....

(3) In the determination of any criminal charge against him, everyone shall be entitled to the following minimum guarantees, in full equality:

(b) To have adequate time and facilities for the preparation of his defence and *to communicate with counsel of his own choosing*;....

(d) To be tried in his presence and to defend himself or *through legal assistance of his own choosing*; to be informed, if he does not have legal assistance, of this right; and to *have legal assistance assigned to him, in any case where the interests of justice so require, and without payment by him in any such case if he does not have sufficient means to pay for it*;....[21]

The ICCPR is also explicit in imposing on States Parties certain obligations in the context of court proceedings in the justice system. Article 23(4) requires States Parties to "take appropriate steps to ensure equality of rights and responsibilities of spouses as to marriage, during marriage and at its dissolution...."

4.3 Additional United Nations Mandates

The United Nations has amplified on some of the rights of criminal defendants to counsel. In the UN Standard Minimum Rules for the Treatment of Prisoners, 1957,[22] Article 93 states:

---

20 Adopted and opened for signature, ratification and accession by General Assembly resolution 2200A (XXI) of 16 December 1966 entry into force 23 March 1976, in accordance with Article 49; ratified by Botswana 8 December 2000.

21 Emphasis added.

22 Adopted by the First United Nations Congress on the Prevention of Crime and the Treatment of Offenders, held at Geneva in 1955, and approved by the Economic and Social Council by its resolutions 663 C (XIV) of 31 July 1957 and 2076 (LXII) of 13 May 1977.

> "For the purposes of his defence, an untried prisoner shall be allowed to apply for free legal aid where such aid is available, and to receive visits from his legal adviser with a view to his defence and to prepare and hand to him confidential instructions. For these purposes, he shall if he so desires be supplied with writing materials. Interviews between the prisoner and his legal adviser may be within sight but not within the hearing of a police or institution official."

The UN Basic Principles on the Role of Lawyers, 1990,[23] in its preamble describes the importance of legal services:

> "[A]dequate protection of the human rights and fundamental freedoms to which all persons are entitled, be they economic, social and cultural, or civil and political, requires that all persons have effective access to legal services provided by an independent legal profession,…."

The Basic Principles include a section on "Access to lawyers and legal services":

1. All persons are entitled to call upon the assistance of a lawyer of their choice to protect and establish their rights and to defend them in all stages of criminal proceedings.
2. Governments shall ensure that efficient procedures and responsive mechanisms for effective and equal access to lawyers are provided for all persons within their territory and subject to their jurisdiction, without distinction of any kind, such as discrimination based on … property….
3. Governments shall ensure the provision of sufficient funding and other resources for legal services to the poor and, as necessary, to other disadvantaged persons.
4. Governments and professional associations of lawyers shall promote programmes to inform the public about their rights and duties under the law and the important role of lawyers in protecting their fundamental freedoms. Special attention should be given to assisting the poor and other disadvantaged persons so as to enable them to assert their rights and where necessary call upon the assistance of lawyers.

The Basic Principles also contain "Special safeguards in criminal justice matters." These include safeguards listed in the ICCPR plus the following two sections:

---

[23] Adopted by the Eighth United Nations Congress on the Prevention of Crime and the Treatment of Offenders, Havana, Cuba, 27 August to 7 September 1990.

7. Governments shall further ensure that all persons arrested or detained, with or without criminal charge, shall have prompt access to a lawyer, and in any case not later than forty-eight hours from the time of arrest or detention.
8. All arrested, detained or imprisoned persons shall be provided with adequate opportunities, time, and facilities to be visited by and to communicate and consult with a lawyer, without delay, interception, or censorship and in full confidentiality.

4.4 The African Charter for Human and Peoples' Rights

The African Charter for Human and Peoples' Rights, 1981/1986,[24] does not require appointment of a lawyer where a criminally accused person is unable to afford one, although it does require, in Article 7,1(c) "the right to defence, including the right to be defended by counsel of his choice." Article 3 specifically requires "equal[ity] before the law" and "equal protection of the law." Article 2 states that "every individual shall be entitled to the enjoyment of the rights and freedoms … in the present Charter without distinction of any kind such as … fortune…." According to the African Charter, as in other international standards and mandates, there shall be no discrimination according to fortune or degree of property and all shall be treated equally before the law and enjoy the equal protection of the law.

The African Commission on Human and Peoples' Rights (ACHPR), which was established by the African Charter, is more explicit in mandating that governments must provide legal assistance for poor people. As has been noted, the Dakar Declaration states that "[i]t is the duty of governments to provide legal assistance to indigent persons in order to make the right to a fair trial more effective."[25]

States parties to the African Charter should:

- "Urgently examine ways in which legal assistance could be extended to indigent accused person, including through adequately funded public defender and legal aid schemes;
- In collaboration with Bar Associations and NGOs, enable innovative and additional legal assistance programs to be established including

[24] Also called the "Banjul Charter", adopted by the OAU in Nairobi, Kenya, 27 June 1981, entered into force 21 October 1986.

[25] Dakar Declaration and Recommendations on the Right to a Fair Trial in Africa, Section 9 (Legal Aid), fn 15, *supra*.

> allowing paralegals to provide legal assistance to indigent suspects at the pre-trial stage and pro-bono representation for accused in criminal proceedings…."[26]

In 2001 the ACHPR adopted ACHPR Principles and Guidelines on the Right to a Fair Trial and Legal Assistance in Africa, that included the following "Legal Aid and Legal Assistance" standards:

1. The accused or a party to a civil case has a right to have legal assistance assigned to him or her in any case where the interest of justice so requires, and without payment by the accused or party to a civil case if he or she does not have sufficient means to pay for it.
2. The interests of justice should be determined by considering:
    a. In criminal matters:
        i. The seriousness of the offence;
        ii. The severity of the sentence.
    b. In civil cases:
        i. The complexity of the case and the ability of the party to adequately represent himself or herself;
        ii. The rights that are affected;
        iii. The likely impact of the outcome of the case on the wider community.
3. The interests of justice always require legal assistance for an accused in any capital case,….
4. An accused person or a party to a civil case has the right to an effective defence or representation and has a right to choose his or her own legal representative at all stages of the case. They may contest the choice of his or her court-appointed lawyer. [27]
5. The ACHPR has mandated the provision of legal assistance to parties in criminal and civil cases. Its reason is because "[l]egal representation is regarded as the best means of legal defence against infringements of human rights and fundamental freedoms."[28]

---

[26] *ibid.*, at Recommendations.

[27] ACHPR Principles and Guidelines on the Right to a Fair Trial and Legal Assistance in Africa, 2001, Section H.

[28] ACHPR Principles and Guidelines on the Right to a Fair Trial and Legal Assistance in Africa, 2001, Section N2(a).

5 Implications for Botswana

The implications for Botswana are clear: Botswana is required to establish a legal aid system for poor litigants under international law. The standards above are intended to be examples but are not intended to be exhaustive. As examples, they illustrate the extent of the international mandate for legal aid. Botswana is a member of the African Union and the United Nations. It has ratified the ICCPR. It is therefore obligated to comply with the international mandates which it has willingly accepted.

5.1 The Absence of a Legal Aid System in Botswana Government Policy Strongly Supports a Legal Aid System

"A national legal aid system should be established to support those in need of legal counseling and court representation services."[29] This is a strategy to accomplish the goal or vision of "an open, democratic and accountable society" in "Vision 2016", Botswana's 20-year blueprint, leading up to the 50th anniversary of independence. The authors and thinkers who developed Vision 2016 wisely recognised the relationship between democracy and accountability and a national legal aid system to support those in need of legal services.

"What can be done to ensure that a legal aid system is designed that is simple, affordable and sustainable and available to all, especially the less privileged?" asked His Excellency Lieutenant General Seretse Khama Ian Khama, when he opened the Access to Justice Workshop in April 2008.[30] Twelve years after Vision 2016 described a strategy of establishing a national legal aid system, the President of Botswana is asking what can be done to establish it, with the criteria that he described: simple, affordable, sustainable, available.

Again, no one in government is questioning the need. The government of Botswana has expressed a commitment to government's providing legal aid in Botswana, consistent with international mandates.

5.2 The Botswana Constitution and Customary Courts Act Prevent a Comprehensive Legal Aid System

The Constitution of Botswana includes a right to legal representation, only in criminal proceedings and only at one's own expense, in Section 10(2)(d).

[29] Vision 2016, Section 5e(v).

[30] Mmegi newspaper, 30 April 2008, p. 22–23.

"Every person who is charged with a criminal offence – shall be permitted to defend himself before the court in person or, at his own expense, by a legal representative of his own choice." This mandate falls short of the international standards above by failing to mandate legal representation at no cost to a poor litigant under any circumstances, even where the interests of justice demand it. Under the Constitution, the only time that an accused person is entitled to legal representation is when the accused pays for the attorney.

But even this limited constitutional right to legal representation is less than it seems. The Constitution sets out a range of rights of criminally accused people in Section 10, "Provisions to secure protection of law," including the right to a legal representative. Then a claw back provision later in the same section says that this right does not apply in customary law criminal proceedings, if legal representation is prohibited in any law dealing with customary court proceedings.[31] The Customary Courts Act specifically states: "Notwithstanding anything contained in any other law, no advocate or attorney shall have a right of audience – (a) in any customary court…."[32]

The prohibition of legal representation in criminal proceedings in the Customary Courts flies in the face of international human rights standards. International law does not only require that criminally accused people have *permission* to have access to legal representation in the courts. In most instances – where justice demands – international law *requires appointment* of counsel and *access to legal assistance* at all important stages of the criminal proceedings. Botswana fails to have any systems that require appointment of counsel. In fact, Botswana actually actively prohibits legal representation in the customary courts, where a large proportion of the criminal cases are heard.[33]

---

[31] Constitution, Section 10(12)(b) says: "Nothing contained in or done under the authority of any law shall be held to be inconsistent with or in contravention of – subsection (2)(d) … of this section to the extent that the law in question prohibits legal representation before a subordinate court in proceedings for an offence under customary law (being proceedings against any person who, under that law, is subject to that law)…."

[32] Customary Courts Act, Chapter 04:05, Section 32. In a case where a person is accused of an offence, such as stock theft, which does not fall to be determined by customary law, the Customary Court is obliged by constitutional considerations relating to the right to legal representation to accede to an application for transfer of the case, for hearing and determination by a Magistrate's Court. In *S. v Ntwayame* [2008] BWCA 37 (1 January 2008), the Botswana Court of Appeal held that the Customary Court of Appeal had been wrong not to have granted an appeal on this ground. The decision is of considerable importance in mitigating some of the harshness of the exclusion of entitlement to legal representation in Customary Courts.

[33] The author has been unable to locate statistics on the number of cases in the customary courts and the common law courts in Botswana. This observation is based on conversations with knowledgeable people, based on their estimates.

5.3 Botswana Law and Practice Do Not Provide a Legal Aid System

Although the Constitution of Botswana does not mandate appointed counsel at no cost to an indigent litigant and prohibits counsel in customary courts, the practice is for the High Court to occasionally appoint defence counsel at no cost to indigent defendants in criminal proceedings, as *pro deo* counsel.[34] The practice is widely recognised as requiring counsel only in capital offences.[35]

Even less frequently the High Court appoints counsel at no cost to indigent litigants in civil proceedings, as *pro bono* counsel. The process of deciding whose case is "worthy" of appointed counsel or who is "most in need" of appointed counsel is not close to a "system" and is haphazard, at best.[36] There is no oversight of counsel whom the Registrar of the High Court appoints, so there are no guarantees of competent and professional counsel, particularly because the payment to the attorneys is far less than what they would receive from paying clients.

There are no laws that establish a system of legal assistance for disadvantaged individuals or groups. There are organisations that do provide various degrees of legal assistance, generally in the form of legal education and advice, but occasionally legal representation in court.

"Several organisations such as The Botswana Center for Human Rights (DITSHWANELO); Botswana Law Society; and The Botswana Network on Ethics, Law and HIV/AIDS provided free legal services but had limited capacity. The University of Botswana Legal Assistance Center provided free legal services for some civil, but not criminal, matters."[37]

Other organisations that do provide or have recently provided limited legal assistance include *Emang Basadi* ("Stand Up Women") and Kagisano Women's Shelter Project, both related to women's rights.

---

[34] See Ditshwanelo (The Botswana Centre for Human Rights), Proceedings of Workshop on Alternatives to the Pro Deo System 'From Arrangement to System', 18 November 2004, Gaborone, Botswana.

[35] U.S. Department of State, Country Reports on Human Rights Practices – 2007 (released March 11, 2008) http://www/state/gpve/g/drl/rls/hrrpt/2007/100467.htm> (3 of 14), last visited 5/30/2008 1:30:54 am.

[36] See Ditshwanelo (The Botswana Centre for Human Rights), Proceedings of Workshop on Alternatives to the Pro Deo System 'From Arrangement to System', 18 November 2004, Gaborone, Botswana.

[37] U.S. Department of State, Country Reports on Human Rights Practices – 2007 (released March 11, 2008) http://www/state/gpve/g/drl/rls/hrrpt/2007/100467.htm> (4 of 14), last visited 5/30/2008 1:30:54 am.

Sadly, considering the great need and the expressed government intent, there is no sustainable, government-funded system of legal assistance in Botswana that meets international human rights standards for access to justice. In fact, there is no *system* of legal assistance – *full stop*.

6 The Way Forward: How Botswana Must Provide Legal Aid

6.1 Why Botswana Must Provide a Legal Aid System: It's the Right(s) Thing to Do

Access to justice through legal aid is a human right that the United Nations and the African Union have defined. Botswana, as a member of the United Nations and the African Union, is obligated to comply with the standards of both bodies.

Legal assistance is so important because without it the other human rights cannot be protected and achieved. Without access to justice through legal assistance, there is no equality before the law; there is no fair trial; there is no protection of the rule of law. That is a given. But a far wider range of rights – to life itself, liberty and security of person, maintenance of family and other relationships, protection of property, free speech and assembly and religion – all are in jeopardy without access to justice. One of the greatest barriers to access to justice is lack of legal assistance, purely because of lack of resources to obtain it.

Why should Botswana provide a legal aid system? Because it is the right thing to do, according to human rights law and according to the vision of the government – Vision 2016 and President Khama's challenges of democracy, development, discipline and *dignity* – and according to Botswana's standards of *botho* – humaneness.

6.2 Specifically, Botswana Must Change Its Law to Allow Legal Representation in All Court Proceedings

A. Botswana's Laws Prohibiting Representation in Customary Courts Are Fatally Flawed

Under human rights standards, particularly where a person's life, liberty or property is in jeopardy or where an individual is involuntarily before the court, the law must permit legal representation by parties. Because Botswana prohibits legal representation in customary courts, it must change its laws. The issue here is not whether Botswana must provide legal representation if a person is unable to afford it. The issue is that the country may not prevent or prohibit a person from having representation under international law.

While there is an argument that rights which require governments to act are always subject to government's ability to act, given its resources and priorities, this argument applies generally to "positive" rights, that is to rights where the government must take some actions that incur costs of monetary and other resources.[38]

> "A positive right is a claim to something – a share to material goods, or some particular good like the attentions of a lawyer or a doctor, or perhaps the claim to a result like health or enlightenment – while a negative right is a right that something not be done to one, that some particular imposition be withheld. Positive rights are inevitably asserted to scarce goods, and consequently scarcity implies a limit to the claims. Negative rights, however … do not appear to have … such inevitable limitations."[39]

Under this argument Botswana's failure, so far, to provide a general system of legal aid for indigent people, supported by government resources, may not be a violation of a positive international right because positive rights are limited and relative, not absolute.

But Botswana's laws *prohibiting* access to counsel, even at the person's own expense, are not related to positive rights. There is no cost to the government to permit access to legal assistance. The cost to the individuals within Botswana's legal systems is extreme. Examples are shown above. International standards are clear that access to legal assistance, particularly for the criminally accused, is required to ensure the most basic human rights, such as the right to a fair trial and equality under the law.

In fact, the Botswana Constitution, read with the Customary Courts Act, violates a "negative" right. Batswana, under international law, may not be prevented from having legal representation. They are entitled, without limitation, to have the government allow them to have legal representation in all court proceedings. Botswana may not impose an unfair trial on people who are brought involuntarily before its courts (including its duly established customary courts) by preventing legal representation in court.

---

[38] Durchslag, Melvyn R., "Constraints on Equal Access to Fundamental Liberties: Another Look at Professor Michelman's Theory of Minimum Protection", 19 Ga L. Rev. 1041, at 1059 (1985).

[39] C. Fried, *Right and Wrong* 110 (1978).

B. The Cure Is to Repeal the Prohibition through Statute

The cure is straightforward: the government should repeal the section of the Customary Courts Act that prohibits representation. As noted above, the Botswana Constitution gives the right of representation by counsel of choice at the party's own expense in criminal proceedings.[40] A provision later in the same Section makes it clear that this right does not apply in customary law criminal proceedings, *if legal representation is prohibited in any law dealing with customary court proceedings*.[41] The Customary Courts Act specifically prohibits an advocate or attorney from "a right of audience … in any customary court."[42] The Constitution's section 10(12)(b) is not self-executing. It requires a law to prohibit legal representation in customary courts. If Section 32 of the Customary Courts Act is repealed, there will be no limit on the right to representation as described in Section 10(2)(d), which says: "Every person who is charged with a criminal offence – shall be permitted to defend himself before the court in person or, at his own expense, by a legal representative of his own choice." It is a simple and elegant cure to a fatal defect in the laws of Botswana.

C. An Alternative Is to Seek Judicial Relief

If there is no change in the law, one could litigate to establish the minimal right to counsel of one's own choice at one's own expense. What tribunal would be appropriate – domestic, African Commission, United Nations' jurisdiction? That is beyond the scope of this paper. But the point is clear that the right to counsel of one's own choice, at one's own expense, is a "negative" right that only requires the government and laws to get out of the way. It would likely be considered favorably by any tribunal that considers the plea.

7 Botswana Can Systematically Provide Legal Assistance in Compliance with Policy and International Standards

This paper will not go into all the ways that legal aid/assistance should and can be provided; but lessons learned from others can help to prevent Botswana from

[40] Constitution, Section 10(2)(d).

[41] Section 10(12)(b) of the Constitution provides:

"Nothing contained in or done under the authority of any law shall be held to be inconsistent with or in contravention of – subsection (2)(d) … of this section to the extent that the law in question prohibits legal representation before a subordinate court in proceedings for an offence under customary law (being proceedings against any person who, under that law, is subject to that law);…."

[42] Customary Courts Act, Chapter 04:05, Section 32.

re-inventing the wheel. Those who do not learn from history are doomed to repeat it. The following three points are well-supported by the experiences of others.

7.1 Define "Legal aid" to Include a Full Range of Legal Assistance and Interventions

It is clear that – in order to provide equality and non-discrimination on the basis of property or fortune before the law and to protect the rights to security of life, liberty and property and freedom of relationships and activities - access to justice through legal aid is essential. That is why "legal aid" is not limited only to representation in court and why it includes a wide range of activities that provide legal information, education, skills, advice, assistance, representation, generally at no cost to the individual who receives the benefit. "Legal aid" is a substantial part of the full range of activities that are necessary to ensure equal access to the legal systems, regardless of the poverty or disadvantage of the recipient of the legal aid services.

A. Legal Aid Must Include a Continuum of Services Provided by a Variety of Personnel

To comply with international standards, the state must devise a continuum of legal aid services that will maximise access to justice, while recognising the very real constraints of resources. The resources involved are not just financial outlays; they include the recognition that there are only about 200 private attorneys admitted to practice in Botswana.[43] As noted earlier, there is just one private attorney for every 8,421 members of the population.

The continuum of services must include community legal education and information, education (in skills and knowledge) within the legal and justice systems and the availability of legal advice and assistance short of full legal representation – in addition to full representation. All should be provided at no cost to the beneficiaries of the services.

The services can be provided by a wide range of personnel, with various degrees of knowledge and skill. If lawyers hold the keys to the courtroom doors, paralegals may hold the keys to the prison (and government) doors.

A specific example of how the use of paralegals and other non-lawyers can provide services that meet the international mandates is the Paralegal Advisory

---

[43] Law Society of Botswana recent figures.

Service Institute (PASI).[44] Through Paralegal Aid Clinics, PASI has reduced the percentage of people who are in prison before trial by about 20 percent, to stabilise the remand population at about 17.5 percent. The Paralegal Advisory Service has been replicated in Benin, Kenya, Uganda and Niger and continues to respond to invitations to develop comparable systems in other states in Africa. The organisation has reduced prison populations (particularly remand detentions), diverted juveniles from the adult systems and ensured access to vital, understandable legal information and assistance from the first encounter with police in Malawi and other countries in Africa.[45]

In Zambia, paralegals are cost-effective for advice and assistance and where the cost of a lawyer's services would outweigh the financial value of the service to the client. Examples include social pensions, worker's compensation benefits and unemployment benefits.[46]

B. Legal aid Services must be Organised to Ensure Independence

The way that legal aid is organised in a country appears to have an impact on its effectiveness in providing the needed assistance. The Legal Aid Board in South Africa is an independent body created by statute, funded by the state and accountable to the government.[47] As compared to the legal aid directorates in Namibia and Zimbabwe, which are within the Ministries of Justice of the governments, the Legal Aid Board of South Africa has established an enviable record of representing indigents, primarily criminal defendants but also a range of civil litigants, accomplishing its goal of providing access to justice to those most in need, according to international and its own constitutional standards. In contrast, the Legal Aid Directorates in Namibia and Zimbabwe are hampered by lack of financial support and organisational agility.[48] The Zambian Constitution, in contrast to Botswana, guarantees all persons accused of a criminal offence the right to legal representation but has not been able to provide free legal aid in criminal cases while that mandate was within the Ministry of Justice.[49] A Legal Aid Board independent of the Ministry of

---

[44] Based in Malawi, its National Executive Director is Clifford Msiska.

[45] Access to Justice Workshop, 29–30 April 2008, presentation by Clifford Msiska.

[46] Access to Justice Workshop, 29–30 April 2008, presentation by Mary Chisanga, Legal Resources Foundation, Zambia.

[47] Access to Justice Workshop, 29–30 April 2008, presentations by Justice Dunstan Mlambo and Patrick Hundermark, Legal Aid Board, South Africa.

[48] Access to Justice Workshop, 29–30 April 2008, presentations by Nelson Zvidzayi, Legal Aid Directorate, Zimbabwe, and Vero Mbahuurua, Legal Aid Directorate, Namibia.

[49] Access to Justice Workshop, 29–30 April 2008, presentation by Mary Chisanga, Legal Resources Foundation, Zambia.

Justice has recently been established with the goal of providing free legal aid, particularly in criminal cases, throughout the country.

There is an important role for civil society organisations and other bodies to continue to provide legal aid and legal advocacy outside of the government-funded official structure or at least with independent decision-making despite receiving government funding. For example, the Legal Resources Foundation in Zambia is an organisation that provides legal aid primarily in cases involving police brutality, false imprisonment, labour disputes and property grabbing. As Mary Chisanga states: "While legal representation in criminal cases is always a major focus for legal aid services, legal aid must also be used to promote social and political change."[50] The Southern Africa Legal Assistance Network is an example of a network of civil society organisations and others that work together to enhance the availability and the scope of legal aid services throughout the region.[51]

7.2 Define When Counsel Must Be Appointed "Where the Interests of Justice Require"

The African Union standards concerning appointment of legal assistance state that:

> "The accused or a party to a civil case has a right to have legal assistance assigned to him or her in any case *where the interest of justice so require*, and without payment by the accused or party to a civil case if he or she does not have sufficient means to pay for it."[52]

This particular section is similar to Article 14, Section 3(d) of the International Covenant on Civil and Political Rights, describing the rights of indigent accused people to appointed counsel.[53] In both documents, the decision on whether to provide legal assistance depends upon whether "the interest of justice so require".

---

[50] *ibid.*

[51] *ibid.*

[52] "ACHPR Principles and Guidelines on the Right to a Fair Trial and Legal Assistance in Africa," "Legal Aid and Legal Assistance," Section 1 (2001). (Emphasis added.)

[53] ICCPR Article 14, Section 3(d): "In the determination of any criminal charge against him, everyone shall be entitled to the following minimum guarantees, in full equality:...and to have legal assistance assigned to him, in any case *where the interests of justice so require*, and without payment by him in any such case if he does not have sufficient means to pay for it ...." (Emphasis added.)

But what are "the interests of justice" and how does one know them when one sees them? The ACHPR Principles add:

2. The interests of justice should be determined by considering:
   a. In criminal matters:
      i. The seriousness of the offence;
      ii. The severity of the sentence.
   b. In civil cases:
      i. The complexity of the case and the ability of the party to adequately represent himself or herself;
      ii. The rights that are affected;
      iii. The likely impact of the outcome of the case on the wider community.
3. The interests of justice always require legal assistance for an accused in any capital case....[54]

Implicit in this listing of considerations is an individualised determination of each case. An individualised determination may be appropriate in civil cases, particularly because the considerations above include the individual capacity of the party, the complexity of the case, the rights affected and the likely impact on others.

There is a problem, though, with determining the interests of justice individually in each case, particularly in criminal cases. There are two aspects to the problem.

A. Because a Criminally Accused is Entitled to Legal Assistance from the First Point of Contact with the Prosecuting Authority, an Individualised Assessment of "Interests of Justice" Violates the Rights of the Accused

The first problem with an individualised assessment of the interests of justice is that criminally accused persons are entitled to a range of protections from the moment that they are arrested, and even before the arrest. For example, they may generally not be arrested without a warrant having been issued. They may be detained after arrest for only 48 hours before they are released or charged. They may not be forced to speak to police officers or other investigating officers. Any statement they make must be witnessed in a

[54] "ACHPR Principles and Guidelines on the Right to a Fair Trial and Legal Assistance in Africa," "Legal Aid and Legal Assistance", Sections 2–3 (2001).

particular way. They are entitled to have counsel present during any parts of the arrest, detention and interrogation.

"Special safeguards in criminal justice matters," within the "Basic Principles on the Role of Lawyers" include very specific mandates related to timing of access to a lawyer and legal assistance:[55]

7. Governments shall further ensure that all persons arrested or detained, with or without criminal charge, shall have *prompt* access to a lawyer, and in any case *not later than forty-eight hours from the time of arrest or detention.*
8. All arrested, detained or imprisoned persons shall be provided with adequate opportunities, time, and facilities to be visited by and to communicate and consult with a lawyer, *without delay*, interception, or censorship and in full confidentiality.

The specificity of the mandate recognises the importance of the timeliness of the legal assistance in state arrests and detentions and criminal charges and prosecutions.

These protections apply to circumstances even before a person is charged with a crime and certainly before an accused person has a first appearance in court. Then who makes the determination that the interests of justice require appointment of counsel? It should be someone who is impartial, not the arresting or investigating police officer. That implies the court. But when someone is arrested, the police take the arrestee to the police station, not to the court. Police work 24 hours each day. The courts do not.

A simpler way of determining eligibility for whom the state should provide legal assistance is to have somebody at the police station at least to give legal information and advice and to provide oversight of compliance with mandatory procedures – for everyone who is arrested. There does not need to be any individual determination. The interests of justice always require that level of legal assistance for everybody at the early stages of the criminal proceedings.

[55] Adopted by the Eighth United Nations Congress on the Prevention of Crime and the Treatment of Offenders, Havana, Cuba, 27 August to 7 September 1990, Sections 7–8. (Emphasis added.)

B. A Bright Line should be Drawn for a Right to Appointed Counsel, to Avoid Individual Determinations Too Late in the Court Representation Process

A second problem with individual case-by-case determinations concerning the interests of justice is that the determination is often made too late in the court process. As noted, a string of rights apply to arrestees, detainees, accused persons throughout the criminal process. This is necessary at least partly because of the power of the state, compared to the individual. All human rights standards recognise the special protections necessary to ensure individual rights in the criminal legal process.

If an individual determination is made of the interests of justice, it will generally be done, at the earliest, at the first court appearance but very likely later in the process, when it becomes apparent to the court that the individual needs legal representation. By that time, the inequalities between the state (or a corporate or personal litigant) and the individual may have become so oppressive that a "fair trial" may be impossible, even with appointed counsel.

An example of a bright line, not individualised, determination of the interests of justice is in the ACHPR Principles on "Legal Aid and Legal Assistance": "The interests of justice always require legal assistance for an accused in any capital case…."[56] It is clear that, where an individual's life is at stake, the interests of justice require appointment of counsel for an accused. No individual determination is necessary.

The criteria for when the interests of justice require appointment of counsel should be written clearly and should be fulfilled whenever a person's human rights are endangered, particularly in court proceedings or other state action. The rights involved should include life (capital offences), liberty (whenever there is risk of involuntary confinement, in prison or in hospital or any other institution), bodily integrity (for example, corporal punishment in school or customary court), association or relationships (when a family relationship is being altered, through divorce, custody, guardianship), when one is involuntarily before the court (as a defendant in a civil action, for instance) and other human rights.

For example, in the United States, appointment of criminal defence counsel is required whenever the criminally accused is charged with a crime that can

[56] *op. cit.*, fn. 27, *supra*, Section 3.

result in any term of imprisonment (loss of liberty).[57] The standard was set by the U.S. Supreme Court because its case-by-case individualised assessment of the "interests of justice" had been too cumbersome and too late to avoid manifest injustice in court proceedings. As Justice Black wrote for the United States Supreme Court in 1963,

> "[R]eason and reflection require us to recognize that in our adversary system of criminal justice, any person hauled into court, who is too poor to hire a lawyer, cannot be assured a fair trial unless counsel is provided for him…. That government hires lawyers to prosecute and defendants who have the money hire lawyers to defend are the strongest indications of the widespread belief that lawyers in criminal courts are necessities, not luxuries."[58]

The result is that legal counsel is appointed for all except minor crimes, that cannot have a prison sentence of even one day, at no cost to an indigent defendant.

Subsequent to the decision on legal counsel appointments in criminal cases, several cases and many statutes have provided the basis for free legal representation in a range of civil cases in the United States. Counsel is made available because of the risk of deprivation of human rights, including the right to a fair trial and equality before the courts, as well as other human rights.

It should not have to take a court decision by the highest court of the land or an international tribunal for Botswana to establish in law the right to appointed counsel, free for those who cannot afford to pay. The standard for who or what case is eligible for appointed counsel should be clearly articulated. It should be mandatory and easily applied. Because the standard is clear, legal assistance should be provided at the earliest possible time in the proceedings, to prevent injustice and to serve the interests of justice.

7.3 Eliminate Other Barriers to Access to Justice

There are other things that Botswana can do to maximise access to justice, at very little cost to the legal system and the government, but at great value to those who are now barred from the justice system. These do not fall within

---

[57] *Gideon v Wainwright*, 372 U.S. 335 (1963), and its successive progeny.

[58] *ibid.*, at 343–344.

the description of "legal aid" but for a little effort they can produce remarkable results in providing access to justice. A few examples follow.

A. Eliminate Financial and Logistical Barriers to Filing in Courts

Even if an individual has legal counsel without cost or does not need counsel in order to access the justice system equally, there are barriers to actually proceeding in court. These include the costs of filing fees that are beyond the reach of many and the difficulty of actually getting to the courthouse to file. In the University of Botswana Legal Clinic, students assist many very poor individuals to get a divorce by drafting all the documents necessary to begin the proceedings and to move the proceedings along to completion. But many documents are never filed. The two most frequent reasons that UB Legal Clinic clients do not start proceedings in courts are: the *cost of filing the documents* in court and the *distance* they must travel to pick up the documents from Gaborone and file them in Lobatse (75 kilometres away) or Francistown (500 kilometres away) where the High Court offices are located.[59]

Liberal waiver of filing fees is one obvious solution to the barrier of cost, unrelated to the cost of legal assistance. A simplified, inclusive system of establishing eligibility for waiver of filing fees will resolve the problem. For instance, in the United States a series of court decisions has required the state to remove the requirement to pay court fees and costs, when the party is indigent, and have even required the state to take on some costs.

The US Supreme Court has agreed with the claimants' arguments that poverty prohibited them from adequately protecting their interests against the state's criminal process, thus violating their rights.[60] In these cases the state had not taken affirmative steps to disadvantage the claimants – it simply had done nothing to equalise their ability to protect themselves. As a result, they were not in an equal position before the law.

Similarly, in a divorce case, the U.S. Supreme Court ruled that a fee for filing a divorce petition foreclosed a judicial forum to one who could not pay the price of admission.[61] The rationale was that "the right to a meaningful

---

[59] Author's observation in her work with the University of Botswana Legal Clinic.

[60] *Griffin v Illinois*, 351 U.S. 12 (1956); *Douglas v. California*, 372 U.S. 353 (1963); *Ake v Oklahoma*, 470 U.S. 68 (1985).

[61] *Boddie v Connecticut*, 401 U.S. 371 (1971).

opportunity to be heard … must be protected against denial by … laws that operate to jeopardise it for particular individuals."[62]

In the United States, as in Botswana, the state has monopolised the process ending marital relationships, as it has monopolised the process of criminal proceedings and many other civil proceedings. Consequently, it can not, by charging admission, deny access to some while permitting it to others.

> "Resort to the judicial process by these plaintiffs is no more voluntary … than that of the defendant called upon to defend his interests in court. For both groups this process is not only the paramount dispute-settlement technique, but … the only … one."[63]

The state should also assume certain costs. For instance, again in the United States, the Supreme Court determined that the state was constitutionally required to assume the cost of paternity testing in affiliation proceedings.[64] The rationale was the same: the claimant's financial predicament prevented access to the tools of his defence against paternity, an exculpatory test.

The courts should provide alternative access to filing at the High Court and magistrate courts. With electronic and facsimile communication so available, even in Botswana, the courts should allow filing electronically or through facsimile through secure methods. For example, a legal assistance office could be registered to do electronic filing, rather than requiring actual delivery, of documents like founding Affidavits and Notice of Summons. After service the Affidavit of Service could be filed with signatures and notarisation through facsimile transmission or scanning and electronic transmission. Even people who live far from legal assistance offices may be able to locate a facsimile machine or scanner that is located closer than the nearest court.

The potential of technology will, no doubt, soon reduce even further the logistical barriers to filing court documents. Creative use of technology will greatly reduce the distance a party would have to travel and the financial and other burdens a party would have to assume to accomplish filing. Secure application of technology can minimise barriers to access to justice.

---

[62] *ibid.*, at 379–80.

[63] *ibid.*, at 376–77.

[64] *Little v Streater*, 452 U.S. 1 (1981).

B. Provide Simple Dispute Resolution Systems where People are

The beauty of customary courts in Botswana is that they are where most people are. If the standards of the customary courts are upgraded to meet international standards, they provide a basis for access to justice on many important issues in people's lives. If they are integrated into the whole justice system, they will maintain their value as the most accessible dispute resolution system in Botswana and increase their value by providing equality before the law.

Small claims courts, distributed throughout the country, with simplified procedures are another means of providing simple dispute resolution systems that provide access to justice. For example, Zimbabwe has a Small Claims Courts Act[65] that has enhanced access.[66]

8 Conclusion: Botswana Must – and Can – Do the Right Thing

What more can be said? Access to justice through legal aid is a human right. Botswana has not yet officially, legally acknowledged that human right through its justice system. Botswana has made a commitment to provide simple, affordable, sustainable, available legal aid to poor and other disadvantaged people. There are many things to do to meet the commitment. It is not easy but it is doable. There is much to learn from the experiences of others.

"The die is cast,"as Chief Justice Nganunu said when he officially closed the Access to Justice Workshop.[67] There is no turning back. Botswana is beginning the journey to a sustainable legal aid system for all. The journey of a thousand miles starts with the first step. It is the human rights thing to do. It is the right thing to do.

[65] Chapter 7:12.

[66] Access to Justice Workshop, 29–30 2008, presentation of Chief Magistrate Herbert Mandeya.

[67] Access to Justice Workshop, 29–30 2008, Closing Speech of Chief Justice Nganunu.

Greasing the Criminal Process with a Human Touch: the Protection of the Accused Person's Right to a Trial within a Reasonable Time

Bugalo Maripe*

1 Introduction

The focus of this paper is on the right of an accused person to have a fair hearing within a reasonable time. The Constitution of Botswana provides as follows:

> "If any person is charged with a criminal offence, then, unless the charge is withdrawn, the case shall be afforded a fair hearing within a reasonable time by an independent and impartial court established by or recognized by law".[1]

This is the provision protecting the accused person's right to a fair trial and is a recognition and expression of the old adage that "justice delayed is justice denied". It is also noteworthy that it falls within Chapter II of the Constitution, which is styled "The Protection of Fundamental Rights and Freedoms of an Individual".

2 Is Trial Within a Reasonable Time a Human Right?

To the extent that it is provided for under the part on fundamental rights and freedoms, then it will be classified as such. To the extent again that it is one of the general conditions of a fair trial, it is submitted that it is a fundamental

---

*LL.B (UB), LL.M (Lond.), Attorney (Botswana) Senior Lecturer, Department of Law, University of Botswana. When I was doing the preliminary research for this paper I had occasion to have a discussion with Mr. Justice Lesetedi of the High Court of Botswana after he delivered judgment in the *Simba Joseph* case. I am grateful to him and in particular for his assistance in pointing out to me and supplying copies of certain relevant cases such as the Lesotho case of *Nomoro Edwin Ketisi v DPP* (CRI) no. 9/06 and the Botswana High Court case of *Mareko v The State*, [2006] BWHC 79, of which I was then unaware.

[1] Constitution of the Republic of Botswana, Section 10(1).

requirement of the criminal justice system and to the extent that it protects a person who is at risk of loss of liberty or of freedom of movement, it properly falls to be described as a human right. More importantly, state practice and general international law would tend to support the above proposition. On the international plane, almost all human rights conventions make provision for a trial within a reasonable time.[2] On the domestic plane, almost every constitution provides for the right in the same language to that employed in human rights instruments or language substantially similar.[3] In all the instruments, provision for trial or hearing within a reasonable time is made under chapters dealing with fundamental rights and freedoms. It is therefore proper to conclude that it is a human right.

2.1 Purpose of the Right

The requirement for a trial or hearing within a reasonable time is an offshoot of the general requirement of a fair trial.[4] Although it appears in its form to be a right vesting in an accused person, it also protects and secures the general societal interest in expediting cases and bringing them to conclusion within reasonable periods, thereby securing some degree of certainty and confidence in the judicial system. The state in criminal proceedings, as the complainant, and therefore a necessary party to proceedings, is also interested in the speedy disposal of cases.

From the standpoint of the accused, a speedy disposal of the case brings with it numerous advantages. In a Zimbabwean case, *In re Mlambo*,[5] the full bench of the Zimbabwe Supreme Court had to consider the purpose underlying the constitutional guarantee of a fair trial within a reasonable time,[6] and equated the purpose thereunder with that under the speedy trial guarantee under the Sixth Amendment to the Constitution of the United States of America. It

---

[2] See Article 71(d) of the African Charter on Human and People's Rights; Article 8(1) of the American Convention on Human Rights; Article 6(1) of the European Convention for the Protection of Human Rights and Fundamental Freedoms; Article 67(1)(c) of the Rome Statute on the International Criminal Court (1998), which provides for the right of an accused "to be tried without undue delay"; Article 6(1) of the Commonwealth of Independent States Convention on Human Rights and Fundamental Freedoms.

[3] E.g. Section 10 (1) of the Constitution of Botswana; Section 18(2) of the Zimbabwean Constitution; Section 12(1)(b) of the Namibian Constitution; Section 35(3)(d) of the South African Constitution; Section 42(2)(f)(i) of the Malawian Constitution; Section 12(1) of the Constitution of Lesotho.

[4] See *Simba Joseph v The State*, [2007] 1 BLR 345, *Sejammitlwa and Others v The Attorney General and Others* [2002] 2 BLR 75.

[5] 1992 (4) SA 144 (Zimbabwe Supreme Ct.).

[6] Section 18(2) of the Constitution of Zimbabwe.

borrowed from the jurisprudence of the United States Supreme Court,[7] to the effect that the speedy trial guarantee is

> "...designed to minimize the possibility of lengthy incarceration prior to trial, to reduce the lesser, but nonetheless substantial, impairment of liberty imposed on an accused while released on bail, and shorten the disruption of life caused by arrest and the presence of unresolved criminal charges".[8]

These words have been held to reflect the law of Botswana.[9] Not only does the provision benefit the accused person; it also benefits society in that it assures the community that serious crimes are investigated and tried within a reasonable time frame. Thus the trial of offences within a reasonable time instils confidence in the entire judicial process.

3 The Scope of the Protection

It is necessary to examine the various elements of section 10(1) in order to establish the exact protection intended to be afforded to persons in the circumstances contemplated. Section 10(1) protects (a) a person charged with a criminal offence, (b) in respect of whom the charge has not been withdrawn, (c) and who must be afforded a fair hearing within a reasonable time (d) by an independent and impartial court established or recognised by law.

i) a fair hearing

This requires the observance of the rules of natural justice, and in particular the *audi alteram partem* rule.[10] Although the Constitution makes provision for this right to be heard, the requirement would still have to be observed even in the absence of the provision, for it has its origins in the common law, in terms of which a person who stands to be affected negatively by a decision must not only be served with notice of the charge, but also be allowed the opportunity to make representations against the proposed decision, unless that right is excluded by statute or other considerations. Thus it is a

---

[7] *United States v Macdonald* 456 US 1 at 8 (1982) and *United States v Loud Hawk* 474 US 302, at 311 (1986) .

[8] [1992] 4 SA 144, at 147–148 (*per* Gubbay C J).

[9] *Sejammitlwa and Others v The Attorney General and Others* [2002] 2 BLR 75, at 81 (*per* Tebbutt AJP).

[10] Section 10(2) of the Constitution of Botswana; *Phirinyane v Spie Batignolles* [1995] BLR 1; *Alfred Makgoeng v Attorney General* [1987] BLR 518.

codification of existing rules. This is usually satisfied in every criminal trial in Botswana.

(ii) in respect of whom the charge has not been withdrawn
The intention here is to protect only people facing the potential of criminal sanction. A person who has had charges withdrawn cannot strictly speaking be said to be facing any criminal sanction, unless the charges were withdrawn with a possibility of re-prosecution. Under our law, the prosecution may apply to court for the withdrawal of the case, which withdrawal may be granted by the court subject to the condition that the State (prosecution) retains the liberty to reinstate the charges.[11] It will be shown later that, although the claimant for the right is an accused person who still has not had charges withdrawn or an accused person against whom charges were withdrawn and subsequently reinstated, the time of the first laying of charges will be taken into account in determining not only the time taken to hear the case, but any possible delay and the reasonableness or otherwise of the delay in bringing the accused to trial.

(iii) if any person is 'charged'
The right under section 10(1) of the Constitution can be asserted only by a person who is or has been 'charged' with a criminal offence. It is clear on the terms of this subsection that the requirement for a hearing within a reasonable time is for purposes of determining the guilt or otherwise of the person facing the charge. It is therefore important to determine the exact time when the charge was laid against the accused person, for that will determine whether the time taken to try the matter is reasonable or not. The time of bringing the charge is the time when the 'clock starts ticking' against the State in any assessment for the purposes of section 10(1).[12]

The statute books do not define the word 'charged'. This notwithstanding, the Court of Appeal has provided guidance in this respect. In *Sejammitlwa and Others v Attorney General and Others*, Tebbutt AJP observed:

> "In my opinion when a person is 'charged' is not when he is first arraigned before a court. When a person is 'charged' may occur at a date prior to the case coming before the court, such as the date of arrest, the date when the person concerned was officially notified that he would be prosecuted or the date when preliminary investigations were opened. 'Charged' for the

[11] Criminal Procedure and Evidence Act, Cap 08:02, section 150(A).
[12] *Sejammitlwa and Others v Attorney General and Others*, [2002] 2 BLR 75; *Kelaotswe v Attorney General* [2005] 1 BLR 306; *Ntwa v The State* [2001] 2 BLR 212.

purposes of section 10(1) may be defined as 'the official notification given to an individual by the competent authority of an allegation that he has committed a criminal offence'..."[13]

The court also accepted that while 'charge' may be so defined, "it may in some instances take the form of other measures which carry the implication of such an allegation and which likewise substantially affect the situation of the suspect".[14]

In view of the above, the question arises as to what happens when a charge is withdrawn and subsequently re-instated. Does it affect the computation of time for the purpose of an assessment under section 10(1)? Judicial opinion leans strongly in favour of the view that the time starts ticking when the charge was first laid and not when it was re-instated.[15] It is submitted this approach is the right one, for to hold otherwise would be to allow the State authorities wantonly to bring charges any time even without evidence, then to withdraw the same and to re-instate the charges at will, and repeatedly. It would amount to abuse of authority, and would encourage what was envisaged by the remedy of malicious prosecution at common law.[16] It also has a positive spinoff in that charges will be laid only against people in respect of whom there is some *prima facie* evidence as to the possibility of commission of a criminal offence, thereby discouraging the actions of overly exuberant investigating and prosecuting officials. It also prevents real prejudice to suspects, for in many cases the fact that a person has been charged may lead to his or her suspension from work and other similar or equally negative implications.[17]

(iv) 'within a reasonable time'

This is the basis for the protection accorded to an accused person under section 10(1). It enjoins the prosecuting authorities, once a charge has been laid, to bring the accused person to trial as soon as possible. It prevents the charge from remaining undetermined for an indefinite period of time, occasioning real prejudice to an accused person. The *raisons d'etre* for the

---

[13] [2002] 2 BLR, at 83.

[14] *ibid*, at 84.

[15] *Sejammitlwa v Attorney General and Others (supra); Kelaotswe v Attorney General (supra).*

[16] *Sarefo v Dira* [1985] BLR 306; *Thokwane v Attorney General* [1998] BLR 22.

[17] For example under the General Orders, made under the Public Service Act, a civil servant facing criminal charges may be interdicted from work, either on full salary or some such proportion of the salary (not being less than half the salary) as may be determined by the officer effecting the suspension. General Orders are the conditions of service of the Public service of the Republic of Botswana.

protection and the kind of prejudice an accused person would suffer if it is not provided are best summarised by Gubbay CJ as follows:

> "The right therefore recognises that, with the passage of time, subjection to a criminal charge gives rise to restrictions on liberty, inconvenience, social stigma, and pressures detrimental to the mental and physical health of the individual. It is a truism that the time awaiting trial must be agonising for accused persons and their immediate family. I believe that there can be no greater frustration for an innocent person charged with an offence than to be denied the opportunity of demonstrating his lack of guilt for an unconscionable time as a result of delay in bringing him to trial. The right recognizes also that an unreasonable delay may well impair the ability of the individual to present a full and fair defence to the charge."[18]

Although in law a person remains innocent until proved guilty, once he is charged with an offence, his personal circumstances change immediately. In the eyes of the ordinary citizens, and due to the gullibility of the ordinary human mind, there arises are a belief or presumption of guilt (it is a popular belief that there is no smoke without fire!), which may lead to many kinds of social ostracisation of the accused person. In some cases the accused person may be remanded in custody pending trial, before investigations are complete, thus depriving him of his liberty and freedom of movement. He may even be put on terms restricting the ordinary transaction of business and his normal way of life. It is in recognition of all these, and the desirability of conducting the trial in the shortest manner possible, that is the basis of the protection under section 10(1).

3.1 What then is a Reasonable Time?

Nowhere in the Constitution, or the general legislative framework, is the phrase 'reasonable time' defined. It remains an elastic concept which must be determined of the basis of the particular or special circumstances of each case. The absence of a definite time period is not peculiar to Botswana, for, as shown above, the protection is couched in the same or substantially similar

[18] *In re Mlambo* 1992 (4) SA 144, at 147–8, where the Zimbabwean Supreme Court was considering section 18(2) of the Zimbabwean Constitution, which provision is *in pari materia* to section 10(1). These words were adopted with approval in *Sejammitlwa and Others v Attorney-General* at 81.

language across jurisdictions.[19] There is good reason for the absence of a definite period of time. It is precisely because when a person is finally brought to trial depends on several factors, which are rarely similar in between cases. The elasticity in the language allows for a determination of the peculiarity of the circumstances in each case, for justice, as a societal concept, is never uniform, and the factors that underpin the concept are not immutable. It is submitted that the elasticity of the language is desirable as it allows for judicial discretion to prevail without the limitations that go with fixed period. It is for this reason that Amissah P, in the Court of Appeal decision in *Busi* v *The State*, said:

> "In my view, regard ought to be had to the fact that what the provision requires is not the charge to be heard in a specific time but that the hearing should be within a reasonable time. Such time would therefore vary depending on the circumstances of each case. In determining what is a reasonable time, the period taken to bring and to prosecute the charge will be one, but only one of several factors to be taken into account. The nature of the particular criminal act, the charge, the availability of witnesses, the efforts made to prosecute the charge expeditiously, the availability of judges or magistrates, will all be factors which would have to be taken into consideration."[20]

In adopting these words, and expanding on the same, Mosojane J said;

> "The sum total of these authorities, here and abroad, is that there is no such thing as a reasonable time in abstract. What is reasonable time depends of the circumstance of each case. The period taken to bring charges against the accused is but only one of several factors to be taken into account in determining what a reasonable time is. Some of these factors are those mentioned in the above cited passages in the judgment of Amissah P. which clearly were not intended to be exhaustive. For as long as delay in bringing the accused to trial is attributable to causes beyond the prosecution's control and the state has neither acted negligently nor unreasonably the time taken will not be held to be unreasonable."[21]

---

[19] See notes 2 and 3 above.

[20] [1997] BLR 69, at 72.

[21] *Loso and Another v The State* [1998] BLR 518, at 524–5.

These have been adopted in almost all the cases that have gone before the High Court[22] and the Court of Appeal of Botswana.[23] If a definition be attempted here: reasonable time is a period of time fixed by a court as being reasonable, between the laying of a charge, and bringing of the accused to trial, following a determination by the court upon the exercise of its judicial discretion, in the assessment of all relevant factors having a bearing upon the particular circumstances of each case.

4 Protection of the Right

4.1 Constitutional Provisions

Constitutional and legislative provisions on their own may not provide effective protection until that protection is asserted or claimed. While in some cases they may spur the prosecuting authorities in moving swiftly to avoid delays, thus protecting the accused person, where this is not so the accused person may lose that protection if he or she does not move the court for an appropriate remedy. In the absence of an appropriate order or remedy, the delay will continue.

As a fundamental right, the right to a trial or hearing within a reasonable time falls to be protected in the same manner that such other rights are protected. The Constitution allows a person alleging a violation of fundamental rights to apply to the High Court for redress.[24] In terms of the said constitutional provision, the contravention of the fundamental right must be *in relation* to the person claiming the protection. As such it cannot be any other person but

---

[22] *E.g. Ntwa v The State* [2001] 2 BLR 212, where Marumo J said the Court of Appeal in *Busi v The State (supra)* had never intended these factors to be exhaustive; *Rabana v Attorney General* [2003] 1 BLR 330, *per* Chatikobo J; *Charles v The State* [2005] BLR 421, *per* Mosojane J; *Kelaotswe v Attorney General (supra) per* Molokomme J; *Masoba v The State*, MCHLB-0000110-07 ((unreported) *per* Newman J; *Mareko v The State*, [2006] BWHC 79 *per* Chinhengo J; *Patricia Moyo v The State*, Miscellaneous Criminal Application No. F70 of 2004, *per* Gaongalelwe J.

[23] *Sejammitlwa and Others v Attorney General and Others (supra)* (Court of Appeal, full bench); *The State v Maauwe and Another* [2006] 2 BLR 530 (Court of Appeal, full bench); *Kelaotswe v AG* [2006] 1 BLR 229 (Court of Appeal, full bench); *Simba Joseph v The State*, [2007] 1 BLR 345, *per* Lesetedi AJA (concurred in by Grosskopf and McNally JJA); *Alec Thomas v The State*, [2007] 2 BLR 749, *per* Moore JA (concurred in by Tebbutt JP and Zietsman JA), the most recent and perhaps the most exhaustive case in Botswana so far on the point.

[24] Section 18(1) of the Constitution.

[25] *Dow v AG* [1992] BLR 119. For a full and comprehensive discussion on principles of legal standing in Botswana, see B. Maripe, "*Locus Standi* and access to judicial review : Statutory interpretation and judicial practice in Botswana", 1999 *THRHR* 390.

the person whose right has allegedly been violated who may make application to the High Court for redress. The person must therefore have the necessary *locus standi.*[25] That the High Court is the only court with original jurisdiction to determine allegations of contraventions of fundamental rights is fortified by the provisions of the Constitution which provide:

> "The High Court shall have original jurisdiction – (a) to hear and determine any application made by any person in pursuance of subsection (1) of this Section".[26]

Thus no Subordinate Court[27] has the jurisdiction and would be acting *ultra vires* were it to determine any such application or indeed any question arising as to the alleged contravention of a fundamental right. In Botswana, the bulk of criminal trials commence in the Magistrates' Courts, with the High Court, although having original jurisdiction,[28] usually trying cases at first instance in matters in which the subordinate courts do not have jurisdiction.[29] Thus what happens in practice is that accused persons make allegations of contravention of fundamental rights in the courts where they are being tried, which are subordinate courts. In view of the jurisdictional issue, the Constitution provides for a process of escalation or transfer of the issue of alleged contravention of those rights to the High Court as follows:

> "If in any proceedings in any subordinate court any question arises as to the contravention of any of the provisions of Section 3 to 16 (inclusive) of this Constitution, the person presiding in that court *may*, and *shall* if any party to the proceedings so requests, refer the question to the High Court *unless, in his opinion, the raising of the question is merely frivolous or vexatious.*"[30]

Several observations may be made in respect of this provision. First, the use of the word "*may*" allows the Subordinate Court, on its own motion, and in the exercise of its discretion, to refer any question arising as to the contravention of fundamental rights to the High Court. It does not have to be moved to do

[26] Section 18(2) (a) of the Constitution.

[27] Subordinate Court means "Any Court other that the Court of Appeal, High Court, Court Martial or Industrial Court": Section 127(1) of the Constitution . Such would include Magistrates' Courts under the Magistrates Courts Act, Cap 04:04, and Customary Courts under the Customary Courts Act, Cap. 04:05.

[28] Sections 18(2) and 95(1) of the Constitution.

[29] These include matters in which punishment includes capital punishment, for example murder and treason.

[30] Section 18(3) of the Constitution. (Emphasis added.)

so. The subordinate court may make an assessment of all issues arising and determine whether any such issue merits a referral to the High Court. Secondly, the use of the word "shall" makes it mandatory for the subordinate Court to make a referral of the allegation of contravention of the fundamental right to the High Court if any party so requests. However, the court may decline to make such a referral, whether in cases where it, on its own motion, determines the issue to have arisen, or in cases where it has been requested to do so if, in the opinion of that court, the raising of the question is merely *frivolous* or *vexatious*. Thus the court is again enjoined to exercise a judicial discretion to determine the propriety or otherwise of the request to make a referral to the High Court.[31] It has power to make a determination as to the seriousness of the question only, but not to determine and decide upon the question itself.

The words "frivolous or vexatious", in the context of law, call for a proper determination by a court faced with the question, and require a careful assessment of all the circumstances surrounding the case, for it is that assessment which determines whether or not a referral to the High Court should be made by the Subordinate Court. They need therefore to be defined. It is apposite here to refer to what was said by the Zimbabwean Supreme Court, in construing section 24 of the Zimbabwean Constitution, which is *in pari materia* with section 18(3) of the Constitution of Botswana. The Court said:

> "In the context of Section 24 of the Constitution, the word 'frivolous' connotes in its ordinary and natural meaning, the raising of a question marked by lack of seriousness; one inconsistent with logic and good sense, and clearly so groundless and devoid of merit that any prudent person could not possibly expect to obtain relief from it. The word 'vexatious' in contradistinction, is used in the sense of the question being put forward for the purpose of causing annoyance to the opposing party, in full appreciation that it cannot succeed; it is not raised *bona fide* and a referral would be to permit the opponent to be vexed under a form of legal process that was baseless."[32]

These words were adopted in Botswana in *Mareko v The State*[33]. It is clear, therefore, that although a Magistrates' court or any subordinate court for that matter may not have the jurisdiction to determine a claim based on the right to trial within a reasonable time, it plays a pivotal role in determining the

---

[31] *Mareko v The State*, [2006] BWHC 79.

[32] *Martin v Attorney General* [1993] (1) ZLR 153, at 157.

[33] [2006] BWHC 79, para 12.

preliminary question as to the propriety or otherwise of a request for a referral to the High Court once the question arises. In fact it may even decline a request for a referral if, in its opinion, such request is either frivolous or vexatious. Its role therefore may not be underestimated as, by refusing to make a referral, it effectively determines the enjoyment of the right. It therefore has some jurisdiction in respect of the right, albeit in this preliminary and limited sense.

4.2 Procedure in the High Court

In terms of section 18(4) of the Constitution, Parliament is enabled to confer upon the High Court such powers as are necessary for the purpose of enabling it to exercise its jurisdiction. In terms of section 18(5) the Constitution allows for Rules of Court to be made with respect to the practice and procedure in the High Court for the purposes of matters concerning legal claims against contraventions of fundamental rights provisions. The High Court Act authorises the Chief Justice to make rules, among others, for that purpose.[34] It is in pursuance of these provisions that the High Court Act carries special rules for the enforcement of the protective provisions under Section 18 of the Constitution: They provide:

> "An application by any person for redress in terms of subsection (1) of Section 18 of the Constitution of Botswana shall be by way of notice of motion calling upon the party or parties, against whom redress is sought, to show cause why an order in terms of a draft (to be attached to the notice of motion) should not be granted by the court.[35]
>
> "The notice of motion shall be supported by an affidavit setting out the circumstances and the grounds upon which the applicant relies."[36]

Thus the claimant of relief under section 18, or for breach of the right to a trial or hearing within a reasonable time, must proceed by way of an application. This procedure may be problematic in cases where the Subordinate Court under section 18(3), on its own motion, decides to refer the matter to the High Court, or in the cases where the accused is indigent or unable to read. It is a matter of relief that the High Court does not insist on a rigid compliance with these rules and can deal with the question even if it is raised from the bar or on the date of the hearing. This is to be applauded, for

34 Cap 04:02, section 28.

35 Order 70, Rule 1.

36 Order 70, Rule 2.

otherwise the protection would be formal rather than substantive. Insistence on this compliance with technical rules of procedure, would frustrate the broader judicial policy of protecting fundamental rights.

4.3 Powers of the High Court and the Issue of Remedies

In addition to conferring upon the High Court original jurisdiction to determine any application under section 18(1) and to determine any question referred to it by a Subordinate Court, the Constitution, in section 18(2), gives the High Court power to

> "...make any such orders, issue such writs and give such direction as it may consider appropriate for the purpose of enforcing or securing the enforcement of any of the provisions of sections 3 to 16 (inclusive) of this Constitution."[37]

The High Court is thus at large to issue any order or give any such direction as it considers appropriate. The range of orders it may issue or directions it may give is limitless. It only has to exercise a judicial discretion in doing so. In the case of allegations of violations of the right to be tried within a reasonable time, the Court of Appeal has said:

> "It is now settled law that the powers *include*, in appropriate situations, the power to order a permanent stay of the prosecution, the effect of which would be the equivalent of an acquittal and discharge."[38]

In *Charles v The State*, Mosojane J, declared:

> "The right as I understand it is to a fair trial within a reasonable time or lengthy lapse of time. It is therefore important to emphasise that the true position in applications of this nature is that a stay of proceedings will normally be imposed only where a fair trial would not be possible or where it would be unfair to try the accused at all. It will also be imposed where the effect of the delay or the conduct of the State is such as to render continuation of proceedings an abuse of the process of the court."[39]

---

[37] Section 18(2).

[38] *Sejammitlwa and others v Attorney General and Others* [2002] 2 BLR 75, at 88. (Emphasis added.)

[39] [2005] 1 BLR 421, at 427.

The learned judge proceeded to say:

> "In such a case, the court is obliged to stay the proceedings. But in cases where prejudice falls short of rendering the trial unfair, the court must grant such other remedy as is appropriate to the demonstrated breach of the reasonable time requirement. For example, the court may after conviction reduce the sentence it would normally pass in such a case [or] order that the trial be continued without delay…..or the accused may seek damages for the delay."[40]

These views appear to enjoy the imprimatur of the Court of Appeal where, in *Sejammitlwa*, the Court of Appeal, while acknowledging that in appropriate situations the court has power to order a permanent stay of execution, went on to recognise that:

> "[T]his is not the only competent verdict that can be reached by the court. The court can, for example, order that the trial should be continued without delay, as happened in *Ntwa case*, or the appellants can seek damages for the delay."[41]

Judicial opinion is not entirely uniform in regard to the question of remedies available upon a successful section 10(1) application. In the *Mareko* case, Chinhengo J, while acknowledging that the remedies available under Section 18(2) had not been exhaustively listed by any court, went on to say:

> "In my view, however, where a court has determined that a person's right to a speedy trial has been infringed, *the remedy can only be one i.e. a permanent stay of prosecution.* An order that the trial commences without further delay can not be a remedy where the right under section 10(1) of the Constitution has already been violated. It is rather a refusal of the remedy sought by the applicant though it is coated with some sugar, so to say, in its appearance as a remedy. If a person applies for a stay but the court orders that his trial be commenced immediately, that is, in substance, a refusal of his application."[42]

The learned judge reached his conclusion on at least on three grounds: first,

> "that an order that a person be tried immediately or within such time frame as the court may direct is an order or direction designed to secure the

[40] *ibid.*, at 428.

[41] [2002] 2 BLR 75, at 88.

[42] *Mareko v The State* [2006] BWHC 79, para 35. (Emphasis added.)

> enforcement of the provisions of Sections 3–16 of the Constitution and can only follow upon a determination by the court pursuant to Section 18(1) that the applicant's right 'is being or is likely to be contravened in relation to him'."[43]

Thus, according to the learned judge, it is only appropriate for violations that are continuing or likely to occur, as opposed to those that have already occurred. The problem with this basis is that continuing violations would usually have happened in the past as well, and in many cases a right that is 'being' infringed would also, almost invariably, have been infringed at the time the right is being asserted. It is therefore not easy to demarcate or draw the dividing line between violations that have occurred and those that are continuing. Secondly, the learned judge considers the statement in *Sejammitlwa*, approving of the statement in *Ntwa v the State* on the possible remedies available, to have been *obiter* because (a) the Court of Appeal granted a permanent stay of execution in any event and (b):

> "The Court of Appeal had not been called upon to pronounce on what other remedies are available nor was it pronouncing on remedies peculiar to a finding that section 10 has been violated. Its comment is, in the context, about remedies generally available under Section 18(1) of the Constitution."[44]

This position is also problematic in several respects. To begin with, the Court of Appeal in *Sejammitlwa* was very clear in what it was dealing with. As a matter of fact, the only issue the court was called upon to decide was an application made under Section 10(1) of the Constitution, which application had been dismissed by the High Court. It was pronouncing on matters of trial and on the powers of a court in criminal matters. Were it not otherwise, it would not have used the words "permanent stay of the prosecution", or "acquitted and discharge", nor have stated that the court can "order that the trial should be continued without delay". This language is not consistent with a general pronouncement on remedies of all kinds. It is specific to criminal proceedings. Additionally, statements of law made in decided cases, although not forming the basis of decisions, may nonetheless be authoritative in the context in which they are made. The fact of a proposition's being *obiter dictum* does not, on that account alone, destroy its force as an authoritative pronouncement of law. In any event, it is a matter of debate whether the

---

43 *ibid.*

44 *ibid.*

statement by the Court of Appeal was *obiter* given that it was made in the context of an application which sought relief in terms of Section 18(2), in terms of which the court may "make such orders, issue such as writs and give such direction as it may consider appropriate".[45] Such include a permanent stay of prosecution. That it was ultimately the relief given by the court would not elevate it to the status of the "sole remedy", as other reliefs were equally competent. The consideration of other remedies would therefore not be *obiter*. It is only that in the particular circumstances of *Sejammitlwa*, it turned out, upon the exercise of judicial discretion, that a permanent stay of prosecution was the most appropriate remedy.

Thirdly, having said that the views of the Court of Appeal were not *obiter*, and in some other sense authoritative, the views of Chinhengo J in the *Mareko* case would have to give way to those of the Court of Appeal in the *Sejammitlwa* case in terms of the doctrine of authoritative hierarchy. There is a long line of cases which adopt the views that in a case under section 10(1), there is a variety of remedies available, and so Chinhengo J's views would appear to represent a lone voice. It remains to be seen how the Court of Appeal will comment on the views of Chinhengo J.

4.4 The Approach in Section 10(1) Applications

As said above, the approach usually adopted by the courts to applications for relief where allegations of contravention to section 10(1) are made is to consider not only the period taken between the laying of a charge and the bringing of an accused person to trial, but to consider other factors spelt out above. Again, as already demonstrated above, there is no uniform period. It all depends on the circumstances of each case. A permanent stay of prosecution has been granted in situations of disparate periods of delay: for example, in *Sejammitlwa,* the delay was seven years and the charges were theft and conspiracy to defraud; in *Mareko,* it was over two years and the charge was rape; in *Patricia Moyo* it was four years and the charge was theft; in *Thomas,* it was over six years and the charge was theft. A permanent stay was, however, refused on traffic offence charges in *Simba Joseph* where the delay was 14 months; on a charge of misappropriation of funds by a person employed in the public service in *Ntwa* where the delay was over three years, on several charges including murder in *Charles* where the period was over three years; on charges of stealing by agent in *Masoba*, where the delay was over six years; and on a charge of stealing by a person employed in the public service

[45] See, for example, *Kelaotswe (supra); Masoba (supra).*

in *Kelaotswe* where the delay was over five years. In many of these cases, the relief was still refused in spite of the fact that the period was considered unreasonably or extraordinarily long. To bring in a simplistic comparative analysis: in *Mlambo* the period was over five years and a permanent stay of prosecution was granted; it was refused in the South African cases of *Sanderson*[46] and *Wild*[47], in which the delays were two and three years respectively; the remedy was also refused in the *Ketisi* case in which the delay was over eight years. Where the court held that the period was unreasonably long, but nonetheless declined to grant the remedy sought, it was usually on the basis that the accused person had not suffered prejudice.

Prejudice in this context has usually been held to be a situation where, on account of the lapse of the long period, the accused person's ability to mount an effective defence has been compromised and, by reason of the inordinate delay, a fair trial is not possible.[48] There would not, however, be prejudice where, in spite of the long delay, a fair trial is still possible in the sense that the accused is still able to effectively mount his or her defence. However, this seems to have been denigrated by Moore JA, in *Alec Thomas* who said, in reference to what Mosojane J said in *Charles v The State:*

> "It is arguable that in the passage cited at p. 765 above, His Lordship was postulating that in order to obtain relief under Section 10(1) of the Constitution, an applicant had to show that he had suffered prejudice arising from the delay and further, that as a consequence of the prejudice his trial would be unfair and that despite an inordinate delay, he could nevertheless be denied a stay of his prosecution if a fair hearing was still possible. Thus, according to the judge's thinking, a person whose right to a fair hearing within a reasonable time under section 10(1) had been clearly violated because of inordinate delays, could nevertheless be denied of (sic) of his prosecution, if a fair hearing was still possible, in spite of those delays. However, viewed in the context of the entire

[46] *Sanderson v Attorney General, Eastern Cape*, 1998 (2) SA 38 (Constitutional Court of South Africa).

[47] *Wild and Another v Hoffert NO and Others*, 1998 (3) SA 659 (Constitutional Court of South Africa).

[48] *Kelaotswe (supra); Charles (supra).*

judgment, I do not think this was the intention of the learned judge. *But if it was, then I must respectfully differ.*"[49]

The learned Justice Moore JA, however, does not indicate what would be the appropriate position, or how the pronouncement by Mosojane J deviates from the acceptable and permissible approach to be taken. It would appear later on in his judgment in the *Alec Thomas* case that in fact the position Moore JA favours is quite consistent with the position laid down by Mosojane J in *Charles*, which accords with that propounded by Tebbutt AJP in *Sejammitlwa*, and that laid down by Marumo J in *Ntwa*, and that also adopted by Lesetedi AJA in *Simba Joseph*. Moore JA, in laying out what is the Botswana approach, says:

> "The course for Botswana has been clearly set for all of us by Tebbutt AJP in *Sejammitlwa*. It lays down the path which the judge should follow if he or she has reached the conclusion that there has been a breach of a person's right under Section 10(1) of the Constitution."[50]

---

[49] *Alec Thomas (supra)*, at p. 766 (emphasis added.) Similar sentiments were expressed by Chinhengo J in *State v Lebakeng; State v Ngahino*, [2006] BWHC 28 (26 May 2006), who recorded his respectful dissent from the approach taken by Mosojane J in *Charles v The State*:

> "First I do not think that it is proper to separate the phrase 'within reasonable time' from the words 'afforded a fair hearing' in s.10(1) of the Constitution so as to say that even where it is found that the delay was unreasonable and therefore the 'within reasonable time requirement' in s.10(1) was infringed relative to an applicant, nonetheless, if he cannot demonstrate some particular prejudice which he will suffer a stay would not be granted. In the other cases which I have referred to it was specifically found that the delay was not unreasonable because a satisfactory explanation for it was given. I think that s.10(1) of the Constitution must generally be construed as importing that once it is shown that the delay was so inordinate as to be unreasonable, then the accused would suffer trial related prejudice arising from the whole gamut of possibilities as mentioned in *Sejammitlwa and Others v The Attorney-General and others* [2002] 2 BLR 75 (CA) – impairment of the defence case, due to either memory loss, the death or non availability of the defence witnesses and the disappearance of material exhibits, etc. To require an applicant for a stay of prosecution to show what trial related prejudice he will suffer in addition to his having established that the delay was unconscionable and in violation of this right under s.10(1) of the Constitution, is, to my mind, to set too high a requirement which may make it almost impossible to afford the applicant the right granted to him by s.10(1).
>
> More importantly however, I respectually differ with the learned judge in that after finding that the accused's fundamental right granted by s.10(1) was violated, as the learned judged did …, it would still be open to him to examine if the accused would suffer prejudice. In my view, where there has been a violation of a constitutional right appropriate redress must be granted whether or not prejudice is shown to have existed or to exist."

[50] [2007] 1 BLR 345.

In fact Tebbutt AJP proceeded to hold that a permanent stay is not the only remedy, suggesting that it may be refused in appropriate cases.[51] Proceeding further with the judgment, Tebbutt AJP went to hold that in the circumstances of the case he was considering (*Sejammitlwa)*, that the non-availability of defence witnesses and consequent inability to prepare and conduct an adequate defence due to the lapse of time, were very prejudicial to the applicants, a stay of prosecution was the correct order.[52] Thus in a case where, despite the delay, an accused person is able to call and bring his witnesses and conduct an adequate and effective defence, the court could properly decline a request for a stay of prosecution notwithstanding a finding that there had been unreasonable or inordinate delay. This is the approach adopted in the many cases and is consistent with the pronouncement of Mosojane J in *Charles*. It is submitted it is the Botswana approach; and is not different from the position elsewhere,[53] and in fact the learned Moore JA then went on to put down an elaborate summary of the general findings to be gleaned from the *Sejammitlwa* case. The accused person's right to a speedy trial is to be weighed against the general societal interest in the pursuit of justice that those who break the law must be brought to book. Moore JA accordingly said:

> "A balancing exercise is required involving a consideration of the right to a speedy trial with society's right to see to it that those against whom allegations of wrong doing are made have their guilt or innocence determined according to the dictates of the law after due process."[54]

4.5 The Factors to be Taken into Account

The factors to take into account in performing the balancing exercise, as outlined by the judge, are on the one hand, (a) the nature of the offence(s); (b) the seriousness of the offence(s); (c) whether the offence(s) are such that the public interest requires that the alleged offender should stand his or her trial and on the other; (d) the length of the delay (e) whether the applicant or the State is responsible for the delay; (f) if the State is responsible, whether there is an acceptable explanation for the delay; (g) whether the applicant has

---

51 *Sejammitlwa and Others v The Attorney General and Others* [2002] 2 BLR 75, at 88.

52 *ibid.*

53 *In re Mlambo*, 1992 (4) SA 144 (Zimbabwe Supreme Ct.); *Ketisi v DPP*, C of A (CRI), No 9/06, (Court of Appeal of Lesotho), relying heavily on *Wild and Another v Hoffert NO and Others* 1998 (3) SA 695 (Constitutional Court of South Africa) and *Sanderson v Attorney General, Eastern Cape* 1998 (2) SA 38 (Constitutional Court of South Africa).

54 Page 41.

previously asserted his or her right to a speedy trial; (h) whether the applicant has suffered undue hardship as a result of the delay; (i) whether the ability of the applicant to conduct his or her defence is compromised by the delay; (j) whether it still possible in all the circumstances for the applicant to be afforded a fair trial; (k) whether the applicant has suffered any pre trial incarceration.[55] These factors cannot be said to be exhaustive, and regard must also be had

> "to organic or systematic or institutional weaknesses, to socio-economic conditions, to levels of development of the legal system, to the level of tolerance of society as a whole for delays, the degree of political stability at the relevant time, and any security concerns which the society may be facing'."[56]

These were also alluded to by Lesetedi AJA in *Simba Joseph v The State* thus:

> "There would be those delays inherent in the system. Systemic factors which may impact on the extent of the delay include resource limitations (not least human) which hamper the effectiveness of police investigations, prosecution of the case and or the speedy disposal of cases by judicial offices."[57]

A brief discussion of some of the factors will be appropriate here. The longer the delay, the greater the prospect of that delay's being held unreasonable. This is the primary factor, for "the longer the time that lapses, after the charge, the more the presumption that the accused person would be prejudiced thereby."[58] On the other hand, if the period between the charging of an accused and the bringing of him or her to trial does "not reach the threshold required to constitute unconscionable delay, that is the end of the inquiry and the application would have stood to be dismissed on that basis alone".[59] Thus where there is no undue delay, then *cadit quaestio*, and the court would not enter into an inquiry of all the other factors to determine a possible infringement of section 10(1), for in the circumstances it would not have been violated. It stands to reason therefore that it should always be the first factor to consider,

[55] Page 39.
[56] Page 13. See also *Simba Joseph*, p. 20 and p. 25, *Masoba* , p. 16, *Rabana v AG and Another* [2003] 1 BLR 330, 340.
[57] *Simba Joseph* at p. 353. The same views were expressed in the *Sanderson case*, on which the learned judge relied.
[58] *ibid.*, p. 16.
[59] *ibid.*, p. 20.

and this is borne out by practice. No specific period is laid down. When systemic or institutional considerations have been taken into account, the unreasonableness or otherwise of any delay will be determined by the practice or conditions in the particular system as well as societal expectations based on that practice. It is for this reason that the following words by Mosojane J in *Charles* are apt to quote. The learned judge said:

> "Experience in this country has shown, that a pretrial delay of three years, on average, to bring a murder suspect to court, though long, is not necessarily an unreasonable time delay depending on the circumstances of each case. Manpower constraints all round, among others, are often cited as the major cause and the courts generally accept that as a valid reason in our circumstances."[60]

In the *Ntwa* case, the learned Marumo J found a period of three years five months in a murder case "presumptively prejudicial so as to cry out for an inquiry into the other relevant circumstances forming part of the balancing exercise".[61] Whether the applicant or the State is responsible for the delay would necessarily lead to an order against the side on whom the responsibility falls. A justifiable explanation as to the delay would usually be an exculpatory excuse from the standpoint of the State. Although the practice in Botswana and elsewhere[62] seems to be that the assertion of the right to a speedy trial is a factor to take into account, it seems the courts in other jurisdictions would disregard it.[63] It would seem the court would be more likely, where the applicant has suffered pretrial incarceration, to consider a delay unreasonable than in the case of an accused who is on bail, for a person on bail does not suffer any compromised liberty. The other factors have already been discussed before.

---

[60] [2005] 1 BLR 421, at 425.

[61] [2001] 2 BLR, at 219.

[62] For example in the United States of America (*See Baker v Wingo*, 407 US 514, at 530 (1972)); Zimbabwe (*Mlambo*).

[63] For example in South Africa: in *Sanderson v Attorney General, Eastern Cape* 1998 (2) SA 38, at 56, Kriegler J said: "An accused should not have to demonstrate a genuine desire to go to trial in order to benefit from the right….There is, however, no need for the accused to assert his right or actively compel the State to accelerate the preparation of its case. Provided that he has genuinely suffered prejudice as a result of the State's delay, he cannot be responsible in the State's tardiness". See also the Lesotho Court of Appeal decision of *Ketisi, supra*, p. 10. That Court was composed of three South Africans, which might explain the similarity in positions.

5 Some Disturbing Observations

The above generally represents the law in Botswana and the attitude of the courts towards applications for relief under sections 10(1) and 18 of the Constitution. Rights are usually asserted by people who are aware of them, or at least those who have been advised of their existence. In Botswana, those rights have sometimes been asserted for the sole purpose of avoiding going through a trial; hence the courts take a guarded approach in the determinations of applications for relief in the pursuit of those rights. Alternatively, in terms of Section 18(3), a Subordinate Court can *mero motu* make the assessment that there is need for a determination of a possible infringement of Section 10(1) and thereby refer the matter to the High Court. The question is what happens to the majority of the gullible and ignorant persons who are dragged before Customary Courts for trial. Customary Courts, as Subordinate Courts, have legal responsibilities under Section 18 where there is a possible violation of section 10(1). The lack of legal sophistication at this level of Court, among the adjudicators and those who appear as accused persons at the Customary Courts, means that it is hard to ensure that the relevant constitutional rights are properly protected in the Customary Courts. This creates a discrepancy, for it creates a situation where accused persons before some Subordinate Courts and the High Court can more effectively have their rights protected than those who appear elsewhere. The forum determines the extent to which the right may be enjoyed. This could never have been intended by the framers of the Constitution.

This then calls into question the continued operation of the dual system of criminal justice, and whether a Customary Court should continue to exercise jurisdiction in criminal matters.[64] That raises larger issues, which would require a separate discussion.

6 Conclusion

The right to a fair trial within a reasonable time has received considerable judicial attention. The reason, as has been mentioned, is not difficult to find, as it may, where successfully asserted, lead to an acquittal. Fortunately, the courts have determined the parameters within which it is to be asserted. This development is to be welcomed. It would appear on the ground that some of

---

64 See Duma Gideon Boko. "Fair Trial and the Customary Courts in Botswana: Questions on Legal Representation," 11 (4) Criminal Law Forum 445 (2000).

the systemic constraints leading to delays are now being addressed. The Directorate of Public Prosecutions is now taking active steps to have suspects brought to courts expeditiously. The remaining challenges seem now to lie with the judiciary in terms of resource constraints, although steps are also being taken to arrest the situation on that front.

It is hoped that a debate will be undertaken as to the continued existence of the two-tier system court structure. A criminal justice system that is not uniform in its application can scarcely be perceived to be fair and raises serious questions as to its conformity with of the rule of law.

Gender and the Courts in Botswana: When Human Rights and Customary Law Clash

Samwiri Wakhakha*

1 Introduction

Gender equality has been a feature of global human rights discourse since the advent of the United Nations in 1945, although the concept of equality has been the preoccupation of humanity throughout history.[1] In Botswana gender discrimination has generated considerable academic discourse since the 1980s, underlining the pivotal significance of gender not only as a human rights issue but also as a development issue. The discrimination prohibitions in the Botswana Constitution,[2] juxtaposed against other discriminatory laws, including prejudicial customary practices, have been at the centre of the discourse. Owing partly to efforts by various women's and feminist groups,[3] and partly to legislative action by the post-independence governments, significant progress has been achieved in the alleviation of gender discrimination but more remains to be done.

Judicial intervention was sought for the first time to deal with a discriminatory statute in the celebrated case of *Unity Dow v Attorney General of Botswana.*[4] In this case a Motswana[5] mother successfully challenged the validity of a provision in the Citizenship Act which denied citizenship to two of her three children who were born during her marriage with a non-citizen male whilst the same Act granted citizenship to children fathered by Batswana husbands

---

*LL.B (Hons) (MUK), Dip.LP (LDC) LL.M (UB), Lecturer, Department of Law, University of Botswana.

[1] O Tshosa, "The Application of Non-Discrimination in Botswana in Light of *Attorney General of Botswana v. Unity Dow:* Judicial Approach and Practice", 5 Int'l J. of Discrimination & L. 190 (2001).

[2] Constitution of Botswana Chapter 1.

[3] For example the Emang Basadi "Stand Up Women" is a movement for women's rights in Botswana.

[4] [1992] BLR 119.

[5] Citizens of Botswana are referred to as Batswana (Motswana singular).

with non-citizen wives. This decision led to an amendment of the Constitution[6] as well as the Citizenship Act, outlawing sex-based discrimination in Botswana. Following the constitutional amendment, Section 15(3) provides:

> "In this section, the expression 'discriminatory' means affording different treatment to different persons, attributable wholly or mainly to their respective descriptions by race, tribe, place of origin, political opinions, colour, creed or sex whereby persons of one such description are subjected to disabilities or restrictions to which persons of another such description are not made subject or are accorded privileges or advantages which are not accorded to persons of another such description."[7]

Thus the case turned out to be the trailblazer for judicial interventions in human rights and gender discrimination cases in Botswana. In the aftermath of the decision, the government of Botswana has launched several legal and policy reforms[8] to address gender discrimination as well as uphold the principle of non-discrimination in general.[9] There is no doubt that these and other legal and policy measures have resulted in the establishment of formal equality of women and men. For example women have the same unlimited access to education at all levels as men and there is currently no known legal policy that discriminates against women in terms of access to formal employment and remuneration either in the public or private sector. Botswana is one of the four countries in the world[10] that attained gender parity at tertiary level by 2005.[11] However, formal equality alone without substantive equality may not lead to an egalitarian society to which the nation of Botswana aspires to in its long term Vision 2016,[12] because gender equality cuts across all the seven pillars of the Vision. The national vision itself should in this context be seen as a clarion call to action by all the three branches of

---

6 Section 4 of the Constitution (Amendment) Act, 2005.

7 The original provision had omitted the word "sex", giving rise to a popular perception that it permitted discrimination on the basis of sex.

8 These have mainly consisted of amendments of the Citizenship Act, the Deeds Registry Act and the Penal Code, the re-enactment of the Marriage Act and the enactment of the Abolition of Marital Power Act.

9 For example in July 1997 a consultancy was commissioned by the Ministry of Labour and Home Affairs, whose overall objective was to conduct a comprehensive study of all laws affecting the status of women, with a view to expanding the rights and enhancing the position of women in terms of the law.

10 The others are China, Mexico and Peru.

11 Sarua news bulletin found at http://sample.jdconsulting.co.za/sarua/mailer/SARUA_5_Apr_08.pdf

12 Presidential Task Group for a Long Term Vision for Botswana, *Vision 2016: Towards Prosperity for All*, Government Printing and Publishing Services, Gaborone.

government to deal decisively with any vestiges of gender discrimination and empower women.

It is common cause that there are still some provisions in the Constitution that potentially promote discrimination against women and constrain judicial ability to protect the rights of women in various spheres of life. In principle the Constitution of Botswana as amended disallows discrimination on specified grounds.[13] However, the right to non-discrimination is not absolute and is shackled by numerous claw back clauses provided for in section 15(4) to (8). Specifically, section 15(4) of the Constitution states that subsection (1) shall not apply:

(c) with respect to adoption, marriage, divorce, burial, devolution of property on death or other matters of personal law;
(d) for the application in the case of members of a particular race, community or tribe of customary law with respect to that matter which is applicable in the case of other persons or not.

To the extent that such provisions preserve customary law in order to preserve culture, they resonate with the national policy predicated upon the preservation and promotion of culture for the pride and nationhood as well as future heritage of the nation.[14] The Minister put it succinctly: "It simply stands as a facilitatory strategy for building our nation and our identity as distinct from other nations."[15] Customary law is part of culture and preservation of culture must inevitably entail preservation of customary law. The benefits that derive from preservation of a nation's culture cannot be ignored.

The negative aspect of these provisions is that they serve to validate laws that are discriminatory in the areas of personal or family law, including the devolution of property or in the application of customary law in any matter to the members of a particular race or tribe exclusively.[16] Thus the clash between culture and human rights becomes quite apparent.

---

[13] See s. 15(3) of the Constitution of Botswana as amended by s. 4 of Act 9 of 2005.

[14] See Foreword by the Minister of Labour and Home Affairs, National Policy on Culture, Ministry of Labour and Home Affairs (Department of Culture and Youth) October 2001, Government Printer, Gaborone.

[15] *ibid.*

[16] See C.M. Fombad, "Constitutional Protection Against Discrimination in Botswana", 53 Int'l & Comp. L. Q. 139, at 151 (2004).

These provisions have not so far been tested in the courts of Botswana and therefore judicial opinion on them at this stage can only be a matter of conjecture. The judiciary has, however, set precedents regarding women's rights vis-à-vis culture. In the *Unity Dow* case the Attorney General strenuously argued that it was legitimate to discriminate against women in Botswana because Botswana society was patrilineal and therefore male-oriented. This relic of customary law was rejected by the Court, although the unconstitutional provisions of the Citizenship Act were a codification of customary law. The case is a sound foundation on which the judiciary can protect women's rights notwithstanding the limitations imposed by the constitutional protection of customary law.

This paper is divided into five parts. After the present Introduction in Part 1, Part 2 involves an analysis of international and regional human rights instruments and their relevance to Botswana. Part 3 examines existing customary practices presumptively protected by the Constitution in terms of section 15(4)(d). Part 4 assesses the judicial protection of women's rights in Botswana and Part 5 contains concluding observations.

2 Legal Frameworks for Gender Equality

2.1 International Law

In Africa, gender subordination is still defined in terms of the legal and policy framework as well as the cultural setting. Women in Botswana, as in the rest of Africa, have no alternative but to rely on international law and policy frameworks to define the content and standards of their human rights. International law and policy also form the foundation of advocacy efforts because they set the benchmark to which states and society in general should aspire and to which many states have subscribed by signing and ratifying international treaties. The international legal framework also plays a crucial role in research and documentation on women's issues, particularly the appointment of the UN Special Rapporteur on violence against women who has carried out extensive research and documented women's human rights abuses across the globe.[17]

[17] http:www.ohchr.org/English/issues/women/rapporteur/index.htm. The Special Rapporteur publishes annual reports as well as undertaking country visits to document cases of violence against women.

The post-Second World War period resulted in a plethora of international and regional agreements and declarations aimed at addressing the issue of gender inequality. Most of the international agreements have been made under the auspices of the United Nations while the regional agreements have been substantially inspired by the UN. The concern for equality and non-discrimination was first expressed in the UN Charter of 1945. The Charter in its preamble expresses the need "to reaffirm faith in the fundamental human rights, in the dignity and worth of the human person, and in the equal rights of men and women".[18] The UN set a common standard on human rights with the adoption of the Universal Declaration of Human Rights (UDHR) in 1948.[19]

Articles 6, 7 and 8 of the Declaration are quite instructive. Article 6 provides that everyone has the right to recognition everywhere as a person before the law. Article 7 proclaims that all are equal before the law and are entitled without any discrimination to equal protection of the law. It goes on to provide that all are entitled to equal protection against any discrimination in violation of the Declaration and against any incitement to such discrimination. Article 8 provides that everyone has the right to an effective remedy by the competent national tribunals for acts violating the fundamental rights granted him by the constitution or by law.

Although the Declaration is not legally binding, its acceptance by all countries around the world gives great moral weight to the fundamental principle that all human beings, rich and poor, strong and weak, male and female, of all races and religions, are to be treated equally and with respect for their natural worth as human beings.[20]

Significantly, the UDHR forms the basis of bills of rights of many national constitutions around the world, including the Constitution of Botswana. Two instruments coming out of the UDHR, the International Covenant on Civil and Political Rights (ICCPR), and the International Covenant on Economic, Social and Cultural Rights (ICESCR), also reaffirm global concern for the twin principles of equality and non-discrimination.[21]

---

[18] See also Articles 1(3), 55 and 56 of the United Nations Charter (26 June 1945).

[19] http://www.unicef.org/crc/index_framework.html. The Declaration was adopted by the United Nations General Assembly on 10 December 1948.

[20] *ibid.*

[21] See ICCPR, 999 UNTS, 171, Articles 2, 3 and 26; and ICESCR 999 UNTS 3, Articles 2 and 3.

A more specific Convention dealing with discrimination against women – the Convention on the Elimination of All Forms of Discrimination Against Women (CEDAW)[22] – came into force in 1979. In its preamble, CEDAW restates the obligation of States' Parties to ensure the equal rights of women and men to enjoy all economic, social, cultural, civil and political rights. CEDAW also notes that extensive discrimination against women continues to exist, violating the principles of equality of rights and respect for human dignity, thereby constituting an obstacle to the participation of women. CEDAW defines discrimination against women as:

> "Any distinction, exclusion or restriction made on the basis of sex which has the effect or purpose of impairing or nullifying the recognition, enjoyment or exercise by women, irrespective of their marital status, on the basis of equality for men and women, of human rights and fundamental freedoms in the political, economic, social, cultural or any other field."[23]

State parties are enjoined by CEDAW to take appropriate measures to modify the social and cultural patterns of conduct of men and women, with a view to achieving the elimination of prejudices and customary and all other practices which are based on the idea of inferiority or the superiority of either of the sexes or on stereotyped roles for men and women.[24]

All the regional human rights instruments protect the principle of non-discrimination. In particular, the African Charter on Human and Peoples' Rights (ACHPR) embraces the three principles of equality, equality before the law and non-discrimination in unambiguous language:

> "Every individual shall be entitled to the enjoyment of the rights and freedoms recognized and guaranteed in the present Charter without distinction of any kind such as race, ethnic group, colour, sex, language, religion, political or any other opinion, national or social origin, fortune, birth or other status."[25]

In Article 3 provision is made for equality before the law and equal protection before the law.

---

[22] Adopted and opened for signature, ratification and accession by General Assembly resolution 34/180 of 18 December 1979. Entry into force 3 September 1979.

[23] CEDAW, Article 1.

[24] *ibid.*, Article 5.

[25] African Charter on Human and Peoples' Rights, Article 2.

More significantly, the African Charter on Human and Peoples' Rights, in its Preamble, affirms the cardinal principle of interdependence, interconnectedness and indivisibility of all rights, noting that it is:

> "... essential to pay particular attention to the right to development and that civil and political rights cannot be dissociated from economic, social and cultural rights in their conception as well as universality and that the satisfaction of economic, social and cultural rights is a guarantee for the enjoyment of civil and political rights."

The corresponding Protocol to the ACHPR on the Rights of Women in Africa expresses concern that, despite the ratification of the ACHPR and other international human rights instruments by the majority of states parties and their solemn commitment to eliminate all forms of discrimination and harmful practices against women, women in Africa still continue to be victims of discrimination and harmful practices.[26]

The UN instruments have been followed by international conferences and resolutions that have all sought to refocus attention onto women's human rights. These include the Vienna Human Rights Conference (1993) the Cairo International Conference on Population and Development (1994), the Copenhagen Social Summit (1995) and the Beijing Platform for Action (1995). Botswana not only has participated in these conferences but is also signatory to a substantial number of them, an indication of its endorsement of the underlying principles.

All the treaties to which Botswana is a signatory have as their basis international human rights norms. For example the ICCPR in its Preamble refers to the "recognition of the inherent dignity and of equal and inalienable rights of all members of human family as the foundation of freedom, justice and peace in the world" and to the "obligation of States under the Charter of the United Nations to promote universal respect for, and observance of, human rights and freedoms."[27]

The consistency with which all the international and regional instruments[28] emphasise the equality and non-discrimination principles underscores the

---

26 Preamble, Protocol to the African Charter on Human and Peoples' Rights of Women in Africa (2003/2005) adopted in Maputo, Mozambique on 11 July 2003.

27 See paras 1 and 4 of the Preamble.

28 These include the United Nations Charter, the United Nations Declaration on Human Rights, the International Covenant on Civil and Political Rights, the International Covenant on Social, Economic and Cultural Rights and the African Charter on Human and Peoples' Rights.

pivotal significance of gender equality in national and international developments. It is now common cause that all human rights are universal, indivisible and interdependent and interrelated. The call to the international community to treat human rights globally in a fair and equal manner, on the same footing and with the same emphasis,[29] is unequivocal.

As Justice Molokomme has appositely opined, in view of the now widely accepted concepts of universality, indivisibility and inalienability of human rights, there can be no debate about whether these instruments are relevant to SADC countries.[30]

> Fortunately, that approach finds ample support in the Botswana judiciary. In the *Unity Dow* case Aguda J.A said: I take the view that in all these circumstances a court in this country, faced with the difficulty of interpretation as to whether or not some legislation breached any provisions entrenched in Chapter II of our Constitution which deals with fundamental rights and freedoms of individual, is entitled to look at the international agreements, treaties and obligations entered into before or after the legislation was enacted to ensure that such domestic legislation does not breach any of the international conventions, agreements, treaties, and obligations binding upon this country save upon clear and unambiguous language."[31]

The SADC Chief Justices' Conference on Human Rights urged courts in SADC member states where incorporation of international and regional instruments have not been effected to utilise international customary law and the Bangalore Principles, to remove ambiguity and uncertainty from national constitutions, legislation and common law.[32] It is significant that the initiative to convene this seminal conference came from the Botswana judiciary.

---

[29] World Conference on Human Rights, Vienna, 25 June 1993, Vienna Declaration and Programme of Action, Part 1, paragraph 5 (UN Document A/Conf 157/23 (1993))

[30] Justice Athaliah Molokomme, "Response: International and Regional Human Rights Instruments: Challenges for SADC Countries", Proceedings of the SADC Chief Justices, Conference on Human Rights, Mowana Lodge, Kasane, Botswana, 5–7 July 2004.

[31] *Unity Dow v Attorney General*, [1992] BLR119 at 170.

[32] See paragraph 7.2.3 of the Statement Adopted by the Conference of SADC Chief Justices on Human Rights, Independence of the Judiciary, the Rule of Law, and Access to Justice, Proceedings of the SADC Chief Justices' Conference on Human Rights, Mowana Lodge, Kasane, Botswana 5–7 July 2004, p. 158.

The decision of the South African Constitutional Court in *The State v Makwanyane*[33], which led to the abolition of the death penalty, is a good example of how an African court can rely on western and international jurisprudence without losing sight of the national legal context and customary values to advance the cause of human rights. In this respect, the President of the Court, Chaskalson P., stated:

> "In dealing with comparative law we must bear in mind that we are required to construe the South African Constitution, and not an international instrument or the constitution of some foreign country, and that this has to be done with due regard to our legal system, our history and circumstances, and the structure and language of our own Constitution."[34]

The Court also called into its aid the philosophy of *ubuntu*[35] to justify its reliance on indigenous values:

> "Indeed, there is a need for indigenous concepts like that of *ubuntu* to find appropriate expression in constitutional law judgments so that our jurisprudence can have an autochthonous character."[36]

Ubuntu is the equivalent of the notion of *botho*[37] espoused in Botswana. Further, the Act[38] which provides for the interpretation of the Constitution and other enactments expressly authorises courts to rely *inter alia* on international treaties and agreements in their construction of such enactments.[39]

There is therefore a wide scope for the harmonisation of both customary law and international law.

2.2 National Law

The Constitution of Botswana[40] in its Bill of Rights enshrines only civil and political rights. Unlike other constitutions[41] in the region it is silent about the

---

33 Case no CCT/3/94; [1995] 1 LRC 269.

34 *ibid.*, para 39.

35 An ethic or humanist philosophy focusing on people's allegiances and relations with each other.

36 See the judgments of Mokgoro J and Langa J, paras 300, 307–308, 223–227 respectively.

37 Vision 2016, A Framework for a Long Term Vision for Botswana defines Botho "as a concept of a person who has a well rounded character, who is well mannered, courteous and disciplined."

38 The Interpretation Act Cap. 01:04.

39 *ibid.*, section 24(1).

40 Chapter 1.

41 Such as those of South Africa, Namibia, Angola and Malawi.

place and role of international law in municipal law. Neither does it contain special provisions for women's rights, like other constitutions in the region.[42] Specifically it makes no provision for economic, social and cultural rights. This, however, does not necessarily mean that Botswana is delivering less on human rights than other countries in Africa or in the region. On the contrary, Botswana has an excellent human rights track record.

This Constitution has now been amended several times[43] with a view to removing provisions which entrench discrimination in general and gender discrimination in particular, and is therefore a good backdrop for initiatives aimed at gender equality. The constitutional prohibition against sex-based discrimination is, however, subject to the exceptions already mentioned, with the result that the protection so guaranteed has been severely compromised.

Furthermore, many present laws have incorporated discriminatory elements of customary law, particularly in the areas of marriage, adoption, devolution of property upon death and the ownership and use of property.[44] Until quite recently the list of laws that discriminated against women was quite long and no fewer than 10.[45] One of the terms of reference for the consultancy commissioned by the Women's Affairs Department was to review all statutes and subsidiary legislation affecting women, particularly the following: the Marriage Act (Cap 29:01), the Married Persons' Property Act (Cap 29:03), Abortion: the Penal Code Amendment (Cap 08:01), the Deeds Registry Act (Cap 33:03), the Administration of Estates Act (Cap 31:01), the Employment Act (Cap 47:01), the Deserted Wives and Children Protection Act (Cap 28:03), the Matrimonial Causes Act (Cap 29:06), the Adoption Act (Cap 28:01) and Delicts.[46] Some of these, as already noted, have now been amended, including the Marriage Act, the Penal Code with respect to abortion, and the Deeds Registry Act and the momentous Abolition of the Marital Power Act

[42] See, for example, section 24 of the Constitution of Malawi.

[43] The amendments have been compiled in the Constitution of Botswana (Amendment) Government Printer, Gaborone.

[44] For a full discussion of discrimination against women in Botswana, See Human Rights Watch/ Africa Human Rights Watch Women's Project, *Botswana: Second Class Citizens*, vol. 6 no. 7 (1994).

[45] See the *Report on A Review of All Laws Affecting the Status of Women in Botswana*, September 1998, Department of Women's Affairs, Ministry of Labour and Home Affairs, Government of Botswana, Gaborone p. 1.

[46] *ibid.*

is now law. The Act, however, excludes customary and religious marriages[47] from its application; these constitute the bulk of marriages in Botswana. Nonetheless, such legislative attempts at reform are a clear indication of government's predisposition to remove the remaining obstacles to gender equality.

It is submitted that the ongoing constitutional and legal reforms aimed at bringing about gender parity should serve as an inspiration to the judiciary to do more in support of that process. In this regard the courts in Botswana have set precedents which should serve as an inspiration for future decisions. For example, they have avoided some of the injustices arising out of the traditional rules of customary laws of inheritance[48] by adopting a more purposive interpretation of the law. A similar approach could go a long way towards alleviating the customary law prejudices against women. Further justification for this kind of approach is provided by the Customary Courts Act.[49] The Act defines customary law as meaning:

> "In relation to any particular tribe or tribal community, the customary law of that tribe or tribal community so far as it is not incompatible with the provisions of any written law or contrary to *morality, humanity or natural justice"*.[50]

2.3 Customary Law and Gender

After decades of British imperial rule, Botswana inherited a dual legal system at independence and the indigenous tribes and communities which were resident within the territory of what was then called the Bechuanaland Protectorate.[51] This dual system of law consists of both the received common law[52] and the indigenous customary law. The term 'customary law' refers to

---

[47] See Part I of the Act.

[48] See, for example, the case of *Tshepo Mbenge Mosienyane v Lesetedinyana Lesetedi & 15* Ors, Misca No. F257 of 2005.

[49] Cap 04:05.

[50] Section 2 (emphasis added).

[51] Under Article 4 of the Bechuanaland Protectorate General Administration Order in Council of 9th May (1891), the High Commissioner was to respect Native law and Custom. The Bechuanaland Protectorate Administration Order-in-Council Proclamation of 10th June (1891) introduced the Cape Colonial Laws into the Bechuanaland Protectorate.

[52] Generally referred to as the Roman-Dutch common law. See further Tshosa, *op. cit.*, fn. 1, *supra* at 42. See also A. Molokomme, "The reception and development of Roman-Dutch law in Botswana" (1985) 1 *Lesotho Law Journal* 121.

the variety of rules, principles and usages of the different ethnic groups,[53] which may differ from each other.[54]

In Botswana, the Tswana[55] customary law is full of norms and practices that are either directly or indirectly discriminatory against women. Under Tswana customary law, women are on the whole regarded as socially inferior to men and are always treated as minors.[56] The Tswana customary laws are such that women are disadvantaged in almost all spheres of life including marriage and proprietary rights. For instance, when a married man dies, leaving a wife and children of both sexes, his eldest son becomes the principal heir *(mojaboswa)*, even if there is an older daughter.[57] On the death of their father, daughters formerly received no cattle at all; nor did the widow as she was expected to be maintained and supported by the heir while she lived with him. This is said to be the general rule in most tribes.[58] Thus a historical inequality exists which continues to be accentuated by customary practices as well as unequal power relations.

The preservation of gender inequality which is inherent in the continuous application of customary laws in many of the areas covered by section 15(4)(c) and (d) of the Constitution is clearly a glaring anomaly and an anachronism, which is difficult to reconcile with the spirit, purport and objects of the Bill of Rights.[59] These exceptions are an indication that customary law[60] still holds sway in Botswana. In other words customary law and the Constitution are mutually reinforcing in that, whilst the former influenced some of the latter's provisions, the Constitution has served to protect the continued application of the customary law. It can hardly be imagined that such was the intention of

---

[53] Botswana comprises the dominant Tswana speaking communities such as the Ngwato, Kgatla, Kwena and Ngwaketse and other ethnic communities otherwise known as 'subject communities/ tribes' such as the Kalanga, Birwa, Yei and Sarwa.

[54] See G.O. Radijeng, *Customary Law and Gender Equality: The Legal Status of Women in Botswana*, (Unpublished D. Phil Thesis, University of Oxford. 2004), p. 58.

[55] This refers to the most dominant tribe in Botswana called the Tswana. For the purposes of this paper, any reference to Tswana customary laws or practices should be construed as such unless otherwise specified.

[56] I. Schapera, *A Handbook of Tswana Law and Custom,* p. 28.

[57] *ibid.* p. 230.

[58] *ibid.* p. 231.

[59] C. M. Fombad, op. *cit.,* fn. 15 *supra*, at p. 152.

[60] See *Attorney General v Unity Dow* [1992] BLR 119 at p. 137, where Amissah JP said: "Our attention has been drawn to the patrilineal customs and traditions of the Botswana people to show …..that it was proper for Parliament to legislate to preserve or advance such customs and traditions."

the founders of the present day Botswana who participated in the formulation of the Constitution.

Consequently many of the problems associated with gender-based discrimination in Botswana have to do with customary law and its influence on the formulation of the country's Constitution and statutory legislation after independence. Despite the variations in the customary laws of the different ethnic groups in Botswana, one thing seems to be common to all of them, that is that all of them directly or indirectly discriminate against women.

There is, however, nothing sacrosanct about customary law in Botswana. This is because even the most powerful chiefs in Botswana saw the need to adapt Tswana law and custom to the changing socio-economic circumstances of the country during the colonial era. For example, among the Ngwato, Chief Khama abolished polygamy and modified the customary rules of inheritance so that daughters should also inherit cattle.[61] Likewise Chief Linchwe of Kgatla is said to have handed down a number of decisions in the 1970s to the effect that the property of a deceased man be distributed equally between the children irrespective of gender.[62] It has also been noted that presently the customary courts have made decisions that reflect sensitivity to changing socio-economic conditions[63] in the country as demonstrated by their decisions in the cases of *Mmokele v Ramgale*[64] and *Moswelakgomo v Kekgaretswe*.[65] These laudable gender-sensitive measures, taken together with the recent legal reforms aimed at eliminating inequalities against women, lead unerringly to the conclusion that in Botswana, when culture and human rights clash, the latter prevails. Furthermore, one of the principles of Botswana's development philosophy enshrined in Vision 2016 is *botho,*[66] which disapproves of anti-social, disgraceful and criminal behaviour, and encourages social

[61] See I. Schapera, *op. cit.,* fn. 53, *supra,* pp. 43–44. See also B. Morton, "The evolution of women's property rights in colonial Botswana, 1890–1966" (1998) 12 *Pula: Botswana Journal of African Studies* 5.

[62] See *Report on a Review of All Laws Affecting the Status of Women in Botswana* p. 44, citing Comaroff and Roberts, 1981.

[63] *ibid.* p. 48.

[64] CRB 150/1995, Customary Court of Appeal.

[65] CRB 23/1995, Customary Court of Appeal. For the facts of both cases, see *Report on a Review of All Laws Affecting the Status of Women in Botswana,* p. 48.

[66] Reference has already been made to this concept when discussing *ubuntu*. It involves the notion of a person who has a well-rounded character, who is well-mannered, courteous and disciplined, and realises his or her full potential both as an individual and as part of the community to which he or she belongs. See Presidential Task Group for a Long Term Vision for Botswana, *Vision 2016: Towards Prosperity for All*, September 1997, Government Printing and Publishing Services, Gaborone, p. 2.

justice for all.[67] It envisages a future where no citizen of Botswana will be disadvantaged as a result of gender, age, religion or creed, colour, national or ethnic origin, location, language or political opinions.[68] The future envisaged for Botswana will be one devoid of negative social attitudes towards the status and role of women, the youth, the elderly and the disabled and will be free from all forms of sexual harassment.[69] Despite such welcome declarations of intent, the present situation allows customary law to disadvantage women. In the words of Chief Justice Nganunu, "as the Vision is a national strategy for broad development and social justice the Botswana judiciary has accepted that it is a necessary pillar in this process because it provides the legal services that must keep the wheels of society oiled, enabling society in general to go about its business smoothly."[70]

4 The Judiciary and Gender

Since its seminal decision in the *Unity Dow* case, the Botswana judiciary has been consistent in its protection of women's constitutionally enshrined rights, as demonstrated by a number of landmark cases.[71] This has not only earned the judiciary well-deserved accolades but also heightened expectations from gender activists and other feminist groups in and out of Botswana. The Botswana judiciary is also aware of its responsibility as the custodian but not the overlord of the Constitution.[72] The judiciary's constitutional and primary function is the adjudication of disputes in the community. In a "secondary sense" judges indeed make law,[73] but there are limits of a policy nature on the manner and extent of judicial law-making, since, in the words of Lord Diplock, the courts are invariably influenced by the "underlying political philosophy of a particular nation as to the appropriate limits of law-making functions of a non-elected judiciary".[74]

---

[67] *ibid.*

[68] *ibid.* p. 11.

[69] *ibid.*

[70] Welcome speech by Hon. J.M. Nganunu Chief Justice of Botswana, Proceedings of the SADC Chief Justices' Conference on Human Rights, Mowana Lodge, Kasane, Botswana 5–7 July 2004 p. 8.

[71] These include *Unity Dow v. Attorney General, supra* and *SRC, Molepolole College of Education v. Attorney General of Botswana* [1995] BLR 178. For a commentary on the latter case, see EK Quansah "Is the right to get pregnant a fundamental human right in Botswana?" (1995) 39 *Journal of African Law* 97.

[72] O.K. Dingake, *Key Aspects of the Constitutional Law of Botswana*, p. 143

[73] See Hahlo H.R and Kahn E, *The South African Legal System and its Background*, Cape Town, Juta & Co (1968), p. 306.

[74] *Geelong Harbor Trust Commrs v. Gibbs Bright & Co* 1974 (2) ALR 362, at 369.

The judiciary as the third arm of government[75] in a liberal democracy such as Botswana can play a critical transformative role in fostering a human rights culture. In Marcel Storme's conception of the role and status of the judiciary as a state power, the judiciary has three essential functions:

> "(1) to take an active part in the process of developing the law, whilst at all times doing so with the necessary degree of restraint; (2) to have as its supreme function the safeguarding and protection of human rights, more particularly in terms of the relationship between the citizen and the authorities; and (3) to be the ultimate bulwark in maintaining the rule of law."[76]

This position was echoed by Chief Justice Cullinan of Lesotho when he opined that the judiciary's cardinal duty is to uphold the rule of law and protect human rights and that the persistent exercise of this crucial role ensures that the courts always are defenders of fundamental human rights.[77] The Botswana Constitution expressly authorises the judiciary to be the protector of the constitutionally enshrined human rights protective provisions. Section 18(1) states:

> "Subject to the provisions of subsection (5) of this section, if any person alleges that any of the provisions of sections 3 and 16 (inclusive) of this Constitution has been, is being or is likely to be contravened in relation to him, then, without prejudice to any other action with respect to the same matter which is lawfully available, that person may apply to the High Court for redress."

The importance of this provision is two-fold. It provides the legal basis for the judiciary to deal with the human rights protection cases and it is evidence that the politicians, the elected representatives of the people of Botswana, have in their wisdom decided to ascribe this power to the judiciary. The Botswana judiciary has been steadfast in its protection of human rights

---

[75] According to the celebrated doctrine of *trias politica* the judiciary constitutes the third branch of government. This doctrine was expounded by Montesquieu C.L.J in his celebrated work *L' Espirit des Lois.*

[76] Marcel Storme, President of the International Association for Procedural Law, Role and Status of the Judiciary as a State Power, International Encyclopedia of Laws, Kluwer Law International, "Law in Motion" 1st World Law Conference, Brussels, Belgium, Palais des Congres 9–12 September 1996, General Reports and Conference Papers Part 1 p. 133.

[77] See the opening address by Cullinan, C.J. during the Workshop on Constitutional Government and Human Rights in Africa, Maseru, Lesotho, 4–8 October, 1989.

in general and the rights of women in particular as exemplified by the landmark cases already mentioned. These cases are now well known as substantial academic literature has been generated around them, recognising their liberal and progressive approach in construing the constitutional human rights provisions. The cases also show that the courts in Botswana are loath to accept sex as a basis for discrimination. In *Unity Dow*, Horwitz J. declared:

> "... It is difficult if not impossible to accept [counsel]'s argument that Botswana is a discriminatory society and that the word sex was left out of the section because Botswana believes that there should be discrimination based on sex."[78]

The judiciary has been able to achieve this feat largely because of the enduring democracy and statesmanlike leadership in the country since independence. These are important prerequisites for the judiciary to carry out its function without let or hindrance. Former president, Festus Mogae, put this beyond any shadow of doubt when he said:

> "The judiciaries have a constitutional obligation to constantly remind the executive arm of governments that international agreements and instruments are but meaningful in their implementation."[79]

This is an unequivocal call to action from the highest executive authority in the land. Thus the judiciary in Botswana has a unique opportunity to take advantage of the prevalent democratic environment in the country to build on its earlier work in the protection of human rights.

However, the government has not domesticated most of the international human rights instruments that it has ratified, thus rendering them inapplicable in Botswana courts. The judiciary has not lost sight of this fact. Nonetheless, the judiciary has creatively relied on international instruments in interpreting constitutional human rights provisions.

---

[78] [1991] BLR 231, at 243.

[79] H.E Mr. Festus Mogae, President of Republic of Botswana Official Opening Speech, Proceedings of the SADC Chief Justices' Conference on Human Rights, Mowana Lodge, Kasane, Botswana 5–7 July 2004, p. 18.

In *Unity Dow,* the judiciary was forthright in justifying its reliance on international law in the interpretation of constitutional human rights provisions. Aguda J.A. stated:

> "In my view it is the clear duty of this court when faced with the difficult task of construction of provisions of the Constitution to keep in mind the international obligation. If the constitutional provisions are such as can be construed to ensure the compliance of the state with its international obligations then they must be so construed."[80]

In this case the human rights instruments relied upon included the European Convention on Human Rights and Fundamental Freedoms, CEDAW, the ACHPR and the ICCPR.

The Court of Appeal was emphatic in reaffirming Unity *Dow* when deciding the case of *SRC, Molepolole College of Education v Attorney General of Botswana.*[81] Amissah J.A. said:

> "Any constitutional challenge in our courts on the basis of sex discrimination must begin with the examination of this court's decision in the *Attorney General v. Unity Dow*. It was in this case that this court held that discrimination based on sex is repugnant to sections 3 and 15 of the Constitution of Botswana."[82]

This case has not only continued to inspire courts in Botswana but has also inspired courts in other countries such as Zimbabwe.[83]

4.1 Litigation as a Tool for Social Transformation

For litigation to function as a tool in social transformation there must exist litigation on the one hand and on the other hand there must be a willingness by the judiciary to engage and develop the equality jurisprudence[84] to reflect the transformative needs of society. Litigation is initiated by individuals or a

---

80 [1992] BLR 119 at p. 171.

81 [1995] BLR 178.

82 At p. 195.

83 For a detailed discussion on the impact of this case in Botswana and the Southern African Region: See, O. Tshosa, *op. cit.* fn. 1, *supra*.

84 See Catherine Albertyn, "Substantive Equality and Transformation in South Africa", 23 *South African Journal of Human Rights* 253 (2007) for a detailed discussion.

group of individuals in the form of a case that is properly filed in a court registry. It is this kind of case that triggers judicial intervention in a dispute between the parties. It is widely acknowledged that Botswana has achieved formal equality but substantive equality continues to be elusive.[85] Substantive equality, unlike formal equality, may be difficult to legislate as it takes various social and economic dimensions. It is best dealt with through individual vigilance by rights holders.

In recognition of the significance of vindication of individual rights in the courts, the High Court of Botswana has widened the scope for such claims. Thus, although, in its wording, the Botswana Constitution limits itself to dealing with individual rights[86] and has no reference to collective rights, the High Court has liberally interpreted this provision to include groups of individuals formally or informally organised.[87] This should therefore be an encouragement to the interest groups or women's organisations and other human rights organisations in Botswana in bringing cases to vindicate women's rights in the High Court.

There are, however, obstacles to an individual's ability to enforce his or her rights in a court of law. One such obstacle is that only the High Court (and, by way of appeal, the Court of Appeal) is authorised to hear claims arising out of sections 3 to 16 of the Constitution.[88] Such suits would require legal representation for the applicant to have any realistic chance of success. In the absence of legal aid most rural folk, including women, would be constrained in making such applications. Therefore litigation in this regard, especially by the rural unemployed women, is likely to be limited and the judicial role in social transformation will correspondingly be affected. The legal aid currently provided by the University of Botswana Legal Clinic is not capable of fully meeting the needs of disadvantaged women in Botswana. Divorce and customary inheritance cases constitute the bulk of cases handled by the Legal Clinic,[89] an indication that there is real need for legal aid in this respect.

---

[85] See Ditshwanelo, Examination of the Report of Botswana by the UN Human Rights Committee, List of Issues. In Issue no. 7 it is acknowledged that "[g]enerally, the Government has achieved much in terms of *de jure* aspects of women. However, *de facto* equality and protection continues to be a challenge."

[86] *ibid.*

[87] See *Kamanakao I & 2 others v Attorney General of Botswana* [2001] 2 BLR 654 and [2002]1 BLR 110.

[88] See Section 18(1) of the Constitution.

[89] From my interview with Prof. Louis McKinney, Fulbright scholar attached to the Clinic in 2008.

In dealing with these obstacles it is worth recalling the following seminal statement by former president H.E Festus Mogae:

> "I appreciate the fact that appropriate focus has been placed on the important issue of access to justice. Whereas the executive arms of governments have their share of responsibility to provide human and financial resources and facilities to courts, the judiciaries too could contribute to this requirement by modernizing the processes and procedures of adjudication by making the court environment more user-friendly than it is at present."[90]

In this regard, the High Court's circuit programme is a laudable practice as it takes services nearer to the people and drastically reduces transport costs of litigants.

5 Concluding Observations

Judicial office in Africa can be precarious. In some jurisdictions judges have had to act with the greatest caution, making it hard for them to discharge effectively their duty as defenders of human rights and the rule of law. Fortunately, the Botswana judiciary does not face that prospect of interference by the executive, a fact that has been noted by a recent study on the Judicial Institution in Southern Africa.[91] Neither are the ordinary courts in Botswana alone in this process of transformation. The executive and the legislature as well as the customary courts are also playing their role. What the courts in Botswana can do is to complement those efforts by simply following the path they have charted with such great distinction and honour, guided by the contemporary human rights trends. In the words of Judge Learned Hand:

> "A judge must preserve his authority by cloaking himself in the majesty of an overshadowing past; but he must discover some composition with the dominant trends of his time – at all hazards he must maintain that

[90] H.E Mr. Festus G. Mogae, President of the Republic of Botswana, Official Opening, SADC Chief Justices' Conference on Human Rights, Mowana Lodge, Kasane, Botswana, 5–7 July 2004.

[91] *The Judicial Institution in Southern Africa, Democratic Governance and Rights Unit*, UCT p. 32 where it is stated that "all the literature and all the interviewees were unequivocal about the independence of the Botswana judiciary: there has never been a case in which there was even a suggestion of government influence or interference."

tolerable continuity without which society dissolves, and men must begin again the weary path up from savagery."[92]

It has sometimes taken simple tact on the part of the judiciary to convince the executive and the legislature to remedy a human rights issue, such as happened in the case of *Kamanakao I v Attorney General of Botswana & Anor*,[93] where Chief Justice Nganunu said[94]:

> "We mention .... that the refusal by this court to order as applied for is not an expression that the issues involved in this case must be ignored. On the contrary we wish to emphasize the urgent requirement on the part of the Government of Botswana to attend to them lest they bedevil the spirit of goodwill existing between the different tribes and communities in this country."

The Government has taken legislative action on the issues referred to by the Chief Justice.[95] This rare prompting from the judiciary notwithstanding, judges generally cannot take the initiative towards law reform. Even where doubts may exist about the constitutionality of certain legislation or excessive actions have been taken against an individual or a group, they must wait until a case is presented before them. It is therefore primarily the duty of Batswana women to seek judicial intervention through litigation on issues. Only then can the courts play their proper role to ensure protection of their rights.

[92] Cited in Wallace Mendelson, *Supreme Court Statecraft* at p. 27.

[93] [2001] 2 BLR 654.

[94] *ibid.*, at 678.

[95] See Constitution (Amendment) Act 2005.

Human Rights and HIV/AIDS in Botswana: Current Perspectives and Future Prospects

E.K Quansah*

1 INTRODUCTION

Certain fundamental human rights, the basic rights and freedoms to which all humans are entitled,[1] are guaranteed under the Botswana Constitution.[2] However, these constitutional rights are generally regarded as "first-generation" human rights, that is, rights which deal principally with liberty and participation in political life. They are mainly civil and political in nature, and serve to protect the individual from the excesses of the State.[3]

In recent years there has been a growing recognition that additional protection is required for other rights outside those currently protected, the so-called second and third generation of human rights.[4] The second-generation of human rights cover social, economic, and cultural rights such as, a right to be employed and a right to health care,[5] whilst the third-generation cover such rights as the right to self-determination and the right to a healthy environment.[6]

---

*LLB; LLM (Lond.); LLD (Unisa), Barrister of Gray's Inn, Barrister and Solicitor (Ghana); Attorney (Botswana); Professor of Law, University of Botswana.

1 See Art. 1 of the United Nations Universal Declaration of Human Rights 1948. On the general concept of the protection of human rights in Botswana, see CM Fombad "The Protection of Human Rights in Botswana: An overview of the regulatory framework" in *Essays on the Law of Botswana* CM Fombad (ed.), Cape Town, Juta & Co. (2007) pp. 2–5

2 See Chapter II of the 1966 Constitution (sections 3–19).

3 These rights are mainly derived from the International Convention on Civil and Political Rights, adopted and opened for signature, ratification and accession by the UN General Assembly Resolution 2200A (XXI) of 16 December 1966.

4 See Karl Vasak, "Human Rights: A Thirty-year struggle: The sustained efforts to give force of law to the Universal Declaration of Human Rights" (1977) 30 UNESCO Courier 11.

5 See arts. 22–27 of the Universal Declaration of Human Rights 1948.

6 See, for example, the 1972 Stockholm Declaration of the UN conference on Human Environment (5–16 June 1972) and the 1992 Rio Declaration on Environment and Development (3–14 June 1992). The rights envisaged under these declarations have been hard to enact in legally binding documents because of political and economic considerations.

There is growing international recognition of the universality, interdependence and indivisibility of human rights. The United Nations World Conference on Human Rights held in Vienna in June 1993 emphasised this recognition by proclaiming that "[all] human rights are universal, indivisible and interdependent and interrelated." Consequently, the contemporary resurgence of democratisation and reappraisals of independence constitutions in Africa,[7] has given opportunities for the inclusion of second and third generation human rights in the constitutions of various African countries.[8] Botswana has, however, been insulated from what has been referred to as the "infectious fever of constitutional-making"[9] and has maintained its independence constitution with minimal amendments which do not include any of the second and third generations of human rights.[10]

HIV/AIDS has for some time now been recognised internationally as one of the most serious threats to human rights. For example, the African Commission on Human and Peoples' Rights at its meeting in Tripoli in May 2001 declared that HIV/AIDS pandemic is a human rights issue which is a threat against humanity. At the end of 2007, 33.2 million people worldwide were living with HIV of which 22.5 million live in sub-Saharan Africa. 2.5 million people were newly affected by HIV in the same year.[11] In Botswana, of the estimated population of 1.8 million, 270,000 are estimated to be living with HIV.[12] These figures vividly demonstrate the seriousness of the pandemic and the need to put in place legal instruments to protect the human rights of those affected by the pandemic. As succinctly stated in the foreword to the *HIV/AIDS and Human Rights – International Guidelines* of 2002:

---

[7] See CM Fombad, "Challenges to constitutionalism and constitutional rights in Africa and the enabling role of political parties: Lessons and perspectives from Southern Africa" (2007) 55 Am. J. of Comp. L. 1.

[8] See, for example, South Africa (ss. 23, 24, 26 and 27 1996 Constitution); Namibia (Chapter 11 1990 Constitution, provided as principles of State policy rather than enforceable rights) and Ghana (arts. 22, 24, 25 and 26 1992 Constitution). See also JC Mubangizi, "The constitutional protection of socio-economic rights in selected African countries: A comparative evaluation" 2 Afr. J. of Legal Studies 1 (2006).

[9] See CM Fombad, "The Protection of Human Rights in Botswana: An overview of the regulatory framework" *op. cit.*, p. 1.

[10] See Constitution (Amendment) Act, 2005 dealing with such issues as sex discrimination, reform of the House of Chiefs and the establishment of the office of Director of Public Prosecutions.

[11] See Unaids, "Aids Epidemic Update December 2007" at www.unaids.org accessed on 3 March 2008.

[12] See Botswana- Situation Analysis at www.unaids.org accessed on 3 March 2008.

> "Human rights promotion and protection is central to the response to HIV/AIDS. Denying the rights of people living with HIV, and those affected by the epidemic, imperils not only their well-being, but life itself."

The Botswana Constitution, as alluded to above, contains guarantees of certain fundamental human rights but these rights may not be enough to comprehensively protect the human rights of those infected and affected by HIV/AIDS. This paper therefore aims, firstly, to discuss those human rights in the context of HIV/AIDS that are currently protected, evaluate the adequacy or otherwise of such protection and secondly, to identify areas where there are gaps and the need to advocate change in an attempt to establish a right-based approach to HIV/AIDS.

2 Current Framework for the Protection of the Human Rights of HIV/AIDS Victims

2.1 The Constitution

Sections 3–15 of the Constitution protect fundamental human rights and freedoms. These rights include, *inter alia*, the right to life, liberty, security, privacy, human dignity and equal protection under the law and the prohibition against discrimination. These rights are available to all human beings within Botswana, regardless of race, colour, creed, sex or place of origin, whether they are citizens or non-citizens resident in Botswana. Consequently, it includes persons infected with HIV/AIDS. Such persons retain their status as human beings in spite of their being infected with HIV/AIDS.

In the leading case on the interpretation of section 3 of the Constitution, *Attorney-General v Dow,*[13] it was held that the provisions of section 3 conferred on the individual the right to equal treatment of the law. The section was regarded as key or umbrella provision in Chapter II under which all rights and freedoms protected under that Chapter must be subsumed. The fact that discrimination was not mentioned in section 3 did not mean that discrimination, in the sense of unequal treatment, was not proscribed under the section. With regard to the specific definition of "discriminatory" in section 15(3) of the Constitution, the court held that the definition was expressly stated to be valid "in this section" and consequently, the right conferred by section 3 could not be abridged by section 15 because the word "sex" (which was the issue in the case) was omitted from the definition of

[13] [1992] BLR 119.

"discriminatory" in the section. The court added that a fundamental right conferred by the Constitution on an individual could not be circumscribed by a definition in another section for the purpose of that section. The overall effect of the interpretation of section 15(3) dealing with discrimination is that the categories of groups or classes of people who should be protected against discrimination is not closed. As asserted by Amissah P.:

> "I do not think that the framers of the Constitution intended to declare in 1966 that all potentially vulnerable groups or classes who would be affected for all time by discriminatory treatment have been identified and mentioned in the definition in section 15(3). I do not think that they intended to declare that the categories mentioned in that definition were forever closed. In the nature of things, as far-sighted people trying to look into the future, they would have contemplated that with the passage of time not only the groups or classes which had caused concern at the time of writing the Constitution but other groups or classes needing protection would arise. The categories might grow or change. In that sense, the classes or groups itemised in the definition would be, and in my opinion, are by way of examples of what the framers of the Constitution thought worth mentioning as potentially some of the most likely areas of possible discrimination."[14]

This *dictum* clearly points to the distinct possibility of the Constitution giving protection to HIV/AIDS sufferers if they are discriminated against on the ground of their HIV/AIDS status although no specific mention is made of that fact in the Constitution. Indeed, in *Diau v Botswana Building Society*[15] the court expressed the view, albeit *obiter*, that where an employer terminates the employment of an employee because the latter refused to undergo an HIV test, the employer's conduct undermines the employee's right to privacy.[16] However, on the facts of the case, no actual invasion or infringement of the employee's privacy occurred. In *Makuto v The State,*[17] the Court of Appeal held that although the definition of the expression "discriminatory" in section 15(3) of the Constitution contained no mention of discrimination against a group or class of persons identified on the grounds of health or physical disability, on a broad and generous interpretation of the said section, that definition would cover an identified group or class of persons who

[14] *ibid.*, at 146.
[15] [2003] 2 BLR 409.
[16] *ibid.*, at 431.
[17] [2000] 2 BLR 130 (CA).

suffered discrimination as such group or class for no other reason than the fact of their membership of the group or class; and such group or class would be entitled to challenge a law that they allege discriminated against them.[18]

2.1.1 Right to Privacy

In terms of section 9 a person's right to privacy is protected but this is qualified in the interests of defence, public safety, public order, public morality and public health. The effect of these qualifications is that privacy can be restricted, *inter alia*, in the interest of public health or for the protection of rights of others. These could be used against persons infected with the HIV/AIDS. However, the Constitution makes it explicit that any such restriction on human rights must be prescribed by law and must be reasonably justifiable in a democratic society. Thus under the Statistics Act 1967 a person is compelled to provide information for statistics and census purposes.[19] This could derogate from a person's right to privacy if he/she is required to reveal his/her HIV status, on, for example, a census questionnaire.

Furthermore, under the Botswana Medical Council (Professional Conduct) Regulations 1999[20] a patient's right to confidentiality is guaranteed and generally medical practitioners are prohibited from revealing a patient's medical condition. There are three narrow exceptions to this prohibition, namely, a medical practitioner may furnish such information:

1. to a person taking care of, living with or otherwise coming into close contact with such person, where the person is suffering from a communicable disease or has an infection which, may be passed to such person if appropriate precaution is not taken;
2. to a court of competent jurisdiction in Botswana where the court has ordered the disclosure of the information; or
3. to another medical practitioner or legal representative who requires or is entitled to the information in the course of his professional duties.

Whilst the meaning of these exceptions may not generally pose a problem of interpretation, there are aspects which may do so. For instance, a doctor under these provisions, may disclose a person's HIV status to a number of persons such as wives, nurses other doctors or lawyers, some of whom are not under

---

[18] *ibid.*, at 134.

[19] See s. 6 of the Act.

[20] Art. 21.

any burden to maintain confidentiality of the information passed on to them.[21] Under (3) above, although a medical practitioner or lawyer may "require" or "is entitled" to such information, it is unclear when there is a requirement or entitlement. Furthermore, the language used to describe the introduction of shared confidentiality in (1) above has been criticised as being ambiguous.[22] Firstly, it is said that for the confidentiality to be breached, the patient must be suffering from a communicable disease or an infection, "which may be passed to another person if appropriate caution is not taken." It is arguable that this has limited application to HIV/AIDS taking into account the limited means (sexual intercourse, needle-sharing and exchange of blood) by which the disease is spread. Thus the provision may apply only to sexual partners or care givers who are involved in contact with a patient's blood. Secondly, it is argued that even if the provision applies fully to HIV/AIDS and the person caring for or living with a patient are entitled to medical information, what categories of persons are meant by those who come into "regular close contact" with the patient? It is not clear whether these include friends, family members or even employers. The Regulations do not answer these questions.

2.1.2 Right to Liberty

Section 5 of the Constitution protects the right to liberty.[23] This may be derogated from in terms of preventing the spread of a communicable or infectious disease. In terms of Public Health Act 1981, the Minister is empowered to make regulations to prevent the spread of communicable as well as declaring a disease to be a notifiable disease.[24] The Minister can therefore make regulations to prevent the spread of HIV/AIDS and also declare HIV/AIDS as a notifiable disease. The Minister has up till now not exercised such powers with reference to HIV/AIDS sufferers but this is a potentially measure that may be used to derogate from the right to liberty of sufferers.

Section 18 of the Constitution allows a person who is aggrieved that his/her fundamental right has been infringed or is in the process of being infringed,

---

[21] See generally R. Boland *et al, HIV Testing and Confidentiality: A Review of Policy, In-Service Training Curriculum, and Provider Knowledge of the National HIV/AIDS Policy in Botswana,* BONELA, USAID & POLICY (2006).

[22] *ibid.*, p. 26.

[23] See *Serurubele v The Attorney-General* [1998] BLR 661 (HC) and *Attorney-General Reference: In Re State v Marapo* [2002] 2 BLR 26 (HC).

[24] See ss. 5 and 16 of the Act.

to go to the High Court to seek an appropriate remedy. HIV infected persons may use this section to enforce their rights. However, there is a dearth of case law in which such persons have sought remedy from the courts.

In terms of HIV/AIDS rights protection, the Constitution lacks the right to health, which like other so-called second generation rights are not protected under the Constitution. This combined with the fact that the country has neither signed nor ratified the International Covenant on Economic, Social and Cultural Rights[25] creates a situation whereby people living with or affected by HIV/AIDS have no chance of asserting their right to access to health care.

2.2 Legislation

Currently, there is no HIV/AIDS specific legislation. However, section 3 of the Penal Code (Amendment) Act 1998 inserted a new section 142 into the Penal Code 1964 by which any person convicted of rape shall be required to undergo HIV test before he/she[26] is sentenced. If the resulting test reveals that the convict is HIV positive the court is mandated to sentence the convict to:

(a) a minimum of 15 years' imprisonment or to a maximum term of life imprisonment with corporal punishment, where it is proved that such a person was unaware of being HIV positive; or

(b) a minimum of 20 years' imprisonment or to a maximum term of life imprisonment with corporal punishment, where it is proved that on a balance of probabilities such a person was aware of being HIV positive.

The rationale for these provisions may seem to be an attempt to stem the tide of the spread of the pandemic and to punish those who by design or otherwise infect others with the virus. The constitutionality of these provisions was in

[25] Adopted and opened for signature, ratification and accession by the UN General Assembly resolution 2200A (XXI) 16 December 1966.

[26] The definition of rape in section 141 of the Code is gender-neutral; consequently, a male or female is capable of committing the offence. The said section provides as follows: Any person who has unlawful carnal knowledge of another person, or who causes the penetration of a sexual organ or instrument, of whatever nature, into the person of another for the purposes of sexual gratification, or who causes the penetration of another person's sexual organ into his or her person, without the consent of such other person, or with such person's consent if the consent is obtained by force or means of threats or intimidation of any kind, by fear of bodily harm, or by means of false pretences as to the nature of the act, or, in the case of a married person, by personating that person's spouse, is guilty of the offence termed rape.

issue in *Makuto v The State*.[27] The appellant was convicted of rape and underwent an HIV test the result of which was positive. The appellant was committed to the High Court for sentence and that court accordingly sentenced him to 16 years' imprisonment with two light strokes. On appeal against the conviction and sentence, the appellant contended, *inter alia*, that the provisions of section 142(4)(a) of the Penal Code (as amended) were discriminatory and unjust in so far as they provided stiffer penalties for a person convicted of rape who was found to be HIV positive; that the said section was unconstitutional because it offended against section 15 of the Constitution; and that it is unjust and unfair in so far as it presumed that the convicted person who, after trial and conviction, tested HIV positive must have transmitted the virus to the victim and therefore must be harshly punished. The court held that in so far as section 142(4)(a) of the Code treated persons with HIV syndrome differently in punishment from the rest of men without that syndrome who committed the same offence of rape, it was discriminatory. However, the said section was held not to be unconstitutional. If read in the sense that the convicted person must have the HIV syndrome at the time of the act of rape, whether he was aware of it or not, the legislation was reasonably necessary in a democratic society to abridge the freedom from discrimination provision of the Constitution, in order to combat the spread of the HIV/AIDS pandemic which had afflicted the nation; and to deter the increasing incidence of rape. If he was aware that he was HIV positive at the time, he would qualify for the enhanced punishment in terms of section 142(4)(b).[28]

In *State v Lejony,*[29] the accused was convicted of unlawful carnal knowledge of a person under the age of 16 years. After conviction he was tested for HIV virus in terms of section 147(2) of the Penal Code which makes similar provisions to that of section 142 set out above. The result was positive. The victim was 15 years old when she was defiled by the accused but evidence showed that, despite her age, she was sexually active and sexual intercourse with the accused was consensual. In order for the court to impose the prescribed punishment, it had to satisfy itself that the accused was unaware that he was HIV positive when he committed the offence. The court held that the possibility existed in the instant case, that the accused contracted the virus from the victim. Consequently, it was not the case that he should be punished for that. The accused will only be punished if he was HIV positive

27 *Supra.*

28 [2000] 2 BLR 130, at 140.

29 [2000] 1 BLR 326.

though unaware of it when he committed the offence. The court added that unless it is satisfied that the convicted person was HIV positive though unaware of it at the time of committing the offence, it had no legal basis for imposing the enhanced punishment provided for in those circumstances.[30] In view of the evidence, the court therefore imposed the ordinary sentence of 10 years' imprisonment instead of the enhanced punishment of 15 years. On appeal by the State on the court's interpretation of section 147, the Court of Appeal held that the trial court was right in holding that for a person convicted of the offence of defilement to be liable to the enhanced punishment of 15 years it must be proved that he had HIV syndrome at the time of the offence, and not merely at the time of the test after conviction.[31]

It must be pointed out at this juncture that the use of criminal law as a tool in the fight against HIV/AIDS must be premised on a number of policy considerations. Among the guiding principles suggested are:

1. Preventing the transmission of HIV should be the primary objective;
2. Any legal responses to HIV/AIDS, particularly the coercive use of State power, should not only be pragmatic in the overall pursuit of public health but should also conform to international human rights norms, particularly the principles of non-discrimination and of due process; and
3. State action that infringes on human rights must be adequately justified, such that the impact of the law must be the 'least intrusive' to justify the objective of preventing the transmission of the disease.[32]

When the Penal Code (Amendment) Act 1998 is viewed in the light of these principles, it appears that the enhanced punishment for sexual offence in which the perpetrator is found to be infected by the HIV virus was designed to prevent the spread of the disease. Although aspects of the law has been found to be discriminatory, the courts have viewed it as justifiable in the particular context of the infection rate in Botswana.

The realm of employment is one of the most likely places where HIV/AIDS sufferers will be discriminated against. However, the current Labour legislation, the Employment Act 1982, as amended, does not contain any

---

30 *ibid.*, at 330.

31 See *Lejony v The State* [2000] 2 BLR 145. See also *Makuto v The State* [2000] 2 BLR 130 (CA), *Matlapeng v The State* [2001] 1 BLR 161 (CA), *State v Seithamo* [2003] 1 BLR 147 and *Magapatona v The State* [2006] 2 BLR 510 (CA).

32 See R. Elliott, *Criminal Law, Public Health and HIV Transmission, A Policy Options Paper*, UNAIDS (2002) at p. 5.

provision specifically geared towards the protection of HIV/AIDS persons in the work place. The Act has no provisions on confidentiality although it does have some bearing on confidentiality of medical information. For example, under section 46 of the Act, employees are expected to undergo medical examination before they are employed. Such medical examination may include an HIV test. There have been instances where a positive result has led to a denial of employment.

2.3 State Policy on HIV/AIDS

The first national strategic policy response to the HIV/AIDS pandemic, *The Medium Term Plan for the Prevention and Control of HIV/AIDS in Botswana 1989–1993* (MPT I), was health-based. [33] It outlined the role of the health sector and the Ministry of Health with the support and assistance of other sectors and non-governmental organisations in the control and prevention of the pandemic. This was followed by MPT II (1997–2002), a revised strategic plan that shifted the focus from a health-based approach to HIV/AIDS to a multi-sectoral response. In particular, it outlined the international human rights context for addressing issues of stigma and discrimination against people living with HIV/AIDS. The MPT II specifically made reference to the protection of human rights in the following circumstances:

1. In reducing HIV infection transmission, gender inequalities should be eliminated. Policies must be developed to incorporate the rights and protection of the girl child in all relevant policies and Acts, to enforce the Children's Act to protect the girl child and to review all laws and policies that disadvantage women. It further advocated for Children's rights to be incorporated in school counselling procedures in an effort to address child sexual abuse.[34]
2. In reducing the impact of HIV/AIDS at the macro-economic, social, community, household and personal levels, it stated that HIV-friendly and non-discriminatory workplace policies should be developed in line with the National AIDS policy; anti-discrimination legislation should be developed to protect people living with HIV/AIDS; and, a review should be undertaken of all existing legislation to ensure equal treatment of people infected with HIV and people living with AIDS.[35]

[33] See E.K. Quansah, *HIV/AIDS AND HUMAN RIGHTS IN BOTSWANA*, Pretoria, Centre for the Study of Aids/Centre for Human Rights (2004), p. 18.

[34] See MPT II p. 43.

[35] *ibid.*, p. 62.

Following the MPT II, a new National Strategic Plan for HIV/AIDS 2003–2009 was introduced on 26 September 2002. This strategic plan maps out the country's overall multi-sectoral response to the disease for the mentioned period. The main objectives of the Plan include, *inter alia*, the strengthening of the legal and ethical environment for the protection of all people living with HIV/AIDS in Botswana.[36] Three priority areas were set out to achieve this objective. These are (1) advocate for and review existing legislation, guidelines and policies regarding prisons, homosexuality, orphans and vulnerable children, and people living with HIV/AIDS; (2) Strengthening the legal and regulatory framework regarding alcohol distribution and consumption; and (3) supporting legal reform and enforcement of laws addressing issues of rape and sexual violence in Botswana and educate vulnerable groups (men and women) on relevant behavioural change.

The National Policy on HIV/AIDS (revised in 2002)[37] outlines the national response to the pandemic. It mirrors closely the 2003–2009 Strategic Plan. It describes the role of national leaders, various government ministries, the private sector, non-governmental and community-based organisations, persons living with HIV/AIDS, and individual community members in the national response. The strategic objective of the Ministry of Labour and Home Affairs, for example, is to develop legislation regarding the rights of HIV-infected individuals to employment, social welfare and compensation where relevant. The Labour Department was enjoined to ensure that the rights of workers with HIV/AIDS are not infringed in any labour-related legislation that may be developed, as stipulated in the Policy.[38]

There is an acknowledgment that the country has no specific legislation dealing with HIV/AIDS. It premised the legal and ethical aspects of the Policy on principles expressed in national documents such as the Constitution and Public Health Act.[39] It affirms that persons with HIV/AIDS have the same rights as healthy persons, including the right not to be discriminated against, security of person and protection of the law, privacy, education and information about infections, and access to health and social services. The

---

[36] See p. 7 of the Plan.

[37] Approved and adopted through a Presidential Directive CAB: 33/98 (23 September 1998). Revised in 2002 to incorporate national and international developments in the understanding and management of the disease.

[38] See p. 14 of the Revised Policy.

[39] See section 6 Revised Policy. See also O.K Dingake, *AIDS and Human Rights in Botswana*, Gaborone, Morula Press (2000).

Policy then asserted that "the rights of non-infected persons should not be sacrificed in trying to protect the rights of those infected".[40]

From the above framework, one can conclude that the Constitution provides a broad basis for the protection of the human rights of HIV/AIDS sufferers. However, such rights are mainly in the civil and political spheres which do not in the main help. The social and health rights which would have better protected the rights of HIV/AIDS sufferers are conspicuously absent from the Constitution. Other legislation for augmenting the constitutional provisions is non-existent. Whilst State policy on HIV/AIDS is premised on the principle of protecting the rights of HIV/AIDS sufferers, the lack of legal backing for the policy seriously undermines its effectiveness. There is no doubt therefore that the current framework for the protection of the Human Rights of HIV/AIDS sufferers is woefully inadequate and that, in view of the resilience of the pandemic, there is a need to strengthen the framework to enhance the enjoyment of those rights. The possible ways of doing this will be examined next.

3 Future Prospects for the Protection of Human Rights of People with HIV/AIDS

3.1 Scope of Human Rights Protection under the Botswana Constitution

As discussed earlier, the Constitution sets out certain fundamental rights and freedoms which are to be enjoyed by all persons within the geographical limits of the Botswana. These rights and freedoms fall within the so-called first generation rights. These are generally referred to as negative rights because they merely impose a negative duty on the State to refrain from violating them but do not impose any corresponding duty on the State to ensure that the beneficiaries of the rights and freedoms actually enjoy them. These rights are mainly derived from the International Convention on Civil and Political Rights.[41] There is no universally accepted formula on either the form or content of a Bill of Rights, its constituent elements, as well as it overall effectiveness, are determined by a particular State's commitment to the human rights protection of its people.[42]

---

40 See section 19 Revised Policy.

41 See note 3 *supra*.

42 See Fombad, "The Protection of human rights in Botswana…" *op. cit.*, fn. 1, *supra*, p. 15 and R. Nengwekhulu, "Human Rights, development, and the rule of law in post-colonial Botswana" in W.A. Edge & Lekorwe eds., *Botswana Politics and Society* Pretoria, van Schaik Academic (1998) p. 351.

The scope and range of human rights protection under the Botswana Constitution has been gauged with those of the 53 African countries comprising the African Union.[43] With only 12 recognised rights and freedoms, Botswana was ranked amongst the last five countries.[44] As indicated above, these rights are civil and political in nature and do not include any of the so-called second generation human rights, such as the rights to health, employment and family, which are germane to the plight of those with HIV/AIDS. Consequently, the scope of the rights provided under the Constitution is not as extensive as one would have liked. This is attributable to the fact that, at the time the Constitution was being fashioned, one might surmise that it was the political liberties of the people of Bechuanaland that was uppermost in the minds of the political leaders negotiating for independence from Britain.[45] Subsequent events have not motivated a change in the perceptions of these rights in the contemporary circumstances of the country.[46]

3.2 Possible Future Direction for the Protection of the Human Rights of those with HIV/AIDS

It has been asserted that one of the first paradoxes that emerged with HIV/AIDS was that the most effective means of preventing the spread of the virus was the protection of the human rights of the people most at risk of acquiring the virus.[47] This was a paradox because it was contrary to the intuitive responses to the spread of a dangerous virus in society. The usual instinctive response on the part of public health officials would be to control the spread of the virus and that of the general public's response will be to stigmatise those who had and spread the virus and to impose some form of punishment.[48] Thus, the initiation of a rights-based approach to the spread of the disease was a surprise, to say the least.[49] That notwithstanding, the quick recognition by the international community of the disease as a serious threat to the human rights of sufferers enabled measures to be put in place to safeguard their

---

[43] *ibid.*

[44] See C Heyns & W Kaguongo, "Constitutional Human Rights Law in Africa" (2006) 22 *S.* Afr. J. of Human Rts 673–717, cited in Fombad, "The Protection of Human Rights In Botswana…" *op. cit.*, at pp. 15–16.

[45] N. Parsons *et al Seretse Khama* 1921–1980, Johannesburg, Macmillan Boles (1995) Chap. 9.

[46] See fn. 10 *supra.*

[47] See M. Kirby, "The never-ending paradoxes of HIV/AIDS and human rights" (2004) 4 Afr. Human Rts L.J. 163.

[48] *ibid.*, at 167.

[49] See J. Mann, "Health and Human rights: If not now, when?" (1997) 2 Health and Human Rights 118. See also M.E. Wojcik, "Global aspects of AIDS" in *AIDS and the Law* (D.W. Webber ed.), New York, Wiley Law Publications (1997) p. 454.

rights. This was underscored by the African Commission on Human and People's Rights when it highlighted the difficulties that HIV/AIDS patients face in accessing treatment as a major obstacle to their exercise of their right to health as set out under the African Charter of Human and People's Rights.[50] Although there is currently no international covenant imposing specific obligations on States in this arena, the continuous focus on HIV and related human rights issues has resulted in the adoption of many declarations as well as the development of a general consensus on the UN International Guidelines on HIV/AIDS and Human Rights, which address the state's role vis-à-vis the epidemic.[51]

In the light of the inadequacies pointed out in the existing rights in the Constitution, the following second-generation rights should be considered for incorporation into the Constitution.[52]

3.2.1 The Right to Health

The right to health is fundamental to the physical and mental well-being of all individuals and is a necessary condition for the exercise of other human rights. Thus, article 12 of the International Covenant on Economic, Social and Cultural Rights (ICESCR) provides that the States Parties to the present Covenant recognise the right of everyone to the enjoyment of the highest attainable standard of physical and mental health.[53] This means that health care facilities, goods and services have to be available in sufficient quantity; must be physically and economically accessible to everyone, must be ethically and culturally acceptable, and must be of a medically appropriate quality.

Article 25 of the Universal Declaration of Human Rights (UDHR) emphasises recognition of the right of all persons to an adequate standard of living, including guarantees for health and well-being.[54] It acknowledges the relationship between health and well-being and its link with other rights,

---

[50] See the resolution set out in *Compendium of Key Human Rights Documents of the African Union*, Pretoria, Pretoria University Law Press (2005,) p. 200.

[51] See International Guidelines on HIV/AIDS and Human Rights, UNCHR Res. 1997/33, UN Doc. E/CN.4/1997/150 (1997).

[52] See generally P. Akugizibwe, "Socio-economic rights: The missing link in fighting the HIV/AIDS pandemic" (2007) 1 *The Botswana Review of Ethics, Law and HIV/Aids 21.*

[53] Botswana has not yet ratified the Covenant.

[54] Botswana is a signatory to a number of conventions subsumed under this Declaration, for example, International Covenant on Civil and Political Rights (accession 2000) and the Convention on the Elimination of Racial Discrimination (accession 1974).

such as the right to food and the right to housing, as well as medical and social services. It adopts a broad view of the right to health as a human right, even though health is but one component of an adequate standard of living.

Articles 23 and 24 of the Convention on Rights of Children (CRC) recognise the right to health for all children and identify several steps for its realisation.[55] Similarly, article 12 of the Convention on the Elimination of All Forms of Discrimination against Women (CEDAW) establishes the obligation to adopt adequate measures to guarantee women access to health and medical care, with no discrimination whatsoever, including access to family planning services.[56] It also establishes the commitment to guarantee adequate maternal and child health care. Article 16 of the African Charter on Human and Peoples' Rights enshrines the right to the highest possible level of health, to which end "necessary measures" will be taken, while also guaranteeing medical services in case of illness.[57] The African Charter on the Rights and Welfare of the Child also includes recognition of the right to health.[58]

Numerous other instruments also provide for the right to health. These are: the International Convention on the Elimination of All Forms of Racial Discrimination, the Convention relating to the Status of Refugees, the International Convention on the Protection of the Rights of All Migrant Workers and Members of Their Families, the Convention on the Rights of Persons with disabilities, the Geneva Conventions, the Declaration on the Protection of Women and Children in Emergency and Armed Conflict, the Standard Minimum Rules for the Treatment of Prisoners, the Declaration on the Rights of Mentally Retarded Persons, and the Declaration on the Rights of AIDS Patients.

The provisions in the above international documents make it quite clear that health and human rights are inextricably linked.[59] The right to health is of prime concern to all persons but much more so to HIV/AIDS sufferers. Because as of now there is no cure for the disease and the drugs to manage the disease are in most cases beyond the financial resources of sufferers, there

55 Botswana acceded to this Convention in 1995 with a minor reservation with regard to age of majority.

56 Botswana acceded to this Convention in 1996.

57 Botswana acceded to this Charter in 1986.

58 Botswana ratified this Charter in 2001 with minor reservation.

59 See JM Mann "Human Rights and AIDS: the future of the pandemic" in *Health and Human Rights: A Reader* (JM Mann, S Gruskin, MA Grodin & GJ Annas eds.) New York, Routledge (1999) pp. 216–226.

is a need for the right to health to be made a constitutional right. This will enable sufferers, where provisions are not made available for them to have access to the relevant medicines to manage the disease, to seek enforcement of the right to enable them to have such access. One will concede that in Botswana, the provision of the antiretroviral therapy has been made available to HIV/AIDS Sufferers on a wide scale. However, there are cases in which non-citizens married to citizens have been denied the therapy.

A constitutional guarantee of health may enable this practice/policy to be challenged in the courts. For example, in the South African case of *Treatment Action Campaign v Minister of Health*[60] the plaintiffs brought a suit against the South African government alleging that its restrictions on the availability of nevirapine (limiting it in the public sector to hospitals involved in a pilot study) and its failure to have a reasonable plan to make the drug more widely available violated the right to health of HIV-positive pregnant women and their children guaranteed in the South African Constitution.[61] The trial court, which ruled that restricting nevirapine to a limited number of pilot sites in the public sector "is not reasonable and is an unjustifiable barrier to the progressive realisation of the right to healthcare." In July 2002, the Constitutional Court of South Africa, the country's highest court, affirmed the ruling, stating that the government's nevirapine policy violated the health care rights of women and newborns under the South African Constitution.

3.2.2 Right to Work

The right to work is acknowledged by Article 23 of the UDHR which states that everyone has the right to work, to free choice of employment to just and favourable conditions of work and to protection against unemployment. However, the working environment in Botswana is under stress from the HIV/AIDS epidemic.[62] Workers who suffer from HIV-related illnesses or who are infected with HIV are being arbitrarily dismissed because of stigmatisation and discrimination. Furthermore, workers whose lives are

---

[60] 2002 (10) BCLR 1033. See also *Soobramoney v. Minister of Health* (1997) 12 BCLR 1696.

[61] The right to health is guaranteed by section 27 of the 1996 South African Constitution.

[62] See U. Ndadi, "HIV/AIDS and employment law in Botswana" (2008) 2 *The Botswana Review of Ethics, Law and HIV/AIDS* 43 where the writer concludes that it is clear that HIV/AIDS does present huge challenges in the workplace and that the absence of clear and specific laws compounds the situation. See also R. Kumar & M Raizada, "Realization of Human Rights: A path towards the reduction of vulnerability to HIV/AIDS by the Government of Botswana" (2008) 2 *The Botswana Review of Ethics, Law and HIV/AIDS 71.*

affected by the epidemic are also suffering due to increased absenteeism for caring and for attending funerals.[63]

One of the key problems in this area is the lack of job security/employment protection of HIV-infected workers. Current employment legislation does not comply with international minimum standards set by the International Labour Organisation (ILO).[64] For example, the Discrimination (Employment and Occupation) Convention, 1958 (No. 111)[65] bans any distinction, exclusion or preference which has the effect of nullifying or impairing equality of opportunity or treatment in access to training, access to jobs, promotion processes, security of tenure, remuneration, conditions of work, including leave, rest periods, occupational safety and health measures and social security benefits. It lists seven grounds of banned discrimination, and in Article 1(1)(b), allows ratifying States to add, after consulting representatives of workers' and employers' organisations, additional grounds. Although the Industrial Court has tried to fill the gaps that exist in the legislative framework by reference to ILO conventions[66] and creative decisions,[67] a lot remains to be done. It is submitted that in order to safeguard the employment of HIV/AIDS sufferers there should be legislation providing for the following:

1: Prohibition of non-consensual pre-and post-employment HIV screening.

2: Prohibition of discrimination against HIV-infected workers, that is, no dismissal based on HIV/AIDS until medically unfit to carry out adapted work.

3: Care and support for HIV infected workers, and

4: Prevention of HIV/AIDS in the work place.

If these are implemented, the human rights of HIV/AIDs sufferers will be considerably enhanced for, as rightly put by Dingake J, "In this modern era,

[63] See Draft Policy document of Botswana Network on Ethics, Law, and HIV/AIDS (BONELA) prepared for a Drafting Workshop on HIV/AIDS and Employment held in Gaborone, Botswana 7–9 October 2002.

[64] Botswana is a signatory to a number of Conventions adopted under the auspices of the ILO, for example, Freedom of Association and the Protection of the Right to Organise Convention (No. 87) (Ratified 1997).

[65] Ratified by Botswana on 5 June 1997.

[66] See for example, *Phirinyane v Spie Batignolles* [1995] BLR 1(IC) where the court applied Art. 4 of the Labour Convention 158 of 1983 to an unfair dismissal case.

[67] See *Lemo v Northern Air Maintenance* [2004] 2 BLR 317(IC) at 328.

the right to work is not only a matter of the right to earn a living; it is a matter of human dignity too."[68]

It is worth noting at this point that the idea of recognising these second generation human rights constitutionally has been questioned on the ground, *inter alia*, that their strict judicial enforcement is neither possible nor indeed desirable because they involve resource allocation between competing public demands and are better dealt with in the political arena.[69] Whilst this question may be difficult to fault in some instances, recent jurisprudence in South Africa has shown that constitutionally guaranteed second-generation rights are not merely constitutional platitudes but real rights capable of enforcement.[70] As aptly observed by a learned writer, one of the lessons to be learnt from the South African experience is that the potential unsuitability of such matters to be determined by the courts is no longer an excuse for not incorporating them in the constitution.[71]

4 Conclusion

The onset of the HIV/AIDS pandemic has brought in its wake novel human rights issues hitherto not encountered. The prognosis of the epidemic looks gloomy in that an effective cure is still far from being found. Consequently, it is likely to be around for the foreseeable future. Those afflicted by it should be made to live as normal a life as reasonably possible. The safeguarding of their human rights is one sure way to ensure that they live with dignity in the face of their adversity. The linkage between HIV/AIDS and human rights is now recognised and accepted by all and sundry and positive steps should be taken to make this linkage a reality at the practical level. The current framework for the protection of the rights of HIV/AIDS sufferers is inadequate and has proved ineffective so far. By extensively discussing the issues and

---

[68] See "Expanding the frontiers of fundamental human rights: Judicial protection of human rights in Botswana" at p. 12. A paper presented at the conference: Protecting Human Rights in Botswana: Emerging Issues, Gaborone, June 5 2008.

[69] See generally, Y Ghai & J Cottrell (eds.), *Economic, Social and Cultural Rights in Practice – The Role of Judges in Implementing Economic, Social and Cultural Rights*, London, Interights (2004). See also J.C. Mubangizi, "The Constitutional Protection of Socio-Economic Rights in Selected African Countries: A Comparative Evaluation" 2 Afr .J. of Legal Studies 1 (2006).

[70] See the case of *Government of South Africa v Grootboom* 2001 (1) SA 46 (CC) where the right to adequate housing was discussed by the Constitutional Court and cases mentioned in fn. 60 *supra*.

[71] See CM Fombad, "The protection of human rights in Botswana: An overview of the regulatory framework" in CM Fombad (ed.) *Essays on the Law of Botswana* Cape Town, Juta (2007), p. 26.

adopting the suggestions outlined in this paper, it is submitted that the safeguarding of the human rights of HIV/AIDS sufferers in Botswana will be considerably enhanced. To quote President Seretse Khama Ian Khama:

"…no one should need to live an undignified life as a result of poor shelter or *health* and abuse in a domestic environment. Anything in life that brings you suffering affects your dignity as a person and we shall seek to address and overcome some of these challenges."[72] (Emphasis supplied).

One of the challenges HIV/AIDS sufferers will fervently hope will be tackled with vigour is the enhancement and protection of their human rights. The President will leave a much improved legacy if he is able to translate into practical reality his vision of "dignity as a person" by, *inter alia*, taking the requisite steps to enhance the protection of the human rights of HIV/AIDS sufferers in consonance with the nation's vision of becoming a compassionate and caring nation by 2016.[73]

---

[72] Speech delivered on 1 April 2008 on the occasion of assuming the Presidency of Botswana. See www.gov.bw/docs/InaugurationAddress.pdf accessed on 28 May 2008.

[73] See *Vision 2016, A Framework for a Long Term Vision **for** Botswana*. One of the strategic goals of the vision is that the spread of Human immuno-deficiency virus (HIV) that causes Acquired Immuno-deficiency Syndrome (AIDS), will be stopped. AIDS patients will have access to quality care in health facilities, in their community or workplace.

The Role of the Judiciary in Protecting Freedom of Expression: How Far Should the Courts Go?

Badala Tachilisa Balule*

1 Introduction

Freedom of expression is widely regarded as the lifeblood of every democratic society. The High Court of Botswana has also acknowledged in the case of *Media Publishing (Pty) Ltd v Attorney General and Another* that freedom of expression is a cornerstone of every democratic society.[1] In a democracy, freedom of expression has both an intrinsic and instrumental value. It is valued for its own sake and it also facilitates the free flow of information and ideas that inform political debate.[2]

Botswana, as has been recognised by its Court of Appeal in a number of cases, is a modern liberal democracy,[3] which has a written constitution that guarantees fundamental rights and freedoms, including the right to freedom of expression. The important role that freedom of expression plays in a democracy has been recognised by Botswana's High Court and it has held that this freedom should be jealously guarded by the courts of law.[4] This, however, does not mean that freedom of expression is an absolute right; its exercise must be reconciled with other equally important individual rights and the public interest. The Constitution thus allows restrictions on freedom of expression in order to protect these interests. Restrictions to the right must, however, be in conformity with and not contrary to the provisions of the Constitution. It is the role of the judiciary to ensure that restrictions on

*LLB (UB), LLM, PhD (Edinburgh), Lecturer in Law, Department of Law, University of Botswana.

1 [2001] 2 BLR 485 at 494.

2 See *R v Secretary of State for the Home Department, ex parte Simms* [2000] AC 115 at 126.

3 See, among others, *Attorney General v Dow* [1992] BLR 119 at 168 and *Moatshe v The State; Motshwari and Another v The State* [2004] 1 BLR 1 at 8.

4 *Media Publishing (Pty) Ltd v Attorney General and Another*, [2001] 2 BLR 485, at 495.

fundamental rights and freedoms guaranteed under the Constitution are in conformity with the supreme law of the land.[5]

While it has been observed that the government of Botswana generally respects the right to freedom of expression, there is evidence that immigration laws are often easily resorted to by the government in retaliation against criticism by non-citizens resident in the country. Immigration laws were used in the 1980s to deport South African refugees, especially media practitioners, who were critical of Botswana's foreign policy regarding then-apartheid South Africa.[6] More recently, two Zimbabwean journalists and an Australian-born academic were deported from the country in what many perceived to have been due to the government's displeasure at their critical stance to its controversial relocation of Basarwa (Bushmen) from the Central Kalahari Game Reserve (CKGR).[7] These incidents raise the question of whether the use of immigration laws in this manner is constitutional, and more importantly, whether courts of law in Botswana have done enough to jealously protect the enjoyment of the right to freedom of expression by non-citizens resident in the country.

This paper interrogates whether courts in Botswana have been able to adequately monitor the use of immigration laws by the executive so as to strike a proper balance between the protection of non-citizens' right to freedom of expression on the one hand and the public interest on the other. The paper starts with an overview of the protection of the right to freedom of expression in Botswana. It then focuses on provisions of the Immigration Act[8] that are used to deport non-citizens, highlighting the potential conflict with the right to freedom of expression. The paper will then analyse the Court of Appeal's decision in the case of *Good v Attorney General* to determine whether courts in Botswana have been effectively able to play their role in jealously guarding the right to freedom of expression.

---

[5] *Good v Attorney General* [2005] 2 BLR 337 at 343 (*per* Tebbutt, J.P.).

[6] See B. Otlhogile, 'The Constitutional Rights of the Mass Media in Botswana: An Academic's View' in M. Leepile (ed), *Botswana's Media Democracy: Selected Papers from the Seminar on Media in a Democracy* (Mmegi Publishing House, 1996) 53 at 63.

[7] See Z. Titus, 'Regional Overview of State of Media Freedom and Freedom of Expression in SADC' in MISA, *So This is Democracy? State of Media Freedom in Southern Africa 2005* (MISA, 2006) 10 at 11.

[8] [Cap. 25:02] Laws of Botswana.

2 Protection of Freedom of Expression in Botswana

2.1 Protection under the Constitution

Freedom of expression is expressly guaranteed under the Constitution. Section 12(1) provides:

> 'Except with his own consent, no person shall be hindered in the enjoyment of his freedom of expression, that is to say, freedom to hold opinions without interference, freedom to receive ideas and information without interference, freedom to communicate ideas and information without interference (whether the communication be to the public generally or to any person or class of persons) and freedom from interference with his correspondence'.

The guarantee of freedom of expression under the Constitution is subject to section 12(2), which reads:

> 'Nothing contained in or done under the authority of any law shall be held to be inconsistent with or in contravention of this section to the extent that the law in question makes provision –
>
> (a) that is reasonably required in the interests of defence, public safety, public order, public morality or public health; or
>
> (b) that is reasonably required for the purpose of protecting the reputations, rights and freedoms of other persons or the private lives of persons concerned in legal proceedings, preventing the disclosure of information received in confidence, maintaining the authority and independence of the courts, regulating educational institutions in the interests of persons receiving instruction therein, or regulating the technical administration or the technical operation of telephony, telegraphy, posts, wireless, broadcasting or television; or
>
> (c) that imposes restrictions upon public officers, employees of local government bodies, or teachers,
>
> and except so far as that provision or, as the case may be, the thing done under the authority thereof is shown not to be reasonably justifiable in a democratic society'.

Section 12(2) incorporates a three-part test in the determination of the legitimacy of restrictions to freedom of expression. First, the restriction must be "done under the authority of any law". The Supreme Court of Zimbabwe has held that this phrase, although worded differently from such equivalent phrases as "provided by law", "prescribed by law" or "in terms of the law", used in other constitutional and human rights instruments, carries substantially the same meaning.[9] The court held that, to satisfy this test, the law must be adequately accessible and formulated with sufficient precision to enable a person to regulate his/her conduct.[10] To further satisfy this test, not only must a law that restricts freedom of expression be foreseeable, it must also be compatible with the rule of law. That is, if the law confers discretionary powers on the executive, adequate guidelines as to the exercise of the discretion must be provided and they should be mechanisms to control or limit the exercise of the power.[11]

Second, a restriction must serve one or more of the purposes enumerated in sub-paragraphs (a), (b) and (c) above.

Third, the restriction should be shown to be reasonably justifiable in a democratic society. The determination of whether a restriction is reasonably justifiable in a democracy involves a balancing exercise, whether the benefits to a democratic society resulting from the specific restriction demonstrably outweigh the detriment caused.[12]

The protection of freedom of expression under the Constitution is further buttressed by sections 3 and 18 of same. Section 3(a) guarantees every person in Botswana the protection of the law. This provision has been interpreted to mean that "any penalty or disadvantage inflicted on a person in Botswana by an organ of the state must be in accordance with or capable of being justified in terms of the domestic laws of Botswana".[13] Section 18(1) permits any person to apply to the High Court if he or she alleges that any of the fundamental rights and freedoms of the individual guaranteed under Part II of the Constitution have been contravened in relation to him or her.

2.2 Protection under International Law

The right to freedom of expression is protected in all major international and regional human rights instruments. Those that are relevant for the purpose of this paper include: the Universal Declaration of Human Rights (UDHR);

---

[9] *Chavunduka & another v Minister of Home Affairs* 2000 (4) SA 1.

[10] *ibid,* at 12.

[11] See *The Law Society of Zimbabwe v The Minister of Transport and Communications* (2004) AHRLR 292 at 298 (ZwSC 2004).

[12] *Chavunduka & another v Minister of Home Affairs, supra,* at 15–16.

[13] *Good v Attorney General, supra,* at 363 (*per* Lord Coulsfield).

the International Covenant on Civil and Political Rights (ICCPR); and the African Charter on Human and Peoples' Rights (ACHPR). These three instruments all expressly guarantee the right to freedom of expression.[14]

The UDHR would appear at face value to be guaranteeing an absolute right to freedom of expression. The formulation of the provision has been criticised for its failure to balance the twin concepts of freedom and responsibility. Article 19 must, however, be read in conjunction with Article 29, which provides for the unity of freedom and responsibility. Article 29 permits restrictions on freedom of expression solely for the purpose of securing respect for the rights and freedoms of others and of meeting the just requirements of morality, public order and the general welfare in a democratic society. Furthermore, the rights set forth in the Declaration may not be exercised contrary to the purposes and principles of the UN.[15]

The guarantee of freedom of expression under the ICCPR clearly shows that the right is not absolute, but that its exercise carries with it duties and responsibilities. Under Article 19(3), freedom of expression may be restricted to ensure respect for the rights or reputations of others and for the protection of national security or of public order or of public health or morals. It has, however, been said that where a state party imposes certain restrictions on the exercise of the freedom of expression, these must not put in jeopardy the right itself. Such restrictions must satisfy the conditions laid in Article 19(3), that is, (i) the restriction must be provided by law; (ii) must be imposed for one of the purposes set out in sub-paragraphs (a) and (b); and, must be justified as necessary for that state party for one of those purposes.[16]

The ACHPR, like the UDHR, does not include any express restrictions on freedom of expression. The guarantee of freedom of expression must, however, be read subject to restrictions set forth in Articles 27–29, the most pertinent of which requires the individual to exercise protected freedoms "with due regard to the rights of others, collective security, morality and common interest".[17] The African Commission on Human and Peoples' Rights, has in addition, adopted principles that inform the application of Article 9.[18]

---

[14] See Article 19 UDHR; Article 19 (2) ICCPR; and Article 9 (2) ACHPR.

[15] Article 29 (2) and (3) of the UDHR.

[16] Report of the Human Rights Commission to the General Assembly, 38th Session, Supp. No. 40, 1983 (A/38/40) Annexe VI, General Comment 10.

[17] Article 27 (2).

[18] *Declaration of Principles on Freedom of Expression in Africa* (Adopted by the Commission at its 32nd Ordinary Session, 17–23 October 2002).

These principles require that any restriction on freedom of expression shall be provided by law, serve a legitimate interest and be necessary in a democratic society.[19] Further, the Principles require that no one shall be subject to arbitrary interference with his or her freedom of expression.[20]

In dealing with permissible grounds for restricting freedom of expression, all the instruments discussed above set forth essentially the same three-part test for determining the legitimacy of restrictions: First, any restriction must be prescribed by law; secondly, it must serve one of the legitimate purposes expressly enumerated in their text and, finally, it must be necessary.

International human rights instruments have no automatic operation in Botswana's domestic law unless specifically incorporated by an act of the legislature. This dualistic position has been confirmed by the Court of Appeal in a number of cases, where it held that treaties and conventions do not confer enforceable rights on individuals within the state until Parliament has legislated their provisions into law.[21]

Botswana has ratified the ICCPR and ACHPR[22] but neither has yet been incorporated into the domestic law and in consequence they are not directly enforceable in the country. Judicial activism, has however, gone some way towards altering the strict dualist position in the country. Over the years, courts have in some cases used, as an aid to the interpretation of constitutionally entrenched rights, emerging international human rights norms located in conventions to which their state is or even is not a party. In Botswana, the legal basis for invoking unratified and unincorporated human rights treaties to interpret, not only domestic legislation, but even constitutional provisions is section 24 of the Interpretation Act,[23] which states that, as an aid to the construction of the enactment a court may have regard to any relevant international treaty, agreement or convention.[24] In addition to this canon of

[19] Principle II (2).

[20] Principle II (1).

[21] See, among others, *Attorney General v Dow, supra* at 154 and *Good v Attorney General supra* at 355.

[22] Botswana ratified the ACHPR on 17 July 1986 and the ICCPR on 8 September 2000.

[23] [Cap. 01:04] Laws of Botswana.

[24] In *Attorney General v Dow supra*, the Court of Appeal sought guidance from the provisions of the ACHPR which although ratified, is not incorporated into the domestic law and the UN Convention on the Elimination of All Forms of Discrimination Against Women, to which Botswana was not then a party, in order to interpret some provisions of the Constitution and the *Citizenship Act of 1984*. The court ultimately declared the provisions in question *ultra vires* the Constitution as they allowed sex-based discrimination, which, the Court said, was prohibited by the Constitution.

interpretation, the Court of Appeal has also emphasised that courts must interpret domestic laws in a way as compatible with the state's responsibility not to be in breach of international law as laid down by law creating treaties, conventions, agreements and protocols within the UN and OAU.[25]

Even though the ICCPR and ACHPR have not been incorporated into the domestic law and therefore are not directly enforceable, there is evidence that the jurisprudence on the two treaties serve as a useful guide to the interpretation of similar provisions in the laws of Botswana as evidenced from the case of *Attorney General v Dow*.

3 Is an Alien's Right to Freedom of Expression Adequately Protected Under Botswana Law?

The President is given powers under section 7(f) of the Immigration Act[26] to declare a person a prohibited immigrant in consequence of information received from any source deemed by him to be reliable. The decision by the President to declare someone a prohibited immigrant under the Act cannot be appealed and courts of law are precluded from questioning the adequacy of the grounds for any such declaration.[27] Furthermore, under section 36 of the Act, a person has no right to be heard before or after a decision has been made by the President declaring him a prohibited immigrant. The provision further provides that a person affected by any such decision shall have no right to demand any information as to the grounds of such decision nor shall any such information be disclosed in any court.

There is a general perception, as indicated in the introduction to this paper, that the provisions of the Immigration Act are often used by the government to deport non-citizens who criticise it. The fact that the President is given very wide discretionary powers to declare someone a prohibited immigrant, that he is not required to disclose his reasons to anyone, and the absence of control mechanisms over the exercise of the discretion, makes the exercise of the discretion susceptible to abuse. It means the President may, with impunity, declare someone a prohibited immigrant merely because of that person's views about him or his government and he does not have to account to anyone for his actions. This raises the question of whether the provisions of the Act

[25] *Attorney General v Dow supra* at 169 (*per* Aguda JA).
[26] [Cap. 25:02] Laws of Botswana.
[27] Section 11(6).

are not in conflict with section 3 of the Constitution that accords every person in Botswana the protection of the law. If a person is deported as punishment for criticising the government, this will be a violation of his/her right to freedom of expression as guaranteed under section 12(1) of the Constitution. In terms of the Constitution, if a person is alleging that any of his/her rights guaranteed under the Constitution have been infringed, he/she is entitled to approach the High Court for redress. However, under the provisions of the Immigration Act, a court is precluded from questioning the adequacy of the grounds for declaring one a prohibited immigrant and the information regarding the grounds for the decision shall not be disclosed in court.

Questions have thus been raised over the constitutionality of these provisions of the Immigration Act on the grounds that they conflict with sections 3 and 18 of the Constitution. The Court of Appeal had occasion to deal with challenges to the constitutionality of sections 11(6) and 36 of the Immigration Act in the case of *Good v Attorney General* (supra). The appellant in this case was challenging his deportation from Botswana, which was done under the Immigration Act. At the time of the deportation, the President did not disclose the grounds for his decision to declare Good a prohibited immigrant, a position that is sanctioned by section 36 of the Act. The President only said his decision was in consequence of information received by him from sources he deemed to be reliable, and that the deportation was in the 'interests of peace, stability and national security of Botswana'. A few weeks later, as pressure mounted on the President to disclose his reasons for declaring Good a prohibited immigrant, he told a press conference that Good's sin was his labelling of Botswana diamonds as 'Blood Diamonds'.[28] It would appear that the main reason for Good's deportation may have been his exercise of freedom of expression, but the courts were not able to ascertain the real cause because the law under which the deportation order was made prohibits the disclosure of the grounds in any court.

In challenging the constitutionality of the provisions of the Immigration Act, the appellant set out obligations that the State of Botswana had to carry out as contained in various international treaties and covenants. In particular, the appellant relied on the ICCPR and ACHPR. Article 13 of the ICCPR provides that an alien lawfully in the territory of a state party to the covenant may be expelled therefrom only in pursuance of a decision reached in accordance with the law except where compelling reasons of national security require otherwise. The Article also requires that an affected party be allowed to

[28] See *Afrol News*, 'Botswana President Explains Academic's Deportation' at www.afrol.com.

submit reasons against his/her expulsion and to have his/her case reviewed by a competent authority. Reliance was also placed on Article 12.4 of the ACHPR, which also requires that an alien legally admitted in a territory of a state party to the Charter may only be expelled from it by virtue of a decision taken in accordance with the law. The appellant's case was that sections 11(6) and 36 of the Immigration Act were in violation of the rights embodied in both the ICCPR and ACHPR and therefore deprived a person declared a prohibited immigrant under the Act protection of the law as contained in section 3 of the Constitution.

The majority members of the Court Appeal, per Tebbutt JP, rejected this argument. It was held that the phrase 'protection of the law' as used in section 3 of the Constitution means 'protection of the domestic law of Botswana'[29] The majority members of the Court observed that when Botswana attained independence in 1966, the treaties which the appellant relied on were not in existence. The court opined:

> "The framers of the Constitution that then came into existence no doubt intended that as Botswana was acquiring its own statehood it should have the ethos of the comity of nations and of the international society into which it was entering. The international environmental probably acted as one of the contributory influences which fashioned and informed the framers (see per Amissah JP in *Dow* (*supra*) at p152F). Giving effect to that ethos would embrace those fundamental rights and freedoms that became the foundation of the provisions of s3. The statement of those rights was doubtless influenced by the United Nations' Universal Declaration of Human Rights of 1948. The international treaties such as the ICCPR and the African Charter of Human and Peoples' Rights clearly have their genesis in the latter document but they came into existence in 1976 and 1981 respectively, ie long after the Constitution came into effect and the Immigration Act of 1966 was enacted.
>
> "The rule of law is the very bedrock of the fundamental rights and freedoms contained in s3 and finds reflection in those provisions of ss4 to 16 of the Constitution such as the rights to life, to personal liberty, to a fair and expeditious trial and the freedom of expression and of conscience. *The rule of law is also the cornerstone of the domestic law of the country and its application is not dependent upon some concept of a quality of law inherent in the articles of international treaties or conventions,*

29 *Good v Attorney General, supra,* at 355.

> *which were not in existence when the Botswana Constitution was framed.*
>
> "The specific provisions in the treaties relating to the expulsion of aliens or foreigners were accordingly not then in contemplation. However, in the law of the new Botswana those matters were."[30]

The majority members of the Court concluded that the Immigration Act came into effect on the same day as the Constitution, and that the framers of the latter were fully aware of the Immigration Act and therefore the impugned provisions of the Act could not be said to be inconsistent with the Constitution.

4 Critique of the Decision in Good v Attorney General

The objective of constitutional provisions such as section 3 of Botswana's Constitution that guarantee individuals the protection of the law are intended to protect individuals against arbitrary action by the State. It has been held that protection against arbitrary action requires that, where possible, the individual concerned should be told of the reasons for any action taken against him/her and be given an opportunity to respond.[31] The provisions of the Immigration Act deny an affected person a right to be told the reasons for his/her deportation and opportunity to respond thereto. To this extent, it can be argued that the provisions of the Act are arbitrary. It is further submitted that the provisions of the Act not only violate section 3, but also fail to comply with the first limb of the three-part test laid down in section 12(2) of the Constitution which requires restrictions on freedom of expression to be "done under the authority of law". The Immigration Act gives the President powers that are too broad and overreaching in declaring someone a prohibited immigrant and fails to provide limitations and control mechanisms against the use of these powers to ensure that they are not abused.[32]

The majority of the members of the Court of Appeal in *Good v Attorney General*, however, found the provisions of the Immigration Act to be in conformity with section 3 of the Constitution. An interesting and perhaps controversial statement made by the Court in the course of the judgment is

---

[30] *ibid.*, at 256–7. (Emphasis added.)

[31] *Good v Attorney General, supra,* at 363 (*per* Lord Coulsfield JA).

[32] See *The Law Society of Zimbabwe v The Minister of Transport and Communications, supra,* at 298.

that the application of the domestic law is not dependent upon some concept of a quality of law inherent in articles of international treaties or conventions which were not in existence when the Constitution of Botswana was framed. It is submitted that this restrictive interpretation of fundamental rights and freedoms guaranteed in the Constitution fails to give to individuals the full measure of the rights and freedoms guaranteed. In his dissenting opinion, Lord Coulsfield JA rightly observes that reliance on domestic law alone may be inadequate to protect inhabitants of a territory against arbitrary action by State authorities, since the domestic law itself may be arbitrary. The learned judge went on to observe that it is widely accepted that the right to protection of the law implies that the domestic law must conform to broader standards of fairness.[33]

It is submitted that Lord Coulsfield's approach should be preferred over the majority view. When it comes to the interpretation of the constitution, most Commonwealth jurisdictions have embraced the view that a constitution must be given a generous and purposive construction.[34] Botswana's Court of Appeal has endorsed this approach in the earlier case of *Attorney General v Dow*, where it held that a "generous construction" means that when interpreting the provisions of the Constitution, a court should not whittle down any rights and freedoms unless by very clear and unambiguous words such interpretation is compelling.[35] The court further observed that the Constitution is the supreme law of the land and is meant to serve not only the present generation, but also further generations; therefore, courts must continue to breathe life into it from time to time as the occasion may arise to ensure healthy growth and development of the State through it.[36]

The Court of Appeal in the *Dow* case went on to observe that it is the primary duty of the judges to make the Constitution grow and develop in order to meet the just demands and aspirations of an ever-developing society which is part of the wider and larger human society governed by some acceptable concepts of human dignity. Most notably, it held:

> "At this juncture I wish to take judicial notice of that which is known the world over that Botswana is one of the few countries in Africa where

[33] *Good v Attorney General, supra,* at 363.

[34] See authorities cited in Article 19, International Centre Against Censorship, *The Interpretation of Fundamental Rights Provisions: International & Regional Standards in African and other Common Law Jurisdictions* (Article 19, 1997) pp. 5–12.

[35] *Per* Aguda JA at 165.

[36] *ibid,* at 166.

liberal democracy has taken root. It seems clear to me that all the three arms of the government - the Legislative, the Executive and the Judiciary - must strive to make it remain so except to any extent as may be prohibited by the Constitution in clear terms. It seems clear to me that in so striving we cannot afford to be immuned from the progressive movements going on around us in other liberal and not so liberal democracies such movements manifesting themselves in international agreements, treaties, resolutions, protocols and other similar understandings as well as in the respectable and respected voices of our other learned brethen in the performance of their adjudicatory roles in other jurisdictions."[37]

The Court of Appeal's approach in the *Dow* case in the interpretation of fundamental rights and freedoms should be preferred over the approach in Good's case. As rightly pointed out by Lord Coulsfield in his dissenting opinion in the latter case, reliance on domestic law alone may not be enough to ensure the full enjoyment of the fundamental rights and freedoms of the individual. It therefore becomes important that in giving effect to the fundamental rights and freedoms of the individual, courts should try to interpret domestic law in a way that is compatible with progressive movements as manifested in international treaties and conventions. It is in this light that the decision of the majority members of the Court of Appeal in the *Good* case, that the application of domestic law is not dependent on some concept of a quality of law inherent in international treaties and conventions not in existence when the Constitution was framed, is disappointing as this does not accord individuals the full protection of the law.

Some progressive democratic states have given effect to the principles contained in international treaties and conventions that require that before an alien is expelled from a country, he/she should be informed of the reasons for the action and be given an opportunity to respond. For example, in the United Kingdom, a Special Immigration Appeals Tribunal was established in 1997 to hear appeals from individuals deported by the Secretary of State for the Home Department under its immigration laws. The move was as a result of the UK's obligations emanating from the European Convention on Human Rights and ICCPR, both of which require State parties to ensure that everyone whose fundamental rights and freedoms are violated is accorded an effective remedy before a national authority.[38]

---

[37] *ibid,* at 168.

[38] See Articles 13 of both instruments.

The Court of Appeal of Botswana in the *Good* case held that the creation of tribunals such as the Special Immigration Appeals Tribunal in the UK is dependent on factors such as the desire to have them and the financial and manpower resources available to ensure their creation and continued operation. The Court left the creation of a similar tribunal to the discretion of the government. It is submitted that such an approach is not consistent with a generous interpretation of the Constitution. The Court should have, in line with Botswana's obligations under international treaties and developments in progressive democracies, urged the government to establish a similar tribunal as a matter of urgency. As Aguda JA held in the *Dow* case, the courts have an obligation to ensure that the domestic laws of their countries conform to the international obligations of that country.[39]

5 Conclusion

Laws that give wide discretionary powers to State authorities without providing adequate mechanisms of control over the exercise of the discretion pose serious threats to the enjoyment of individuals' fundamental rights and freedoms. The provisions of Botswana's Immigration Act on the deportation of aliens are a typical example of such laws. In a state that has a constitution, the constitution is the supreme law of the land that provides a framework and sets the limits of governmental power, acting as a controlling instrument against which all other laws may be tested. A constitution by its nature, unlike ordinary legislation, is not meant to be amended as often as the latter. Because of this, it becomes imperative that a constitution should be interpreted as a living instrument taking into account the present day conditions. Courts of law, as the guardians of the constitution, have a duty to ensure its development by interpreting it as a living instrument. In order to do this, as noted by the Botswana Court of Appeal in the *Dow* case, the court cannot be immune from the progressive movements going around in other liberal democracies manifesting themselves in international agreements. When the same court in the *Good* case held that the application of the domestic law is not dependent upon some quality of law inherent in the articles of international treaties, it clearly failed in its duty to interpret the Constitution of Botswana as a living instrument.

The provisions of Botswana's Immigration Act that empower the President to deport aliens from the country are arbitrary and have no place in a modern

39 *AG v Dow, supra,* at 169.

liberal democracy. There is evidence that the Act is used to curtail the freedom of expression of aliens in the country. The wide discretionary powers conferred on the President and the lack of adequate control mechanisms over the exercise of the power mean that aliens always tread with caution when it comes to the exercise of their right to freedom of expression lest they rub the authorities in the wrong way, which may lead to their deportation. Freedom of expression, it must be emphasised, is essential in every democratic society and, as such, it should be jealously guarded by the courts. The conservative approach taken by the Court of Appeal in the *Good* case clearly leaves aliens in a precarious position. It is submitted that the court should have adopted a more progressive approach, as it did in the *Dow* case, by judging the impugned provisions of the Immigration Act against emerging international standards. Such an approach would have demonstrated that the provisions of the Act are regressive and have no place in a modern liberal democracy.

Perspectives on the Interface Between Human Rights and the Environment in Botswana in the Light of the Basarwa Case

K.K. Lebotse*

Abstract

The Basarwa case generated a lot of excitement both locally and internationally. The Basarwa challenged their forced removal from the Central Kalahari Game Reserve (CKGR). This paper seeks to interrogate the question whether the decision of the court marked a paradigm shift in judicial enforcement of fundamental Human Rights. The Court pointed to the violation of the right to life to affirm what is essentially a claim to the right to a healthy environment. The paper suggests that indeed the decision of the court marked the dawn of a new approach in which the right of citizens to a healthy environment suitable for their survival is recognised. That the right to a healthy environment overlaps with other rights, such as "native rights", is immaterial. In any case, these rights do not have to be mutually exclusive. In their nature they are by and large complementary, indivisible and interdependent as they have a common goal: to secure and better human life.

1 Introduction

On the 13 December 2006, the High Court of Botswana delivered its ruling in the marathon case[1] concerning the relocation of some Basarwa (also derogatively described by colonialists as Bushmen), from their ancestral lands in the Central Kgalagadi Game Reserve (CKGR). The court found in favour of the Basarwa on the fundamental issues in dispute.

---

*LL.B (UB), LL.M (Lond), Attorney (Botswana), Senior Lecturer, Department of Law, University of Botswana.

[1] *Sesana v Attorney General* [2006] 2 BLR 633. The case is reputed to be the longest in the history of the administration of justice in Botswana, having lasted some four years.

The facts of the case were that the applicants belonged to a tribe called the Basarwa, and were also known as Bushmen. They were the indigenous inhabitants of the Kalahari Desert, having built their settlements in an area which was to be declared as the Central Kalahari Game Reserve in 1961. Before the establishment of the game reserve, the applicants and their ancestors hunted, gathered wood and kept small stock in the settlements. They were, however, prohibited from hunting and keeping stock after the declaration of the game reserve. The government provided basic and essential services to the applicants in their settlements. In the latter part of the last century, the government tried to move the applicants from their settlements and to relocate them in new settlements built by the government outside the game reserve. The new settlements were provided with water, schools, clinics and other essential services. Those who agreed to relocate were compensated for vacating their old settlements. They were given land to grow vegetables and rear small stock.

Some of the inhabitants refused to relocate to the new settlements. The government informed those who refused to relocate that basic and essential services being provided for old settlements would be terminated within six months. On 31 January 2002, the government terminated the provision of basic and essential services to those who refused to relocate to the new settlements.

The applicants applied for an order declaring that the termination by the government of the provision of basic and essential services to the applicants was unlawful and unconstitutional; that the government was obliged to restore such basic and essential services; that those individuals forcibly removed by the government from the Central Kalahari Game Reserve had been unlawfully despoiled of their possession of land and that such possession should immediately be restored; and that the refusal to issue the applicants with special game licences or allow them access to the reserve without a permit was unlawful and unconstitutional. The following questions were put before the court for determination:

(a) Whether termination of the provision of basic and essential services in the CKGR with effect from 31 January 2002 was unlawful and unconstitutional;

(b) Whether government is obliged to restore the provision of such services;

(c) Whether subsequent to 31 January 2002 the appellants were:

  (i) In possession of land which they lawfully occupied in their settlements in the CKGR and:

   (ii) Deprived of such possession by the government's forcibly or wrongly and without their consent;

(d) Whether government's refusal to:

   (i) Issue special game licenses to the appellants and

   (ii) Allow the appellants to enter the CKGR unless with a permit is unlawful and unconstitutional.

This paper takes a critical look at two issues in the case, one concerning the termination of the provision of essential services and the refusal to issue the Basarwa with hunting licences and the requirement that they should possess an entry permit in order to enter the CKGR. The paper interrogates the question whether a case could be made that the court in a way recognized the right of the Basarwa to a healthy environment. In the process a brief overview of the nature of Human Rights shall be made and juxtaposed with environmental rights.

2 Nature of Human Rights

Human rights are understood as rights which belong to any individual as a consequence of being human, independently of acts of law. They are neither obtained nor granted through any human actions. They are inalienable. The first identical sections of the preambles to the Universal Declaration of Human Rights (UDHR)[2] and the International Covenants of Human Rights[3] read:

> "Recognition of the inherent dignity and of the equal and inalienable rights of all members of the human family is the foundation of freedom, justice and peace in the world."

The preamble to the Covenants adds that, "these rights derive from the inherent dignity of the human person". Equality is another major element of the conception of human rights. The UDHR declares, "All human beings are born free and equal in dignity and rights". [4]

Equal dignity requires equal respect for an individual related to his or for his or her personal development and for his or her rights. Respect for equality

[2] Adopted by the United Nations on 10 December 1948.

[3] International Covenant on Civil and Political Rights, 1966; and the Covenant on Economic, Social and Cultural Rights, 1966.

[4] Article 1.

does not mean an equal treatment in the way of imposing equal aims and equal circumstances of action. Differences are desirable if there are proportional reasons justifying them. Equality may sometimes be expressed in terms of non-discrimination if discrimination means differentiating without proper reason.

Another important feature of the contemporary conception of human rights is the recognition of indivisibility and interdependence of rights:

> "All human rights are universal, indivisible and interdependent and interrelated. The international community must treat human rights globally in a fair and equal manner, on the same footing, and with the same emphasis."[5]

There are several different ways of categorising human rights. One common method of listing rights is according to subject matter — as in civil, political, economic, social or cultural rights. Civil and political rights include the right to life, privacy, equality and non-discrimination. All these rights may be impacted by environmental conditions.

Human rights can further be divided into substantive and procedural rights. The following substantive rights may be affected by environmental degradation:

- The right to life. In its broadened scope it entails the right to health and well being. This will be elaborated upon later.
- The right to respect for private and family life and home;
- The right to use and enjoy property;
- The right to a decent environment[6];
- The right to cultural expression (particularly important to indigenous peoples.

Procedural rights are a critical complement to substantive rights. Procedural rights are enabling rights in that they make it possible for people to contribute actively to the protection of the environment. Procedural rights that further the environmental cause include:

- The right to information;
- The right to participation;

---

[5] Vienna Declaration, art 1.5.

[6] Expressly recognised by two regional human rights treaties: the African (Banjul) Charter on Human and Peoples' Rights and the San Salvador Protocol to the American Convention on Human Rights.

- The right to equal protection and to be free from discrimination; and
- The right to judicial remedy.

Human rights may also be categorised according to the scope of the protection afforded. Some rights are deemed so fundamental that they may never be suspended whatever the national emergency. The "non-derogable" rights common to all human rights instruments are the right to life, the right to be free from torture, the right of non-discrimination and freedom from slavery. Other rights are drafted in precise terms without qualification or limitation, but they may be suspended when strictly required by the exigencies of a national emergency threatening the life of the nation. A third category of rights is normally defined and its scope set forth, but it is accompanied by a "limitations" clause setting forth the permissible grounds for the state to qualify the right or balance it against other public interests, including public order, health, safety, morality etc.

3 What is Environmental Law?

Environmental law for purposes of this paper will be construed as a body of rules and regulations which have as their object or effect the protection of the environment from environmental hazards as well as to ensure sustainable development.

Environmental law is a relatively new but rapidly growing and expanding field of law which aims at protecting nature, natural resources and the total context within which they exist from major deterioration that could impair their utilisation by the present and future generations. Its development originated from the growing awareness that our planet is endangered by population explosion, over-exploitation of natural resources, loss of biological diversity, ozone depletion, climate change, acid rain, deforestation, desertification, air and water pollution, hazardous waste disposal and the list can go on and on.[7]

There is also recognition that environmental problems transcend national borders and this has resulted in the development of international environmental

[7] See generally N.A. Robinson, "Environmental Law: The Bedrock for sustainability", a paper presented at the Global Judges' Symposium on Sustainable Development and the Rule of Law, Johannesburg, South Africa, 18–20 August 2002.

law to meet particular concerns where consensus has been garnered.[8] Nation States have realised that *ad hoc*, unco-ordinated and reactive policy responses by individual states have not and will not be adequate to address the rapidly growing problems faced by the international community. Environmental law has thus grown from a body of national rules, or bilateral rules to an area governed by a large and expanding body of regional and global treaties.[9]

4 Nature and Scope of Environmental Rights

The setting for environmental rights discourse is arguably the 1972 Stockholm UN Conference on the Human Environment. The conference declared that, "Man has the fundamental right to freedom, equality and adequate conditions of life in an environment of a quality that permits a life of dignity and well-being."[10] Twenty years later, at the Rio Conference on Environment and Development there was once again mention of the link between human rights and the environment. The conference declared: "Human beings are the centre of concerns for sustainable development. They are entitled to a healthy and productive life in harmony with nature."[11] Though this formulation of the need to guarantee a healthy and productive environment has been criticised for taking an anthropocentric view of environmental protection, it nonetheless evidenced a paradigm shift in so far as the interaction between human beings and the environment is concerned. There is acknowledgment that human beings need a healthy environment for their existence.

It is important to stress that environmental rights do not fit neatly into any single category or generation of human rights, rather they straddle all categories. Hence there have been efforts in some quarters to derive

[8] For a comparative view of the multinational nature of Environmental Law, *see Comparative Environmental Law and Regulation*, (N.A. Robinson ed.) New York, OUP (2007).

[9] See for example, African Convention on the Conservation of Nature and Natural Resources (1968), Convention on International Trade in Endangered Species of Wild Fauna and Flora (CITES) (1973), Convention on Wetlands of International Importance especially as Waterfowl Habitat (RAMSAR) (1971), Convention to Combat Desertification in those Countries Experiencing Serious Drought and/or Desertification, Particularly in Africa (1994) and Kyoto Protocol to the UN Framework Convention on Climate Change (1997).

[10] Principle 1, Declaration on the Human Environment, Report of the United Nations Conference on the Human Environment (New Your), UN Doc. A/CONF. 48/14/Rev. 1

[11] Principle 1, Declaration on Environment and Development, Report of the UN Conference on Environment and Development, 1 (New York, 1992), UN Doc.A/CONF.151/26/Rev. 1

environmental rights from other internationally protected rights, such as life, private life, or property.[12]

4.1 The Right to a Safe and Healthy Environment

The concept of a right to a healthy and safe environment has generated debate in international human rights discourse. Clearly, not every social problem must result in a claim becoming expressed as a human right and there remains disagreement even about some of the human rights already enunciated. However, the recognition that human survival depends upon a safe and healthy environment places the claim of a right to environment fully on the human rights agenda. However, it has become clear that without a constitutionally guaranteed right to healthy environment it is difficult to enforce or claim the right to a healthy environment. The right is not justiciable. Hence emerging democracies have made a right to a decent or healthy environment a constitutional right.[13] The absence of a constitutional right to a healthy environment has caused litigants to ride over surrogate rights, that is, use accepted fundamental rights, such as right to life, to advance what is essentially a claim to a healthy environment. Petitioners have put their complaint of violation of the right to a clean environment in the context of violation of right to life.

4.2 Case Law from Other Jurisdiction on Interpretation of the Right to Life

In Africa Tanzania appears to be the first African nation in which courts addressed the scope and constitutional right to life provisions in the context of environmental protection. The Tanzanian Constitution provides, "Everyone has the right to live and to the protection for his life by the society in accordance with law."[14] In *Joseph D. Kessy v Dar es Salaam City Council*[15] citizens of Tabata, a suburb of Dar es Salaam, brought a suit against the city council of Dar es Salaam, seeking to enjoin the City Council from operating a garbage dump that created severe air pollution in the nearby neighbourhood.

---

[12] 1981 African Charter on Human and Peoples' Rights, Article 24, 21 ILM (1982), 52; 1966 UN Covenant on Economic and Social Rights, Article 12, 6 ILM (1967), 360; UNGA Res. 45/94 (1991); 1992 World charter for Nature, Principles 23, 23 ILM(1983), 455; *Powell and Rayner v UK* (1990) 12 EHRR 355, *Lopez Ostra v Spain* (1994) 20 EHRR 277, *Gronus v Poland* (1999) ECHR Case no. 29695/96.

[13] See, for example, South Africa s. 24 1996 Constitution, Uganda s. 39 1995 Constitution.

[14] See s. 14 1977 Constitution.

[15] Civil Case No. 229 of 1998 (High Court of Tanzania, 9 September 1991).

The foul smell and air pollution had caused respiratory problems to residents in the area, particularly in children, pregnant women, and the elderly. The court noted that the air pollution created by the garbage dump endangered the health and lives of nearby residents.

The same approach has been espoused by the Indian courts. Article 21 of the Indian Constitution provides that, "no person shall be deprived of his life or personal liberty except according to procedural issues established by law". Thus in *L.K. Koolwal v Rajasthan*[16] the court found that a city had violated residents' right to life by failing to implement adequate sanitation measures. The court held that maintenance of health, preservation of sanitation, and environmental protection fall within the purview of Article 21's right to life. It found the problem of sanitation to be "very acute in Jaipur City…creating hazard to life of the citizens".

In *Vellore Citizens Welfare Reform v Union of India*[17], the Indian Supreme Court found that tanneries in the state of Tamil Nadu had violated citizens' right to life by discharging untreated effluents into agricultural land making it unfit for cultivation.

In *General Secretary, West Pakistan Salt Miners Labour Union (CBA) Khewra, Khelum v The Director, Industries and Mineral Development, Punjab Lahore*[18], the Supreme Court of Pakistan found that mining companies had violated the right to life of citizens residing near mining operations by polluting local drinking water supplies.

In *Shehla Zia and Others v WAPDA*,[19] the Pakistan Supreme Court found that the constitutional right to life is broad enough to include "protection from being exposed to the hazards of electromagnetic field or any other such hazards which may be due to installation and construction of any grid station, any factory, power station or such like installations". The petitioners opposed the construction of a power grid station near the residential area in which they lived (Islamabad). The Malaysian case of *Kajing Tubek v Ekran and others*[20] is instructive in analysing cases such as the Basarwa Case. Of particular interest is the pronouncement of the court in that case which is similar to

[16] 1988 A.I.R. Raj 2 (High Court of Rajasthan).

[17] (1996) 5 SCC 647.

[18] Human Rights Case No. 120 of 1993, 1994 SCMR 2061 (1994).

[19] Human Rights Case No. 15-K of 1992 P.L.D. 1994, Supreme Court, 693 (1994).

[20] [1996] 2 MLJ 388 (High Court, 19 June 1996).

those made in *Sesana*'s case, especially that of Dow J. In the Malaysian case, the plaintiffs were residents of longhouses in Belaga, Sarawak who were affected by the government's proposed development of a hydroelectric project. They sought a declaration that before the project could be implemented the defendants had to comply with the Environmental Quality Act of 1974 requiring an Environmental Impact Assessment (EIA) for prescribed activities. By an order the Minister had excluded the application of this Act to Sarawak and instead subjected the project to a procedure, which, unlike the 1974 Act, did not provide for public participation in the EIA process. The defendants challenged the plaintiff's standing to bring the suit. The court's rejection of this challenge has been summarised as follows:

> "The plaintiffs claim that their homes and land would be destroyed, their lives uprooted by the project and that they would suffer far more greatly and directly than other members of the public as their 'land and forest are not just a source of livelihood but constitute life itself, fundamental to their social cultural and spiritual survival as native peoples', was sufficient to justify the plaintiffs having a substantial or genuine interest to have a legal position declared."[21]

In *Sesana*'s case, Dow J. quoted with approval the words of Jose R. Martninez Cobo[22]:

> "It is essential to know and understand the deeply spiritual relationship between indigenous peoples and their land as basic to their existence as such and to all their beliefs, customs, traditions and culture. For such peoples the land is not merely a possession and a means of production. The entire relationship between the spiritual life of indigenous peoples and Mother Earth, and their land, has a great many deep-seated implications. Their land is not a commodity which can be acquired, but a material element to be enjoyed freely."[23]

The learned judge took the view that uprooting the Basarwa from their ancestral land not only infringed upon their right to liberty and movement but amounted to a destruction of a community's life. The relocations, she stressed, affected the very essence of the existence of the Basarwa.[24]

---

21 *Compendium of Judicial Decisions on Matters Related to Environment*: National Decisions Volume 1, p. 47 (1998).

22 [2006] 2 BLR, at 705. Quoting from "The Study of the Problem of Discrimination Against Indigenous Populations", Vol. V No E. 86. XIV. 3 (United Nations publications).

23 *ibid.*, at 705.

24 *ibid.*, at 730–731.

5 Decision of the Court on Issues Touching on Environmental Rights

5.1 Termination of the Provision of Basic and Essential Services

The basic and essential services that the Government stopped providing to the residents of the CKGR with effect from 30 January 2002 included: provision of food rations to registered destitute and orphans; provision of healthcare through mobile clinics and ambulance services and provision of transport for children attending school outside the reserve. Two judges, Phumaphi and Dibotelo JJ., (Dow J. dissenting) found that the termination was not unlawful and unconstitutional because the applicants failed to establish either a legitimate expectation based on promise made to them or on practice. Dow J. was, however, moved by the consideration that the termination included water and food rations for destitute and orphans. These, she noted, were essential for the survival of the recipients. She observed that their termination endangered life, a constitutionally guaranteed right.

5.2 Stoppage of the Supply of Food Rations and the Refusal to Issue Special Game Licenses

The court found that the simultaneous stoppage of the supply of food rations and the refusal to issue special game licenses to the applicants was "tantamount to condemning the applicants remaining in the reserve to death by starvation.[25] This violated the applicants' constitutional right to life."[26] The reasoning here was that the survival of some of these people depended on food rations and they as a people depended on hunting game for meat and the refusal to issue game licenses went to the root of their survival. In fact, the refusal actually made their survival difficult.

The second issue should be distinguished from the first in that the essential services in the first included stoppage of provision of healthcare through mobile clinics and ambulance services and provision of transport to children attending school outside the reserve. Dibotelo and Phumaphi JJ. felt termination of these services was not unlawful and unconstitutional. Judge Dow, in minority, was of the view that these were unlawfully and unconstitutionally terminated. She observed that these services were terminated or withheld to force the Basarwa to move out of the CKGR. This,

[25] *ibid.*, at 635.

[26] *ibid.*

it is submitted, violated the applicant's right to live in their natural environment.

5.3 Refusal to Allow the Appellants to Enter the CKGR unless with a Permit

The court again held that this was unlawful and unconstitutional and that it went to the root of their survival. Phumaphi J. observed that this requirement violated the appellants' rights of freedom of movement guaranteed by section 14 of the constitution of Botswana.[27]

5.4 Deprivation of the Basarwa of Possession of their Land

All the three judges held that the Basarwa were deprived of possession of their land unlawfully and forcibly. It is important to note that the court recognised the Basarwa's aboriginal title to their land. The court emphatically stated that the applicants were aboriginal inhabitants of the area over which the CKGR was established; that the establishment of colonial rule and appropriation of the land in the area for the Crown did not extinguish their right or title to the land; neither did the establishment of a game reserve and the imposition of some restriction on hunting and access to the area, or re-designation of the area as State Land after independence affected their vested rights. This aspect of the case has been hailed as probably the first decision in the Roman-Dutch law jurisdiction to expound on the core elements of the doctrine of native or aboriginal title to land.[28] It also shows that whilst government has a right to protect the environment by restricting the killing of game and protecting fauna from over-utilisation by the Basarwa, there is a need to strike a balance between environmental concerns and rights of the Basarwa to live in their natural environment. In their nature these concerns are by and large complementary, indivisible and interdependent as they have a common goal: to secure and better human life.

6 Conclusion

The Basarwa case was a case in which a people defended themselves against forced removal from the CKGR and, most importantly, their way of life. The hurdles put before them to make life difficult only served to strengthen their

[27] *ibid.*, at 774.

[28] See Ng'ong'ola "Sneaking Aboriginal Title into Botswana's Legal system through a side Door: Review of *Sesana and Others v The Attorney General*" 6 U. of Botswana L.J. 107, at 128 (2007).

resolve to fight for their dignity. These hurdles came in the form of stoppage of essential services and refusal to issue them with special hunting licences and the requirement that they can only enter the CKGR if they had entry permits. These issues gave rise to constitutional issues and issues touching on fundamental human rights and the relationship of those human rights to the right of the Basarwa to live in an environment which is healthy and suitable for their survival.

It is the argument of this paper that the decision of the court in this case will go a long way to securing the right of citizens to a decent environment. This case also illustrates the difficulty faced by litigants when they try to enforce a right to a decent environment when such right is not guaranteed by the constitution. The case also illustrates the reluctance of the court to pronounce on violation of a right which is not guaranteed by the constitution. Instead the court used a surrogate rights (the right to life, liberty and movement) to affirm what in essence is a claim to a right to a decent environment. As Dow J neatly put it:

> "The case is thus, ultimately about a people demanding dignity and respect. It is a people saying in essence, 'our way of life may be different but it's worthy of respect. We may be changing and getting closer to your way of life, but give us a chance to decide what we want to carry with us into the future'."[29]

[29] [2006] 2 BLR, at 729.

Property Guarantees in the Constitution and Implications for Land Tenure Policy in Botswana

Clement Ng'ong'ola*

1 Introduction

In debates, disputes and other contestations over land in Botswana, time and again, reference must be made to the questions whether, and to what extent, does the Constitution protect land or property rights? Some of the property guarantees clauses in the Constitution are well–known, but probably not sufficiently understood. They have occasionally been misconstrued, even by the High Court in landmark cases. This paper is first a compendium of all the provisions in the Constitution that protect, deal with, or have a bearing on, protection of property. It is secondly an assessment of the implications of these guarantees for post colonial land tenure policy in Botswana. The paper will offer suggestions on policy shifts required to better accommodate the constitutional dictates. It should also logically offer suggestions as to what constitutional adjustments might be required on some of the policy preferences, but it is loath to do so. In Botswana, we have often heard, in response to clamors for constitutional reform, the retort, in American slang, that "if it isn't broke, why fix it?" The question the paper seeks to leave with the audience is whether or not in this area we are dealing with a broken instrument that might or might not require fixing?"

2 The Land Tenure System in Historical Perspective

In Botswana, as elsewhere in sub-Saharan Africa, a plural land tenure system emerged almost from the onset of colonial at the turn of the last century. The main categories of land are Tribal or customary land, covering over 70 per cent of the total land area of the country, estimated at 582,000 square kilometres; State land, covering about 25 per cent of the total land area; and

* LL.B. (Malawi), LL.M. (Exeter), Ph.d. (Lond.), Associate Professor of Law, University of Botswana.

Freehold or private land, covering about 5 per cent of the total land area.[1] At independence on 30th September 1966, the relative sizes of the three categories were: Tribal land, 48 per cent; State land, 47 per cent; and Freehold land, 6 per cent.[2]

As the nomenclature suggests, Tribal land was land originally occupied by indigenous communities under customary forms of tenure. It is now held under both customary and statutory forms of tenure. State land was designated as Crown lands during the colonial era. It was land appropriated from the tribal pool by the colonial administration for government use, and vested in the Crown as Head of State and Government. It was re-designated as the State land at independence. It is held under forms of tenure prescribed by statute. Most of it comprises of national parks, wildlife management areas and forest reserves, and a small percentage is urban land for commercial and residential use.[3] Freehold land was also initially appropriated from the tribal pool, and allocated to settlers of European descent or their enterprises, under forms of tenure that acknowledged the existence of "a freehold estate in land,"[4] a concept regarded as akin to dominion or individual or private ownership of the land.[5] It was, and still is, predominantly held or regulated under statute law and common law concepts introduced with colonial rule

[1] Republic of Botswana, *National Development Plan 9, 2003–2009,* Ministry of Finance and Development Planning, Gaborone, 2002, Para. 17.1, p. 332.

[2] B. Machacha, "Botswana's land tenure: institutional reform and policy formulation", in Arntzen, Ngcongco and Turner (eds.), *Land Policy and Agriculture in Eastern and Southern Africa*, Tokyo, 1986, p. 39.

[3] Republic of Botswana, NDP 9, Para. 17.1, p. 332 gives the following breakdown of State land: national parks and wildlife management areas, 19.4%; forest reserves, 1%; and urban land, 4.6%.

[4] This is an English property law concept. For its meaning see F.H. Lawson and B. Rudden, *The Law of Property*, 2nd ed., Clarendon Law Series, Oxford, 1982, p. 93. English common law, however, was not the residual common law applied in the Bechuanaland Protectorate. Section 19 General Administration Proclamation of 10 June 1891 provided for the application of the law for the time being in the colony of the Cape of Good Hope. This was presumed to be Roman Dutch law, brought to the Cape by the original Dutch settlers in 1652. See J.H. Pain, "The reception of English and Roman Dutch Law in Africa with reference to Botswana Lesotho and Swaziland," XI (1978) *Comparative and International Law Journal of Southern Africa, (CILSA)*, pp. 137–167, and A.J.G.M. Sanders, "Legal Dualism in Lesotho, Botswana and Swaziland", 1, 1(1985) *Lesotho Law Journal*, pp. 47–67.

[5] For a discussion of concepts of ownership and dominium under the common law applicable in Botswana see A.M. Honore, "Ownership", in A.E. Guest (ed.), *Oxford Essays in Jurisprudence*, Oxford, 1961, pp. 107–147; P. Birks, "The Roman law concept of dominium and the idea of absolute ownership", (1985) *Acta Juridica,* pp. 1–37; D.P. Visser, "The 'absoluteness' of ownership: the South African common law in perspective", (1985) *Acta Juridica* pp. 39–52; and C. Lewis, "The modern concept of ownership of land" (1985) *Acta Juridica*, pp. 245–266.

This law and land tenure matrix has given rise to some of the same types of policy concerns and issues in Botswana as elsewhere in Southern Africa, some of which have required consideration or invocation of the property guarantees in the Constitution. The more intractable of these issues, to be revisited later on in this discussion, include reclamation of freehold agricultural land from settler or alien control, and indigenisation or localisation of parcels not reclaimed. In respect of State land, the issues are re-discovery and assertion of aboriginal or historical land rights overlooked in the appropriation of Tribal land for the Crown, and perpetuation of freehold titles in the disposal of State land for urban use. In respect of tribal or customary land, the issues are reform or modernisation of customary forms of tenure and administrative arrangements, and regulation of squatting or self provisioning of land.

In discussions of these and other land tenure issues, some of which I have led,[6] account is not always taken of what the Constitution provides, and what the implications should be for land tenure policy and reform. This paper is intended to address this omission in the literature. It seeks to provide a more comprehensive review of constitutional provisions that have a bearing on familiar property and land tenure themes and issues in Botswana. The discussion must inevitably lead to suggestions on constitutional reforms and land tenure policy modifications. Through my other writings and publications,[7] some of my views on land tenure reforms might be well known. The paper therefore will focus on and tease out possible areas for constitutional reform. The paper in this way seeks to provoke wider reaction to the view obtaining in some political circles that Botswana has been well served by its fairly old constitution and, in the colourful language of mechanics and technicians, "why fix it, if its is not broken?"

---

[6] See, for example, C. Ng'ong'ola, "Land tenure reform in Botswana: post colonial developments and future prospects" (1996) 11 *South African Public Law*, pp. 1–29; and S. Morolong and C. Ng'ong'ola "Revisiting the notion of ownership of tribal land in Botswana," in C. Fombad (ed) Essays on Law in Botswana, (Juta & Co., Cape Town, 2007), pp. 147–175.

[7] My other notable publications on land issues in Botswana include: "Land problems in some peri-urban villages in Botswana, and problems of conception, description and transformation of tribal land tenure", 36,2(1992), *Journal of African Law*, pp. 140–167"Land rights for marginalised ethnic groups in Botswana, with special reference to Basarwa", 41, 1(1997) *Journal of African Law*, pp. 1–26. "Legal and practical problems in the administration of Tribal land in Botswana", Ditshwanelo, Botswana Centre for Human Rights, *Report on the Conference on Human Rights and Democracy, 17–19 November 1998*, Gaborone 2000, pp. 163–174; and "Sneaking aboriginal title into Botswana's legal system through a side door: Review of *Sesana and Others v The Attorney General*" 6(2007) *University of Botswana Law Journal*, pp. 107–130.

3 An Overview of Property Clauses in the Constitution

There are two clauses in Chapter II of the Constitution, on "protection of fundamental rights and freedoms of the individual," that explicitly refer to protection of property. Two other clauses, on protection of other rights, are pertinent to debates and discussion of land tenure policy in Botswana, as are three clauses in Chapter V, Part III, on the establishment and composition of the second House of Parliament, previously called the House of Chiefs, and now called "*Ntlo ya Dikgosi*", the vernacular equivalent of the previous appellation.

An important political detail in the assessment of protection of property and other fundamental rights in Botswana is that unlike some of its neighbours in Southern Africa, Botswana had a relatively trouble free transition from colonial rule to independence. There was no war of independence; no civil disobedience, or the type of agitation or campaigning that would have compelled colonial authorities to restrain or incarcerate nationalist leaders.[8] Constitutional arrangements under which power was ultimately transferred evolved between 1963 and 1966. Negotiations on the side of the nationalists were dominated by Seretse Khama's Botswana Democratic Party (BDP),[9] a pro-capital, right of centre outfit that has since won all elections held in the country. In the negotiations, land issues were overshadowed by concerns such as racial discrimination, and the role of chiefs and tribal leaders under the proposed new dispensation. At the end of the last constitutional conference in 1966, at Marlborough House, the chair of the working sessions, not surprisingly, remarked that this was "one of the briefest and most peaceful constitutional conferences for some time."[10]

Although the "independence struggle" in Botswana was not a "struggle for land", the independence Constitution nevertheless incorporated strong property guarantees, aimed at assuring the comparatively small settler community that their freehold land rights would be secure.[11] Section 3, the opening clause in Chapter II, provides:

---

[8] Sir Ketumire Masire, "Foreword" in P. Fawcus and A. Tilbury, *Botswana: The Road to Independence*, Pula Press and The Botswana Society, Gaborone, 2000, p. ix.

[9] P. Fawcus and A Tilbury, *Botswana: The Road to Independence*, especially Ch. 10, pp. 123–128, and Ch 18, pp. 196–207.

[10] N. Parsons, W. Henderson and T. Tlou, *Seretse Khama, 1921–1980*, Macmillan Boleswa, Bramfontein, South Africa, 1995, 243.

[11] T. Allen, *The Right to Property in Commonwealth Constitutions*, Cambridge University Press, 2000, at pp. 58–59 observes that there was no illusion in Britain that a Bill of Rights would deter a

> "Whereas every person in Botswana is entitled to the fundamental rights and freedoms of the individual, that is to say, the right, whatever his race, place of origin, political opinions, colour, creed or sex, but subject to respect for the rights and freedoms of others and for the public interest to each and all of the following, namely –
>
> (a) life, liberty, security of the person and the protection of the law;
>
> (b) freedom of conscience, of expression and of assembly and association;
>
> (c) protection for the privacy of his home and other property and from deprivation of property without compensation,
>
> the provisions of this Chapter shall have effect for the purpose of affording protection to those rights and freedoms subject to such limitations of that protection as are contained in those provisions, being limitations designed to ensure that that the enjoyment of the said rights and freedoms by any individual does not prejudice the rights and freedom of others or the public interest."

In *Attorney General v Dow*,[12] Amissah P, in the main speech for the majority of a full bench of the Court of Appeal, regarded this as the "key or umbrella provision in Chapter II under which all rights and freedoms protected under that Chapter must be subsumed." The Court suggested that the other clauses in Chapter II, elaborating on the fundamental rights or freedoms guaranteed, should not be interpreted in a manner that restricts a right covered by the section. Thus, section 15, elaborating on protection from discrimination, could not be interpreted in a manner that restricts interpretation of section 3, so that discrimination on the basis of gender could be regarded as permissible.[13] In a dissenting opinion, however, Schreiner JA regarded section 3 as "declaratory, in general terms, of the goal which it is sought to be reached by the provisions of the Chapter as a whole …"[14] In his view, section 3 did not "create specific rights and freedoms which do not fall specifically within the more detailed provisions of sections 4 to 15."[15]

determined nationalist government from proceeding against settler proprietary interests, but strong property guarantees had an important psychological value. They provided the assurance to settlers that there might be economic and political stability in the new nations.

12 [1992] BLR 119 (Court of Appeal).

13 [1992] BLR 119, at 133–134.

14 [1992] BLR 119, at 187.

15 *ibid.*

If we take, as we should, the majority view as the correct legal position, then section 3(c) could be interpreted as offering a particular and distinct type of property protection, "from deprivation without compensation"; and section 8, the second property clause, as offering protection from "compulsory acquisition" or expropriation. If Schreiner's view is the correct one, and the side note to section 8 suggests that it may be, the Constitution offers only protection from deprivation of property by way of compulsory acquisition, as elaborated in section 8. Section 3 does not create a property protection clause, distinct and separate from what is in section 8. This is the first ambiguity in the property clauses of the Constitution. It is not clear whether the Constitution offers freedom "from deprivation of property without compensation", as well as protection from "compulsory acquisition of property" except where, among other conditions, there is payment of compensation.[16] Compulsory acquisition traditionally involves the State or some authorised agency interfering with proprietary rights through dispossession of the holder. Deprivation refers to a wider category of interferences, which may not entail dispossession of the holder. The Constitution would offer even stronger protection of proprietary rights if Section 3(c) is interpreted as offering protection from deprivation of property even where there is no dispossession.

The other ambiguity in section 3, arising from the majority decision in *Attorney General v. Dow*, has now been clarified. If section 3 is a key provision, under which must be subsumed all the other rights in the Chapter, was it the intention that it should prevail in the event of conflict or inconsistencies with other provisions in the Chapter, or the Constitution? In *Kamanakao I and others v The Attorney – General and Another*,[17] the High Court acknowledged that sections 77, 78 and 79 of the Constitution, as originally drafted, abridged rights of the Wayei tribe to equal protection of the law, contrary to section 3(a) of the Constitution. But the Court refused to hold that sections 77, 78 or 79 were in consequence unconstitutional. One part of the Constitution could not be interpreted as invalidating another part of the Constitution, unless this was explicitly so provided for in the Constitution. The Court in effect ruled that there was no ranking on the basis of superiority of the clauses in the Constitution, or indeed in the Chapter on protection of fundamental rights and freedoms. The Court, on the other hand, was prepared to hold that provisions in the Chieftainship Act (Cap. 41:04) or

---

[16] For a detailed discussion of these and other troublesome elements of property clauses of this nature see A.J. Van der Walt, "Double property guarantees: a structural and comparative analysis," (1998) 14 *South African Journal on Human Rights*, pp. 560–586.

[17] [2001] 2 BLR 654.

the Tribal Territories (Cap. 32:03) that were inconsistent with Section 3(a) could be invalidated.

The first paragraph of section 8, the second property guarantee clause in Chapter II, or the clause elaborating on the protection from deprivation of property provided for in section 3(c), starts with the following words:

> "No property of any description shall be compulsorily taken possession of, and no interest in or right over property of any description shall be compulsorily acquired, except where the following conditions are satisfied ..."

Two sets of conditions are then specified, which severely cut down what would have been excessively strong protection of property rights. These are that: (a) the taking of possession or acquisition must be necessary or expedient for certain specified public purposes; and (b) provision must be made by a law applicable to the taking of possession or acquisition "for the prompt payment of adequate compensation", and for access to the High Court, directly or on appeal from any other authority, for determination of disputes pertaining to the legality of the acquisition or the amount or payment of any compensation.

Section 8(2) adds another condition for a valid expropriation which may now be time worn. It states:

> "No person who is entitled to compensation under this section shall be prevented from remitting, within a reasonable time after he or she has received any amount of that compensation, the whole of that amount (free from any deduction, charge or tax made or levied in respect of its remission), to any country of his or her choice outside Botswana."

Section 8(3) provides that the requirement for prompt payment of adequate compensation shall be deemed satisfied if the law providing for the taking of possession of minerals or the acquisition of rights to minerals provides for "the payment at reasonable intervals of adequate royalties".

Subsections (4), (5) and (6) of section 8 are the claw-back provisions. Subsection (4) permits attachment of compensation or the imposition of reasonable restrictions on its externalisation, if so authorised by an order of a competent court. Subsection (5) has the effect of excluding the application of the property guarantees in section 8 to takings or acquisitions authorised by laws relating, *inter alia*, to the following: enforcement of payment of taxes, rates or other taxes that may be due; enforcement of judgments, penalties or orders issued in civil or criminal proceedings; prescription or limitation of actions; or the taking over of property of enemies, insolvents, deceased persons, and other persons that are by law disabled from administering their own affairs. Subsection (6) precludes the application of the property guarantees to acquisition in the public interest of any property, interest or right held by "a body corporate established by law for public purposes in which no moneys have been invested other than moneys provided by Parliament." It will be suggested below that land boards are among the bodies corporate affected by this subsection.

The third property guarantee clause in Chapter II of the Constitution is embedded in section 14, which offers "protection from freedom of movement." Section 14(1) states that "no person shall be deprived of his or her freedom of movement," which for these purposes "means the right to move freely throughout Botswana, the right to reside in any part of Botswana, the right to enter Botswana and immunity from expulsion from Botswana." It is in the claw-back provisions in section 14(3) that allusions are made to protection, or lack of protection, of property rights related to residence in Botswana. First, paragraph (a) acknowledges that it may be necessary to impose restrictions on freedom of movement that are reasonably required "in the interests of defence, public safety, public order, public morality or public health." It also acknowledges that restrictions may be imposed "on the acquisition or use by any person of land or other property in Botswana". It should be noted that the restrictions permitted under this paragraph may be contested if "shown not to be reasonably justifiable in a democratic society".

Paragraph (b) of section 14(3), secondly, acknowledges that freedom of movement shall not be violated by an act done under a law that provides for the imposition of restrictions on movement of any person who is not a citizen of Botswana. But it is not suggested that the restriction may be contested if shown not to be reasonably justifiable in a democratic society. Does this mean that Government will be less constrained in restricting the right of non-citizens to enter or move freely within Botswana, as well as to acquire property for the purpose of residing in any part of the country?

Paragraph (c) of section 14(3), thirdly, acknowledges that freedom of movement shall not be violated by a law providing "for the imposition of restrictions on entry into or residence within defined areas of Botswana of persons who are not Bushmen to the extent that such restrictions are reasonably required for the protection or well–being of Bushmen." As will be taken up later, the High Court in *Sesana and Others v The Attorney General*,[18] relied on this provision to find that some Basarwa communities indigenous to the Central Kgalagadi Game Reserve (CKGR) had aboriginal title to their land and settlements, and it was unlawful and constitutional to force them to relocate.[19]

What paragraphs (b) and (c) of section 14(3) provide on possibilities of restricting freedom of movement for persons identified in reference to citizenship or ethnicity, indicates that section 15 of the Constitution, on protection from discrimination on the basis sex, gender, race ethnicity or citizenship, may be relevant to the debate on protection of property. Section 15 purports to outlaw discriminatory laws as well as discriminatory treatment of persons under any law.[20] Section 15(3) describes discriminatory as "affording different treatment to different persons, attributable wholly or mainly to their respective descriptions by race, tribe, place of origin, political opinions, colour, creed or sex." It involves either subjecting persons of one such description to disabilities or restrictions, or according them privileges or advantages not available to persons of another such description. Section 15(4) is the claw-back clause. It provides that the prohibition of discriminatory laws and discriminatory treatment shall not apply to certain laws. In the context of this debate, the notable examples of discriminatory laws that may be permissible include those providing for discriminatory treatment of persons who are not citizens; discriminatory treatment in "matters of personal law," such as adoption, marriage, divorce, burial, or devolution of property on death; discriminatory treatment in the application of customary law to members of a "particular race, community or tribe"; and discriminatory and differential treatment that in the special circumstances of those affected could be said to be reasonably justifiable in a democratic society.[21] This last example could justify 'positive discrimination' in favour of persons such as the Bushmen referred to in 14(3)(c), or other groups otherwise in need of preferential treatment.

The derogation authorised by section 15(9) should also be underlined. It states that "nothing contained in or done under the authority of any law shall be held to be inconsistent with the provisions of this section," if that law was in force

---

[18] [2006] 2 BLR 633.

[19] For a review and discussion of this case, see C. Ng'ong'ola, "Sneaking aboriginal title into Botswana's legal system through a side door: Review of *Sesana and Others v The Attorney General*," 6 UBLJ (2007) pp. 107–130.

[20] Sections 15(1) and (2).

[21] Sections 15(4)(b), (c), (d) and (e).

immediately before the coming into force of the Constitution, and has at all times thereafter continued in force; or to the extent that such a law repeals and re-enacts any provision in a written law that was in force immediately prior to the coming into force of the Constitution. It was on the basis of the first part of this derogation that the Court held in *Kamanakao I and Others v The Attorney General and Another* that the Chieftainship Act and the Tribal Territories, although discriminatory against Wayei, could not be invalidated under Section 15.[22] The Court, however, noted that section 15(9)(a) saved acts or laws inconsistent with Section 15, but not any other provision prohibiting discrimination, such as section 3, for example. The Court therefore found that section 2 of the Chieftainship Act was inconsistent with section 3, and unconstitutional. It ordered amendment of the section, so that Wayei could be afforded equal treatment and equal protection under that law. The finding and order were not replicated in reference to the Tribal Territories Act, apparently because the Court was not properly addressed on the issue. The spectre therefore remains that the Tribal Territories Act, a law on which post colonial reforms of tribal land tenure were predicated, may one day be declared unconstitutional, unless revisited in the manner suggested for the Chieftainship Act. As for post colonial legislation on tribal land tenure reforms, the derogations in Sections 15(9) of the Constitution would not in any event be available.

In the *Kamanakao I* case, as suggested above, the basic contention was that sections 77, 78 and 79, on the establishment and composition of the House of Chiefs in chapter V of the Constitution, discriminated against the Wayeyi tribe and were in consequence unconstitutional. Section 77(2) at that time provided that the House of Chiefs shall consist of eight *ex-officio* Members; four Elected Members; and three Specially Elected Members.[23] Section 78 provided that the ex officio members "shall be such persons as are for the time being performing the functions of the office of chief in respect of Bakgatla, Bakwena, Bamalete, Bamangwato, Bangwaketse, Barolong, Batawana and Batlokwa Tribes, respectively." Section 79(1) provided that the four Elected Members shall be elected from among their own number by persons for the time performing functions of the office of Sub-Chief in the Chobe, North East, Ghanzi and Kgalagadi districts. Section 79(2) provided that the Specially Elected Members shall be elected by the *ex officio* and the

---

[22] See Nganunu CJ, Dibotelo J, and Dow J, *Kamanakao I and Others v The Attorney General and Another*, [2001] 2 BLR, 654, especially pp. 672–680.

[23] Sections 85 and 88(2) of the Constitution described the core functions of the House as debating and advising the National Assembly on Bills and other matters pertaining to customary law, tribes and tribal organization.

Elected Members of the House from among persons who have not been active in politics within the preceding five years. The complaint by Wayeyi was that section 78 provided for *ex officio* membership only for the eight so called major Tswana tribes.[24] Kamanakao I, their chief, had no seat or place in the House. The High Court, as noted, readily agreed that this was discriminatory, but the sections could not be invalidated as unconstitutional by reference to other provisions of the Constitution.

A Commission of Inquiry reporting at about the same time confirmed that a significant proportion of citizens in the country found sections 77, 78 and 79 discriminatory of other tribes not referred to or mentioned in these sections.[25] The Commission recommended, and Government initially accepted, that there should be no reference to tribes and chiefs in the description of the composition of the House of Chiefs; that the House should be described using the vernacular, *Ntlo ya Dikgosi*, without any English translation; that it should substantially be composed of members "designated" from the nine administrative districts of the country and from regions identified within some of the larger districts; and that districts that still had names with tribal connotations should be given geographical names. After much debate, some of it emotionally charged, Government decided to retain tribal names for some of the affected administrative districts; and to opt for a mechanism for designating and selection of Members that deferred to local customs and practices in some areas.

A revised section 77(1) now provides that the *Ntlo ya Dikgosi* shall consist of not less than 33, but not more 35 members identified by designation, appointment and selection. Section 77(1)(a) provides that one person performing the functions of the office of *Kgosi* in each of 12 specified areas shall be designated as a member. Section 77(1)(b), secondly, authorises the President to appoint five members. Section 77(1)(c), thirdly, provides that up to 20 members shall be selected by Regional Electoral Colleges to be established for 20 regions of the country. The areas for which Dikgosi may be designated as members in terms of section 77(1)(a) are: Barolong farms in the Southern District; Chobe in the North West District; Ga Malete in the South East District; Ga Mmangwato in the Central District; Ghanzi District;

---

[24] Section 2 of the Chieftainship Act also described the words "tribe" and "chief" in reference to the so called eight principal Tswana tribes.

[25] Republic of Botswana, *Report of the Commission of Enquiry into Sections 77, 78 and 79 of the Constitution of Botswana*, Government Printer Gaborone, November 2000, and Republic of Botswana, *Draft Government White Paper of NO. of 2001, Presidential Commission of Inquiry into Sections 77, 78 and 79 of the Constitution of Botswana*, Government Printer, Gaborone, November 2001.

Goo Tawana in the North West District; Kgalagadi District; Kgatleng District; Kweneng District; Ngwaketse in the Southern District; North East District; and Tlokweng in the South East District. Section 78(1) now states that except for the areas of Ghanzi, Chobe, Kgalagadi and North East, the persons to represent the other areas shall be designated according to the norms and practices for those areas. This would appear to be a concession to the eight principal Tswana tribes that they could decide for themselves whether to designate a paramount chief as a member of the house. Section 79, in its revised form describes qualifications for designation, appointment and selection as a member of the house.

It follows from above that doubts still linger as to whether revisions to sections 77 and 78 now assure all tribes and ethnic groups of equal treatment and protection, and whether the vestigial distinctions between some administrative districts and areas, or the ethnic groups living in those areas, would pass muster under sections 3 and 15 of the Constitution. The difficulties encountered in what were commendable efforts to amend sections 77, 78 and 79 of the Constitution also regrettably suggest that ethnic identities are still very strong in Botswana. It is worthy recalling that the role of chiefs and tribal leaders under the proposed new political dispensation was one of the issues that pre-occupied and delayed the making of the Independence Constitution.[26] It is a puzzle that Botswana is still grappling with such issues so many years after independence. As we will see later, this puzzle has an equivalent on reform and modernisation of customary or tribal land tenure.

4 Land Tenure Policy Implications

There is no single official document from which to gauge all the post colonial land tenure policy options for Botswana. The issues and concerns identified at the beginning of this essay can be gathered from a variety of sources, including legislation, reports of inquiries and investigations periodically commissioned, National Development Plans, positions taken by Government in important litigation, and academic and other commentaries and essays.

4.1 Reclamation and Indigenisation of Freehold

Post colonial policy thrusts on freehold land can be gleaned from at least two pieces of legislation on the statute book, and from changes in the amount of

---

[26] P. Fawcus and A. Tilbury, *Botswana: The Road to Independence*, (2000) p. 203.

freehold land in the figures presented earlier. It should be recalled that amount of freehold land has been reduced from 6 per cent of the total land area at independence to about 5 per cent. We can presume that this has largely been due to the application of the Acquisition of Property Act, (Cap. 32: 10), which authorises compulsory acquisition or expropriation of land in the manner regulated by section 8 of the Constitution. Perhaps because compulsory acquisition processes are strictly regulated by the Constitution, Government evolved another strategy for indigenisation of freehold agricultural land that does not involve expropriation. This is in the Land Control Act, (Cap. 32:11).

4.1.1 Compulsory Acquisition of Freehold Land

The law authorising expropriation of freehold land was passed during the colonial era,[27] and revised in the run – up to independence, mainly for the purpose of accommodating the property guarantees secured in constitutional negotiations for independence.[28] As with the property guarantees in the Constitution, the main features of the Acquisition of Property Act have not been revised after independence. For purposes of this discussion these elements relate to the justification for expropriation and the measure of compensation.

In compliance with the protection afforded under section 8(1)(a) of the Constitution, section 3(1) of the Acquisition of Property Act empowers the President to expropriate "any real property"[29] where this is necessary or expedient:

"(a) in the interests of defence, public safety, public order, public morality, public health, town and country planning or land settlement; or

(b) In order to secure the development or utilization of that or other property for a purpose beneficial to the community…"

Section 9 states that any person "holding or claiming any interest or title" in the property who "disputes the legality of the proposed acquisition" may

[27] Bechuanaland Protectorate Acquisition of Property Proclamation, 80 of 1954.

[28] See HMC Order 1 of 1963; L.N. 28 of 1965; Law 26 of 1966; and L.N. 84 of 1966.

[29] This is defined in section 2 as meaning "any real right in immovable property in Botswana, other than a mortgage bond over immovable property". It also includes "any lease of immovable property, any rights to the use of public water …, any servitude, …, and any land granted or ceded to any corporation, company or person; but shall not include Tribal Territories as defined by the Tribal Territories Act. From this definition, the scope of the Act covered real rights in the freehold sector, real rights in land allocated or granted from Crown lands or State land, but not rights in tribal land.

apply to the High Court for the determination of the issue. This, however, should not be lightly contemplated. First, the public needs are so widely drawn that Government can hardly fail to justify an expropriation. The Courts, secondly, are not inclined to probe, query or evaluate the assessment of the public need by public officers. Courts are inclined to assume that public officers exercise their judgement or discretion in such matters in good faith.

In *Tati Company Ltd v The High Commissioner for the Bechuanaland Protectorate*,[30] the only reported case from the colonial era on this topic, the High Court held that it would not interfere with an expropriation decision on the basis that it was in fact wrong, inequitable or taken in ignorance of a relevant fact. The Court of Appeal adopted a similar approach after independence in *President of the Republic of Botswana and Others v Bruwer and Another*.[31] The case involved Government acquisition in 1996 of the Molopo Ranch, a huge 121 613 hectare freehold farm, originally allocated to the Commonwealth Development Corporation (CDC) during the colonial era. Government initially showed no interest when the CDC advertised its intention to dispose of its entire shareholding in a company registered as the owner of the ranch. When negotiations for the sale of the shares to two citizens of Boer (Afrikaner) extraction were about to conclude, Government hurriedly published an expropriation notice for the farm as well as the cattle on it. Government acted with such haste that the Attorney General's office failed to notice that the Act under which the notice was issued only authorised expropriation of "real property", but not cattle, shares or other movable assets. Court documents suggested that the ranch and the cattle were required for restocking in Ngamiland, an administrative district where all cattle had been exterminated on Government orders to control an outbreak of cattle lung disease. The Court of Appeal quickly confirmed that this was a legitimate public purpose. It rejected the contention accepted in the High Court that relevant Government officers had acted in bad faith, or with the ulterior or improper motive of pre-empting the transfer of shares to the applicants, and thereby depriving them of a legitimate bargain.[32] The applicants unfortunately did not help their cause by displaying an insulting, acerbic disposition towards Government officers, even in official court documents. But, as it turned out

[30] (1959) *High Commission Territories Law Reports (HCTLR)*, 32–53.
[31] [1998] BLR 86.
[32] The High Court decision is reported as *Bruwer and Another v President of the Republic of Botswana and Others*, [1997] BLR 477.

after the conclusion of the case, the ranch was never used for the purpose for which it was expropriated.[33]

Attempts by Government to expropriate the Molopo ranch, and the cattle on it, rebuffed by the Courts as regards the cattle, revealed an important lacuna in the law of expropriations in Botswana. If the reference in section 8(b) of the Constitution to provision being made in "a law applicable to that taking of possession or acquisition" refers to a written law, then Botswana has no such written law. In the absence of such a law, compulsory acquisition of other than real rights in immovable property would be unconstitutional. It must be remembered that protection of property offered under section 8(1) is wide-encompassing. The section regulates or imposes conditions for compulsory acquisition of "property of any description" and an "interest in or right over property of any description". It probably would be advisable for Government to amend the Acquisition of Property Act to accommodate expropriation of other forms of property, instead of seeking an adjustment of the Constitution.

Any amendment of the Acquisition of Property Act would also have to address the provisions on compensation for expropriation. It should be recalled that the Constitution calls for prompt payment of adequate compensation. Section 16 of the Act suggests measuring adequacy in reference to the market value of the property at the date of service of the expropriation notice. In the only case so far to reach the High Court on this issue,[34] the concept of market value was interpreted as referring to "market price" or the price that the property would realise if sold in an open market between a willing seller and a willing buyer. The Court further suggested that assessment of "adequate compensation" must take into account potential uses to which the property could be put. The price of comparable property in the market would not be adequate.[35] Botswana law thus allows a claimant to recover much more than what was paid for or invested in the land. This is what makes expropriation expensive, and a not so viable strategy for the reclamation of freehold land in some countries in Southern Africa. In Botswana, this is

---

[33] For a more detailed discussion of this case see Clement Ng'ong'ola, "Challenging the legality of an expropriation notice in Botswana", Vol. 115, Part IV (1998) *The South African Law Journal (SALJ)*, 616–628.

[34] *Attorney General v Western Trust (Pty) Ltd*, Civil Appeal No 12 of 1981, belatedly reported in [2006] 2 BLR 1.

[35] For a more detailed discussion of this case and the law on compulsory acquisition in Botswana see Ng'ong'ola, 'Compulsory acquisition of private land in Botswana: the Bonnington Farm case', XXII (1989) *CILSA*, 298–319.

compounded by the constitutional requirements on prompt payment and repatriation of compensation. Section 21(b) of the Acquisition of Property Act requires that compensation must be paid upon registration of the title in the name of the expropriating authority, or within two months of the settlement of a contested award. These are luxurious constitutional requirements, which even a solvent country like Botswana can ill-afford.

4.1.2 Control of Transfers of Freehold Agricultural Land

Through an Act passed and enacted in 1975, the Government of Botswana established a mechanism aimed at facilitating transfer of agricultural land in the freehold sector to citizens. The Land Control Act seeks to provide citizens with an opportunity to pre-empt sale and transfer of agricultural land to a person who is not a citizen of Botswana. Agricultural land "means land other than tribal land or land within a township".[36] This is what suggests that the concern was mainly with dealings with agricultural land in the freehold sector. The Act imposes requirements for prior Ministerial approval and wide publicity of every "controlled transaction". Such a transaction includes: "the sale, transfer, lease capable of running for a period of five years or more, exchange, partition or other disposal or dealing with any agricultural land; the division of any such agricultural land into two or more parcels to be held under separate titles; [and] the issue, sale, transfer, mortgage or any other disposal of or dealing with any share in a private company owning any agricultural land", where the person acquiring the land or interest in land or shares is not a citizen of Botswana. [37] The citizenship of a company is for these purposes determined by reference to incorporation in Botswana as well as the nationality of individuals beneficially holding the majority of all classes of shares in the company.[38]

Before Ministerial consent is sought, a notice of intention to enter into a controlled transaction must be published for a period of not less than 90 days in the Government Gazette and local newspapers.[39] In addition to essentials such as the parties, price, and the property, the notice must specify that any citizen of Botswana interested in entering into a similar transaction has the right to receive priority in the matter. Any interested person is also entitled to give the Minister written notice of his objections to a proposed transaction.[40]

---

[36] Section 2.
[37] Section 3(1).
[38] Section 3(4).
[39] Section 5(1).
[40] Section 5(2).

When deciding whether to grant or refuse consent, the Minister must take into consideration any expressions of interest or objections, and factors such as the potential or prospects for development or proper utilization of the land.[41] The Minister's decision, whether to give or to refuse consent, is described as "final and conclusive" and not to be "questioned in any in any court." These are extravagant assertions. As the Courts have observed on more than one occasion, Ministerial decisions can and will be reviewed, especially where fundamental rights guaranteed by the Constitution are allegedly infringed.[42]

In similarly extravagant language, section 3(1) asserts that a controlled transaction shall be "void for all purposes" if consent is not given. Section 3(2) further asserts that an agreement to be a party to controlled transaction shall become void for all purposes at the expiration of three months if an application for consent has not been made, or at the expiration of 30 days if an application was made, but the consent was refused. Section 4, then clarifies that any money or valuable consideration paid under a transaction that becomes void shall be recoverable as debt by the person who paid it, from the person to whom it was paid. The money or valuable consideration is not recoverable only where payment was intentionally effected in furtherance of an avoided transaction.[43]

The Land Control Act raises several interesting constitutional conundrums. First does it involve deprivation of property, as a distinct constitutional right in terms of section 3 of the Constitution, or compulsory acquisition of an interest in property, in terms of section 8(1)? Second, would the discrimination against non-citizen purchasers or transferees pass muster under the provisions prohibiting discrimination? As regards the first conundrum, my tentative assessment is that it depends on whether consent is refused, and the transferor is compelled to dispose of the property at a price or value lower than what he would have initially received. It must be noted that the main effect of the Act is to qualify the owner's *ius disponendi,* by interposing a different purchaser. If the purchaser matches the consideration proposed by a non-citizen transferee, this can hardly be described as deprivation of property. It is also probably not compulsory acquisition, since nothing is taken possession of. If however, the Minister refuses to grant consent, and the property must then

---

41 Section 7.

42 See, for example, *Kamanakao I and Others v The Attorney-General and Another,* [2001] 2 BLR 654, at p. 686.

43 Section 10.

subsequently be disposed of at a lower value to a citizen purchaser, then the owner would have lost the difference between two values. The qualification of his *ius disponendi* would thus probably be a deprivation of a proprietary right. This tentative assessment thus suggests that the constitutionality of the scheme put in place depends on either the Minister routinely giving consent, or authorising pre-emption by citizens only where the consideration in the proposed controlled transaction can be matched.

As for the conundrum relating to discriminatory treatment of non-citizen transferees, it should be recalled that this is clearly accommodated under section 15(4)(b) of the Constitution. It could also be accommodated under section 14(3)(a) if shown to be reasonably justifiable in a democratic society. Under section 3, the umbrella clause in the Human Rights Chapter, the consideration would also be whether it is in the public interest to so discriminate. There are probably not many Batswana who would not regard this as justifiable and constitutional discrimination.

The Land Control Act, finally, has been operation for over three decades, but there are no readily accessible public records and statistics to guide us in assessing its effectiveness. We can only judge from its textual weaknesses that it would have been of marginal utility. First, the Minister can ignore an expression of interest by a citizen to pre-empt a controlled transaction, and the Minister's determination is supposed to be beyond scrutiny. The Act, secondly, does not regulate the price element of a controlled transaction. The transaction can always be priced beyond the means of aspiring citizens, and the land thereby retained under foreign ownership. The selling of freehold land at inflated prices is not illegal in Botswana. The only mild deterrent for the parties is the fact that an inflated price attracts a commensurately higher level of transfer duty.[44] The third weakness is that there are no effective mechanisms for monitoring controlled transactions that do not require registration in the Deeds Registry, such as short leases and share transfers. Shares in companies that own agricultural land may change hands without the knowledge of the Registrar Deeds, the officer charged with the responsibility of collecting duties upon such transactions, and ensuring that all aspects of the Land Control Act have been complied with. The Act, finally, is also limited in scope to agricultural land. It is not applicable for the

[44] Section 2(3) of the Transfer Duty Act, Cap. 53:01, Laws of Botswana, provides for the payment of duty calculated on the basis of the declared price or the value of the land, which ever is higher. The rate for controlled transactions is 30 per cent. Citizens pay duty calculated at the rate of 5 percent, and are additionally to an exemption on first Pula 100 000 of the purchase price.

reclamation of freehold land put to non-agricultural uses. This is therefore a rather mild and conservative strategy for indigenisation of freehold land, unlikely to be emulated in other countries with a more serious settler land problem to redress.

4.2 State Land Tenure Policies

The State Land Act of 1966 is the starting point in the discussion of land policy concerns affecting this category. This is a brief statute, devoid of indication of the relevant policy thrusts and concerns. Its chief merit is that it defines State land as comprising of unalienated state land and reacquired state land.[45] Unalienated State land is land yet to be allocated to a particular person. This is the residual category of land in the country, within which falls any piece of land that cannot be regarded as part of the other land categories. Reacquired state land is predominantly land reclaimed from the freehold pool. The land policy concerns to be discussed here relate to tenure conditions for allocation or disposal of reacquired state land and unalienated State land delineated for urban use, and the survival of indigenous rights in or in or over unalienated State land now designated as national parks and game reserves.

4.2.1 Tenure Conditions for the Allocation of State Land

In addition to the identification of State land categories, section 2 of the State Land Act indicates that "its ownership … is vested in the Republic". Sections 3 and 4 indicate that the President, or any person authorised by him by notice published in the Government Gazette, may make and execute grants or other dispositions of any state land or interests therein. Section 10 provides that no contract for the sale or other disposition of State land or any interest therein "shall be of any force or effect" unless it is in writing and signified under the hand of the President or the person duly authorised by him in terms of section 4. No tenure conditions are specified in the Act or the Regulations.

Even without backing legislation, two types of grants have been conceived for allocations of State land in urban areas. These are a Certificate of Rights (COR), which offers indefinite occupancy rights, and a Fixed Period State Grant (FPSG), which ostensibly offers rights of ownership, but for a

[45] Section 2 of Law 29 of 1966, Cap 32:01, Laws of Botswana.

specified period.[46] The COR is for our purposes the less important of the two concepts. It was conceived as title for low cost housing units in townships and urban areas, partly as a way of regularising squatting and self allocation of land. As the title is not recorded or registered in the Deeds Registry, it is somewhat lowly regarded in the commercial land market. Holders are indeed encouraged to convert the Certificate into a FPSG for purposes of accessing funds. The FPSG is now the standard, popular and dominant form of tenure for allocation of State land in urban settings. The grant typically vests ownership in the purchaser for a period of either 99 years for residential use, or 50 years for commercial use. It also states that the purchaser "shall have the right to cede, assign, transfer, lease, sell, mortgage or otherwise deal with the property during the period of ownership, always provided that at the end of the [specified period] the property together with the improvements thereon shall (in whose name so ever they may then be registered) revert to the State absolutely without compensation payable for improvements or otherwise." The grant also contains a development covenant, requiring the construction of a building of specified value within a specified period. It further states that for as long as the covenant is not fulfilled, the property shall not be sold or transferred to any person other than the State. Other controversial conditions in the grant require the purchaser or his successors in title to maintain buildings and improvements in good order and repair, and to surrender the property with all buildings and improvements in good repair and condition. Again, "no compensation shall be payable by the State for any improvements on the property." The last of these controversial conditions reserves for the state or any authorised public authority the right to construct on any part of the property pipe lines, aqueducts, drains or telephone or telegraph lines required for public purposes. No compensation shall be payable by the Government or the public authority for the exercise of these rights, except for the value of any damage to improvements actually sustained by reason of the exercise of these rights.

---

[46] Documents indicating policy thrusts on state land tenure include Republic of Botswana, *Report of the Presidential Commission on Land Tenure*, Government Printer, Gaborone, December 1983; *National Policy on Land Tenure*, Government Paper No.1 of 1985, Government Printer, Gaborone; *Report of the Presidential Commission of Inquiry into the allocation of state land plots and aspects of Botswana Housing Corporation*, Government Printer, Gaborone, 1986; and *Report of the Judicial Commission of Inquiry into State Land Allocations in Gaborone*, Government Printer, Gaborone, 2004.

FPSGs were apparently conceived around 1972, initially for the development of a township in the mining area of Selibe Phikwe.[47] Government was keen to attract private land developments to the area. The allocation of State land under leasehold titles was not regarded as sufficiently attractive to investors, but Government was also not keen to grant rights of ownership or freehold titles, especially to foreign entrepreneurs. The solution settled upon was a "grant of ownership for a fixed period," upon payment of a lump sum at the beginning of the term. This makes the grant a legal oddity. It is neither a lease, nor a grant of ownership. Ownership in property law and theory is supposed to be absolute and potentially perpetual; absolute in the sense that no greater interest may exist in a thing beyond it.[48] Although terminable through processes such as expropriation or prescription, the grant should also be capable of running for an indefinite period. The FPSG lacks these critical elements of ownership. The state arguably retains the absolute interest in the land granted. The grantee acquires a real right less than ownership, akin to, but more burdensome in some respects, than a lease. First, the rentals are converted into capital to be paid up front. Second, termination and reversion provisions of a normal lease can allow for conventional or tacit relocation, and for payment of compensation for improvements that cannot be removed.[49]

The FPSG can also be described as a legal and political time bomb, ticking away as the period for the first reversions draws closer. In less than 22 years the political resolve of the State to take over developed urban commercial and residential properties will be tested. The constitutionality of the reversion clause is also likely to be tested. Resumption of ownership of land and improvements, without payment of compensation, surely, will amount to compulsory acquisition or taking of possession of an "interest in or right over property of any description" in the language of section 8(1) of the Constitution. The exercise of the right to construct on the property public works, without compensation, can also amount to deprivation of property in a manner that does not involve a taking, contrary to section 3 of the Constitution, if it is read as creating a distinct property guarantee. Government probably was not properly advised when the FPSG was conceived, but its legal and constitutional

[47] W. Dickson, *Land tenure and management in a developing country. The case of Botswana 1966–1985*, University of Botswana, NIR Working Paper No. 54, May 1990, 21–23.

[48] See P. Birks, 'The Roman law concept of dominium and the idea of absolute ownership', (1985) *Acta Juridica*, 25–31.

[49] See W.E. Cooper, *Landlord and Tenant*, 2nd ed., Juta, 1994, Ch. 21.

oddities should now be well known.[50] There is no reason in law why the State continues to make grants subject to the same constitutionally odious terms and conditions. It should also be appreciated that as the period for the expiry of the earlier grants draws closer, the affected properties increasingly become less marketable, and not so attractive to investors, thus counteracting the rationale for the introduction of the grants in the first place. The case for a complete rethink of this aspect of land tenure policy, and for replacement of the FPSG with more conventional leasehold or freehold titles cannot be more compelling.

4.2.2 Indigenous Titles in or Over Unalienated State Land

The Government of Botswana espouses a policy of public ownership of natural resources, so that they may be utilised for the development of the whole country, and not only for the benefit or enrichment of communities fortunate to be located where the resources are.[51] This policy is manifested by the vesting of ownership of unalienated State land in Republic; the vesting of ownership of Tribal land in Tribal Territories in land boards, public institutions that are mandated to manage and hold it trust for the benefit of all citizens of Botswana[52]; and by the separation of ownership of surface land rights from ownership of mineral rights, so that the latter may be vested in the Republic, and Government can ensure proper exploration and beneficial exploitation.[53] In some parts of the country, implementation of this policy preference leads to conflicts between the State and Communities in whose areas resources are located. The widely publicised dispute between the Government and some Basarwa or Bushmen communities over land and other resources in the CKGR is a case in point.

The CKGR was proclaimed in 1961,[54] on lands appropriated for the Crown as *terra nullius* or *terra incognita*, but which were also known to contain traditional territories or ranges of several Basarwa communities. The original

[50] The 1983 *Report of the Presidential Commission on Land Tenure* recommended that negotiations for the renewal of the FPSGs should begin 15 years before the date of their expiration.

[51] His Excellency President Festus Mogae, "The role of natural resources in Botswana's socio – economic development", Address delivered at the University of Botswana, Gaborone, on 14 September 2007.

[52] Section 10(1) of the Tribal Land Act, Cap. 32:02.

[53] Section 3 of the Mines and Mineral resources Act, No. 17 of 1999.

[54] The CKGR was proclaimed under High Commissioner's Notice No. 33 included in section 5 of the First Schedule of the Fauna Conservation Proclamation No. 22 of 1961. At about 52,800 square kilometres, it was at the time one of the largest game reserves in Africa.

plan was that the CKGR should be a sanctuary for game, as well as for "several thousand Bushmen" desirous of maintaining their traditional hunting and gathering modes of existence, unmolested by other people or communities.[55] The relevant laws and regulations however only managed to secure for "Bushmen indigenous to the CKGR" the right to enter the reserve "without having first obtained a permit in writing from the District Commissioner Ghanzi"[56] Subsequent laws, regulations and policies on fauna conservation also accommodated their right to hunt game, albeit with restrictions requiring licenses, and regulating what could be hunted, and with what weapons. This status quo was passed on at independence when Crown lands became State land. The additional legal dimensions, however, was the insertion of section 14(3)(c) in the Constitution, ostensibly to underscore that the CKGR was always intended as a reserve for the Bushmen.

The figures on land classification presented in the introduction show that there was nearly as much State land as Tribal land at independence. Later figures from the NDP 9 Report show that the amount of State land reduced from 47 per cent of the total land area to 25 percent, and the amount of Tribal land increased correspondingly from 48 per cent to 70 per cent. These changes are largely due to reclassification of chunks of State land in Chobe, Ghanzi and Kgalagadi districts into Tribal land,[57] to create tribal territories for indigenous communities whose land or territorial rights were not accommodated when native reserves were created, and the remainder of the land appropriated as Crown lands. This solution to an age-old land problem was not replicated for the CKGR Bushmen.

Towards the end of the 1990's, Government conceived a policy of persuading and encouraging communities still in the reserve to relocate to permanent settlements outside the reserve. In August 2001, perhaps to facilitate the relocation process, Government terminated supply and provision of essential services, such as drinking water, destitute rations and health care to those still remaining in the reserve. This triggered an application to the High Court alleging that the termination of the supply of such basic and essential services was unlawful and unconstitutional; and that the underlying attempt to forcibly

---

[55] G. Silberbauer, *Report to the Government of Bechuanaland on the Bushman Survey*, Gaborone, 1965, 132.

[56] Clive Spinage, History and Evolution of Fauna Conservation Laws of Botswana, Botswana Society, Gaborone, 1991, 31; Fauna Conservation Proclamation, 22 of 1961, especially sections 4, 7, 34 and 57; and Section 2 of the Central Kalahari Game Reserve (Control of Entry) Regulations, GN 38 of 1963.

[57] Tribal Land (Amendment) Act, No. 21 of 1976.

relocate the applicants was also unlawful despoliation of their land rights and unconstitutional.[58] The High Court, by a majority of two to one, found for the applicants on both grounds. It found that the applicants were in lawful possession of their land from time immemorial. This was not affected by the appropriation of the land for the Crown; the establishment of the CKGR; or the conversion of Crown lands into State land at independence. Indeed, the effect of the inclusion of section 14(3)(c) in the independence Constitution was to acknowledge their indigenous rights or title to their settlements in the reserve. To attempt to force them to relocate, through the termination of the supply of services, was indeed unlawful and unconstitutional despoliation. As for the later contention, the Court held that the applicants had a legitimate expectation that supply of services would not be terminated without proper consultation.

It should be underlined in this discussion that section 14(3)(c) anchored the finding that the applicants had indigenous or aboriginal title to land in their settlements in the CKGR. Such rights can only be taken away in a constitutionally permissible manner. At common law, indigenous rights can for example be extinguished by Government action that is inconsistent with their exercise. An example in the area of dispute would be allocation by the colonial administration of freehold titles to settlers of European descent on the Ghanzi ridge. After independence, whether relocation amounts to deprivation or expropriation, compensation would be payable. The two conundrums here would be whether the State can expropriate where it already has title to the land, and what would be adequate compensation for extinguished indigenous rights. These issues were sadly not considered or broached in the case.

In contrast to the findings on aboriginal title, there were no constitutional provisions to buttress findings on rights of the applicants to the supply of basic and essential services. The Court made references to surrogate or related rights, such as the right to life in section 4 of the Constitution, but it ultimately relied on an administrative law notion, that the applicants had a legitimate expectation that services would not be terminated without proper consultations. It would appear that Government would have fulfilled its constitutional responsibilities had it taken decisions on the supply of basic and essential services in a manner consistent with the administrative law notion invoked, even if the decisions were adverse to the applicants. This aspect of the case

[58] For an extensive review and discussion of the case, see C. Ngongola, "Sneaking aboriginal title into Botswana's legal system through a side door", 6 UBLJ (2007) 107–130.

reveals or confirms the existence of a serious gap in the scheme for the protection of fundamental rights in Chapter II of the Constitution. There is no protection or guarantee of socio economic and cultural rights, some of which are obviously necessary for meaningful exercise of property, civic and other political rights guaranteed by the Constitution.

4.3 Tribal Land Reforms and Modernization

Of all the land policy concerns identified in this work, it is in this area that policy has advanced further in Botswana. The Tribal Land Act, the law proposing radical changes to tribal or customary land tenure was passed and implemented within a short time of the attainment of independence.[59] Although refinements and adjustments are required from time to time, the reformed system has endured and become an accepted feature of Botswana's tenure landscape. Comparable land tenure reform or modernization projects in other sub-Saharan African countries would appear to have petered out.[60]

The reforms have succeeded or endured in Botswana partly due to the unique social and political milieu in which they were attempted. The reforms were introduced in or over areas that were previously native reserves and tribal territories. Native reserves in the Bechuanaland Protectorate were proclaimed mainly for the Tswana – speaking tribes or ethnic groups, led by powerful chiefs, three of whom were central in entreating for British protection.[61] After the proclamation of each reserve, colonial administrators chose to interfere as little as possible in tribal land matters.[62] In consequence, a fairly uniform picture of Tswana land tenure emerged all over the Protectorate, which Schapera diligently researched and ably described in his works.[63] It was essentially over the system described by Schapera that post colonial reforms were crafted.

---

[59] The Act was passed as No. 54 of 1968. It entered into force on 30 January 1970.

[60] C. Ng'ong'ola, "Customary, land tenure and policy in some African countries at the threshold of the twenty-first Century", in G.E. van Maanen and A.J. van der Walt, eds. *Property Law on the Threshold of the Twenty – First Century*, MAKLU, Antewerpen, 1996, pp. 391–494, especially 409–414.

[61] Native Reserves, later called Tribal territories, were proclaimed incrementally over a period of more than three decades. The first five reserves were created under Proclamation No. 9 of 1899. Other reserves were created under Proclamations No. 2 of 1911; 28 of 1909; 44 of 1933; and 77 of 1935. Only Proclamation No. 2 of 1911 created a reserve for a non-Tswana ethnic group, on reacquired freehold land in the Tati District.

[62] Lord Hailey, *Native Administration in British African Territories, Part V,* London, 1953, p. 311.

[63] I. Schapera, *Native Land Tenure in the Bechuanaland Protectorate*, Lovedale, 1943, and *A Handbook of Tswana Law and Custom*, Frank Cass and Co., 1984, especially 196–211.

4.3.1 Characteristic Features of Tswana Land Tenure

The characteristic features of Tswana customary land tenure, as described by Schapera, can be recounted using terms and concepts that were in vogue among legal and social anthropologists describing African land tenure systems.[64] Schapera subscribed to characterisation of Tswana land tenure as communal in nature. Some would have said of it that land rights vested in the community, but not in the individual; or that the notion of "individual ownership of land" was not countenanced.[65] This is best regarded as an indication that access to land and its resources depended on membership of a particular group, community or social group, and that in the invent of conflict between individual and group rights and interests, the latter were likely to prevail.[66] It is inaccurate to read references to communal and individual rights as suggesting that no individual land rights were acknowledged, or that all members of the community had equal rights to land. Among the Tswana, as recorded by Schapera, land was generally allocated for three types of use: for residential units, cultivation, and cattle grazing. Land for the first two purposes could be allocated to individuals or sub units of the community, such as family groups, but most members of the community were entitled to access to tribal grazing ranges for their cattle. In due course, however, the sinking of a well in grazing ranges could lead to assertion of exclusive rights to grazing in the surrounding area.

Among the Tswana, the community or social group to which land rights and entitlements were generally ascribed was a tribe, defined by Schapera as a "politically independent unit", under the leadership of a chief, and occupying a fairly distinct geographical territory.[67] A tribe was not a closed group, and it was not necessarily homogenous, culturally or linguistically. Tribal membership could be acquired by descent or by consensual or coercive incorporation. Through such processes some of the 'Tswana tribes' identified by Schapera became extremely heterogeneous entities, incorporating several

---

[64] For a detailed and more critical reflection on Schapera's description of Tswana land tenure see Ng'ong'ola, 'Land problems in some peri-urban villages in Botswana and problems of conception, description and transformation of 'tribal' land tenure,' 36, 2(1992) *J.A.L.* 141–148.

[65] This language is lifted from a remark on native or African customary land tenure made by Viscount Haldane in *Amodu Tijani v Secretary, Southern Nigeria*, [1921] 2 AC 399, at pp. 404–405.

[66] See fn. 64, *supra*.

[67] I. Schapera, *The Tswana*, International African Institute, monograph, London 1976, p. 10.

sub-groups with distinct cultural and linguistic traits.[68] But even with such tribes, a chief was the central figure around whom all aspects of tribal life revolved. His position in the political and social structure was such that some of Schapera's informers described land in the tribal territory as belonging to the chief. Schapera cautioned that this did not mean the chief was the "owner of the land" in a common law sense. His position was more akin to that of a trustee holding the land for and on behalf of a tribe.[69]

4.3.2 Reform and Modernisation of Tribal Land Tenure

Modernisation and democratisation were the two themes, or catchwords, in speeches in the National Assembly supporting enactment of a new law on Tribal land tenure, so soon after independence. It was suggested that the prevailing system was not able to accommodate more modern practices of land use, such as exclusive allocation and utilisation of tribal grazing ranges.[70] It was also suggested, but not over emphasized, that it was necessary to provide a young country with a land administration system that could assure all Batswana of access to land, and would be more accountable to elected politicians.[71] These themes, and the constitutional implications arising therefrom, can be appreciated from the parts and provisions of the Tribal Land Act[72] on establishment and composition of land boards, the new institutional arrangements for the administration and management of tribal land; the core duties and functions of the land board; and on expropriation of tribal land.

4.3.2.1 Establishment and Composition of Land Boards

The Tribal Land Act replaced chiefs and tribal leaders with land boards as the custodians and administrators of Tribal land. These institutions could in theory be constituted and composed in a democratic and politically accountable manner. In its original form, section 3(1) in Part II of the Tribal Land Act provided for the establishment of what are now termed "main land boards"

[68] The Ngwato tribe in the expansive Central Ditsrict offered an extreme example of such heterogeneity, and incorporated non- Tswana groups such as the San, Herero, Kalanga and Birwa and Kgalagadi. I. Schapera, *A Handbook of Tswana Law and Custom*, pp. 4–5 estimated that the non-Tswana groups comprised about four – fifths of the tribe.

[69] I. Schapera, *A Handbook of Tswana Law and Custom*, pp. 4–5.

[70] Sir Seretse Khama, *National Assembly, Official Report, Hansard 23*, 2nd session, 1st Meeting, 8–17 January 1968, 14.

[71] See, for example, the speeches during the second reading of the Bill in *National Assembly, Official Report, Hansard 25*, 2nd session, 3rd Meeting, 6–9 August 1968.

[72] No. 58 of 1968, now Cap 32:02.

for specified "tribal areas"; and section 19(1) in Part III provided for the establishment of "subordinate land boards" for "any area within a tribal area". Nine main land boards were initially established, for areas corresponding with the native reserves or tribal territories recognised by the colonial administration.[73] The number increased to 12 after the reclassification of State land as Tribal land for purposes of creating tribal territories in Chobe, Ghanzi and Kgalagadi districts in 1976.[74] The total number of subordinate land boards, on the other hand, was not pre-fixed, or the areas of jurisdiction predetermined. As many subordinate boards as were necessary could be created to operate within designated sections of the tribal territory of the main board.[75]

After the amendments to section 77 and 78 of the Constitution described above, one would have expected an attempt to re-designate tribal areas for land boards in reference to criteria that would not be regarded as discriminatory of other tribes. The outcomes of the efforts to amend the Constitution are also indicative of resistance and difficulties that would be have been encountered in some tribal areas. Perhaps this is why nothing much has been done so far. The Tribal land Act thus remains prone to criticism that it perpetuates unconstitutional discrimination against tribes or ethnic groups that are not associated with any of the 12 main land boards. On the authority of *Kamanakao I and Others v The Attorney General and Another*, we can conclude that the relevant provisions of the Tribal Land Act offend both sections 3 and 15 of the Constitution. We have noted above that the Tribal Territories Act, from which the Tribal Land Act derives descriptions of tribal areas, like the Chieftainship Act, would have been declared inconsistent with section 3 of the Constitution, if the matter had been properly argued. As an Act carried over from the colonial era, however, it would not have been inconsistent with section 15 of the Constitution, because of the derogation in section 15(9). The Tribal Land Act, on the other hand, as a post colonial piece of legislation, cannot be accommodated by the derogation in section 15(9). Even if it could be so accommodated, it probably would still be inconsistent with section 3 the Constitution.

---

[73] The tribal areas were indicated in the First Column of the First Schedule of the Act.

[74] Tribal Land (Amendment) Act, No. 21 of 1976.

[75] The Establishment of Subordinate Land Boards Order, SI No. 47 of 1973 established 27 boards. The number grew to 38 in 1995. See Republic of Botswana, *Handbook, The Tribal Land Act, The Tribal Land Regulations, and Subordinate Land Board Regulations,* Government Printer, Gaborone, (undated), 6; and B.M. Mathuba, 'Overview of land administration systems in Botswana,' Paper prepared for the conference on land administration reform, Pretoria, July 1995, 2.

Each main land board under the original Act comprised of 6 members. These members were the chief or tribal authority for the area, as an *ex officio* member; one member appointed by the chief; two elected by the District Council; and two appointed by the Minister responsible for land matters.[76] The Minister was also empowered to designate the chairman of the board from the members, and to appoint a secretary to act as a chief executive.[77] In the *Kamanakao I* case, the Wayeyi, justifiably, would have been entitled to contend that this was discriminatory, as Kamanakao was not entitled to sit as an *ex officio* member of the main land board. The composition of the subordinate land boards, on the other, was probably satisfactory. They comprised of 4 members, being: one Ministerial appointee, and one member each elected by the main land board, the District Council, and the headmen and sub-chiefs of villages within the area of jurisdiction of the board.[78] The main land board was responsible for the appointment of a clerk for each subordinated board, whose duties included the maintenance and preservation of board records and acting as secretary to the subordinate board.[79]

It would appear that it was initially regarded as neither feasible nor desirable to completely exclude chiefs and tribal authorities from land board membership, and to provide for land administration institutions that could truly be regarded as democratically constituted and composed. Land boards would have been completely handicapped without the involvement or participation in their operations of those who were supposed to be repositories of knowledge on tribal or customary land matters. It was possible however to exclude chiefs and tribal authorities from land board membership by 1994.[80] The main land boards now have a variable composition of between 14 and 18.[81] One board has a total of 18 members; three have 16 members each; and the rest have a composition of 14.[82] Although these variations may be logical and justifiable, those responsible must always be wary of discriminating against some tribes. On each of the main land boards, regardless of the total

---

[76] The composition of each main board was indicated in the Third Column of the First Schedule to the Act.

[77] Regulation 3 of the Tribal Land Regulations, SI No 7 of 1970, and section 8 of the Act.

[78] Regulation 4 of the Establishment of Subordinate Land Boards Order, SI No 47 of 1973.

[79] Regulation 9 of Tribal land (Subordinate Land Boards) Regulations, SI 48 of 1973.

[80] Tribal Land (Amendment of Schedule) Order, SI No. 63 of 1994, and Tribal Land (subordinate Land Boards)(Amendment) Regulations, SI No. 65 of 1994.

[81] Tribal Land (Amendment of Schedule) Order SI No. 92 of 1999.

[82] The 18 members are specified for the Ngwato land board. The Tawana, Kweneng, and Ngwaketse land boards have 16 members each. The Kgatleng, Malete, Tlokweng, Barolong, Tati, Chobe, Kgalagadi and Ghanzi land boards have 14 members each.

membership, two members are representatives of the Ministries of Agriculture and Commerce and Industry. The rest are equally divided between members elected to hold office for a 4-year renewable term, and members appointed by the responsible Minister for a 3-year renewable term. The membership for all subordinate land boards is set at 10; comprising of 2 members representing the Ministries of Agriculture and Commerce and Industry, 4 members appointed from a slate of elected candidates, to hold office for a 4-year renewable term, and 4 members directly appointed by the Minister to hold office for a 3-year renewable term.[83]

Although, on the face of the legal texts, a preponderant number of members are ministerial appointees, considerable progress has been made towards democratisation of these institutions. Although it is not so explicitly stated, the Minister may indeed choose to appoint only elected persons. After considerable criticisms, the methods of conducting land board elections have also improved. In the past, for example, the regulations required voters to "indicate their vote for a candidate by standing in a queue behind that candidate" at the *kgotla*.[84] The regulations now state that voting "at a *kgotla* shall be by simplified secret ballot box, and every person who has cast a vote shall have the tip of his or her thumb dipped into indelible ink to indicate that he or she has voted."[85] Additional improvements that could enhance democratization of the process, and quell some of the criticism that surface after each round of land board elections, might include transfer of the management of the process from Land Board Selection Committees to the Electoral Commission, and conduct of elections strictly in accordance with laws governing conduct of other elections. It is however unlikely that Government would prefer to fully democratize the process in this manner, and to completely surrender the composition of land boards to the vagaries of electoral politics and processes. The concern in some Government circles is that even with fairly stringent eligibility conditions and strict vetting of candidates,[86] current processes still lead to the identification of candidates

[83] Tribal Land (Subordinate Land Boards)(Amendment) Regulations, SI No. 90 of 1999.

[84] Regulation 2(7) of the Tribal Land Regulations, as amended by the Tribal Land (Amendment)(No. 2) Regulations, 1999.

[85] Regulation 2(4) of the Tribal Land Regulations, introduced by the Tribal Land (Amendment) Regulations, SI 87 of 200.

[86] Regulation 2(2) of the Tribal Land Regulations, as amended by the Tribal Land (Amendment) (No.2) Regulations, 1999, SI No. 91 of 1999, indicated that candidates for election and appointment as land board members must be citizens of Botswana, who have attained the age of 25 years and are not over 65 years old; holding an academic qualification equivalent to a secondary school Junior Certificate; residing within the tribal area in which elections are sought; and are not actively involved

who may on account of age, qualifications or experience be unsuitable for appointment. It is therefore necessary to retain the Minister's power to appoint to the land board persons with special skills and abilities, who may not be identified through electoral processes.[87] This suggests that it will perpetually remain a challenge, resulting in repeated tinkering with the law, to strike the right balance between democratisation, ensuring efficiency, bureaucratic control, political accountability and local legitimacy of the land boards.

4.3.2.2 Title, Powers and Functions of Main Land Boards

Section 9 in Part II of the Act described each main land boards as "a body corporate, capable of suing and being sued in its own name." Section 10(1), in its original form, also stated that "all the rights and title to land in each tribal area … shall vest in the land board set out in relation to it … in trust for the benefit and advantage of the tribesmen of that area and for the purpose of promoting the economic and social development of all the peoples of Botswana." Section 10(2), however, attempted to clarify that the vesting did not include "any land or right to water held by any person in his personal and private capacity."

Section 13 in Part III of the Act further stated that each main land board shall have "all the powers vested in a chief under customary law in relation to land," including those necessary for the making or cancellation of grants of land rights, and the resolution of disputes relating to such activities. Sections 22 to 31 in Part III of the Act also gave the main land boards powers to make grants of land under common law forms of tenure, subject to Ministerial approval. Provision was made for the allocation of rights of ownership and leasehold rights, but it was apparently never the intention to re-create freehold titles in Tribal Territories through grants of rights of ownership. Thus, no such rights were ever granted to any person other than the State.[88] Long leases, for residential or commercial use, arable farming, and establishment ranches on tribal grazing lands, were the most common type of common law grants ever made. It was through grants of leasehold rights over demarcated

---

in party politics. The Tribal Land (Amendment) Regulations 2006 have increased the age requirement to 26 years and specified the academic qualification only as a Secondary School Junior Certificate.

[87] Republic of Botswana, *Report of the Second Presidential Commission on the Local Government Structure in Botswana*, Government Printer, Gaborone (2001), pp. 85–87.

[88] Republic of Botswana, *Report of the Presidential Commission on Land Tenure*, Government Printer, Gaborone, December 1983, para 2.03, p. 5.

portions of tribal grazing ranges that the law was expected to fulfil its modernisation objectives.[89]

The replacement of chiefs and tribal leaders with land boards as the custodians, guardians, trustees, managers or administrators of tribal land, and the vesting of more concrete legal titles and extensive powers in the land boards, should have excited debate as to whether this was consistent with the property guarantees in the Constitution. Sections 10, 13 and 24 of the Tribal Land Act arguably regulated or interfered with rights in property, in a manner which would call for compensation if section 3(c) is interpreted as protecting property from interferences that do not involve takings. If protection from deprivation is interpreted in the manner elaborated in section 8, still, an argument could be made that the replacement of chiefs with tribal leaders in such matters involved the taking of possession of rights or interests in property. Even in this scenario, the Constitution calls for payment of adequate compensation. It is a puzzle what adequate compensation would have been for these purposes. It is also a puzzle whether this issue can be resurrected and revisited over 30 years after the implementation of the land board system.

An issue that did excite considerable legal debate, with constitutional undertones, was the meaning and effect of section 10(2). In *Kweneng Land Board v Matlho and Another*, the High Court held, and the Court of Appeal affirmed,[90] that the effect of section 10(2) was to exclude from the supervisory jurisdiction of main land boards land and water rights acquired by a person prior to the establishment of land boards in 1970. The Courts held that the Kweneng Land Board had no right or power to evict as a trespasser a party who purchased a piece of land from a person claiming that his family held and possessed the land prior to the establishment of the land boards. The courts in effect held that land and water rights acquired prior to the establishment of land boards were an example of rights held in a personal and private capacity in terms of section 10(2). Land so held could be dealt with and disposed of without the sanction of the land board. The Courts further discounted strong evidence suggesting that it still was not permissible to sell land under local customary law. The High Court in effect suggested that land

[89] See Republic of Botswana, *National Policy on the Tribal Grazing Land Policy*, Government Paper No. 2 of 1975; and B. Mathuba, "Land policy in Botswana" paper prepared for the workshop on Land policy in Eastern and Southern Africa, Maputo, February 1992, p. 13.
[90] [1992] BLR 292, upholding the decision of Horwitz AJ in *Kweneng Land Board v Matlho and Others*, Misc. No. 137 of 1990, which does not appear to have been reported.

rights acquired prior to the establishment of land boards were comparable to unregistered freehold rights, which the holder had the right to deal with, without the involvement of the relevant board.

The conclusions in the *Matlho* case had profound implications on the ability of land boards to oversee dispositions of tribal land and, particularly, in peri urban settings, where the problem was most acute, to check unauthorised transfers and self provisioning of land. Parliament responded with fairly swift amendments to the Tribal Land Act.[91] First Section 10(2) was deleted from the Act. At the same time, section 10(1) was amended to clarify that title to land in specified tribal areas shall vest in designated land boards "in trust for the benefit and advantage of citizens of Botswana and for the purpose of promoting the economic and social development of all the peoples of Botswana." The mandate or trust of each main land board was in this way "detribalised". Amendments to sections 13 and 15 in Part III of the Act, secondly, clarified that all powers previously vested in chiefs and subordinate land authorities shall vest in land boards, including powers enabling cancellation of grants where the land is not utilised for its intended purpose or is utilised in contravention of customary law. Several new provisions were also inserted in Part VII of the Act, to clarify that customary or common law rights granted under the Act, whether prior to or after the coming into operation of the Act, shall not be transferred, whether by way of sale or otherwise, without the consent of the land board concerned. It is only in three instances that the consent or permission of the relevant land board is dispensed with.[92] In the case of common law rights, the Registrar of Deeds is prohibited form registering any conveyance of such rights without satisfying himself of compliance with the restrictions now imposed on transfers.[93] The Act finally makes it an offence punishable by fairly hefty penalties to attempt to deal

[91] The Tribal Land (Amendment) Act, No 14 of 1993 dealt with other aspects of the law, not part of this discussion focusing only on the implications of the property guarantees on tribal land tenure policy. For more detailed commentaries on the Tribal Land Act, the 1993 amendments, and the litigation they gave rise to see: C. Ng'ong'ola, "Land Problems in peri urban villages in Botswana and problems of conception, description and transformation of tribal land tenure", 36, 2 [1992] J.A.L., 140–167; and S.T. Morolong and C. Ngongola, "Revisiting the notion of ownership of Tribal land in Botswana", in Fombad (ed), *Essays on the Law of Botswana*, Juta, Cape Town, 2007, pp. 142–175.

[92] Section 38(1) of the Act states that consent of the land board shall not be required for a sale in execution to a citizen; for hypothecation by a citizen; upon devolution of land by way of inheritance; or where the land has been developed to the satisfaction of the land board concerned. This last example in effect still requires seeking the board's approval.

[93] Section 38(2).

with tribal land in contravention of the law as clarified by these amendments.[94]

After years of vacillation and prevarication in the Courts as to what the law should be, the Court of Appeal decided in *Kweneng Land Board v Mpofu and Another*[95] that the High Court was not bound by the *Matlho* decision, and that the law on this matter was closer to the intention of the Legislature as revealed by the unmistakable thrusts of the 1993 amendments. It took a full bench of the Court of Appeal to debunk *Matlho* as a precedent, but the law is still unclear as to what Parliament intended to achieve through the original section 10(2), (excluding from the title or jurisdiction of the main land boards land or rights to water held by any person in his personal and private capacity). The full ramifications of the deletion of the section from the Act in 1993 are also not clear. It seems unlikely that Parliament intended to signal that no rights in land or water in tribal areas are held in a personal and private capacity. The makers of the Tribal Land Act in 1968 must have regarded such rights as capable of existence, hence the inclusion of section 10(2) in the law. If Parliament was suggesting that any such rights have now ceased to exist, this would probably be deprivation of property, contrary to section 3 of the Constitution, if this is interpreted as giving rise to a distinct property guarantee. If, as is more likely, Parliament only intended to signal that if such rights exist, they must henceforth be dealt with in a manner requiring approval by the land board, still the dictates of section 3 of the Constitution must be observed. Deprivation of property in this manner under the Botswana Constitution might require payment of compensation. The State may only be able to avoid this problem by arguing that deprivation in section 3 of the Constitution refers to taking, compulsory acquisition, or expropriation as elaborated in section 8, and there is no deprivation if the State interferes with property rights without taking them over. As suggested earlier, this argument may be sustained by showing that the interpretation of section 3 by the majority in the *Attorney General v Dow* is either wrong or inapplicable to protection of property. We probably have to wait much longer for this to take occur place than we did for the debunking of the *Matlho* precedent.

4.2.2.3 Tribal Land Required for Public Purposes

As indicated earlier, the Acquisition of Property Act did not authorise compulsory acquisition of land in Tribal Territories. This meant that there

[94] Section 39.

[95] [2005] 1 BLR 3.

was no law at independence authorising compulsory acquisition of tribal land required for public purposes, as required by section 8(1)(b) of the Constitution. Sections 31 to 35 in Part V of the Tribal Land Act sought fill this gap in the law, and to provide for expropriation of land in tribal areas, in a manner that would satisfy the Constitution. This part of the Act mainly dealt with the procedure to be followed when Tribal land was required for public purposes, and the measure of compensation to be paid.

Section 32 of the Tribal Land Act, in its original form, as under the Acquisition of Property Act, identified the President as the appropriate expropriating authority. The procedure to be followed was fairly simple. If the President determined that it was in the public interest for the State to acquire land from a land board, he was required to serve a notice on the land board, copied to the District Council, requesting the land board, after ascertaining the views of the District Council, to grant ownership of the land to the State. If the land board was not inclined to make the grant, or if it failed to decide upon the matter within three months, or if it imposed terms and conditions unacceptable to the Minister, the latter could refer the matter to a Commission of Inquiry. The task of the Commission was to investigate and determine whether the land was indeed required for a public purpose, and if so, whether the requirements of the State are in other respects reasonable. It could also assess any objections by the land board or District Council to the request.[96] After receiving the Commission's report on the matter, section 33(3) stated that the Minister may "give such direction in the matter as he shall think, fit, being a direction not inconsistent with the finding of the Commission, and it shall be the duty of land board to comply with such direction." If the land board failed or neglected to comply, section 32(4) stated that "the Minister may himself execute the grant for and on behalf of the land board."

The tenor of these provisions suggests that it was not envisaged or expected that the decision to request the grant of land required for public purposes could be contested in the Courts. It would have indeed been in keeping with bureaucratic inclinations at the time, clearly manifested in some of the provisions in the Land Control Act, to keep such matters beyond the purview of the Courts. If this was so, the procedure in section 32 of the Tribal Land Act would have fallen short of the requirement in section in Section 8(1)(b)(ii) of the Constitution. There should have been provision in Section 32 or Part V of the Act for reference of appeals against decisions or findings of a Commission of Inquiry to the High Court. It should however be acknowledged

[96] Section 35(2) of the Tribal Land Act.

that reference of requests for land to a Commission of Inquiry was a commendable procedure. It is consistent with good practice in the processing of expropriation demands in other countries. It is a procedure that gives the public at large an opportunity to influence decision taking in such matters.

When the Tribal Land Act was amended in 1993, section 32, unfortunately, was not regarded as in need of clarification on the issue of taking appeals to a Court of law after investigation by a Commission of Inquiry. It was probably regarded as not necessary to clarify the issue since, in any event, Courts would not regard a ministerial decision on such matters as final and beyond their purview. The introduction of land tribunals, (quasi-judicial bodies), under the 1993 amendments, however, called for rationalisation of all procedures in the Act relating to appeals and dispute settlement. It should be noted in this respect section 40 of the Tribal Land Act did not envisage that the tribunals to be established could have a role to play in such matters. Section 40(3) was drafted in a manner suggesting that a tribunal would only have jurisdiction to entertain appeals from decisions of land boards, which under the previous dispensation were taken to the Minister. There is nothing in the provision suggesting that an appeal could lie to a tribunal against a decision of the Minister, or against the finding of a Commission of Inquiry in a contested expropriation.

What the 1993 amendment of the Act addressed was section 33, on compensation for customary rights in land required for public purposes. Section 33 in its original form provided that the holder of customary rights of use in land required for public purposes shall be granted rights "to the use of land of equivalent value elsewhere," and to compensation for standing crops and for certain types of improvements on the land. With the passage of time, it increasingly became difficult for land boards to locate land of equivalent value that could be offered.[97] Policy makers also took cognisance of the fact that section 8(1)(b)(i) of the Constitution requires "prompt payment of adequate compensation" for rights or interests in property taken possession of. It was debatable whether the compensation proposed under section 33 met this standard, especially where no land of equivalent value was available for allocation.

[97] Republic of Botswana, *Report of the Presidential Commission of Inquiry into Land Problems in Mogoditshane and Other Peri-urban Villages in Botswana*, Government Printer, Gaborone, 1992, pp. 85–89.

Section 33(2) was in consequence revised in 1993 to provide that the person required to vacate land required for public purposes “may be granted the right to use other land, if available, and shall be entitled to adequate compensation from the State” for the value of standing crops taken over; improvements effected; costs of resettlement; and the loss of the right of use of the land. Section 33(3) provides for reference of disputes as to the amount or adequacy of compensation, the right or interest affected, or the legality of the acquisition, to the High Court or a Magistrate’s court of competent jurisdiction. The part of this provision on resolution of disputes as to the legality of the acquisition does not appear to accommodate the role of the Commission of Inquiry. It is again notable that no role is envisaged for land tribunals in these matters. As for the revised measure of compensation, it is interesting to speculate over what would be “adequate compensation” in areas where the sale of land is prohibited or frowned upon, and there is no open market price to guide the assessment of the adequacy of compensation. It is also notable that no provision is made for compensation of a land board for loss of its right of ownership in the land. This is not an infringement of the Constitution. In the language of the derogation in section 8(5) of the Constitution, land boards may qualify as “bodies corporate established by law for a public purpose in which no monies have been invested other than moneys provided by Parliament”.

5 Concluding Observations

This paper has revisited the property guarantees in the Botswana Constitution and the implications arising therefrom for post colonial land tenure policy. As stated earlier, the objective is to provoke reaction to the view that Botswana has done well with its decades – old Constitution. There is no need to fix what may not be broken. From the litigation generated by the property guarantees and the other clauses on fundamental rights, it might be a gross exaggeration to equate the Constitution with a broken machine that requires fixing. It should indeed be conceded that Botswana has generally been well-served by its Constitution, and politicians are entitled to be proud of what the country has achieved under a Constitution that has not changed much from what was bequeathed at independence. Botswana has recorded achievements unparalleled in sub-Saharan Africa in the areas of democracy, political accountability, good governance, respect for human rights, observance of the rule of law, and general economic, social, human and spatial development. A closer analysis of the property guarantees, and their implications particularly for post colonial land policy, suggests, however, that these parts may be broken. They certainly do require fixing. Sections 3, 8, 14 and 15 are the parts requiring attention, but it may not be advisable to fix only these parts. A review and modernization of the entire human rights chapter, or the Constitution would be commendable.

On section 3 of the Constitution, the main problem is lack of clarity as to whether the protection from deprivation of property offered is a distinct and separate guarantee from the protection from compulsory acquisition more elaborately described in section 8. This ambiguity percolates through and affects almost every aspect of post colonial land policy. It is therefore suggested that clarity must be sought through constitutional review, and not through the type of judicial pronouncements that confirmed the existence of the problem in the first place. The interpretation of section 3 preferred by the majority in the land mark case of *Attorney General v Dow* leads to the conclusion that the clause secures protection from deprivation of property without compensation as a separate and distinct right from protection from compulsory acquisition in section 8. This would amount to strong protection of property, but there would be lack of clarity as to what the measure of compensation should be. If the compensation must be assessed in reference to the parameters in section 8, then the minority view on the interpretation of section 3 in the *Dow* case might well be the correct elucidation of the law.

If indeed it is necessary to clarify through constitutional review whether Botswana has, or should have, a single or a combined property guarantee clause, it would also be opportune to revisit some of the conditions laid down in section 8 as mandatory requirements for a valid expropriation. This paper suggests that it is no longer necessary to guarantee the right to remit compensation to any country outside Botswana. This may have been necessary at independence for the protection of settler freehold land interests. There is not much freehold land now under the control of settlers. The majority of land holders to be protected now are likely to be citizens, with common law grants in tribal land. They may not need this type of protection. If they do, Botswana, in any event, probably has the most liberal exchange control regime in sub Saharan Africa.

The requirement for prompt payment of adequate compensation in section 8 of the Constitution is also overdue for reconsideration. The interpretation of adequate compensation as referring to market value is problematic in a country where the bulk of the land is not supposed to be bought or sold openly. This measure also inevitably leads to extravagant awards that may exceed the real, true, fair or appropriate value of the property. As in other countries where this measure has proved obstructive of genuine and equitable land reform and redistribution, Botswana should long have reconsidered this aspect its expropriation laws.

Section 14(3) has been revealed or confirmed as a property guarantee clause only through bold and highly imaginative judicial activism in *Sesana and Others v The Attorney General*. It cannot otherwise be regarded as good constitutional practice to acknowledge and accommodate aboriginal title or land rights through a derogation from the right of every person to move freely within Botswana and to live in any part of the country. The conclusion of this paper on this issue is that land rights or title secured or protected in this case cannot be meaningfully exercised without additional responsibilities on the part of Government to provide other amenities in the CKGR. This can best be secured through provisions that directly guarantee socio economic and cultural rights. Since Chapter II of the Botswana Constitution only secures civic, political and property rights, this paper, like most other commentaries, advocates for review of the Constitution, if need be, only for the purpose of modernizing and expanding the Human Rights Chapter.

Section 15 of the Constitution, like section 14, has attracted censure in this review not because of the substantive right it secures, but because of the derogations it permits from the protection of the right, and the implications thereof for post colonial land policy. It should be recalled that section 15 effectively proscribes discrimination on grounds of race, tribe, place of origin, political opinions, colour, creed or gender. This ideally ought to be reflected in all written laws. It is for this reason that the strenuous efforts to expurgate ethnic distinctions from sections 77, 78 and 79 of the Constitution deserve commendation, notwithstanding that the final outcome is a little disappointing. It is suggested and acknowledged in this paper that expurgation of ethnic distinctions from laws and policies relating to customary or tribal land tenure is likely to be more problematic and divisive, partly because of the nature of customary land tenure. This is a subject to be approached with extreme caution. What, however, may not be acceptable is the perpetuation of ethnic distinctions in land tenure and other laws on account of the derogation in section 15(9). It should be recalled that this provision potentially saves every discriminatory law in force at independence, which has remained in force after independence. Surely, Botswana has sufficiently matured as an independent country to decide for itself what discriminatory laws from its colonial past should remain in force today.

The other derogation from the protection against discrimination that should probably be reconsidered is in section 15(4)(b). This provision effectively states that it shall not be unconstitutional to discriminate in any written law against persons who are not citizens of Botswana. Land tenure policy appears to be a preferred area for constitutional discrimination against non-citizens. The Government of Botswana, like any other government, is entitled to prioritize the well – being of citizens in its programmes and activities. If this must entail discriminating against non-citizens under any law, ideally, one would expect that this would pass muster under other conventional derogations, such as discrimination that might be reasonably justifiable in a democratic society, or the saving of laws effecting what may be termed positive discrimination, (Section 15(4)(e)). It is galling and somewhat xenophobic for a human rights clause to proclaim in advance that any law that discriminates against persons who are not citizens shall not be unconstitutional.

African Charter on Human and Peoples' Rights

PREAMBLE

The African States members of the Organisation of African Unity, parties to the present Convention entitled "African Charter on Human and Peoples' Rights,"

Recalling Decision 115 (XVI) of the Assembly of Heads of State and Government at its Sixteenth Ordinary Session held in Monrovia, Liberia, from 17 to 20 July 1979 on the preparation of "a preliminary draft on an African Charter on Human and Peoples' Rights, providing inter alia for the establishment of bodies to promote and protect human and peoples' rights";

Considering the Charter of the Organisation of African Unity, which stipulates that "freedom, equality, justice and dignity are essential objectives for the achievement of the legitimate aspirations of the African peoples";

Reaffirming the pledge they solemnly made in Article 2 of the said Charter to eradicate all forms of colonialism from Africa, to coordinate and intensify their cooperation and efforts to achieve a better life for the peoples of Africa and to promote international cooperation having due regard to the Charter of the United Nations and the Universal Declaration of Human Rights;

Taking into consideration the virtues of their historical tradition and the values of African civilization which should inspire and characterize their reflection on the concept of human and peoples' rights;

Recognizing on the one hand, that fundamental human rights stem from the attitudes of human beings, which justifies their international protection and on the other hand that the reality and respect of peoples' rights should necessarily guarantee human rights;

Considering that the enjoyment of rights and freedoms also implies the performance of duties on the part of everyone;

Convinced that it is henceforth essential to pay particular attention to the right to development and that civil and political rights cannot be dissociated from economic, social and cultural rights in their conception as well as universality and that the satisfaction of economic, social and cultural rights is a guarantee for the enjoyment of civil and political rights;

Conscious of their duty to achieve the total liberation of Africa, the peoples of which are still struggling for their dignity and genuine independence, and undertaking to eliminate colonialism, neo-colonialism, apartheid, zionism and to dismantle aggressive foreign military bases and all forms of discrimination, language, religion or political opinions;

Reaffirming their adherence to the principles of human and peoples' rights and freedoms contained in the declarations, conventions and other instruments adopted by the Organisation of African Unity, the Movement of Non-Aligned Countries and the United Nations;

Firmly convinced of their **duty** to promote and protect human and peoples' rights and freedoms and taking into account the importance traditionally attached to these rights and freedoms in Africa;

HAVE AGREED AS FOLLOWS:

PART 1

RIGHTS AND DUTIES

CHAPTER 1

HUMAN AND PEOPLES' RIGHTS

ARTICLE 1

The Member States of the Organisation of African Unity, parties to the present Charter shall recognise the rights, duties and freedoms enshrined in the Charter and shall undertake to adopt legislative or other measures to give effect to them.

Article 2

Every individual shall be entitled to the enjoyment of the rights and freedoms recognised and guaranteed in the present Charter without distinction of any kind such as race, ethnic group, colour, sex, language, religion, political or any other opinion, national and social origin, fortune, birth or any status.

Article 3

1. Every individual shall be equal before the law
2. Every individual shall be entitled to equal protection of the law

Article 4

Human beings are inviolable. Every human being shall be entitled to respect for his life and the integrity of his person. No one may be arbitrarily deprived of this right.

Article 5

Every individual shall have the right to the respect of the dignity inherent in a human being and to the recognition of his legal status. All forms of exploitation and degradation of man, particularly slavery, slave trade, torture, cruel, inhuman or degrading punishment and treatment shall be prohibited.

Article 6

Every individual shall have the right to liberty and to the security of his person. No one may be deprived of his freedom except for reasons and conditions previously laid down by law. In particular, no one may be arbitrarily arrested or detained.

Article 7

1. Every individual shall have the right to have his cause heard. This comprises:
   a) The right to an appeal to competent national organs against acts of violating his fundamental rights as recognized and guaranteed by conventions, laws, regulations and customs in force;
   b) The right to be presumed innocent until proved guilty by a competent court or tribunal;
   c) The right to defence, including the right to be defended by counsel of his choice;
   d) The right to be tried within a reasonable time by an impartial court or tribunal.
2. No one may be condemned for an act or omission which did not constitute a legally punishable offence at the time it was committed. No penalty may be inflicted for an offence for which no provision was made at the time it was committed. Punishment is personal and can be imposed only on the offender.

Article 8

Freedom of conscience, the profession and free practice of religion shall be guaranteed. No one may, subject to law and order, be submitted to measures restricting the exercise of these freedoms.

Article 9

1 Every individual shall have the right to receive information.
2. Every individual shall have the right to express and disseminate his opinions within the law.

Article 10

1. Every individual shall have the right to free association provided that he abides by the law.

2. Subject to the obligation of solidarity provided for in Article 29, no one may be compelled to join an association.

Article 11

Every individual shall have the right to assemble freely with others. The exercise of this right shall be subject only to necessary restrictions provided for by law, in particular those enacted in the interest of national security, the safety, health, ethics and rights and freedoms of others.

Article 12

1. Every individual shall have the right to freedom of movement and residence within the borders of a State provided he abides by the law.
2. Every individual shall have the right to leave any country including his own, and to return to his country.

   This right may only be subject to restrictions, provided for by law for the protection of national security, law and order, public health or morality.
3. Every individual shall have the right, when persecuted, to seek and obtain asylum in other countries in accordance with the law of those countries and international conventions.
4. A non-national legally admitted in a territory of a State Party to the present Charter, may only be expelled from it by virtue of a decision taken in accordance with the law.
5. The mass expulsion of non-nationals shall be prohibited. Mass expulsion shall be that which is aimed at national, racial, ethnic or religious groups.

Article 13

1. Every citizen shall have the right to participate freely in the government of his country, either directly or through freely chosen representatives in accordance with the provisions of the law.
2. Every citizen shall have the right of equal access to the public service of the country.

3. Every individual shall have the right of access to public property and services in strict equality of all persons before the law.

Article 14

The right to property shall be guaranteed. It may only be encroached upon in the interest of public need or in the general interest of the community and in accordance with the provisions of appropriate laws.

Article 15

Every individual shall have the right to work under equitable and satisfactory conditions, and shall receive equal pay for equal work.

Article 16

1. Every individual shall have the right to enjoy the best attainable state of physical and mental health.
2. State Parties to the present Charter shall take the necessary measures to protect the health of their people and to ensure that they receive medical attention when they are sick

Article 17

1. Every individual shall have the right to education.
2. Every individual may freely take part in the cultural life of his community.
3. The promotion and protection of morals and traditional values recognized by the community shall be the duty of the State.

Article 18

1. The family shall be the natural unit and basis of society. It shall be protected by the State which shall take care of its physical health and moral.
2. The State shall have the duty to assist the family which is the custodian of morals and traditional values recognized by the community.

3. The State shall ensure the elimination of every discrimination against women and also ensure the protection of the rights of women and the child as stipulated in international declarations and conventions.
4. The aged and the disabled shall also have the right to special measures of protection in keeping with their physical or moral needs.

Article 19

All peoples shall be equal; they shall enjoy the same respect and shall have the same rights. Nothing shall justify the domination of a people by another.

Article 20

1. All peoples shall have the right to existence. They shall have the unquestionable and inalienable right to self-determination. They shall freely determine their political status and shall pursue their economic and social development according to the policy they have freely chosen.
2. Colonized or oppressed peoples shall have the right to free themselves from the bonds of domination by resorting to any means recognized by the international community.
3. All peoples shall have the right to the assistance of the State Parties to the present Charter in their liberation struggle against foreign domination, be it political, economic or cultural.

Article 21

1. All peoples shall freely dispose of their wealth and natural resources. This right shall be exercised in the exclusive interest of the people. In no case shall a people be deprived of it.
2 In case of spoilation, the dispossessed people shall have the right to the lawful recovery of its property as well as to an adequate compensation.
3. The free disposal of wealth and natural resources shall be exercised without prejudice to the obligation of promoting international economic cooperation based on mutual respect, equitable exchange and the principles of international law.

4. State Parties to the present Charter shall individually and collectively exercise the right to free disposal of their wealth and natural resources with a view to strengthening African Unity and solidarity.

   State Parties to the present Charter shall undertake to eliminate all forms of foreign exploitation particularly that practised by international monopolies so as to enable their peoples to fully benefit from the advantages derived from their national resources.

Article 22

1. All peoples shall have the right to their economic, social and cultural development with due regard to their freedom and identity and in the equal enjoyment of the common heritage of mankind.
2. States shall have the duty, individually or collectively, to ensure the exercise of the right to development.

Article 23

1. All peoples shall have the right to national and international peace and security. The principles of solidarity and friendly relations implicitly affirmed by the Charter of the United Nations and reaffirmed by that of the Organisation of African Unity shall govern relations between States.
2. For the purpose of strengthening peace, solidarity and friendly relations, State Parties to the present Charter shall ensure that:
   a) any individual enjoying the right of asylum under Article 12 of the present Charter shall not engage in subversive activities against his country of origin or any other State Party to the present Charter;
   b) their territories shall not be used as bases for subversive or terrorist activities against the people of any other State Party to the present Charter.

Article 24

All peoples shall have the right to a general satisfactory environment favourable to their development.

Article 25

State Parties to the present Charter shall have the duty to promote and ensure through teaching, education and publication, the respect of the rights and freedoms contained in the present Charter and to see to it that these freedoms and rights as well as corresponding obligations and duties are understood.

Article 26

State Parties to the present Charter shall have the duty to guarantee the independence of the Courts and shall allow the establishment and improvement of appropriate national institutions entrusted with the promotion and protection of the rights and freedoms guaranteed by the present Charter.

CHAPTER II

DUTIES

Article 27

1. Every individual shall have duties towards his family and society, the State and other legally recognised communities and the international community.
2. The rights and freedoms of each individual shall be exercised with due regard to the rights of others, collective security, morality and common interest.

Article 28

Every individual shall have the duty to respect and consider his fellow beings without discrimination, and to maintain relations aimed at promoting, safeguarding and reinforcing mutual respect and tolerance.

Article 29

The individual shall also have the duty:

1. To preserve the harmonious development of the family and to work for the cohesion and respect of the family; to respect his parents at all times, to maintain them in case of need.
2. To serve his national community by placing his physical and intellectual abilities at its service;
3. Not to compromise the security of the State whose national or resident he is;
4. To preserve and strengthen social and national solidarity, particularly when the latter is strengthened;
5. To preserve and strengthen the national independence and the territorial integrity of his country and to contribute to his defence in accordance with the law;
6. To work to the best of his abilities and competence, and to pay taxes imposed by law in the interest of the society;
7. To preserve and strengthen positive African cultural values in his relations with other members of the society, in the spirit of tolerance, dialogue and consultation and, in general, to contribute to the promotion of the moral well being of society;
8. To contribute to the best of his abilities, at all times and at all levels, to the promotion and achievement of African unity.

PART II

MEASURES OF SAFEGUARD

CHAPTER 1

ESTABLISHMENT AND ORGANISATION OF THE AFRICAN COMMISSION ON HUMAN AND PEOPLES' RIGHTS

Article 30

An African Commission on Human and Peoples' Rights, hereinafter called "the Commission", shall be established within the Organisation of African Unity to promote human and peoples' rights and ensure their protection in Africa.

Article 31

1. The Commission shall consist of eleven members chosen from amongst African personalities of the highest reputation, known for their high morality, integrity, impartiality and competence in matters of human and peoples' rights; particular consideration being given to personshaving legal experience.
2. The members of the Commission shall serve in their personal capacity.

Article 32

The Commission shall not include more than one national of the same State.

Article 33

The members of the Commission shall be elected by secret ballot by the Assembly of Heads of State and Government, from a list of persons nominated by the State Parties to the present Charter.

Article 34

Each State Party to the present Charter may not nominate more than two candidates. The candidates must have the nationality of one of the State Parties to the present Charter. When two candidates are nominated by a State, one of them may not be a national of that State.

Article 35

1. The Secretary General of he Organisation of African Unity shall invite State Parties to the present Charter at least four months before the elections to nominate candidates;
2. The Secretary General of the Organisation of African Unity shall make an alphabetical list of the persons thus nominated and communicate it to the Heads of State and Government at least one month before the elections;

Article 36

The members of the Commission shall be elected for a six year period and shall be eligible for re-election. However, the term of office of four of the members elected at the first election shall terminate after two years and the term of office of three others, at the end of four years.

Article 37

Immediately after the first election, the Chairman of the Assembly of Heads of State and Government of the Organisation of African Unity shall draw lots to decide the names of those members referred to in Article 36.

Article 38

After their election, the members of the Commission shall make a solemn declaration to discharge their duties impartially and faithfully.

Article 39

1. In case of death or resignation of a member of the Commission, the Chairman of the Commission shall immediately inform the Secretary General of the Organisation of African Unity, who shall declare the seat vacant from the date of death or from the date on which the resignation takes effect.
2. If, in the unanimous opinion of other members of the Commission, a member has stopped discharging his dutiesfor any reason other than a temporary absence, the Chairman of the Commission shall inform the Secretary General of the Organisation of African Unity, who shall then declare the seat vacant.
3. In each of the cases anticipated above, the Assembly of Heads of State and Government shall replace the member whose seat became vacant for the remaining period of his term, unless the period is less than six months.

Article 40

Every member of the Commission shall be in office until the date his successor assumes office.

ARTICLE 41

The Secretary General of the Organisation of African Unity shall appoint the Secretary of the Commission. He shall provide the staff and services necessary for the effective discharge of the duties of the Commission. The Organisation of African Unity shall bear cost of the staff and services.

ARTICLE 42

1. The Commission shall elect its Chairman and Vice Chairman for a two-year period. They shall be eligible for re-election.
2. The Commission shall lay down its rules of procedure.
3. Seven members shall form the quorum.
4. In case of an equality of votes, the Chairman shall have a casting vote.
5. The Secretary General may attend the meetings of the Commission. He shall neither participate in deliberations nor shall he be entitled to vote. The Chairman of the Commission may, however, invite him to speak.

ARTICLE 43

In discharging their duties, members of the Commission shall enjoy diplomatic privileges and immunities provided for in the General Convention on the Privileges and Immunities of the Organisation of African Unity.

ARTICLE 44

Provision shall be made for the emoluments and allowances of the members of the Commission in the Regular Budget of the Organisation of African Unity.

CHAPTER II

MANDATE OF THE COMMISSION

ARTICLE 45

The functions of the Commission shall be:

1. To promote human and peoples' rights and in particular:

a) to collect documents, undertake studies and researches on African problems in the field of human and peoples' rights, organise seminars, symposia and conferences, disseminate information, encourage national and local institutions concerned with human and peoples' rights and, should the case arise, give its views or make recommendations to Governments.

b) to formulae and lay down, principles and rules aimed at solving legal problems relating to human and peoples' rights and fundamental freedoms upon which African Governments may base their legislation.

c) cooperate with other African and international institutions concerned with the promotion and protection of human and peoples' rights.

2. Ensure the protection of human and peoples' rights under conditions laid down by the present Charter.
3. Interpret all the provisions of the present Charter at the request of a State Party, an institution of the OAU or an African Organisation recognised by the OAU.
4. Perform any other tasks which may be entrusted to it by the Assembly of Heads of State and Government.

CHAPTER III

PROCEDURE OF THE COMMISSION

Article 46

The Commission may resort to any appropriate method of investigation; it may hear from the Secretary General of the Organisation of African Unity or any other person capable of enlightening it.

COMMUNICATION FROM STATES

Article 47

If a State Party to the present Charter has good reasons to believe that another State Party to this Charter has violated the provisions of the Charter, it may draw, by written communication, the attention of that State to the matter. This Communication shall also be addressed to the Secretary General of the OAU and to the Chairman of the Commission. Within three months of the receipt of the Communication, the State to which the Communication is addressed shall give the enquiring State, written explanation or statement elucidating the matter. This should include as much as possible, relevant information relating to the laws and rules of procedure applied and applicable and the redress already given or course of action available.

Article 48

If within three months from the date on which the original communication is received by the State to which it is addressed, the issue is not settled to the satisfaction of the two States involved through bilateral negotiation or by any other peaceful procedure, either State shall have the right to submit the matter to the Commission through the Chairman and shall notify the other States involved.

Article 49

Notwithstanding the provisions of Article 47, if a State Party to the present Charter considers that another State Party has violated the provisions of the Charter, it may refer the matter directly to the Commission by addressing a communication to the Chairman, to the Secretary General of the Organisation of African unity and the State concerned.

Article 50

The Commission can only deal with a matter submitted to it after making sure that all local remedies, if they exist, have been exhausted, unless it is obvious to the Commission that the procedure of achieving these remedies would be unduly prolonged.

Article 51

1 The Commission may ask the State concerned to provide it with all relevant information.

2. When the Commission is considering the matter, States concerned may be represented before it and submit written or oral representation.

Article 52

After having obtained from the States concerned and from other sources all the information it deems necessary and after having tried all appropriate means to reach an amicable solution based on the respect of human and peoples' rights, the Commission shall prepare, within a reasonable period of time from the notification referred to in Article 48, a report to the States concerned and communicated to the Assembly of Heads of State and Government.

Article 53

While transmitting its report, the Commission may make to the Assembly of Heads of State and Government such recommendations as it deems useful.

OTHER COMMUNICATIONS

Article 54

The Commission shall submit to each Ordinary Session of the Assembly of Heads of State and Government a report on its activities.

Article 55

1. Before each Session, the Secretary of the Commission shall make a list of the Communications other than those of State Parties to the present Charter and transmit them to Members of the Commission, who shall indicate which Communications should be considered by the Commission.
2. A Communication shall be considered by the Commission if a simple majority of its members so decide.

Article 56

Communications relating to Human and Peoples' rights referred to in Article 55 received by the Commission, shall be considered if they:

1. Indicate their authors even if the latter requests anonymity,
2. Are compatible with the Charter of the Organisation of Afri- can Unity or with the present Charter,
3. Are not written in disparaging or insulting language directed against the State concerned and its institutions or to the Organisation of African Unity,
4. Are not based exclusively on news disseminated through the mass media,
5. Are sent after exhausting local remedies, if any, unless it is obvious that this procedure is unduly prolonged,
6. Are submitted within a reasonable period from the time local remedies are exhausted or from the date the Commission is seized with the matter, and
7. Do not deal with cases which have been settled by those States involved in accordance with the principles of the Charter of the United Nations, or the Charter of the Or- ganisation of African Unity or the provisions of the present Charter.

Article 57

Prior to any substantive consideration, all communications shall be brought to the knowledge of the State concerned by the Chairman of the Commission.

Article 58

1. When it appears after deliberations of the Commission that one or more Communications apparently relate to special cases which reveal the existence of a series of serious or massive violations of human and peoples' rights, the Commission shall draw the attention of the Assembly of Heads of State and Government to these special cases.
2. The Assembly of Heads of State and Government may then request the Commission to undertake an in-depth study of these cases and make a factual report, accompanied by its finding and recommendations.
3. A case of emergency duly noticed by the Commission shall be submitted by the latter to the Chairman of the Assembly of Heads of State and Government who may request an in-depth study.

Article 59

1. All measures taken within the provisions of the present Chapter shall remain confidential until the Assembly of Heads of State and Government shall otherwise decide.
2. However the report shall be published by the Chairman of the Commission upon the decision of he Assembly of Heads of State and Government.
3. The report on the activities of the Commission shall be published by its Chairman after it has been considered by the Assembly of Heads of State and Government.

CHAPTER IV

APPLICABLE PRINCIPLES

Article 60

The Commission shall draw inspiration from international law on human and peoples' rights, particularly from the provisions of various African instruments on Human and Peoples' Rights, the Charter of the United Nations, the Charter of the Organisation of African Unity, the Universal Declaration of Human Rights, other instruments adopted by the United Nations and by African countries in the field of Human and Peoples' Rights, as well as from the provisions of various instruments adopted within the Specialised Agencies of the United Nations of which the Parties to the present Charter are members.

Article 61

The Commission shall also take into consideration, as subsidiary measures to determine the principles of law, other general or special international conventions, laying down rules expressly recognised by Member States of the Organisation of African Unity, African practices consistent with international norms on Human and Peoples' Rights, customs generally accepted as law, general principles of law recognised by African States as well as legal precedents and doctrine.

Article 62

Each State Party shall undertake to submit every two years, from the date the present Charter comes into force, a report on the legislative or other measures taken, with a view to giving effect to the rights and freedoms recognised and guaranteed by the present Charter.

Article 63

1. The present Charter shall be open to signature, ratification or adherence of the Member States of the Organisation of African Unity.
2. The instruments of ratification or adherence to the present Charter shall be deposited with the Secretary General of the Organisation of African Unity.
3. The present Charter shall come into force three months after the reception by the Secretary General of the instruments of ratification or adherence of a simple majority of the Member States of the Organisation of African Unity.

PART III

GENERAL PROVISIONS

Article 64

1. After the coming into force of the present Charter, members of the Commission shall be elected in accordance with the relevant Articles of the present Charter.
2. The Secretary General of the Organisation of African Unity shall convene the first meeting of the Commission at the Headquarters of the Organisation within three months of the constitution of the Commission. Thereafter, the Commission shall be convened by its Chairman whenever necessary but at least once a year.

Article 65

For each of the States that will ratify or adhere to the present Charter after its coming into force, the Charter shall take effect three months after the date of the deposit by that State of the instrument of ratification or adherence.

Article 66

Special protocols or agreements may, if necessary, supplement the provisions of the present Charter.

Article 67

The Secretary General of the Organisation of African Unity shall inform members of the Organisation of the deposit of each instrument of ratification or adherence.

Article 68

The present Charter may be amended if a State Party makes a written request to that effect to the Secretary General of the Organisation of African Unity. The Assembly of Heads of State and Government may only consider the draft amendment after all the State Parties have been duly informed of it and the Commission has given its opinion on it at the request of the sponsoring State. The amendment shall be approved by a simple majority of the State Parties. It shall come into force for each State which has accepted it in accordance with its constitutional procedure three months after the Secretary General has received notice of the acceptance.

Adopted by the eighteenth Assembly of Heads of State and Government,

June 1981 - Nairobi, Kenya

Protocol to the African Charter on Human and Peoples' Rights on the Rights of Women in Africa

The States Parties to this Protocol,

Considering that Article 66 of the African Charter on Human and Peoples' Rights provides for special protocols or agreements, if necessary, to supplement the provisions of the African Charter, and that the Assembly of Heads of State and Government of the Organization of African Unity meeting in its Thirty-first Ordinary Session in Addis Ababa, Ethiopia, in June 1995, endorsed by resolution AHG/Res.240 (XXXI) the recommendation of the African Commission on Human and Peoples' Rights to elaborate a Protocol on the Rights of Women in Africa;

Considering that Article 2 of the African Charter on Human and Peoples' Rights enshrines the principle of non-discrimination on the grounds of race, ethnic group, colour, sex, language, religion, political or any other opinion, national and social origin, fortune, birth or other status;

Further Considering that Article 18 of the African Charter on Human and Peoples' Rights calls on all States Parties to eliminate every discrimination against women and to ensure the protection of the rights of women as stipulated in international declarations and conventions;

Noting that Articles 60 and 61 of the African Charter on Human and Peoples' Rights recognise regional and international human rights instruments and African practices consistent with international norms on human and peoples' rights as being important reference points for the application and interpretation of the African Charter;

Recalling that women's rights have been recognised and guaranteed in all international human rights instruments, notably the Universal Declaration of Human Rights, the International Covenant on Civil and Political Rights, the International Covenant on Economic, Social and Cultural Rights, the Convention on the Elimination of All Forms of Discrimination Against Women and its Optional Protocol, the African Charter on the Rights and

Welfare of the Child, and all other international and regional conventions and covenants relating to the rights of women as being inalienable, interdependent and indivisible human rights;

Noting that women's rights and women's essential role in development, have been reaffirmed in the United Nations Plans of Action on the Environment and Development in 1992, on Human Rights in 1993, on Population and Development in 1994 and on Social Development in 1995;

Recallingalso United Nations Security Council's Resolution 1325 (2000) on the role of Women in promoting peace and security;

Reaffirming the principle of promoting gender equality as enshrined in the Constitutive Act of the African Union as well as the New Partnership for Africa's Development, relevant Declarations, Resolutions and Decisions, which underline the commitment of the African States to ensure the full participation of African women as equal partners in Africa's development;

Further Noting that the African Platform for Action and the Dakar Declaration of 1994 and the Beijing Platform for Action of 1995 call on all Member States of the United Nations, which have made a solemn commitment to implement them, to take concrete steps to give greater attention to the human rights of women in order to eliminate all forms of discrimination and of gender-based violence against women;

Recognising the crucial role of women in the preservation of African values based on the principles of equality, peace, freedom, dignity, justice, solidarity and democracy;

Bearing in Mind related Resolutions, Declarations, Recommendations, Decisions, Conventions and other Regional and Sub-Regional Instruments aimed at eliminating all forms of discrimination and at promoting equality between women and men;

Concerned that despite the ratification of the African Charter on Human and Peoples' Rights and other international human rights instruments by the majority of States Parties, and their solemn commitment to eliminate all forms of discrimination and harmful practices against women, women in Africa still continue to be victims of discrimination and harmful practices;

Firmly Convinced that any practice that hinders or endangers the normal growth and affects the physical and psychological development of women and girls should be condemned and eliminated;

Determined to ensure that the rights of women are promoted, realised and protected in order to enable them to enjoy fully all their human rights;

HAVE AGREED AS FOLLOWS:

ARTICLE 1

Definitions

For the purpose of the present Protocol:

a) "African Charter" means the African Charter on Human and Peoples' Rights;

b) "African Commission" means the African Commission on Human and Peoples' Rights;

- "Assembly" means the Assembly of Heads of State and Government of the African Union;
- "AU" means the African Union;
- ''Constitutive Act'' means the Constitutive Act of the African Union;
- "Discrimination against women" means any distinction, exclusion or restriction or any differential treatment based on sex and whose objectives or effects compromise or destroy the recognition, enjoyment or the exercise by women, regardless of their marital status, of human rights and fundamental freedoms in all spheres of life;
- "Harmful Practices" means all behaviour, attitudes and/or practices which negatively affect the fundamental rights of women and girls, such as their right to life, health, dignity, education and physical integrity;
- ''NEPAD'' means the New Partnership for Africa's Development established by the Assembly;
- "States Parties" means the States Parties to this Protocol;
- "Violence against women" means all acts perpetrated against women which cause or could cause them physical, sexual, psychological, and economic harm, including the threat to take such acts; or to undertake the imposition of arbitrary restrictions on or deprivation of

fundamental freedoms in private or public life in peace time and during situations of armed conflicts or of war;

- "Women" means persons of female gender, including girls;

Article 2

Elimination of Discrimination Against Women

1. States Parties shall combat all forms of discrimination against women through appropriate legislative, institutional and other measures. In this regard they shall:
   a) include in their national constitutions and other legislative instruments, if not already done, the principle of equality between women and men and ensure its effective application;
   b) enact and effectively implement appropriate legislative or regulatory measures, including those prohibiting and curbing all forms of discrimination particularly those harmful practices which endanger the health and general well-being of women;
   c) integrate a gender perspective in their policy decisions, legislation, development plans, programmes and activities and in all other spheres of life;
   d) take corrective and positive action in those areas where discrimination against women in law and in fact continues to exist;
   e) support the local, national, regional and continental initiatives directed at eradicating all forms of discrimination against women.
2. States Parties shall commit themselves to modify the social and cultural patterns of conduct of women and men through public education, information, education and communication strategies, with a view to achieving the elimination of harmful cultural and traditional practices and all other practices which are based on the idea of the inferiority or the superiority of either of the sexes, or on stereotyped roles for women and men.

Article 3

Right to Dignity

- Every woman shall have the right to dignity inherent in a human being and to the recognition and protection of her human and legal rights;

- Every woman shall have the right to respect as a person and to the free development of her personality;
- States Parties shall adopt and implement appropriate measures to prohibit any exploitation or degradation of women;
- States Parties shall adopt and implement appropriatemeasures to ensure the protection of every woman's right to respect for her dignity and protection of women from all forms of violence, particularly sexual and verbal violence.

Article 4

The Rights to Life, Integrity and Security of the Person

1. Every woman shall be entitled to respect for her life and the integrity and security of her person. All forms of exploitation, cruel, inhuman or degrading punishment and treatment shall be prohibited.
2. States Parties shall take appropriate and effective measures to:
   a) enact and enforce laws to prohibit all forms of violence against women including unwanted or forced sex whether the violence takes place in private or public;
   b) adopt such other legislative, administrative, social and economic measures as may be necessary to ensure the prevention, punishment and eradication of all forms of violence against women;
   c) identify the causes and consequences of violence against women and take appropriate measures to prevent and eliminate such violence;
   d) actively promote peace education through curricula and social communication in order to eradicate elements in traditional and cultural beliefs, practices and stereotypes which legitimise and exacerbate the persistence and tolerance of violence against women;
   e) punish the perpetrators of violence against women and implement programmes for the rehabilitation of women victims;
   f) establish mechanisms and accessible services for effective information, rehabilitation and reparation for victims of violence against women;
   g) prevent and condemn trafficking in women, prosecute the perpetrators of such trafficking and protect those women most at risk;
      - prohibit all medical or scientific experiments on women without their informed consent;

- provide adequate budgetary and other resources for the implementation and monitoring of actions aimed at preventing and eradicating violence against women;
- ensure that, in those countries where the death penalty still exists, not to carry out death sentences on pregnant or nursing women.
- ensure that women and men enjoy equal rights in terms of access to refugee status, determination procedures and that women refugees are accorded the full protection and benefits guaranteed under international refugee law, including their own identity and other documents;

Article 5

Elimination of Harmful Practices

States Parties shall prohibit and condemn all forms of harmful practices which negatively affect the human rights of women and which are contrary to recognised international standards. States Parties shall take all necessary legislative and other measures to eliminate such practices, including:

- creation of public awareness in all sectors of society regarding harmful practices through information, formal and informal education and outreach programmes;
- prohibition, through legislative measures backed by sanctions, of all forms of female genital mutilation, scarification, medicalisation and para-medicalisation of female genital mutilation and all other practices in order to eradicate them;
- provision of necessary support to victims of harmful practices through basic services such as health services, legal and judicialsupport, emotional and psychological counselling as well as vocational training to make them self-supporting;
- protection of women who are at risk of being subjected to harmful practices or all other forms of violence, abuse and intolerance.

Article 6

Marriage

States Parties shall ensure that women and men enjoy equal rights and are regarded as equal partners in marriage. They shall enact appropriate national legislative measures to guarantee that:

- no marriage shall take place without the free and full consent of both parties;
- the minimum age of marriage for women shall be 18 years;
- monogamy is encouraged as the preferred form of marriage and that the rights of women in marriage and family, including in polygamous marital relationships are promoted and protected;
- every marriage shall be recorded in writing and registered in accordance with national laws, in order to be legally recognised;
- the husband and wife shall, by mutual agreement, choose their matrimonial regime and place of residence;
- a married woman shall have the right to retain her maiden name, to use it as she pleases, jointly or separately with her husband's surname;
- a woman shall have the right to retain her nationality or to acquire the nationality of her husband;
- a woman and a man shall have equal rights, with respect to the nationality of their children except where this is contrary to a provision in national legislation or is contrary to national security interests;
- a woman and a man shall jointly contribute to safeguarding the interests of the family, protecting and educating their children;
- during her marriage, a woman shall have the right to acquire her own property and to administer and manage it freely.

Article 7

Separation, Divorce and Annulment of Marriage

States Parties shall enact appropriate legislation to ensure that women and men enjoy the same rights in case of separation, divorce or annulment of marriage. In this regard, they shall ensure that:

- separation, divorce or annulment of a marriage shall be effected by judicial order;
- women and men shall have the same rights to seek separation, divorce or annulment of a marriage;
- in case of separation, divorce or annulment of marriage, women and men shall have reciprocalrights and responsibilities towards their children. In any case, the interests of the children shall be given paramount importance;

- in case of separation, divorce or annulment of marriage, women and menshall have the right to an equitable sharing of the joint property deriving from the marriage.

Article 8

Access to Justice and Equal Protection before the Law

Women and menare equal before the law and shall have the right to equal protection andbenefit of the law. States Parties shall take all appropriate measures to ensure:

- effective access by women to judicial and legal services, including legal aid;
- support to local, national, regional and continental initiatives directed at providing women access to legal services, including legal aid;
- the establishment of adequate educational and other appropriate structures with particular attention to women and to sensitise everyone to the rights of women;
- that law enforcement organs at all levels are equipped to effectively interpret and enforce gender equality rights;
- that women are represented equally in the judiciary and law enforcement organs;
- reform of existing discriminatory laws and practices in order to promote and protect the rights of women.

Article 9

Right to Participation in the Political and Decision-Making Process

1. States Parties shall take specific positive action to promote participative governance and the equal participation of women in the political life of their countries through affirmative action, enabling national legislation and other measures to ensure that:
   a) women participate without any discrimination in all elections;
   b) women are represented equally at all levels with men in all electoral processes;
   c) women are equal partners with men at all levels of development and implementation of State policies and development programmes.

2. States Parties shall ensure increased and effective representation and participation of women at all levels of decision-making.

Article 10

Right to Peace

1. Women have the right to a peaceful existence and the right to participate in the promotion and maintenance of peace.
2. States Parties shall take all appropriate measures to ensure the increased participation of women:
   a) in programmes of education for peace and a culture of peace;
   b) in the structures and processes for conflict prevention, management and resolution at local, national, regional, continental and international levels;
      - in the local, national, regional, continental and international decision making structures to ensure physical, psychological, social and legal protection of asylum seekers, refugees, returnees and displaced persons, in particular women;
      - in all levels of the structures established for the management of camps and settlements for asylum seekers, refugees, returnees and displaced persons, in particular, women;
      - in all aspects of planning, formulation and implementation of post conflict reconstruction and rehabilitation.
3. States Parties shall take the necessary measures to reduce military expenditure significantly in favour of spending on social development in general, and the promotion of women in particular.

Article 11

Protection of Women in Armed Conflicts

- States Parties undertake to respect and ensure respect for the rules of international humanitarian law applicable in armed conflict situations which affect the population, particularly women.
- States Parties shall, in accordance with the obligations incumbent upon them under the international humanitarian law, protect civilians including women, irrespective of the population to which theybelong, in the event of armedconflict.

- States Parties undertake to protect asylum seeking women, refugees, returnees and internally displaced persons, against all forms of violence, rape and other forms of sexual exploitation, and to ensure that such acts are considered war crimes, genocide and/or crimes against humanity and that their perpetrators are brought to justice before a competent criminal jurisdiction.
- States Parties shall take all necessary measures to ensure that no child, especially girls under 18 years of age, take a direct part in hostilities and thatno child is recruited as a soldier.

Article 12

Right to Education and Training

1. States Parties shall take all appropriate measures to:
   a) eliminate all forms of discrimination against women and guarantee equal opportunity and access in the sphere of education and training;
   b) eliminate all stereotypes in textbooks, syllabuses and the media, that perpetuate such discrimination;
      - protect women, especially the girl-child from all forms of abuse, including sexual harassment in schools and other educational institutions and provide for sanctions against the perpetrators of such practices;
      - provide access to counselling and rehabilitation services to women who suffer abuses and sexual harassment;
      - integrate gender sensitisation and human rights education at all levels of education curricula including teacher training.
2. States Parties shall take specific positive action to:
   a) promote literacy among women;
   b) promote education and training for women at all levels and in all disciplines, particularly in the fields of science and technology;
   c) promote the enrolment and retention of girls in schools and other training institutions and the organisation of programmes for women who leave school prematurely.

Article 13

Economic and Social Welfare Rights

States Parties shall adopt and enforce legislative and other measures to guarantee womenequal opportunities in work and career advancement and other economic opportunities. In this respect, they shall:

a) promote equality of access to employment;

b) promote the right to equal remuneration for jobs of equal value for women and men;

c) ensure transparency in recruitment, promotion and dismissal of women and combat and punish sexual harassment in the workplace;

d) guarantee women the freedom to choose their occupation, and protect them from exploitation by their employers violating and exploiting their fundamental rights as recognised and guaranteed by conventions, laws and regulations in force;

e) create conditions to promote and support the occupations and economic activities of women, in particular, within the informal sector;

- establish a system of protection and social insurance for women working in the informal sector and sensitise them to adhere to it;

g) introduce a minimum age for work and prohibit the employment of children below that age, andprohibit, combat and punish all forms of exploitation of children, especially the girl-child;

h) take the necessary measures to recognise the economic value of the work of women in the home;

i) guarantee adequate and paid pre and post-natal maternity leave in both the private and public sectors;

j) ensure the equal application of taxation laws to women and men;

k) recognise and enforce the right of salaried women to the same allowances and entitlements as those granted to salaried men for their spouses and children;

l) recognise that both parents bear the primary responsibility for the upbringing and development of children and that this is a social function for which the State and the private sector have secondary responsibility;

m) take effective legislative and administrative measures to prevent the exploitation and abuse of women in advertising and pornography.

Article 14

Health and Reproductive Rights

1. States Parties shall ensure that the right to health of women, including sexual and reproductive health is respected and promoted. This includes:
    a) the right to control their fertility;
    b) the right to decide whether to have children, the number of children and the spacing of children;
    c) the right to choose any method of contraception;
    d) the right to self protection and to be protected against sexually transmitted infections, including HIV/AIDS;
    e) the right to be informed on one's health status and on the health status of one's partner, particularly if affected with sexually transmitted infections, including HIV/AIDS, in accordance with internationally recognised standards and best practices;
    f) the right to have family planning education.
2. States Parties shall take all appropriate measures to:
    a) provide adequate, affordable and accessible health services, including information, education and communication programmes to women especially those in rural areas;
    b) establish and strengthen existing pre-natal, delivery and post-natal health and nutritional services for women during pregnancy andwhile they are breast-feeding;
    c) protect the reproductive rights of women by authorising medical abortion in cases of sexual assault, rape, incest, and where the continued pregnancy endangers the mental and physical health of the mother or the life of the mother or the foetus.

Article 15

Right to Food Security

a) provide women with access to clean drinking water, sources of domestic fuel, land, and the means of producing nutritious food;
b) establish adequate systems of supply and storage to ensure food security.

ARTICLE 16

Right to Adequate Housing

Women shall have the right to equal access to housing and to acceptable living conditions in a healthy environment. To ensure this right, States Parties shall grant to women, whatever their marital status, access to adequate housing.

ARTICLE 17

Right to Positive Cultural Context

1. Women shall have the right to live in a positive cultural context and to participate at all levels in the determination of cultural policies.
2. States Parties shall take all appropriate measures to enhance the participation of women in the formulation of cultural policies at all levels.

ARTICLE 18

Right to a Healthy and Sustainable Environment

1. Women shall have the right to live in a healthy and sustainable environment.
2. States Parties shall take all appropriate measures to:
   a) ensure greater participation of women in the planning, management and preservation of the environment and the sustainable use of natural resources at all levels;
      - promote research and investment in new and renewable energy sources and appropriate technologies, including information technologies and facilitate women's access to, and participation in their control;
      - protect and enable the development of women's indigenous knowledge systems;

   c) regulate the management, processing, storage and disposal of domestic waste;
      - ensure that proper standards are followed for the storage, transportation and disposal of toxic waste.

ARTICLE 19

Right to Sustainable Development

Women shall have the right to fully enjoy their right to sustainable development. In this connection, the States Parties shall take all appropriate measures to:

a) introduce the gender perspective in the national development planning procedures;

b) ensure participation of women at all levels in the conceptualisation, decision-making, implementation and evaluation of development policies and programmes;

  - promote women's access to and control over productive resources such as land and guarantee their right to property;
  - promote women's access to credit, training, skills development and extension services at rural and urban levels in order to provide women with a higher quality of life and reduce the level of poverty among women;
  - take into account indicators of human development specifically relating to women in the elaboration of development policies and programmes; and
  - ensure that the negative effects of globalisation and any adverse effects of the implementation of trade and economic policies and programmes are reduced to the minimum for women.

ARTICLE 20

Widows' Rights

States Parties shall take appropriate legal measures to ensure that widows enjoy all human rights through the implementation of the following provisions:

a) that widows are not subjected to inhuman, humiliating or degrading treatment;

b) a widow shall automatically become the guardian and custodian of her children, after the death of her husband, unless this is contrary to the interests and the welfare of the children;

c) a widow shall have the right to remarry, and in that event, to marry the person of her choice.

ARTICLE 21

Right to Inheritance

1. A widow shall have the right to an equitable share in the inheritance of the property of her husband. A widow shall have the right to continue to live in the matrimonial house. In case of remarriage, she shall retain this right if the house belongs to her or she has inherited it.
2. Women and men shall have the right to inherit, in equitable shares, their parents' properties.

ARTICLE 22

Special Protection of Elderly Women

The States Parties undertake to:

- provide protection to elderly women and take specific measures commensurate with their physical, economic and social needs as well as their access to employment and professional training;
- ensure the right of elderly women to freedom from violence, including sexual abuse, discrimination based on age and the right to be treated with dignity.

ARTICLE 23

Special Protection of Women with Disabilities

The States Parties undertake to:

- ensure the protection of women with disabilities and take specific measures commensurate with their physical, economic and social needs to facilitate their access to employment, professional and vocational training as well as their participation in decision-making;
- ensure the right of women with disabilities to freedom from violence, including sexual abuse, discrimination based on disability and the right to be treated with dignity.

Article 24

Special Protection of Women in Distress

The States Parties undertake to:

- ensure the protection of poor women and women heads of families including women from marginalized population groups and provide the an environment suitable to their condition and their special physical, economic and social needs;
- ensure the right of pregnant or nursing women or women in detention by providing them with an environment which is suitable to their condition and the right to be treated with dignity.

Article 25

Remedies

States Parties shall undertake to:

- providefor appropriate remedies to any woman whose rights or freedoms, as herein recognised, have been violated;
- ensure that such remedies are determined by competent judicial, administrative or legislative authorities, or by any other competent authority provided for by law.

Article 26

Implementation and Monitoring

- States Parties shall ensure the implementation of this Protocol at national level, and in their periodic reports submitted in accordance with Article 62 of the African Charter, indicate the legislative and other measures undertaken for the full realisation of the rights herein recognised.
- States Parties undertake to adopt all necessary measures and in particular shall provide budgetary and other resources for the full and effective implementation of the rights herein recognised.

ARTICLE 27

Interpretation

The African Court on Human and Peoples' Rights shall be seized with matters of interpretation arising from the application or implementation of this Protocol.

ARTICLE 28

Signature, Ratification and Accession

1. This Protocol shall be open for signature, ratification and accession by the States Parties, in accordance with their respective constitutional procedures.
2. The instruments of ratification or accession shall be deposited with the Chairperson of the Commission of the AU.

ARTICLE 29

Entry into Force

1. This Protocol shall enter into force thirty (30) days after the deposit of the fifteenth (15) instrument of ratification.
2. For each State Party that accedes to this Protocol after its coming into force, the Protocol shall come into force on the date of deposit of the instrument of accession.
3. The Chairperson of the Commission of the AU shall notify all Member Statesof the coming into force of this Protocol.

ARTICLE 30

Amendment and Revision

1. Any State Party may submit proposals for the amendment or revision of this Protocol.
2. Proposals for amendment or revision shall be submitted, in writing, to the Chairperson of the Commission of the AU who shall transmit the same to the States Parties within thirty (30) days of receipt thereof.

3. The Assembly, upon advice of the African Commission, shall examine these proposals within a period of one (1) year following notification of States Parties, in accordance with the provisions of paragraph 2 of this article.
4. Amendments or revision shall be adopted by the Assembly by a simple majority.
5. The amendment shall come into force for each State Party, which has accepted it thirty (30) days after the Chairperson of the Commission of the AU has received notice of the acceptance.

Article 31

Status of the Present Protocol

None of the provisions of the present Protocol shall affect more favourable provisions for the realisation of the rights of women contained in the national legislation of States Parties or in any other regional, continental or international conventions, treaties or agreements applicable in these States Parties.

Article 32

Transitional Provisions

Pending the establishment of the African Court on Human and Peoples' Rights, the African Commission on Human and Peoples' Rights shall be the seized with matters of interpretation arising from the application and implementation of this Protocol.

Adopted by the 2nd Ordinary Session of the Assembly of the Union

Maputo, 11 July 2003

Constitution of Botswana

Chapter II

Protection of Fundamental Rights and Freedoms of the Individual (ss 3-19)

3. Fundamental rights and freedoms of the individual

Whereas every person in Botswana is entitled to the fundamental rights and freedoms of the individual, that is to say, the right, whatever his race, place of origin, political opinions, colour, creed or sex, but subject to respect for the rights and freedoms of others and for the public interest to each and all of the following, namely—

(a) life, liberty, security of the person and the protection of the law;

(b) freedom of conscience, of expression and of assembly and association; and

(c) protection for the privacy of his home and other property and from deprivation of property without compensation,

the provisions of this Chapter shall have effect for the purpose of affording protection to those rights and freedoms subject to such limitations of that protection as are contained in those provisions, being limitations designed to ensure that the enjoyment of the said rights and freedoms by any individual does not prejudice the rights and freedoms of others or the public interest.

4. Protection of right to life

(1) No person shall be deprived of his life intentionally save in execution of the sentence of a court in respect of an offence under the law in force in Botswana of which he has been convicted.

(2) A person shall not be regarded as having been deprived of his life in contravention of subsection (1) of this section if he dies as the result of the use, to such extent and in such circumstances as are permitted by law, of such force as is reasonably justifiable—

(a) for the defence of any person from violence or for the defence of property;

(b) in order to effect a lawful arrest or to prevent the escape of a person lawfully detained;

(c) for the purpose of suppressing a riot, insurrection or mutiny; or

(d) in order to prevent the commission by that person of a criminal offence, or if he dies as the result of a lawful act of war.

5. Protection of right to personal liberty

(1) No person shall be deprived of his personal liberty save as may be authorized by law in any of the following cases, that is to say—

(a) in execution of the sentence or order of a court, whether established for Botswana or some other country, in respect of a criminal offence of which he has been convicted;

(b) in execution of the order of a court of record punishing him for contempt of that or another court;

(c) in execution of the order of a court made to secure the fulfilment of any obligation imposed on him by law;

(d) for the purpose of bringing him before a court in execution of the order of a court;

(e) upon reasonable suspicion of his having committed, or being about to commit, a criminal offence under the law in force in Botswana;

(f) under the order of a court or with the consent of his parent or guardian, for his education or welfare during any period ending not later than the date when he attains the age of 18 years;

(g) for the purpose of preventing the spread of an infectious or contagious disease;

(h) in the case of a person who is, or is reasonably suspected to be, of unsound mind, addicted to drugs or alcohol, or a vagrant, for the purpose of his care or treatment or the protection of the community;

(i) for the purpose of preventing the unlawful entry of that person into Botswana, or for the purpose of effecting the expulsion, extradition or other lawful removal of that person from Botswana, or for the purpose of restricting that person while he is being conveyed through Botswana in the course of his extradition or removal as a convicted prisoner from one country to another;

(j) to such extent as may be necessary in the execution of a lawful order requiring that person to remain within a specified area within Botswana or prohibiting him from being within such an area, or to such extent as may be reasonably justifiable for the taking of proceedings against that person relating to the making of any such order, or to such extent as may be reasonably justifiable for restraining that person during any visit that he is permitted to make to any part of Botswana in which, in consequence of any such order, his presence would otherwise be unlawful; or

(k) for the purpose of ensuring the safety of aircraft in flight.

(2) Any person who is arrested or detained shall be informed as soon as reasonably practicable, in a language that he understands, of the reasons for his arrest or detention.

(3) Any person who is arrested or detained—

(a) for the purpose of bringing him before a court in execution of the order of a court; or

(b) upon reasonable suspicion of his having committed, or being about to commit, a criminal offence under the law in force in Botswana,

and who is not released, shall be brought as soon as is reasonably practicable before a court; and if any person arrested or detained as mentioned in paragraph (b) of this subsection is not tried within a reasonable time, then, without prejudice to any further proceedings that may be brought against him, he shall be released either unconditionally or upon reasonable conditions, including in particular such conditions as are reasonably necessary to ensure that he appears at a later date for trial or for proceedings preliminary to trial.

(4) Any person who is unlawfully arrested or detained by any other person shall be entitled to compensation therefor from that other person.

6. Protection from slavery and forced labour

(1) No person shall be held in slavery or servitude.

(2) No person shall be required to perform forced labour.

(3) For the purposes of this section, the expression "forced labour" does not include—

(a) any labour required in consequence of the sentence or order of a court;

(b) labour required of any person while he is lawfully detained that, though not required in consequence of the sentence or order of a court, is reasonably necessary in the interests of hygiene or for the maintenance of the place at which he is detained;

(c) any labour required of a member of a disciplined force in pursuance of his duties as such or, in the case of a person who has conscientious objections to service as a member of a naval, military or air force, any labour that that person is required by law to perform in place of such service;

(d) any labour required during any period of public emergency or in the event of any other emergency or calamity that threatens the life and well-being of the community, to the extent that the requiring of such labour is reasonably justifiable in the circumstances of any situation arising or existing during that period or as a result of that other emergency or calamity, for the purpose of dealing with that situation; or

(e) any labour reasonably required as part of reasonable and normal communal or other civic obligations.

7. Protection from inhuman treatment

(1) No person shall be subjected to torture or to inhuman or degrading punishment or other treatment.

(2) Nothing contained in or done under the authority of any law shall be held to be inconsistent with or in contravention of this section to the extent that the law in question authorizes the infliction of any description of punishment that was lawful in the country immediately before the coming into operation of this Constitution.

8. Protection from deprivation of property

(1) No property of any description shall be compulsorily taken possession of, and no interest in or right over property of any description shall be compulsorily acquired, except where the following conditions are satisfied, that is to say—

(a) the taking of possession or acquisition is necessary or expedient—

(i) in the interests of defence, public safety, public order, public morality, public health, town and country planning or land settlement;

(ii) in order to secure the development or utilization of that, or other, property for a purpose beneficial to the community; or

(iii) in order to secure the development or utilization of the mineral resources of Botswana; and

(b) provision is made by a law applicable to that taking of possession or acquisition—

(i) for the prompt payment of adequate compensation; and

(ii) securing to any person having an interest in or right over the property a right of access to the High Court, either direct or on appeal from any other authority, for the determination of his interest or right, the legality of the taking of possession or acquisition of the property, interest or right, and the amount of any compensation to which he is entitled, and for the purpose of obtaining prompt payment of that compensation.

(2) No person who is entitled to compensation under this section shall be prevented from remitting, within a reasonable time after he has received any amount of that compensation, the whole of that amount (free from any deduction, charge or tax made or levied in respect of its remission) to any country of his choice outside Botswana.

(3) Subsection (1)(b)(i) of this section shall be deemed to be satisfied in relation to any 30 of 1969 Law applicable to the taking of possession of minerals or the acquisition of rights to minerals if that law makes provision for the payment at reasonable intervals of adequate royalties.

(4) Nothing contained in or done under the authority of any law shall be held to be inconsistent with or in contravention of subsection (2) of this section to the extent that the law in question authorizes—

(a) the attachment, by order of a court, of any amount of compensation to which a person is entitled in satisfaction of the judgment of a court or pending the determination of civil proceedings to which he is a party; or

(b) the imposition of reasonable restrictions on the manner in which any amount of compensation is to be remitted.

(5) Nothing contained in or done under the authority of any law shall be held to be inconsistent with or in contravention of subsection (1) of this section—

(a) to the extent that the law in question makes provision for the taking of possession or acquisition of any property—

  (i) in satisfaction of any tax, rate or due;

  (ii) by way of penalty for breach of the law whether under civil process or after conviction of a criminal offence under the law in force in Botswana;

  (iii) as an incident of a lease, tenancy, mortgage, charge, bill of sale, pledge or contract;

  (iv) in the execution of judgments or orders of a court in proceedings for the determination of civil rights or obligations;

  (v) in circumstances where it is reasonably necessary to do so because the property is in a dangerous state or injurious to the health of human beings, animals or plants;

  (vi) in consequence of any law with respect to the limitation of actions; or

  (vii) for so long only as may be necessary for the purposes of any examination, investigation, trial or inquiry or, in the case of land, for the purposes of the carrying out thereon of work of soil conservation or the conservation of other natural resources or work relating to agricultural development or improvement (being work relating to such development or improvement that the owner or occupier of the land has been required, and has without reasonable excuse refused or failed, to carry out),

  and except so far as that provision or, as the case may be, the thing done under the authority thereof is shown not to be reasonably justifiable in a democratic society; or

(b) to the extent that the law in question makes provision for the taking of possession or acquisition of—

  (i) enemy property;

  (ii) property of a deceased person, a person of unsound mind, a person who has not attained the age of 21 years, a prodigal, or a person who is absent from Botswana, for the purpose of its administration for the benefit of the persons entitled to the beneficial interest therein;

(iii) property of a person declared to be insolvent or a body corporate in liquidation, for the purpose of its administration for the benefit of the creditors of the insolvent or body corporate and, subject thereto, for the benefit of other persons entitled to the beneficial interest in the property; or

(iv) property subject to a trust, for the purpose of vesting the property in persons appointed as trustees under the instrument creating the trust or by a court, or by order of a court, for the purpose of giving effect to the trust.

(6) Nothing contained in or done under the authority of any law shall be held to be inconsistent with or in contravention of subsection (1) of this section to the extent that the law in question makes provision for the compulsory taking of possession in the public interest of any property, or the compulsory acquisition in the public interest in or right over property, where that property, interest or right is held by a body corporate established by law for public purposes in which no moneys have been invested other than moneys provided by Parliament.

9. Protection for privacy of home and other property

(1) Except with his own consent, no person shall be subjected to the search of his person or his property or the entry by others on his premises.

(2) Nothing contained in or done under the authority of any law shall be held to be inconsistent with or in contravention of this section to the extent that the law in question makes provision—

(a) that is reasonably required in the interests of defence, public safety, public order, public morality, public health, town and country planning, the development and utilization of mineral resources, for the purpose of any census or in order to secure the development or utilization of any property for a purpose beneficial to the community;

(b) that is reasonably required for the purpose of protecting the rights or freedoms of other persons;

(c) that authorizes an officer or agent of the Government of Botswana, a local government authority or a body corporate established by law for a public purpose to enter on the premises of any person in order to inspect those premises or anything thereon for the purpose of any tax, rate or duty or in order to carry out work connected with any property that is lawfully on those premises and that belongs to that Government, authority or body corporate, as the case may be; or

(d) that authorizes, for the purpose of enforcing the judgment or order of a court in any civil proceedings, the search of any person or property by order of a court or entry upon any premises by such order,

and except so far as that provision or, as the case may be, anything done under the authority thereof is shown not to be reasonably justifiable in a democratic society.

10. Provisions to secure protection of law

(1) If any person is charged with a criminal offence, then, unless the charge is withdrawn, the case shall be afforded a fair hearing within a reasonable time by an independent and impartial court established or recognized by law.

(2) Every person who is charged with a criminal offence—

(a) shall be presumed to be innocent until he is proved or has pleaded guilty;

(b) shall be informed as soon as reasonably practicable, in a language that he understands and in detail, of the nature of the offence charged;

(c) shall be given adequate time and facilities for the preparation of his defence;

(d) shall be permitted to defend himself before the court in person or, at his own expense, by a legal representative of his own choice;

(e) shall be afforded facilities to examine in person or by his legal representative the witnesses called by the prosecution before the court, and to obtain the attendance and carry out the examination of witnesses to testify on his behalf before the court on the same conditions as those applying to witnesses called by the prosecution; and

(f) shall be permitted to have without payment the assistance of an interpreter if he cannot understand the language used at the trial of the charge,

and except with his own consent the trial shall not take place in his absence unless he so conducts himself as to render the continuance of the proceedings in his presence impracticable and the court has ordered him to be removed and the trial to proceed in his absence.

(3) When a person is tried for any criminal offence, the accused person or any person authorized by him in that behalf shall, if he so requires and subject to payment of such reasonable fee as may be prescribed by law, be given within a reasonable time after judgment a copy for the use of the accused person of any record of the proceedings made by or on behalf of the court.

(4) No person shall be held to be guilty of a criminal offence on account of any act or omission that did not, at the time it took place, constitute such an offence, and no penalty shall be imposed for any criminal offence that is severer in degree or description than the maximum penalty that might have been imposed for that offence at the time when it was committed.

(5) No person who shows that he has been tried by a competent court for a criminal offence and either convicted or acquitted shall again be tried for that offence or for any other criminal offence of which he could have been convicted at the trial for that offence, save upon the order of a superior court in the course of appeal or review proceedings relating to the conviction or acquittal.

(6) No person shall be tried for a criminal offence if he shows that he has been pardoned for that offence.

(7) No person who is tried for a criminal offence shall be compelled to give evidence at the trial.

(8) No person shall be convicted of a criminal offence unless that offence is defined and the penalty therefor is prescribed in a written law:

Provided that nothing in this subsection shall prevent a court of record from punishing any person for contempt of itself notwithstanding that the act or omission constituting the contempt is not defined in a written law and the penalty therefor is not so prescribed.

(9) Any court or other adjudicating authority prescribed by law for the determination of the existence or extent of any civil right or obligation shall be established or recognized by law and shall be independent and impartial; and where proceedings for such a determination are instituted by any person before such a court or other adjudicating authority, the case shall be given a fair hearing within a reasonable time.

(10) Except with the agreement of all the parties thereto, all proceedings of every court and proceedings for the determination of the existence or extent of any civil right or obligation before any other adjudicating authority, including the announcement of the decision of the court or other authority, shall be held in public.

(11) Nothing in subsection (10) shall prevent the court or other adjudicating authority from excluding from the proceedings persons other than the parties thereto and their legal representatives to such extent as the court or other authority—

(a) may consider necessary or expedient in circumstances where publicity would prejudice the interests of justice or in interlocutory proceedings; or

(b) may be empowered by law to do so in the interests of defence, public safety, public order, public morality, the welfare of persons under the age of 18 years or the protection of the private lives of persons concerned in the proceedings.

(12) Nothing contained in or done under the authority of any law shall be held to be inconsistent with or in contravention of—

(a) subsection (2)(a) of this section to the extent that the law in question imposes upon any person charged with a criminal offence the burden of proving particular facts;

(b) subsection (2)(d) or (2)(e) of this section to the extent that the law in question prohibits legal representation before a subordinate court in proceedings for an offence under customary law (being proceedings against any person who, under that law, is subject to that law);

(c) subsection (2)(c) of this section to the extent that the law in question imposes reasonable conditions that must be satisfied if witnesses called to testify on behalf of an accused person are to be paid their expenses out of public funds;

(d) subsection (5) of this section to the extent that the law in question authorizes a court to try a member of a disciplined force for a criminal offence notwithstanding any trial and conviction or acquittal of that member under the disciplinary law of that force, so, however, that any court so trying such a member and convicting him shall in sentencing him to any punishment take into account any punishment awarded him under that disciplinary law;

(e) subsection (8) of this section to the extent that the law in question authorizes a court to convict a person of a criminal offence under any customary law to which, by virtue of that law, such person is subject.

(13) In the case of any person who is held in lawful detention, the provisions of subsection (1), subsection (2)(d) and (e) and subsection (3) of this section shall not apply in relation to his trial for a criminal offence under the law regulating the discipline of persons held in such detention.

(14) In this section "criminal offence" means a criminal offence under the law in force in Botswana.

11. Protection of freedom of conscience

(1) Except with his own consent, no person shall be hindered in the enjoyment of his freedom of conscience, and for the purposes of this section the said freedom includes freedom of thought and of religion, freedom to change his religion or belief, and freedom, either alone or in community with others, and both in public and in private, to manifest and propagate his religion or belief in worship, teaching, practice and observance.

(2) Every religious community shall be entitled, at its own expense, to establish and maintain places of education and to manage any place of education which it wholly maintains; and no such community shall be prevented from providing religious instruction for persons of that community in the course of any education provided at any place of education which it wholly maintains or in the course of any education which it otherwise provides.

(3) Except with his own consent (or, if he is a minor, the consent of his guardian) no person attending any place of education shall be required to receive religious instruction or to take part in or attend any religious ceremony or observance if that instruction, ceremony or observance relates to a religion other than his own.

(4) No person shall be compelled to take any oath which is contrary to his religion or belief or to take any oath in a manner which is contrary to his religion or belief.

(5) Nothing contained in or done under the authority of any law shall be held to be inconsistent with or in contravention of this section to the extent that the law in question makes provision which is reasonably required—

(a) in the interests of defence, public safety, public order, public morality or public health; or

(b) for the purpose of protecting the rights and freedoms of other persons, including the right to observe and practise any religion without the unsolicited intervention of members of any other religion,

and except so far as that provision or, as the case may be, the thing done under the authority thereof is shown not to be reasonably justifiable in a democratic society.

12. Protection of freedom of expression

(1) Except with his own consent, no person shall be hindered in the enjoyment of his freedom of expression, that is to say, freedom to hold opinions without interference, freedom to receive ideas and information without interference, freedom to communicate ideas and information without interference (whether the communication be to the public generally or to any person or class of persons) and freedom from interference with his correspondence.

(2) Nothing contained in or done under the authority of any law shall be held to be inconsistent with or in contravention of this section to the extent that the law in question makes provision—

(a) that is reasonably required in the interests of defence, public safety, public order, public morality or public health; or

(b) that is reasonably required for the purpose of protecting the reputations, rights and freedoms of other persons or the private lives of persons concerned in legal proceedings, preventing the disclosure of information received in confidence, maintaining the authority and independence of the courts, regulating educational institutions in the interests of persons receiving instruction therein, or regulating the technical administration or the technical operation of telephony, telegraphy, posts, wireless, broadcasting or television; or

(c) that imposes restrictions upon public officers, employees of local government bodies, or teachers,

and except so far as that provision or, as the case may be, the thing done under the authority thereof is shown not to be reasonably justifiable in a democratic society.

13. Protection of freedom of assembly and association

(1) Except with his own consent, no person shall be hindered in the enjoyment of his freedom of assembly and association, that is to

say, his right to assemble freely and associate with other persons and in particular to form or belong to trade unions or other associations for the protection of his interests.

(2) Nothing contained in or done under the authority of any law shall be held to be inconsistent with or in contravention of this section to the extent that the law in question makes provision—

(a) that is reasonably required in the interests of defence, public safety, public order, public morality or public health;

(b) that is reasonably required for the purpose of protecting the rights or freedoms of other persons;

(c) that imposes restrictions upon public officers, employees of local government bodies, or teachers; or

(d) for the registration of trade unions and associations of trade unions in a register established by or under any law, and for imposing reasonable conditions relating to the requirements for entry on such a register (including conditions as to the minimum number of persons necessary to constitute a trade union qualified for registration, or of members necessary to constitute an association of trade unions qualified for registration) and conditions whereby registration may be refused on the grounds that any other trade union already registered, or association of trade unions already registered, as the case may be, is sufficiently representative of the whole or of a substantial proportion of the interests in respect of which registration of a trade union or association of trade unions is sought,

and except so far as that provision or, as the case may be, the thing done under the authority thereof is shown not to be reasonably justifiable in a democratic society.

14. Protection of freedom of movement

(1) No person shall be deprived of his freedom of movement, and for the purposes of this section the said freedom means the right to move freely throughout Botswana, the right to reside in any part of Botswana, the right to enter Botswana and immunity from expulsion from Botswana.

(2) Any restriction on a person's freedom of movement that is involved in his lawful detention shall not be held to be inconsistent with or in contravention of this section.

(3) Nothing contained in or done under the authority of any law shall be held to be inconsistent with or in contravention of this section to the extent that the law in question makes provision—

(a) for the imposition of restrictions that are reasonably required in the interests of defence, public safety, public order, public morality or public health or the imposition of restrictions on the acquisition or use by any person of land or other property in Botswana and except so far as that provision or, as the case may be, the thing done under the authority thereof, is shown not to be reasonably justifiable in a democratic society;

(b) for the imposition of restrictions on the freedom of movement of any person who is not a citizen of Botswana;

(c) for the imposition of restrictions on the entry into or residence within defined areas of Botswana of persons who are not Bushmen to the extent that such restrictions are reasonably required for the protection or well-being of Bushmen;

(d) for the imposition of restrictions upon the movement or residence within Botswana of public officers; or

(e) for the removal of a person from Botswana to be tried outside Botswana for a criminal offence or to undergo imprisonment in some other country in execution of the sentence of a court in respect of a criminal offence under the law in force in Botswana of which he has been convicted.

(4) If any person whose freedom of movement has been restricted by order under such a provision as is referred to in subsection (3)(a) of this section (other than a restriction which is applicable to persons generally or to general classes of persons) so requests at any time during the period of that restriction not earlier than six months after the order was made or six months after he last made such request, as the case may be, his case shall be reviewed by an independent and impartial tribunal presided over by a person, qualified to be enrolled as an advocate in Botswana, appointed by the Chief Justice.

(5) On any review by a tribunal in pursuance of this section of the case of a person whose freedom of movement has been restricted, the tribunal may make recommendations, concerning the necessity or expediency of continuing the restriction to the authority by which it was ordered but, unless it is otherwise provided by law, that authority shall not be obliged to act in accordance with any such recommendations.

15. Protection from discrimination on the grounds of race, etc.

(1) Subject to the provisions of subsections (4), (5) and (7) of this section, no law shall make any provision that is discriminatory either of itself or in its effect.

(2) Subject to the provisions of subsections (6), (7) and (8) of this section, no person shall be treated in a discriminatory manner by any person acting by virtue of any written law or in the performance of the functions of any public office or any public authority.

(3) In this section, the expression "discriminatory" means affording different treatment to different persons, attributable wholly or mainly to their respective descriptions by race, tribe, place of origin, political opinions, colour or creed whereby persons of one such description are subjected to disabilities or restrictions to which persons of another such description are not made subject or are accorded privileges or advantages which are not accorded to persons of another such description.

(4) Subsection (1) of this section shall not apply to any law so far as that law makes provision—

(a) for the appropriation of public revenues or other public funds;

(b) with respect to persons who are not citizens of Botswana;

(c) with respect to adoption, marriage, divorce, burial, devolution of property on death or other matters of personal law;

(d) for the application in the case of members of a particular race, community or tribe of customary law with respect to any matter whether to the exclusion of any law in respect to that matter which is applicable in the case of other persons or not; or

(e) whereby persons of any such description as is mentioned in subsection (3) of this section may be subjected to any disability or restriction or may be accorded any privilege or advantage which, having regard to its nature and to special circumstances pertaining to those persons or to persons of any other such description, is reasonably justifiable in a democratic society.

(5) Nothing contained in any law shall be held to be inconsistent with or in contravention of subsection (1) of this section to the extent that it makes reasonable provision with respect to qualifications for service as a public officer or as a member of a disciplined force or for the service of a local government authority or a body corporate established directly by any law.

(6) Subsection (2) of this section shall not apply to anything which is expressly or by necessary implication authorized to be done by any such provision of law as is referred to in subsection (4) or (5) of this section.

(7) Nothing contained in or done under the authority of any law shall be held to be inconsistent with or in contravention of this section to the extent that the law in question makes provision whereby persons of any such description as is mentioned in subsection (3) of this section may be subjected to any restriction on the rights and freedoms guaranteed by sections 9, 11, 12, 13 and 14 of this Constitution, being such a restriction as is authorized by section 9(2), 11(5), 12(2) 13(2), or 14(3), as the case may be.

(8) Nothing in subsection (2) of this section shall affect any discretion relating to the institution, conduct or discontinuance of civil or criminal proceedings in any court that is vested in any person by or under this Constitution or any other law.

(9) Nothing contained in or done under the authority of any law shall be held to be inconsistent with the provisions of this section—

(a) if that law was in force immediately before the coming into operation of this Constitution and has continued in force at all times since the coming into operation of this Constitution; or

(b) to the extent that the law repeals and re-enacts any provision which has been contained in any written law at all times since immediately before the coming into operation of this Constitution.

16. Derogation from fundamental rights and freedoms

(1) Nothing contained in or done under the authority of any law shall be held to be inconsistent with or in contravention of section 5 or 15 of this Constitution to the extent that the law authorizes the taking during any period when Botswana is at war or any period when a declaration under section 17 of this Constitution is in force, of measures that are reasonably justifiable for the purpose of dealing with the situation that exists during that period.

(2) Where a person is detained by virtue of such an authorization as is referred to in subsection (1) of this section the following provisions shall apply—

(a) he shall, as soon as reasonably practicable and in any case not more than five days after the commencement of his detention, be furnished with a statement in writing in a language that he understands specifying in detail the grounds upon which he is detained;

(b) not more than 14 days after the commencement of his detention, a notification shall be published in the Gazette stating that he has been detained and giving particulars of the provision of law under which his detention is authorized;

(c) not more than one month after the commencement of his detention and thereafter during his detention at intervals of not more than six months, his case shall be reviewed by an independent and impartial tribunal established by law and presided over by a person, qualified to be enrolled as an advocate in Botswana, appointed by the Chief Justice; and

(d) he shall be afforded reasonable facilities to consult and instruct, at his own expense, a legal representative and he and any such legal representative shall be permitted to make written or oral representations or both to the tribunal appointed for the review of his case.

(3) On any review by a tribunal in pursuance of this section of the case of a detained person, the tribunal may make recommendations, concerning the necessity or expediency of continuing his detention, to the authority by which it was ordered but, unless it is otherwise provided by law, that authority shall not be obliged to act in accordance with any such recommendations.

17. Declarations relating to emergencies

(1) The President may at any time, by Proclamation published in the Gazette, declare that a state of public emergency exists.

(2) A declaration under subsection (1) of this section, if not sooner revoked, shall cease to have effect—

(a) in the case of a declaration made when Parliament is sitting or has been summoned to meet within seven days, at the expiration of a period of seven days beginning with the date of publication of the declaration; or

(b) in any other case, at the expiration of a period of 21 days beginning with the date of publication of the declaration,

unless before the expiration of that period, it is approved by a resolution passed by the National Assembly, supported by the votes of a majority of all the voting members of the Assembly.

(3) Subject to the provisions of subsection (4) of this section, a declaration approved by a resolution of the National Assembly under subsection (2) of this section shall continue in force until the expiration of a period of six months beginning with the date of its being so approved or until such earlier date as may be specified in the resolution:

Provided that the National Assembly may, by resolution, supported by the votes of a majority of all the voting members of the Assembly, extend its approval of the declaration for periods of not more than six months at a time.

(4) The National Assembly may by resolution at any time revoke a declaration approved by the Assembly under this section.

18. Enforcement of protective provisions

(1) Subject to the provisions of subsection (5) of this section, if any person alleges that any of the provisions of sections 3 to 16 (inclusive) of this Constitution has been, is being or is likely to be contravened in relation to him, then, without prejudice to any other action with respect to the same matter which is lawfully available, that person may apply to the High Court for redress.

(2) The High Court shall have original jurisdiction—

(a) to hear and determine any application made by any person in pursuance of subsection (1) of this section; or

(b) to determine any question arising in the case of any person which is referred to it in pursuance of subsection (3) of this section,

and may make such orders, issue such writs and give such direction as it may consider appropriate for the purpose of enforcing or securing the enforcement of any of the provisions of sections 3 to 16 (inclusive) of this Constitution.

(3) If in any proceedings in any subordinate court any question arises as to the contravention of any of the provisions of sections 3 to 16 (inclusive) of this Constitution, the person presiding in that court may, and shall if any party to the proceedings so requests, refer the question to the High Court unless, in his opinion, the raising of the question is merely frivolous or vexatious.

(4) Parliament may confer upon the High Court such powers in addition to those conferred by this section as may appear to be

necessary or desirable for the purpose of enabling that court more effectively to exercise the jurisdiction conferred upon it by this section.

(5) Rules of court making provision with respect to the practice and procedure of the High Court for the purposes of this section may be made by the person or authority for the time being having power to make rules of court with respect to the practice and procedure of that court generally.

19. Interpretation and savings

(1) In this Chapter, unless the context otherwise requires—

"court" means any court of law having jurisdiction in Botswana other than a court established by a disciplinary law, and in sections 4 and 6 of this Constitution a court established by a disciplinary law;

"disciplinary law" means a law regulating the discipline of any disciplined force;

"disciplined force" means—

(a) a naval, military or air force;

(b) a police force; or

(c) a prison service;

"legal representative" means a person entitled to practise in Botswana as an advocate or attorney;

"member", in relation to a disciplined force, includes any person who, under the law regulating the discipline of that force, is subject to that discipline.

(2) In relation to any person who is a member of a disciplined force raised under an Act of Parliament, nothing contained in or done under the authority of the disciplinary law of that force shall be held to be inconsistent with or in contravention of any of the provisions of this Chapter other than sections 4, 6 and 7.

(3) In relation to any person who is a member of a disciplined force raised otherwise than as aforesaid and lawfully present in Botswana, nothing contained in or done under the authority of the disciplinary law of that force shall be held to be inconsistent with or in contravention of any of the provisions of this Chapter.

Index